THE RED WARRIOR

U.S. PERCEPTIONS OF STALIN'S STRATEGIC ROLE IN THE ALLIED JOURNEY TO VICTORY IN THE SECOND WORLD WAR

Reagan Fancher, M.A., Ph.D

Texas Woman's University

Author of *The Holy Warrior: Osama Bin Laden and His Jihadi Journey in the Soviet-Afghan War*

Series in World History

 **VERNON PRESS**

www.vernonpress.com

In the Americas:	*In the rest of the world:*
Vernon Press	Vernon Press
1000 N West Street, Suite 1200	C/Sancti Espiritu 17,
Wilmington, Delaware, 19801	Malaga, 29006
United States	Spain

Series in World History

Library of Congress Control Number: 2024936942

ISBN: 979-8-8819-0007-6

To my Bramerican Queen, Graziele, with all my love

TABLE OF CONTENTS

PREFACE

"This is a very suggestive age…but it will always be found in the end that the only way to whip an army is to go out and fight it."- Ulysses S. Grant in 1865, quoted by Peter G. Tsouras in *Civil War Quotations: In the Words of the Commanders*[1]

Only days after Adolf Hitler's armies launched their summer 1941 offensive against Joseph Stalin's Soviet Union, U.S. President Franklin D. Roosevelt initiated a process of delivering vast amounts of American Lend-Lease aid to help the beleaguered Red Army repulse the Nazi invaders and prevent Berlin from overrunning Moscow's strategic resources. Initially, the Anglo-American Arctic convoys delivered most of this Lend-Lease aid to Stalin's fighting men and women, preventing a separate peace between the Nazi and Soviet tyrannies and helping to fuel the Red Army's wartime struggle. Underestimating Stalin's determination to fight Hitler to the finish, U.S. officials also opened two other supply routes through Iran and Alaska in a desperate effort to demonstrate their goodwill and ironclad commitment to the Soviet aid program. Perceiving Stalin's Red Army as indispensable to achieving Hitler's demise, American Lend-Lease officials helped to hasten the Allied victory yet failed to induce the Soviet leader to pursue a peaceful postwar path as hoped, setting the stage for the Cold War and a precedent for later U.S. martial aid programs.

The above opening quote attributed to Union Lieutenant General Ulysses S. Grant in 1865 speaks volumes about the U.S. strategy to defeat the Axis Powers led by Nazi Germany, Fascist Italy, and Imperial Japan in the Second World War between 1941 and 1945. As pointed out by historian Russell F. Weigley, Grant's strategic thinking that helped U.S. forces to ultimately crush both their Confederate and Native American opponents during the American Civil War (1861-1865) and the Plains' Indian Wars (1866-1890) appears to have strongly influenced the strategy adopted by U.S. leaders, from Roosevelt down, following the Japanese attack on Pearl Harbor. As the U.S. leadership entered the Second World War that raged globally 80 years after Grant's, "strategy of annihilation" had helped decisively cripple the Confederacy and end the bloody futility of Americans killing each other and, subsequently, their Native opponents, they again turned to the Union commander's strategic approach in facing an Axis enemy that they regarded as potentially indestructible.[2]

Hoping to avoid a mechanized version of the prolonged, bloody stalemate that had characterized the First World War's Western Front, U.S. leaders zealously adhered to what they perceived as the practical path to unquestioned victory, a victory that could not have been achieved without the ruthlessness and determination of Stalin's Red Army fighting Hitler's forces in the east. As Roosevelt and his senior officials worked to achieve this goal and poured massive resources into their Soviet Lend-Lease program from early 1942 forward, U.S. General Dwight David "Ike" Eisenhower, reflecting Grant's strategic thinking from eight decades earlier, wrote, "We've got to quit wasting resources all over the world – and still worse – wasting time. *If we're to keep Russia in* [the war against Germany], save the Middle East, India and Burma; we've got to begin slugging with air at West Europe; to be followed by a land attack as soon *as possible.*" [3] The zealously-executed U.S. Lend-Lease program for the struggling Soviets helped to ensure that Stalin's soldiers could indeed whip Hitler's army in the way that Grant recommended, rendering the Second World War shorter and setting a precedent for later U.S. leaders backing resistance to aggression abroad.

This work is the edited and re-edited result of my doctoral dissertation, "The Arsenal of the Red Warriors: U.S. Perceptions of Stalin's Red Army and the Impact of Lend-Lease Aid on the Eastern Front in the Second World War" that I completed while pursuing my Ph.D. in History at the University of North Texas (UNT), and, accordingly, it was initially intended primarily for an academic audience. In researching this work, I found many primary sources, such as Roosevelt's "Map Room Papers", to be immensely helpful in unmasking the U.S. leadership's motives for keeping Stalin's troops well-supplied.[4] Other excellent primary sources that I have found to be especially helpful include the online archival collections of the U.S. Navy Department Library, the War Department's Chief of Finance records, and the U.S. Department of State's *Soviet Supply Protocols.*[5] The *Congressional Record* and the *Wilson Center Digital Archive* also provided useful insights into U.S. wartime perceptions of Stalin's strategic importance and the reasons for which the Roosevelt administration prioritized Lend-Lease aid to the Red Army.[6]

I have also found Hero of the Soviet Union Dmitriy Loza's memoir *Commanding the Red Army's Sherman Tanks: The World War II Memoirs of Hero of the Soviet Union Dmitriy Loza* to be insightful.[7] Other interesting perspectives are provided by Red Army private Nikolai Litvin in his memoir *800 Days on the Eastern Front: A Russian Soldier Remembers World War II* and by biology professor Vadim Medish in his January 2008 interview with Justin Pastorfield-Li.[8] Several other insightful primary sources include British Prime Minister Winston Churchill's *Memoirs of the Second World War,* Field Marshal Lord Alanbrooke's *War Diaries 1939-1945,* the second volume of Sir Henry Pownall's *Chief of Staff: The Diaries of Lieutenant-General Sir Henry Pownall,* and several archival collections housed at *The National Archives of the UK.*[9]

In 1959, Raymond Dawson introduced scholars to the roots of Lend-Lease aid to the Soviet Union in *The Decision to Aid Russia, 1941,* arguing that the first six months after the German surprise assault proved crucial to Roosevelt's efforts to generate U.S. support for Stalin's beleaguered forces.[10] A decade later, in 1969, Robert Huhn Jones launched the first scholarly inquiry into Lend-Lease's effect on the Soviet war effort in contrast to Dawson's focus on the domestic debate in the United States in *The Roads to Russia: United States Lend-Lease to the Soviet Union,* crediting the Iranian route or "Persian Corridor" with delivering the most Lend-Lease transport vehicles and concluding that Lend-Lease served as a far greater contribution to the Red Army's anti-Nazi struggle than the Soviet leadership wished to admit.[11] In 1973, George Herring, Jr. revisited Dawson's emphasis on the diplomatic role of the Soviet Lend-Lease program in *Aid to Russia, 1941-1946: Strategy, Diplomacy, the Origins of the Cold War,* largely dismissing Jones's arguments regarding the program's effectiveness as a military tool in Stalin's war effort.[12]

Revisiting Jones's claim that Lend-Lease played a key role in the Red Army's victory over Hitler, Hubert P. van Tuyll argues in his 1989 book *Feeding the Bear: American Aid to the Soviet Union, 1941-1945* that Lend-Lease aid greatly hastened Germany's defeat.[13] In the 1996 book *Accounting For War: Soviet Production, Employment, and the Defence Burden, 1940-1945,* Mark Harrison adds his conclusions to Soviet Lend-Lease historiography, arguing that, "Without it [U.S. Lend-Lease aid to the Soviets], everyone on the side of the Allies would have had a worse war," contrary to most Cold War Soviet officials' claims to the contrary.[14] In contrast to van Tuyll, Jones, and others, Harrison's 1996 work benefited from access to key Russian archival sources that seem to have just become available during the time in which he conducted his research and which had previously been denied to Western scholars during the Cold War. Likewise consulting both Russian and Western archival sources for his 2004 book *Russia's Life-Saver: Lend-Lease Aid to the U.S.S.R. in World War II,* Albert Weeks reexamines the scholarly debate surrounding Lend-Lease's role on the Eastern Front. Establishing the total of U.S. $12,500,000,000 as the correct monetary value of the war material contributed by the United States to supply Stalin's war effort, Weeks concludes that Lend-Lease aid played a critical role in aiding the Red Army and hastening the Allied victory over the Axis.[15]

In 2021, Sean McMeekin contributed a new and highly controversial perspective to Soviet Lend-Lease historiography, arguing that Lend-Lease deliveries to the Soviet Union should have been severely curtailed or perhaps ended altogether in 1943 in *Stalin's War: A New History of World War II.* McMeekin's conclusions, which are, like those of Harrison, Weeks, and others, based on his consultation of previously unavailable Russian archival sources in addition to Western sources, have since attracted both considerable commendation and controversy, receiving enthusiastic praise from some scholars such as Geoffrey Wawro and heavy criticism from others such as Vojin Majstorovic and Geoffrey Roberts.[16] While his conclusions regarding Soviet Lend-Lease have proved controversial enough, the criticism leveled at McMeekin's work also appears to result, in part, from the other half of his argument emphasizing Stalin's role, rather than Hitler's alone, in helping ignite the Second World War.[17]

Perhaps adding further to the ongoing firestorm of criticism is that McMeekin's already controversial arguments in this regard also appear to be somewhat similar, but in no way identical, to the earlier thesis of former Soviet GRU agent and defector Vladimir Rezun, also known as Viktor Suvorov, whose 2008 book *The Chief Culprit: Stalin's Grand Design to Start World War II* laid the responsibility for the Second World War's outbreak primarily at Stalin's feet.[18] Like McMeekin's more recent work, Suvorov's thesis remains immensely controversial, attracting intense criticism from David Glantz and other top academics, as he theorizes that Stalin initially planned an attack on Nazi Germany in 1941 until Hitler's brutal invasion of the Soviet Union allegedly and inadvertently wrecked the Soviet premier's supposed scheme.[19] Although he seems to part with Suvorov's most hotly contested claims, McMeekin nevertheless continues generating academic ire by adding in *Stalin's War* that, "What these Special [Soviet] Files do reveal, if not a smoking gun about Stalin's [alleged 1941] offensive intentions vis-à-vis Hitler, is a positively breathtaking ramp-up in Soviet military preparations from April to June 1941."[20]

In keeping with my focus on U.S. perceptions of Stalin's role in the Allied war effort and the importance of effectively supplying the Red Army, this work does not delve into either McMeekin's or Suvorov's arguments regarding Stalin's alleged prewar military preparations, his documented aggression against smaller countries, or his overall part in the conflict. Nor will our subject include an in-depth assessment of Lend-Lease's possible impact on the Soviet war effort, other than occasional observations on either the findings or arguments of expert scholars of the Eastern Front such as David Glantz and Alexander Hill, as a deep discussion of these issues would greatly distract from this work's main purpose of exploring Stalin's perceived strategic importance from the wartime American perspective, and these controversies are not, therefore, discussed in the chapters that follow. All the previously mentioned works discussing U.S. Lend-Lease aid to the Soviet Union, however, whether generally held in high academic regard or roundly criticized by scholars, will be cited where relevant throughout the following chapters. Such a course is both necessary and proper in attempting to paint as complete a picture as possible of the American wartime leadership's perceptions of Stalin and the Red Army's key role in the Allied strategy in defeating Hitler, in which nearly all above-mentioned sources agree that U.S. Lend-Lease served as a crucial component.

This work expands upon the findings of the experts by not only exploring wartime Washington's prevailing contemporary views of Stalin's forces and their role in the anti-Axis struggle but by emphasizing the Arctic convoys' key contribution to aiding the Red Army's early efforts and, in contrast to many previous works, calling attention to their importance and perseverance during the late war period as well. While McMeekin proposes that Soviet Lend-Lease aid could reasonably have been discontinued in 1943, this work, in contrast to my dissertation, refrains, to the greatest extent that I have found possible, from in-depth commenting on the Soviet war effort and Lend-Lease's possible battlefield impact therein and proposes the possibility that it was not Soviet Lend-Lease aid in and of itself that sowed the Cold War's seeds, but was, if anything at all on the American side, the naivete of Roosevelt, Hopkins, and other U.S. leaders in their misperception that they could effectively inculcate a moderate attitude in Stalin. In turn, the findings of this work strongly suggest that it was the American leadership's misplaced belief that by furnishing unconditional aid to the Red Army, which was a strategic wartime necessity, Washington could achieve not only its primary goal of preventing a separate peace but essentially "buy" Stalin into moderating and committing to a peaceful postwar world, even supplying the Soviet premier with some of the key components for atomic bomb construction.[21]

While this work, like others, discusses Stalin's infiltration of Roosevelt's White House through the effective planting of spies in the U.S. administration and the president's naivete and misplaced affection for the Soviet premier, it also tackles several questions that have, until now, remained unanswered. In emphasizing the Arctic convoys' vital contribution to the Red Army's struggle even during the late war period, Roosevelt's underestimation of Stalin's duplicitous character and anti-Western tendencies, and the fears of a second Treaty of Brest-Litovsk in Washington, I hope to help explain how and why U.S. leaders came to embrace the Soviet premier and his fighting forces as a crucial part of the Allied struggle.[22]

The shadow of Brest-Litovsk continued to haunt the American leadership as the war on the Eastern Front raged across Nazi-occupied Soviet Europe and Stalin, whether subjectively for better or worse, appears to have sought to exploit these fears to ensure the continued procurement of U.S. Lend-Lease aid. While not presenting Roosevelt and Churchill with an open, outright threat to conclude a separate peace with Hitler, the Soviet premier nevertheless seems to have strongly implied that he could be forced to do so by events at the front in his telegrams with his Allied counterparts. His insistence that Allied material aid paled in comparison to the sacrifices being made by the Soviet government and people, even if subjectively true, appears to have amplified U.S. perceptions that the Red Army, if not sufficiently supplied by the West, could collapse in a repeat of 1918, removing the threat to Hitler's eastern borders and delivering massive Soviet resources to the Nazi war machine.[23]

In his memoir, U.S. Secretary of State Cordell Hull recalls that British Foreign Secretary Sir Anthony Eden and other British officials shared American fears of Stalin feeling alienated by the West and concluding a separate peace with Hitler, just as the Soviet premier had done in August 1939 while assigning the blame for his action to the alleged failure of London and Paris to negotiate with Moscow in earnest.[24] Recalling, "They feared lest, in those circumstances, Stalin might negotiate a separate peace with Germany," Hull suggests that Churchill and Eden shared the concerns of their U.S. counterparts regarding the possibility of a second Brest-Litovsk and felt, like Roosevelt and Hopkins, that the Red Army could not be allowed to falter.[25] Stung by Stalin's claims that former Prime Minister Neville Chamberlain's allegedly insincere attempts at negotiating with Moscow had supposedly led the Soviet premier to conclude his 1939 pact with Hitler, Churchill and Eden likewise labored to keep the Red Army supplied and in the war.[26]

For his part, Stalin appears to have detected these fears and implicitly and repeatedly raised the specter of a second Brest-Litovsk in his dealings with Roosevelt and Churchill to ensure the shipping of unconditional aid to the Red Army.[27] In his 1975 memoir *Special Envoy to Churchill and Stalin 1941-1946*, W. Averell Harriman strongly implies that Roosevelt continued to fear the possibility of a second Brest-Litovsk and sought to prevent this by assuring Stalin of further unconditional aid even as Soviet forces crushed the Germans at Stalingrad.[28] Stalin is said to have coldly declined to meet with the president at Casablanca, Morocco due to, "affairs connected with the front" that demanded his presence in Moscow, a claim that he repeated after Roosevelt proposed moving the meeting to March.[29] "Concerned over Stalin's absence [at Casablanca]" according to Harriman, Roosevelt offered to send U.S. Secretary of State General George C. Marshall to Moscow to help boost Soviet morale and to assure the Soviet premier in the strongest possible terms that he and Churchill intended to carry on the war to Berlin while seeking no terms but Germany's unconditional surrender.[30]

Having already refused to attend the Casablanca Conference at which Roosevelt and Churchill publicly declared their unconditional surrender and total war policy against Germany, Stalin rejected the president's offer to send Marshall to Moscow.[31] Harriman recalls that Roosevelt expressed deep concern at Stalin's absence during the Casablanca Conference and states that the president confided to him at the time that he feared repeating President Woodrow Wilson's perceived mistake in not ensuring Germany's total and unquestioned defeat by taking the war into Berlin in 1918.[32] With Wilson's earlier perceived failures weighing heavily on his mind at Casablanca, Roosevelt appears to have regarded Stalin's absence as an indication that the Soviet leader may seek a separate peace and desperately sought to demonstrate his resolve in keeping him in the war against Hitler.[33]

Although limited to the American leadership's wartime perceptions of Stalin and the Red Army's importance to the Allied war effort, the chapters that proceed reveal how and why the U.S. leaders arrived at important strategic decisions in their efforts to arm their wartime Soviet allies while also overestimating the White House's ability to charm the Soviet premier into moderating his dedication to rigid Communist orthodoxy and expansionism. This work's first and second chapters explore the impact of Brest-Litovsk and early U.S.-Soviet relations on the origins of Lend-Lease, while the third, fourth, and fifth chapters closely examine U.S. perceptions of Stalin's Red Army, the importance of the Arctic convoys, the Persian Corridor, and ALSIB, and the often-overlooked exploits of the Allied Arctic mariners in the last years of the war.

In what I regard as a very important concluding section, I have also conducted a comparative analysis of Roosevelt's Soviet Lend-Lease program with U.S. President Ronald Reagan's support for the Afghan resistance during the 1980s as an example of how Lend-Lease set a historical precedent for U.S. aid programs intended to arm resistance movements fighting aggression during later periods of history up to the present time and the current war in Ukraine. Just as this work refrains from commenting too much on the Soviet war effort and Lend-Lease's possible role therein, however, the reader will find that this book's Conclusion does not delve into the popular allegations that Reagan's CIA trained Osama bin Laden and al-Qaeda as this is a topic that I thoroughly explore in my earlier book and a claim that other authors and I have deftly debunked.

Finally, I would like the reader to understand that this work – unlike my above-mentioned book on bin Laden – is not intended to serve as a biographical account of any of the historical figures discussed throughout its pages (although it would not disappoint me at all if it were to be regarded as such). Nor is this work intended to be another history of either the Second World War or the Eastern Front, of which there are already numerous splendid volumes, many of which served as invaluable sources for my research into our subject. This is a book about U.S. wartime perceptions of Stalin's strategic importance as a key ally in the Second World War and how American leaders viewed him and the need to keep him in the war at the time, about the Arctic convoys' contributions to this goal even during the war's later years. While the early Arctic convoy crews persevered against the odds, the tragic 1942 fates of several convoys and the precedent of Brest-Litovsk in 1918 led many U.S. leaders to fear that Hitler's forces, which remained deep inside Soviet territory in 1943, might still prevail and force Stalin into concluding a separate peace. Their fears were enhanced by Stalin's constant complaints, however justified these may have been, and his consistent postponing of a meeting with Roosevelt, a meeting that did not occur until the Tehran Conference in late 1943. As a result of these concerns, Roosevelt and his chief subordinates expanded the Lend-Lease supply routes through Iran and Alaska even as he and Churchill continued their Arctic aid voyages, brilliantly boosting Stalin's fighting forces and hastening Hitler's downfall while underestimating their ability to "purchase" the Soviet leader's commitment to peaceful postwar policies.[34]

ACKNOWLEDGEMENTS

Turning my dissertation into this book, and researching it to begin with, was a very difficult and, at times, immensely daunting task for me, and it would not have happened without the kindness and support of many wonderful people who not only made the task possible, but worthwhile. My precious wife and greatest treasure, Graziele Fancher, to whom this work is dedicated, merits mention here first and foremost. Grazi's hard work, patience, and perseverance in tolerating and sharing my many stresses, frustrations, and fears as I labored to complete the dissertation that became this work, and then revise it again into the current work, made my research into it possible to begin with. Had she not labored to help provide for us and supported my efforts while I studied, conducted research, and worked as a Teaching Fellow while earning my Ph.D., and then continued urging me to see it through to revision and publication, this project would not have become what it is.

My mother and stepfather, Rebecca Fancher and Keith Kimball, and my father-in-law and mother-in-law, Vanderlei and Suzel Boleli, have also helped to make this work a reality by supporting us with their love, phone calls, text messages, and so much more as I intellectually fought my way through graduate school, for the second and last time. Mom and Keith, along with my brother, Lincoln Fancher, and several other close family friends, first helped us move from Monroe, Louisiana to Denton, Texas in the sweltering, uncertain days of August 2019 and made this five-hour trek once again to help us move to our new home in the stifling July heat of 2021. Through our weekly phone conversations and their prayers, Senhor and Senhora Boleli have been equally supportive of my efforts all the way from Brazil's Sao Paulo state, and I hope that the work I have now produced is one that they can look upon with approval.

My not-so-little brother and best man, Lincoln, is not only a brilliant computer scientist and gifted athlete, but a wonderful, adventurous person, and I want to thank him here for always being an important part of my adventure through history and for his toleration of my numerous and constant history ramblings when we were growing up. I also want to thank my sweet, thoughtful sister, Laura Hinton, for being equally supportive of my lifelong passion for history. Like Linc, Laura endured many of my rambling "lectures" on various historical topics when we were kids, and her moral support throughout my academic career has been truly invaluable and is a greater gift than any big brother could ask for.

My hard-working, thoughtful father, James Douglas Fancher, caring, considerate aunt, Karen Treadway, and loving grandma, Wanda Mae

Treadway, have more than earned my deepest thanks through their love and prayers for my efforts to succeed, as did my late, courageous grandpa, James Harold Treadway, who fought in Korea, spent decades traveling globally and helping to save lives as a pastor, and was the greatest storyteller I have ever known. Aunt Karen's delicious desserts that she consistently mailed to us, her detailed nursing knowledge and experience, and her "green thumb" gardening expertise have always brought smiles to mine and Grazi's faces. The entire team of aces at Vernon Press, particularly Blanca Caro Duran, Isabel Penalba Rodriguez, Irene Ceballos Benavides, Javier Rodriguez, and Argiris Legatos, more than deserve my immense thanks. They have all been consistently positive, professional, and pleasant to work with, and their kindness and generosity to me as an author have motivated my efforts to edit, improve, and finally produce this work. Regarding the completion of this book in particular, Assistant Editor Isabel Penalba was especially helpful, kind, and encouraging, and I wish to offer her my deepest thanks here for her approachability, patience, and encouragement of my efforts to revise and resubmit this work despite my initial discouragement during parts of the peer review process.

UNT History Department Professors Drs. Courtney Welch, Nancy Stockdale, and Michael Wise, and University of Louisiana Monroe (ULM) History Department Professors Drs. Monica Bontty and Jeffrey Anderson have all been true friends and mentors over the years and each of them deserves my tremendous thanks for not only being excellent scholars, but for being amazing people. Equally, my two wonderful Saudi friends and brothers, Eissa Nasraldeen and Ammar al-Qahtani, have been invaluable in generously sharing their culture with me for many years, and their support for my deep, lifelong interest in their country's history helped launch my scholarly writing career by encouraging me to produce my previously-mentioned, first peer-reviewed book, *The Holy Warrior: Osama Bin Laden and His Jihadi Journey in the Soviet-Afghan War*, despite the doubts expressed by others at the time. Sham'Paige Holladay and Luke Holloway are, respectively, a wonderful sister and brother in history and teaching, both of whom I wish to thank here for their many years of friendship. I also want to thank Raluca Oprean, Head Researcher and Founder of Rotra Retrieval, for her invaluable assistance in photographing for me some helpful documents located at several British archives. Raluca is not only kind, professional, and approachable, but her efforts made it possible for me to explore the key role and late war successes of the Arctic convoys while working every day and conducting research from the comfort and safety of home.

Last but most certainly not least, I want to thank both of this book's two anonymous peer reviewers, both of whose time and efforts are greatly appreciated and one of whom was particularly thoughtful and considerate in providing encouraging, constructive criticism that helped me to improve this work. Working with them both, and other such professionals in the past, has truly been an honor. There are many others whose support over the years has helped to make this work possible, more than I can mention here. Yet those I have mentioned have gone above and beyond, and a simple "thank you" does not, from my perspective, sufficiently express my gratitude for their efforts on my behalf, and I can only express my hope that the work I have produced here brings nothing but honor to them in some way. They are the people who made the completion of this project more than worth the difficulties involved, and I cannot thank them enough for proving me wrong, whether knowingly or not, in my fears that the task would not be successful or worth the effort.

INTRODUCTION

My name is James Reagan Fancher. I was born in Monroe, Louisiana in 1985 and, in addition to working various outdoor odd jobs for several loved ones and acquaintances as a teenager, I have worked as a grocery store service clerk, emergency room registration clerk, front office clerk, and more while earning my associate degree, bachelor's degree, master's degree, and doctoral degree, the latter three of which are all in History. When possible, I have traveled, although my adventures have all been family-related journeys of love that remain limited to the Western Hemisphere. My academic journey that culminated in my Ph.D., the major field of which is in European History as it was the closest field to a World History concentration available, began in my childhood and took me across three college campuses in two states, an experience that, together with my working in retail and other industries since my high school years, brought me into contact with many interesting people who reacted to me in different ways, giving me a practical education about life. My lifelong love for history, which was influenced by my grandparents and my mother reading to me as a child and encouraging my genuine interest in other peoples and cultures, truly began in the fourth grade when, at a little Christian school in my father's tiny North Louisiana hometown, the teacher instructed our class to turn to Chapter 9 in our Social Studies textbook.

The image spread across the pages to which I turned immediately captured my attention as it was an action-packed, colorful painting of the Battle of the Wilderness that ignited the French and Indian War, as we have historically called it in the United States of America, in July 1755. The image of Native American warriors and their French allies dressed in woodland brown, frontier-style clothes firing from behind the trees, rocks, and bushes at the ambushed mass of red-coated British regulars and colonial American militiamen captivated me immediately. On one evening at around roughly the same time, I began digging into an encyclopedia article on the First World War and marveled at the black-and-white photographs and, to my young eyes, intriguing appearances and exotically-decorated uniforms of the Allied and Central Powers leaders after watching a science fiction cartoon episode in which the protagonists discovered and rescued a German submarine crew from a giant squid's clutches, the members of which were miraculously alive and well after being frozen inside an iceberg since the end of the conflict in 1918.

From that time forward, my interest in history only grew deeper, and, by the time that my preteen years began in the late 1990s, I was regularly devouring numerous encyclopedia articles on the Second World War, the Cold War, and many other historical subjects, regularly renting my favorite novel, Armstrong Sperry's *Call It Courage*, from the school library at the public school I was then attending in my hometown of West Monroe, Louisiana, and taking my sixth-grade history textbook home with me and reading ahead for fun even when there was no assigned homework, much to the horror of many of my classmates. When I was 15 going on 16, the exiled Saudi al-Qaeda leader Osama bin Laden executed the 9/11 terror attacks, and the various photos of the planet's most hunted man that subsequently appeared in media reports, online encyclopedia articles, and, to my greatest interest, on book covers, catapulted my historical passion onto a different topic as I developed a deep interest in learning about this elusive, white-turbaned, and submachine gun-wielding ethnic Yemeni Salafist militant. Bin Laden's wartime record of fighting the Soviets in Afghanistan as a young guerrilla fighter and leader led to my lifelong fascination with him as a historical figure, and my research, which technically began between 2003 and 2004 – long before I was a trained historian but at a time in which I began buying and consuming numerous books on him and al-Qaeda – culminated in the 2022 publication of my first book.

On moving from my North Louisiana hometown with my beautiful, Brazilian-born bride, Grazi, in the fall of 2019 to pursue my Ph.D. at UNT, my initial intention was to write my doctoral dissertation on bin Laden's wartime exploits fighting the Soviets in Afghanistan. After having uprooted us from our previous jobs and connections in the small town in which I had lived for nearly 34 years, my entire life at that point in time, I was deeply disappointed to find that many (but not all) of the faculty members and peers with whom I spoke attempted, unsuccessfully, to discourage me from pursuing my professional, historically centered fascination with bin Laden and his guerrilla exploits. The doubts that they expressed to me about turning my lifelong interest into my dissertation worked to my advantage, however, and they vastly underestimated my stubbornness as I nevertheless proceeded to complete my manuscript with the goal of publishing it as a book even as I decided on a different dissertation topic.

I am forever thankful to say that the book that I authored, without the knowledge or support of most (again, not all) of my betters and colleagues at the time, became my first peer-reviewed monograph as Vernon Press published the first edition of *The Holy Warrior* in January 2022 while I channeled my efforts into researching an unrelated subject for my dissertation. Before this, however, after meeting with several kind and helpful professors back at the beginning of 2020 as the COVID-19 pandemic erupted into the world and forced many of us into quarantine, I settled, reluctantly but with few other options, on the idea of writing a dissertation exploring U.S. Lend-Lease aid to the Soviet Union in the Second World War. This subject deeply depressed me, because I had chosen it not out of any genuine interest or passion, but in the hopes of writing a dissertation that could possibly win my betters' approval, yet I knew very little about it.

I had studied the Second World War's Eastern Front since my preteen days of bringing home my sixth-grade history textbook when I had first learned about Hitler's attack on Stalin's Soviet Union and the Red Army's dogged defiance of the Nazi assault. Yet I was painfully aware, and constantly reminded, that without having the sufficient language skills, a talent that I had not acquired while working my way through school and learning what I could in my "spare" time, I could not write an acceptable historical account of the Eastern Front unless I approached it from a strictly U.S. perspective. I had done quite well in Spanish in both high school and college and had learned even more from several of my close Mexican, Dominican, and Puerto Rican friends, and my Portuguese had improved to doctoral-level proficiency thanks to my brilliant, gifted wife at home and my in-laws in Brazil, in addition to my own intense studying. Yet being fluent in these beautiful Romance languages did little to ease my stresses and struggles as they were not the Germanic or Slavic languages necessary for the task. Resigning myself to what I feared to be a total academic failure, I settled for what I found to be a boring topic, fearing that I would be misjudged as being yet another "Amero-centric" U.S. historian. I also dreaded that I might be labeled as such in some ways, perhaps, because of having several prominent, controversial nineteenth-century ancestors, one being widely considered among the very worst U.S. presidents and the other being a tenacious, talented American commander once revered and respected as a skilled, leading tactician but who has long since been popularly mischaracterized. I fretted that such a label would only compound others' prejudices against me in addition to me being a Louisiana-born-and-raised scholar, despite my lifelong, deep, and genuine interest in and love for the histories of many other countries and peoples.

As I have often taught my students, however, we cannot allow either our ancestors' actions or others' opinions to limit or otherwise determine our personal destinies, which are influenced by our own important, independent choices. I was thankful and relieved to have subsequently discovered that my work on U.S. Lend-Lease aid to the Red Army received high commendations from all my committee members, most of whom were enthusiastically supportive in many of their comments. Instead of shying away from the subject that helped me earn my doctorate, a hard-earned accomplishment that neither I nor my loved ones could have imagined me achieving in our wildest dreams during my youth, I am thankful to now be the author not only of one scholarly book, but two, through both of which I hope to have contributed something worthwhile to the field of history, a judgment that remains, of course, in the eye of the reader.

Another reason, among many, for my concerns and reluctance when approaching the subject of U.S. Lend-Lease aid to the Soviet Union was the assumptions that I would have to tackle along the way in proving my point, arguments in which I had no genuine interest whatsoever to involve myself. A major claim popularized by both Second World War and Cold War Soviet officials and traditionally subscribed to by many academics, Western and Russian alike, is that Lend-Lease played little to no role in the Soviet war effort and the Red Army's success in crushing Nazi Germany.[1] As if encountering this rigid, propagandized assertion was not disturbing enough, I also knew, as a 100-percent-American in all branches of my family, that there remains a rather small but equally stubborn viewpoint among some of us that "we" won the Second World War, a notion that I long ago knew to be equally incorrect. The truth, as I had already found while researching bin Laden's life and actions, is infinitely more nuanced and interesting.

Although it is derived from the same initial manuscript, the work that I have hopefully produced here differs significantly from the original dissertation that, to my great relief, won the approval of my committee members. In a sincere effort to properly address and satisfy the criticisms from one of this work's two anonymous peer reviewers, I have now labored to shift this book's subject away from its original inclusion of a discussion of Lend-Lease's impact on the Soviet war effort for better or worse and have, instead, attempted to recenter it on U.S. perceptions of Stalin's strategic importance to the Allied war effort and how this, in turn, affected Washington's execution of the Soviet Lend-Lease program. As a result, this work, in addition to discussing to a certain extent the Lend-Lease supply routes over which Red Army-bound U.S. war supplies arrived in the Soviet Union, homes in on the motivations and rationale of the American leaders in keeping Stalin's fighting forces in the war while misjudging both his commitment to orthodox Communism and their own abilities to essentially "purchase" his goodwill, so to speak, through unconditional wartime aid.[2]

During a brief consultation visit at the White House in December 1942, Ambassador William H. Standley voiced his concerns to Roosevelt, Hopkins, Marshall, and General Henry "Hap" Arnold that while the Red Army may triumph at the ongoing Battle of Stalingrad, he dreaded, "what course of action Stalin would take if the war continued into the next summer without tangible help from the Western Allies."[3] Standley's remarks inadvertently undermined his subsequent attempts to persuade the White House to obtain concessions from the Soviets in exchange for continued Lend-Lease aid rather than persisting in providing unconditional support to Moscow as he advised Roosevelt to, "Stop acting like a Santa Claus, Chief …. And let's get something from Stalin in return" rather than continuing to supply, through Lend-Lease War Supply Mission Advisor General Philip R. Faymonville, "everything in the world they [the Soviets] ask for."[4] Yet Standley appears to have succeeded only in reinforcing Roosevelt and Hopkins's shared contemporary conviction that the Lend-Lease supply routes in Iran and Alaska needed urgent expansion to hasten the delivery of supplies to the Red Army to keep its troops fighting, a perspective that American First World War fighter ace Edward "Eddie" Rickenbacker recalls that he and many U.S. officials shared at the time.[5]

Accordingly, the results of this work demonstrate that the wartime American leadership's chief mistake lay not in supplying the Red Army to carry the war into Germany, a policy that doubtlessly hastened the Allied victory and saved countless lives, but simply in Roosevelt and Hopkins's assumptions that Stalin's inherent hostility to the West could be moderated somehow by the unconditional assistance they provided in the Red Army's hour of desperate need.[6] History has shown that Stalin, rather than succumbing to the peaceful postwar intentions that American leaders ascribed to him as they affectionately dubbed him "Uncle Joe" during the war, not only broke his wartime promise to Roosevelt to allow free, democratic elections in East Central Europe, but militarily strengthened the strategic position of Communist forces in China and northern Korea, thereby creating a situation that continues contributing to regional instability and threatens to engulf the world in a nuclear Third World War at a moment's notice.[7] Acknowledging this basic historical fact requires no overcomplicated analysis of Soviet strategic intentions or highly developed Russian language abilities, but a simple understanding that American Lend-Lease officials successfully aided in the defeat of the far greater contemporary totalitarian threat while gambling, incorrectly but with no better alternatives, that their wartime assistance would influence Stalin to pursue a peaceful postwar path.[8]

Perhaps someone might pose a question at this point asserting these global results of the war to be hindsight issues and asking if it is, therefore, unfair to fault wartime Washington for straining to see only the best in Stalin and for hoping and trusting in the idea that the Soviet leader could be influenced into moderating his policies toward the "capitalist" West? To this question, my answer is no. Roosevelt and his senior officials had ample knowledge of Stalin's record of diplomatic duplicity, military aggression, and his rise to power as a notorious bank robber whose violent terrorist acts had flooded the Communist Party with cash during the days of its underground revolutionary activities against Russia's tsarist monarchy while reportedly escaping seven times from the tsar's lax-security prisons.[9] Yet U.S. leaders, with the shadow of Brest-Litovsk weighing on their shoulders, nevertheless rightly ensured a constant flow of aid to the Red Army while overconfidently erring in thinking they could somehow influence or change Stalin, contributing to the Allied victory and setting a precedent for later U.S. aid programs to foreign fighting forces resisting tyrannical aggression abroad.

Brest-Litovsk's ramifications, Wilson's North Russian debacle, and the origins of American Lend-Lease aid to the Soviets

Throughout the Second World War, Roosevelt's Soviet Lend-Lease program appears to have been driven in large part by his concern that Stalin could potentially seek a separate peace with Hitler if the Soviet premier deemed Allied aid insufficient and continued suffering costly defeats. These fears were rooted in history and based largely on the Allied experience in the First World War, in which the German leaders had obtained a peace treaty from the young Soviet regime that eliminated the two-front war they had been waging contrary to Berlin's strategic prewar planning. Allied strategy in the Second World War focused on the total defeat of Hitler and his Axis partners, and concerns over Moscow forging a separate peace pact seem to have motivated not only Roosevelt's apparent zeal in aiding Stalin but that of his senior advisers as well. While Soviet spies within his administration are now known to have played a role in helping to shape U.S. wartime policy in a pro-Soviet direction, Roosevelt's emphasis on aiding Stalin seems to have been largely influenced by the Treaty of Brest-Litovsk's frightening shadow.

The Brest-Litovsk Treaty not only provided First World War Germany with crucial resources that threatened to undermine the British naval blockade of German ports but allowed Berlin to refocus the bulk of its armed might on the Western Front with no fear of being attacked from the east.[1] To avoid a repeat of this dangerous situation and ensure Nazi Germany's ultimate defeat, Roosevelt and other U.S. leaders sought to keep Stalin's soldiers armed, fed, and motivated to carry on the anti-Nazi struggle and drive deep into the Reich's heartland. Accordingly, it is necessary that we first examine early U.S.-Soviet relations and the reasons for which the specter of a potential second Brest-Litovsk seems to have later haunted U.S. leaders, steeling their resolve to aid Stalin while asking little in return and hoping to mold him. This chapter also discusses the extent to which Stalin managed to attract prominent American businessmen and skilled technicians to strengthen his industrialization program in the 1930s, forging connections that later enhanced Soviet Lend-Lease.

The roots of Russia's 1917 revolutions that overthrew the country's monarchy, swept the Communists into power, and triggered an Allied military intervention in the ensuing Civil War and subsequent U.S.-Soviet hostility lie in the country's military disasters suffered in the First World War.[2] Accordingly, it is necessary to first briefly explore the seeds of this mutual hostility and distrust that occurred between the early Soviet leaders and their U.S. counterparts that date back to the decade of diplomatic tensions between the United States and Tsarist Russia before the outbreak of the First World War. During the "Progressive Era" of U.S. Presidents Theodore "Teddy" Roosevelt, William Howard Taft, and Thomas Woodrow Wilson, relations soured between Washington and St. Petersburg as U.S. leaders criticized tsarist autocracy.[3] This overall downward diplomatic spiral appears to have initially served as a major factor in preventing an earlier U.S. entry into the First World War on the side of the Allied Powers.

After reluctantly accepting the imperial crown following his father's death on 1 November 1894, Tsar Nicholas II proved to be a weak and indecisive ruler. His Romanov royal family had reigned over a vast empire spanning two (and, including the period of Russian rule in Alaska, three) continents for nearly three centuries, but as Russia's royal and elite classes prospered, most Russian peasants and workers labored under appalling conditions.[4] An 1885 study of factory conditions conducted by a royal inspection team revealed highly unsanitary conditions at many workers' settlements. In their report, the inspectors cited the billowing smoke columns polluting the air, the cramped tents in which most workers lived, and the "loose boards" that three or four workers at a time were forced to share as beds.[5]

The tsarist rule also made life extremely difficult for Russia's Jewish population, particularly as state-tolerated anti-Semitism grew as the monarchy sought to scapegoat its Jewish subjects while suppressing the country's underground socialist movement during the late nineteenth century. On 1 March 1881, members of the revolutionary "People's Will" terrorist group assassinated Tsar Alexander II (r. 1855-1881), known as the "Tsar Liberator" for his 1861 emancipation of Russia's serf class, in a bomb attack on his royal carriage in the imperial capital, St. Petersburg.[6] The significant social reforms that Alexander II had enacted during his quarter-century reign died with him as his son and successor, Tsar Alexander III, immediately reinstituted harsher and more autocratic rule.[7]

Presiding over the hangings of many revolutionaries during his reign, Alexander III's secret police, the *Okhrana*, also instigated numerous violent mob attacks or *pogroms* against Russia's Jewish communities, leaving a bloody legacy for his son and heir Nicholas II to inherit in 1894.[8] Better known by his pseudonym Lenin, Vladimir Ilyich Ulyanov, the brother of one executed revolutionary, later exacted horrific revenge on the Romanovs after ordering the murders of the then-deposed Nicholas II and his entire family. Perceived by many Russian workers to be a reluctant ruler with little genuine interest in the suffering of his subjects, Nicholas II reputedly remained aloof as conditions continued deteriorating into his reign.[9]

In 1903, many Jewish residents of the city of Kishinev were brutally massacred in a particularly bloody *pogrom*, prompting President Teddy Roosevelt to castigate the Romanov dynasty for its tolerance of such cruelty while privately acknowledging Washington's own problems with the ongoing lynchings of African American southerners in some parts of the American south.[10] In stark contrast to his distant cousin Franklin's later conciliatory approach to Stalin's bloodstained Soviet regime starting in 1933, Teddy used his position at the presidency's helm to level severe criticism at the tsar's dismal human rights record in Russia. Despite his criticism of the Romanov monarchy, however, Roosevelt subsequently played a key role in brokering peace between Russia and Japan after the tsar's army and navy suffered staggering defeats at the hands of their opponents during the Russo-Japanese War in 1905.[11] Along with the January 1905 "Bloody Sunday" massacre of peaceful protesters led by Russian Orthodox priest Father Georgy Gapon, Japan's victory helped ignite a failed revolution launched by various revolutionary political factions in Russia that year.[12]

Tasting the bitter, stinging humiliation resulting from Russia's crushing defeat at the hands of the Imperial Japanese forces, Nicholas II struggled to suppress the 1905 Russian Revolution as the military largely remained loyal, and he subsequently enacted a series of limited reforms.[13] These reforms, such as the establishment of a State *Duma* or parliament that included representatives from various political parties, proved unsatisfactory to the Russian revolutionary leaders and U.S. officials alike. Nicholas II often used his royal authority to dissolve and prevent *Duma* sessions, leading Roosevelt and his two "Progressive" White House successors to maintain a largely negative view of human rights in Tsarist Russia despite presiding over a racial caste system in many southern states.[14]

Following the assassinations of Austro-Hungarian Archduke and heir-to-the-throne Franz Ferdinand and his wife, Duchess Sofie, by the Bosnian Serb militant Gavrilo Princip in June 1914, Austria-Hungary's aging Emperor Franz Josef I demanded reparations from Serbia.[15] Seeking to aid Slavic Serbia following Germany's official support of the Austrian demands, Nicholas II began mobilizing Russia's vast army, triggering a German ultimatum and declaration of war on 1 August 1914.[16] Launching an invasion of East Prussia on 17 August 1914, Nicholas II's army initially advanced quickly into enemy territory before being repulsed by German forces at the Battles of Tannenberg and the Masurian Lakes fought between 30 August and 14 September.[17] From an invading army initially numbering more than 400,000 men, the tsar's generals reportedly suffered 142,000 casualties at Tannenberg and another 120,000 at the Masurian Lakes.[18] While the German, French, and British armies soon settled into immobile trench warfare following the initial engagements in Western Europe, the Eastern Front largely remained a fluid battle zone.[19]

Infighting between the tsar's top generals and corruption in the Imperial Russian High Command or *Stavka* continued leading to unnecessary military disasters as the bloodshed raged across the Eastern Front. While Nicholas II's uncle, Grand Duke Nikolai, remained the army's official commander-in-chief, the tsar preferred the advice of War Minister Vladimir Sukhomlinov due to the general's intense loyalty to the monarchy rather than his military competence.[20] The personal conflicts between Sukhomlinov, Nikolai, and many of their subordinate officers widened the rifts within the tsarist Russian army.[21]

The regular use of uncoded radio messages between Russian commanders also provided enemy interceptors with detailed knowledge of *Stavka's* operational planning and Russian troop concentrations, allowing the German and Austrian commanders to thwart countless offensives.[22] In 1915, German and Austrian forces reportedly captured more than 1,000,000 Russian troops during separate operations in Galicia and the Carpathian Mountains.[23] With each massive loss of men and material at the front, peasant frustration with the tsar's military incompetence and his perceived indifference to the sufferings of ordinary soldiers continued to intensify.[24]

By early 1916, the endless fighting and Russia's inability to achieve a decisive victory over the Central Powers had inflamed the prewar tensions between the Romanov monarchy and most Russian workers and peasants.[25] Seeking to relieve the besieged French forces at Verdun by forcing German Kaiser Wilhelm II's generals into refocusing their attention on Germany's eastern borders, General Alexei Brusilov launched a powerful offensive on 4 June, driving deep into Galicia.[26] While Brusilov's attack further forced Wilhelm II to deploy larger troop concentrations to the Eastern Front, it also resulted in more than 490,000 Russian casualties.[27]

Class tensions within the Imperial Russian Army continued to rise as the war continued, exacerbating the mutual resentment between the army's infantry units and the artillery branch as some tsarist commanders allegedly treated their men as cannon fodder as supplies began to dwindle.[28] While most soldiers serving in the Russian infantry generally hailed from the country's peasant class, the artillery remained dominated by the aristocracy. The aristocratic artillerists are said to have often refused to "waste" their shells on the peasant infantrymen, failing to support them with a bombardment of enemy positions before an infantry assault commenced.[29] In one instance, several surviving

Russian soldiers reportedly raised a white flag after most of their comrades had been killed by enemy fire, only to be shelled by their own artillerymen as they were marched into captivity.[30]

By the beginning of 1917, Russia's military failures and enormous battlefield losses had only succeeded in deepening the country's internal problems and pushing relations between the ruling Romanov monarchy and much of the Russian population to the breaking point.[31] Nicholas II's enforcement of food rationing and his family's perceived indifference to the suffering that the war brought to ordinary Russians strengthened revolutionary movements such as the Socialist Revolutionary Party, or Trudoviks, and Bolshevik Party, later renamed the Communist Party.[32] On 15 March 1917, Nicholas II abdicated the Romanov throne on his own behalf and that of his 12-year-old son and heir, Alexei, in favor of his cousin, Grand Duke Michael Alexandrovich, following a week of mass rioting and demonstrations in the country's capital, Petrograd.[33]

Grand Duke Michael immediately declined the imperial crown, effectively ending three centuries of Romanov royal rule in the Russian Empire.[34] Under the leadership of Socialist Revolutionary President Alexander Kerensky, the Provisional Government of Russia placed the Romanovs under protective custody at their former royal palace in Petrograd. In April, Kerensky's new government vowed to honor the previous regime's commitments to the Allies and continued prosecuting the war against the Central Powers on the Eastern Front.[35]

Until this point in the war, President Woodrow Wilson had continually reassured Americans that he intended to keep their country neutral despite escalating tensions with Germany because of Berlin's policy of unrestricted submarine warfare.[36] Enacted by Wilhelm II, this policy targeted the Allies' Atlantic trade as Great Britain's Royal Navy tightened its blockade of Germany's ports, and it gradually began angering many Americans. Despite his growing frustration with the German submarine menace, Wilson is said to have expressed unease about entering the war on the side of the Allies due to the autocratic nature of Russia's tsarist regime.[37] Nicholas II's perceived disinterest in introducing more effective democratic reforms contributed heavily to Wilson's initial attempts to remain neutral, and for several years, he continued resisting Allied pressure to join the war even as tensions with Berlin mounted.[38]

In January 1917, British cryptographers' discovery and decoding of the Zimmermann Telegram, in which the German leadership promised support for a Mexican campaign into the southwestern United States, pushed relations between Washington and Berlin to the edge.[39] Wilhelm II's escalation of his submarine campaign the following month strained relations further as domestic U.S. support for entry into the war as a member of the Allies increased, pressuring Wilson to act.[40] Even as war appeared increasingly unavoidable, the president expressed his concern that the United States could not claim to be supporting "democracy" because of the tsar's membership in the ranks of the Allied Powers.[41]

Russia's February Revolution and the resulting overthrow of Romanov imperial rule had profound consequences that significantly altered the course of the First World War by rendering the Allied cause more appealing to officials in Washington. Expressing his relief that U.S. involvement no longer required an alliance with the autocratic Romanov dynasty, Wilson appears to have regarded the new Kerensky government as a democratic force worth aiding.[42] Praising, "the wonderful and heartening things that have been happening within the last few weeks in Russia," Wilson portrayed Russian society as having been, "always democratic at heart," while implying tsarist autocracy to be Germanic in origin in his pro-war speech to Congress on 2 April 1917.[43] Combined with public outrage over the Zimmerman Telegram and Berlin's continued submarine attacks, the latter being a mistake repeated by Hitler that allowed Roosevelt to generate support for Soviet Lend-Lease, the tsar's removal proved decisive in the U.S. declaration of war on Germany on 6 April 1917.[44]

Wilson immediately issued Proclamation 1364 aimed at preempting sabotage operations by supposed "alien enemies" aged 14 and older living in the United States, an act that appears to have contributed to a strong domestic fear of Germans and an association of them with anti-American activities.[45] Foreshadowing the popular prejudice against Eastern and Southern European immigrants during the Red Scare, this hysteria culminated in lynchings and threats against German immigrants in some parts of the country as patriotic fervor swept the public.[46] According to Mary J. Manning, suspicions and fears of the disloyalty allegedly harbored by German immigrants and Americans of German origin continued to mount throughout 1918 with the administration's codifying of the Alien Enemy Act of 1798.[47] Similarly, Roosevelt later helped shift Americans' fears away from Communism and refocused them on immigrants and children of immigrants from Axis countries, signing an order that led to the incarceration of thousands of Japanese-Americans in internment camps.[48]

Shortly after the congressional declaration of war, Bolshevik Party leader Vladimir Lenin returned to Russia armed with $5,000,000 in German gold marks to rally his followers and lead a Communist revolution against the Provisional Government.[49] Sensing a crucial opportunity to exploit Russia's turbulent atmosphere and force the country out of the war, Generals Paul von Hindenburg and Erich von Ludendorff had earlier concluded that Germany's strategic interests lay in financially backing Lenin's bid for power.[50] Lenin immediately began calling for the overthrow of Kerensky's Provisional Government and the rule of *soviets* or "councils" of soldiers and workers to represent the people and implement Communist reforms.[51]

Mass demonstrations against the Provisional Government erupted following more military defeats in July 1917, prompting Kerensky to order Lenin's arrest as a German agent, and the Bolshevik leader fled into hiding in Finland. From Bolshevik safehouses in Helsinki, Lenin continued agitating for a Communist revolution and gained many more supporters after three years of devastating conflict with his promises of, "Peace, land, and bread!"[52] His success in exploiting the growing agony of ordinary Russians that resulted from military defeats and food shortages later motivated Roosevelt's prioritizing of Soviet Lend-Lease, as the president sought to save Stalin from sharing Kerensky's fate.[53]

On 7 November 1917, a fleet of Bolshevik sailors entered Petrograd harbor after Lenin's deputy and leader of the city's *soviet* Lev Davidovich Bronstein, popularly known by his pseudonym Leon Trotsky, promised to organize Bolshevik support for a military coup.[54] Fighting erupted as thousands of soldiers organized into *soviets*, abandoning their officers and occupying government buildings. On the following day, the soldiers captured the Winter Palace, overthrowing the Provisional Government while Lenin and Trotsky announced the formation of the Russian Soviet Federative Socialist Republic (RSFSR).[55]

On Lenin's orders, soldiers abandoned their battlefield posts and organized *soviets* to support the victorious Bolsheviks' "October Revolution" against the threat of counterrevolution by the Party's socialist, democratic, and monarchist rivals.[56] Lenin's deputies immediately acted on their proposed programs, issuing a peace declaration, confiscating private property, and nationalizing the country's industries.[57] In December, they initiated a series of peace talks with German officials, yet negotiations temporarily collapsed, and German forces immediately resumed their offensive, driving deep into Russian territory and capturing a large swathe of land between the Baltic and Black Seas.[58]

On 3 March 1918, Lenin and Trotsky surrendered this enormous area, populated by 56,000,000 people from Estonia to Ukraine, to Wilhelm II in the Treaty of Brest-Litovsk.[59] Lenin's treaty with Berlin triggered an immediate and dramatic shift in the overall strategic situation in Europe, carrying ramifications that reverberated across the continent and onto the French and Belgian battlefields. By concluding peace with the Bolsheviks, the German High Command had effectively neutralized the threat from the east and proceeded to concentrate its military efforts on a major offensive against the Western Allies.[60]

In March 1918, Ludendorff launched Germany's Spring Offensive against the increasingly exhausted Anglo-French armies.[61] Yet, as pointed out by Professor Geoffrey Wawro in *Sons of Freedom: The Forgotten American Soldiers Who Defeated Germany in World War I*, U.S. troops had begun arriving in France in large numbers by the spring of 1918.[62] Under General John J. "Blackjack" Pershing, the fighting men of the American Expeditionary Force (AEF) gradually emerged as outstanding soldiers and played a crucial role in delivering the fatal blow that felled Berlin's armies later in the year.[63] As Wawro explains, however, the German troops initially gained ground as Wilson's beleaguered British and French allies (who had been, after all, fighting the Germans tenaciously and courageously while persevering for nearly four long years by this point) began to falter and collapse in several key locations.[64] In the first week of their grand offensive, German forces captured 963 Allied artillery guns and 100 tanks and destroyed 93 aircraft while advancing on the town of Maisonnette and striking Paris with long-range artillery fire.[65]

The Brest-Litovsk Treaty also provided Germany with vital access to the abundant resources of the former Russian Empire, including Ukraine's vast wheatfields, and appeared to Allied leaders at the time as a frightening development that had altered the strategic situation to their detriment.[66] Facing no further resistance from the east, Berlin could potentially reinvigorate its war effort by exploiting the resources of the territories surrendered by Lenin, thereby supplying its armies to fight on indefinitely and reducing the effectiveness of Great Britain's naval blockade. Allied fears grew in April as German troops arrived in Finland following Berlin's 7 March 1918 peace treaty with Helsinki, triggering concerns that the kaiser could now seize Russia's strategic Arctic port of Murmansk and nearby Archangel on the White Sea.[67]

Fearing a German attack, the local Murmansk *soviet* requested assistance from the British government, and Prime Minister David Lloyd George landed a small contingent of troops on the morning after Lenin and Trotsky signed the Brest-Litovsk Treaty.[68] To counter the rise of domestic anti-Communist opposition groups, Trotsky began organizing thousands of soldiers and peasants into a new military force that he called the Red Army in honor of the Bolshevik Party's flag.[69] Upon joining Trotsky's Red Army, soldiers swore an "Oath of the Red Warrior" in which they promised to fight to uphold, enforce, and expand the government's political ideology.[70] Although they represented a diverse range of ideologies ranging from tsarism to democratic socialism and sometimes fought each other, the Russian anti-Communists became collectively known as the White Army.[71]

Angered by Lenin's treaty with the kaiser, British, French, and Japanese leaders reacted with hostility towards the young Soviet regime, perceiving its separate peace as a deadly act of betrayal and fearing its aggressive calls for a worldwide Communist revolution.[72] Dismissing Allied fears, Wilson initially praised Lenin's efforts against tsarist autocracy and monarchism in general in an 11 March 1918 telegram delivered to the Seventh Party Congress at which the Bolsheviks officially changed their party's name to the Russian Communist Party.[73] Wilson appears to have initially welcomed the Communists as an ideologically progressive political party, yet he increasingly expressed alarm over Lenin's handing over of Ukraine's abundant resources to Berlin.[74]

During Russia's years of participation in the struggle against the Central Powers, both Nicholas II and Kerensky had stockpiled large amounts of excess war material provided by the Western Allies in the Arctic ports of Murmansk and Archangel and Vladivostok on the Pacific coast.[75] First utilized for this purpose in the First World War, these three ports later served as key destinations for the Allied deliveries of a much greater amount of Lend-Lease aid to the Red Army. Wilson shared Allied fears that if German forces in Finland again resumed the offensive to seize what Berlin might not gain through diplomacy, they could capture the first two ports, located in the far north of European Russia, and the Allied war material stored in them.[76] Regarding the Pacific Ocean port of Vladivostok, he also feared the possibility of the Allied supplies there either falling into Japanese hands or being given to Germany by a victorious, pro-Berlin Soviet government.[77]

At a 27 May 1918 meeting of the British War Cabinet, Prime Minister Lloyd George and Lord Robert Cecil addressed the ongoing carnage unleashed by Ludendorff's Spring Offensive and spoke hopefully of the incoming U.S. divisions that they viewed as critical Allied reinforcements.[78] Addressing the situation in Russia, Lord Cecil voiced concern over the fate of the Czechoslovak Legion, stating that its men sought to avoid embroilment in Russia's Civil War and to somehow reach the Western Front to fight in the Allied ranks. Announcing that he planned to meet with the French Secretary of State that night, Lord Cecil informed the War Cabinet that Allied officials intended to hold a crucial discussion on Lenin's perceived pro-German stance and how they hoped to reopen the Eastern Front.[79]

Alarmed at these developments and increasingly concerned that Allied supplies in Russia could fall into German hands, the Anglo-French leaders began urging their American counterparts to support a military intervention against Lenin's Bolsheviks.[80] Initially reluctant, Wilson voiced his concern that such action could result in the restoration of the Romanovs and refused to commit U.S. forces to a campaign focused on overthrowing Communism. The president had framed the U.S. war mission as a crusade to preserve and protect democracy in his speeches to the American public, and he initially refused to send troops.[81]

As the fighting between the Allied and German forces in France and the Red and White Armies in Russia raged throughout the summer of 1918, Allied officials continued urging Wilson to dispatch a contingent of U.S. troops to North Russia and Siberia.[82] The Allied leadership desperately sought to restore the Eastern Front to again force Berlin into a two-front war and grew increasingly fearful that the Soviet government constituted a pro-German regime. As daily clashes with German troops continued, Wilson gradually decided to aid the White Army, hoping that a limited U.S. presence could help train its troops, promote democratic values, and ensure the safe passage of the Czechoslovak Legion to the Western Front.[83] The pre-revolutionary Russian High Command had authorized these former Czech and Slovak prisoners-of-war (POWs) to be trained to return and overthrow Habsburg rule and restore national independence to their respective homelands in Vienna's floundering empire.[84]

In March 1918, Lenin's Commissar for Nationalities, the dropout Georgian Orthodox Church seminarian and bank robber Iosib Vissarionovich Dzugashvili, then known by his pseudonym "Stalin" meaning "Man of Steel," authorized free passage for the Czechoslovak Legion to travel to Vladivostok and board ships to sail for the Western Front.[85] A hostile encounter with a local Bolshevik commander in Chelyabinsk led to violence, and, in an insubordinate act for which Stalin appears to have never forgiven him, Trotsky subsequently ordered the legionnaires to be disarmed, arrested, and executed.[86] Trotsky's rash reaction provoked Czechoslovak defiance, and the men subsequently seized a large part of the Trans-Siberian Railroad and advanced upon the Ural Mountain town of Ekaterinburg in July 1918 as the Soviet forces there ruthlessly executed the imprisoned Nicholas II and his Romanov royal family.[87]

Emphasizing his staunch support for "self-determination" and democracy, Wilson grew increasingly concerned about the plight of the legionnaires and sought to help facilitate their safe passage to the Western Front by sending U.S. troops.[88] He also began expressing distaste for Communism after Lenin and Trotsky launched the Red Terror at the hands of their *Cheka* secret police agency, later renamed the NKVD during Stalin's rule, in August 1918.[89] Following peasant resistance to the Soviet regime's seizure of private property and farms, Lenin's secret police organized the mass executions and incarcerations of those suspected of harboring counterrevolutionary thoughts.[90]

From the Soviet capital, Moscow, U.S. Ambassador DeWitt Clinton Poole expressed alarm following a 3 August 1918 speech in which Lenin declared Soviet Russia to be at war with the Allies as more British and French reinforcements arrived in Archangel. The following month, a successful coup by an uneasy alliance of democratic-socialist White Army factions in Archangel and Murmansk led to the establishment of the Provisional Government of the Northern Region.[91] As the Russian Civil War and Red Terror raged, with Lenin and Trotsky voicing increasingly hostile anti-Allied sentiments, Ambassador Poole's reports from Moscow appeared to lend credence to Allied fears that the Communists were German puppets.[92] These concerns were amplified by Poole's alarm at the Soviets' signing of several, "supplementary treaties of Brest-Litovsk" on 27 August, rendering a reopening of the Eastern Front more urgent from the contemporary Allied perspective.[93]

After a discussion with U.S. Secretary of State Robert Lansing, Wilson agreed to dispatch a limited force of about 13,000 troops to assist the White Army in North Russia and Siberia through guard duty, recruitment, and training.[94] He then authored an "aide memoire" stating that he intended the limited and temporary U.S. effort to bolster the White Army's democratic factions while focusing on protecting Allied supplies from falling into German hands.[95] Wilson's stated objectives later created confusion and led to many problems for the U.S. troops that he deployed to aid the Allied forces assisting the White Army in North Russia and Siberia. The president expressly forbade U.S. forces from launching sustained offensive operations against the enemy while imploring them to remain officially neutral in the Russian Civil War and simultaneously train the White Army's often-reluctant soldiers to defeat the Bolsheviks.[96]

On 15 August 1918, 7,950 troops of the American Expeditionary Force, Siberia (AEF-Siberia) under U.S. General William S. Graves landed to somewhat support, but also cautiously observe, the ongoing Japanese military campaign under General Baron Otani Kikuzo and Lieutenant General Yui Mitsue at Russia's strategic Pacific Ocean port of Vladivostok.[97] Serving in the ranks of these men, U.S. Army ordnance officer Philip Faymonville later became a key Lend-Lease official in Moscow between 1941 and 1943. Faymonville's great personal rapport with Soviet officials and his faith in the Red Army's martial talents, an unconventional U.S. view at the time, later earned him the trust and appreciation of Roosevelt's friend Harry Hopkins.[98]

Totaling 4,500 troops in three battalions, the men of the U.S. Polar Bear Expedition landed in Archangel on 4 September 1918 to help their British and French Allies guard the Arctic port and the surrounding villages against the Red Army's raids.[99] Placed under the overall command of British General Frederick C. Poole, the "Polar Bears" initially found themselves involved in several attacks on the enemy against Wilson's orders.[100] After a U.S. State Department complaint to London and Poole's subsequent replacement by General Edmund Ironside in October, the men assumed a static, defensive role. After several meetings with his superiors in London before his North Russian deployment, Ironside quickly realized that he could expect no reinforcements and vowed to honor Wilson's wishes by refraining from an aggressive campaign.[101]

Throughout the winter months of 1918 and 1919, Trotsky's forces struck the White Army and the Allies in North Russia as many local villagers proved reluctant to join the anti-Communists and rallied to the red flag of the Soviet cause.[102] Playing on nationalist sentiments, the Communists portrayed themselves as Russia's true defenders and successfully incited mutinies in the White Army's ranks while turning some local populations against the Allies.[103] Denied further reinforcements from Washington and London and restrained from launching sustained offensive operations against the Red Army's strongholds, U.S. forces in North Russia and Siberia suffered 424 casualties before their withdrawal on 1 April 1920.[104]

While Trotsky's small cadres of Soviet partisans largely ceased their operations against AEF-Siberia during the harsh winter months of late 1918 and early 1919, his Red Northern Army increased its activities against the Polar Bears. As White Army defections to the Soviets mounted during the winter months, swelling the Red Army's ranks to more than 600,000 men by June 1919, United States Senators Hiram Johnson (R-CA), Robert M. LaFollette (R-WI), and William E. Borah (R-ID) challenged Wilson's Russian policy.[105] Arguing that the Allied armistice with Germany and the Czechoslovak Legion's recent neutrality pact with the Soviet government rendered the intervention's initial purpose obsolete, the senators urged the president to withdraw all U.S. forces from Russian soil.[106]

Johnson also pointed out that recent expressions of resentment and open hostility towards the Allied presence in North Russia highlighted the foolishness of leaving small bodies of U.S. troops to guard isolated village outposts whose inhabitants may suddenly turn against them.[107] Wilson's supporters countered that the United States had entered the war to promote democratic governments and the self-determination of nations and argued that the U.S. soldiers were fulfilling this mission by temporarily remaining in Russia.[108] Dismissing the growing unrest and desertions in the White Army's ranks as isolated incidents, the president's allies echoed his argument that the limited U.S. effort could help inspire many Russians to embrace democracy.[109]

As the Allies continued engaging a growing number of enemy forces that were inadvertently bolstered by Wilson's restraints on the Polar Bears and rising local support for the Bolsheviks, Senator Johnson and his colleagues continued arguing for a U.S. troop withdrawal. In a 14 February 1919 Senate session, Johnson introduced a motion to withdraw all U.S. forces from Russia that quickly gained momentum as more lawmakers began voicing their support.[110] Johnson convincingly argued that not only had the fighting in Europe already ended with Germany's defeat but that the growing strength of the Bolsheviks, accompanied by mounting resistance to the Allies in North Russia, amplified the level of danger faced by the Americans.[111]

Johnson proceeded to opine that unless Wilson intended to authorize a far larger force to enter Russia and decisively defeat the Red Army, the decision to maintain such a small number of men in an increasingly hostile country constituted the height of arrogance and folly and could only boomerang to Washington's detriment.[112] Shortly after the California senator's appeal, Wilson committed to a "phased withdrawal" of the Polar Bears and AEF-Siberia from Russian soil.[113] Due to the much higher level of violence in North Russia, the Polar Bears' exit from Archangel and Murmansk received priority and concluded in the summer of 1919, while AEF-Siberia completed its pullout the following spring.[114]

Although a very limited and reluctantly executed military campaign, Wilson's brief intervention proved sufficiently helpful in playing into Lenin and Trotsky's hands and their propagandized portrayal of the United States as a land of imperialist aggressors.[115] In addition to the souring of relations between Washington and Moscow, the campaign also marked a shift in U.S. foreign policy regarding Russia as a crucial strategic theater of war due to the temporarily detrimental strategic impact of Brest-Litovsk. Despite eventually viewing the Communists as a threat, Wilson's motives for the intervention originated in the Allies' desire to reopen the Eastern Front and challenge Germany's unhindered access to Russia's vast resources.[116] Allied animosity toward the early Soviet regime resulted more from its treaty with Berlin rather than its political ideology, a factor that later fueled Roosevelt's quest to keep the Soviets sufficiently armed and kill the Nazis in the field at all costs.[117]

Beginning with the U.S. military intervention in Russia's Civil War, fear of Communism became widespread in the American public, resulting in prejudice against immigrants from Eastern and Southern Europe during the Red Scare of the early 1920s. The slogans of revolutionary political movements such as the International Workers of the World (IWW) also reminded some U.S. veterans of the North Russian campaign of Bolshevik slogans.[118] These fears increased after Lenin and Trotsky successfully reconquered many of the Russian Empire's former territories and declared the birth of the Soviet Union on 30 December 1922 after emerging victoriously in the country's Civil War.[119] During the Red Scare, mistrust of Eastern Europeans in particular became so pronounced that many African American jobseekers fleeing segregation in some of the southern U.S. states found work in northern cities preferring them over immigrants during the "First Great Migration."[120]

Between 1919 and 1921, U.S. Attorney General A. Mitchell Palmer oversaw a series of law enforcement raids by the Wilson administration, known as the "Palmer Raids," on the offices of U.S. labor unions and the Communist and Socialist Parties as the wartime anti-German hysteria evolved into postwar fears of a Communist takeover.[121] Emphasizing the outrages committed by Lenin and Trotsky's regime as they consolidated their power in Russia, Palmer portrayed the American Communist Party as a foreign force seeking to undermine the government and advocated the arrest and deportation of all alleged, "reds."[122] Just as Trotsky's propagandists had undermined the White Army's cause to an extent and utilized xenophobic tactics by portraying its leaders as Western-backed puppets, Palmer's statements appear to have led to the labeling of almost any labor movement or Eurasian immigrants as Communist.[123]

In his position as Wilson's Attorney General, Palmer also publicized a collection of various speeches and writings attributed to Communist politicians to make his case for deporting Eastern and Southern European immigrants, labor union activists, and other alleged Communists in 1920.[124] The specific statements to which Palmer's Justice Department called attention included not only those of actual Communist leaders, but members of the IWW and other political movements as well.[125] These actions appear to have led many U.S. government officials and civilians at the time to associate most organized labor movements with Communism, despite the competing and often hostile relations between rival socialist political parties both domestically and abroad.[126]

Throughout the 1920s, American presidents consistently refused to recognize the Soviet regime and discouraged private entrepreneurs from conducting business with Soviet officials. In the Soviet Union, Stalin steadily rose to the heights of power in the Communist Party's ranks following Lenin's death in January 1924.[127] By 1927, he had fully consolidated his position, established the office of General Secretary of the Communist Party, and exiled many political rivals, including Trotsky, before eventually having him assassinated by the icepick-wielding Spanish Communist Ramon Mercader in Mexico City in 1940. Stalin perfected the dictatorship established by Lenin and Trotsky, and despite his public claims of withdrawing from their aggressive policies, many Americans remained fearful of Soviet Communism.[128]

While counting on his public denials of expansionist motives to allay the fears of Western leaders, Stalin appears to have remained committed to strengthening the Soviet Union militarily while abandoning Trotsky's loud, boastful rhetoric threatening the imminent export of Communist revolution. Through a mass industrialization campaign, Stalin appears to have sought to modernize the country and the Red Army while hoping for the West to lower its guard.[129] Throughout the following decade, he successfully exploited the global economic turmoil to the Red Army's advantage by attracting U.S. industrialists to invest in Soviet military power, convincing some Americans, including future Lend-Lease officials, that he had abandoned Lenin's aggressive strategy. Developments in the 1930s provided Stalin with more opportunities to forge relations with the West and motivated U.S. diplomats and private citizens alike to reach out to the Soviet Union, a process that began as the 1920s ended.[130]

In May 1929, the architect Albert Kahn of the Detroit, Michigan-based firm Albert Kahn Associates signed a contract with the Soviet government's trading company, Amtorg Trading Corporation, to build the Stalingrad Tractor Plant with U.S. steel components and machinery.[131] Although officially a tractor factory only, the Stalingrad plant also served later as a mass production center for tanks and armored vehicles. Christina E. Crawford of Harvard University's Weatherhead Center for International Affairs states that Kahn's designs also led to the construction of the Kharkov Tractor Plant, the structure of which closely resembled the Stalingrad location.[132] Before signing his contract with Amtorg, Kahn had designed and built the Ford Motor Company's massive River Rouge Plant, and he based his work on the designs he had produced for his friend and business acquaintance, Henry Ford.[133]

Shortly after Kahn began his work building Soviet industry, reportedly constructing 531 factories and training more than 4,000 of Stalin's engineers, Ford himself became interested in the project as U.S. firms reeled from the financial sting of the October 1929 Stock Market Crash and the Great Depression's onset.[134] According to Professor Boris M. Shpotov of the Russian Academy of Sciences, Ford Motor Company's technicians completed work on an "automobile" assembly plant, actually another tank and armored car factory, at Nizhny Novgorod on 1 February 1930.[135] Later that year, another assembly plant in Moscow began production as Soviet engineers toiled alongside their U.S. counterparts, using American steel and technical skills to help meet the industrialization goals dictated in Stalin's first "Five-Year Plan."[136]

Ford's representatives agreed to supply technical expertise until 1938, while Stalin committed to purchasing U.S. $13,000,000 worth of Ford vehicles and parts, providing business for the Detroit entrepreneur while upgrading the Soviet Union's military production capabilities. Engineers completed work on another plant, known as Gorki, in 1933, and the Red Army began producing the GAZ and BA series of armored combat vehicles based on the chassis of the Ford Model-A.[137] For his investment in Soviet industrial production, Ford received the honorific title of "Hero of the Soviet Union," and the U.S. industrialist later contributed to the Allied victory through war production at his Detroit plant, eventually shipping an entire factory to Stalin in 1943.[138]

The conditions created by the Great Depression enabled Stalin to continue channeling U.S. ingenuity to the Soviet Union's advantage, attracting the attention of inventors and industrialists seeking to make a profit as the Great Depression destroyed the livelihoods of many Americans. He delivered speeches referring to the growth of Communist parties in the West and ordered the Red Army's commanders to begin developing powerful weaponry while preaching his allegedly peaceful intent and simple goal of national survival.[139] Stalin's desire to strengthen the Red Army motivated Amtorg's purchasing of two prototype tanks disguised as tractors and built by U.S. engineer John Walter Christie, whose invention had previously been rejected by U.S. Army officials, on 30 December 1930.[140] Improving upon Christie's revolutionary suspension system and overall design, Soviet engineers subsequently produced two series of tanks based on his prototypes, equipping the vehicles with sloped frontal armor and developing them into the fast-moving BT-7 and powerful T-34 tanks.[141]

In 1930 alone, more than 600 Americans from the Ford and Hercules Motor Companies arrived in the Soviet Union to provide technical expertise and manual labor for Stalin's factories, setting a precedent for his later procurement of U.S. aid as his diplomats became acquainted with prominent Americans.[142] This is not in any way, shape, or form to say that these American specialists alone built the Soviet Union's interwar industrial base, a claim that would be both ridiculously absurd and inaccurate at best. To be sure, the population of American workers in Stalin's factories built by Ford and other U.S. industrialists utterly paled in comparison to the numbers of Soviet laborers whose strenuous efforts helped the Soviet premier to achieve his goal of industrializing the country and strengthening its military production capabilities. According to Professor Peter Kenez, a scholar of Eastern European and Soviet history, the number of Soviet factory workers and technicians rose from 11,500,000 in 1928 to roughly 24,000,000 in 1932, and their contribution to Stalin's industrialization program naturally dwarfed the efforts of the comparatively miniscule number of American workers at the Ford and Hercules production plants.[143] Yet while the American engineers were few in number compared to their Soviet counterparts, the expertise that the U.S. industrialists provided nevertheless played a key part in boosting Stalin's production capabilities and, as recalled by John Scott, an American chemist, foreman, and welder who worked at the Magnitogorsk factory between 1932 and 1941, Soviet engineers had mastered the techniques of modern industrial production by the time of his arrival in the country.[144]

Following the example of his recently deceased father, the former U.S. Assistant Secretary of War, Vice President Edward R. Stettinius, Jr. of General Motors also invested in Stalin's industrialization, working with Soviet officials such as the Armenian-born Anastas Mikoyan.[145] A key Politburo member to whom Stalin entrusted the Soviet regime's major international business agreements, Mikoyan later served in a key role as Moscow's top diplomat involved in overseeing the procurement of specific Lend-Lease items. With a reputation for being a shrewd negotiator, Mikoyan appears to have forged an effective working relationship with Stettinius, and the two men later cooperated closely as the latter served as Roosevelt's Lend-Lease Administrator between March 1941 and September 1943.[146]

The investments made by U.S. industrialists in helping to industrialize the Soviet Union may have been partially influenced by the normalization of Soviet society as portrayed for American audiences by the documentary photographer Margaret Bourke-White. In 1930, Bourke-White received the Soviet government's permission to enter the country and photograph various factories and industrial projects in the Stalingrad area and elsewhere under the watchful eyes of Soviet officials.[147] By her admission, Bourke-White's photographic documentation of the enormous leaps in Soviet industry resulted from her fascination with capturing the historic development of a society in transition from a medieval peasant past into a modern, mechanized world of industrial efficiency.[148]

Stalin's approval of her government-guided tour of the Soviet Union, a rare opportunity for Westerners at the time, appears to have originated in his desire to advertise the successes of the first Five-Year Plan, and she enjoyed a rare visit with the Soviet premier's mother in his mountainous, Georgian homeland.[149] Noting that, "The Stalingrad [factory] group has been designed by Albert Kahn of Detroit," Bourke-White observed that, "All the machinery has come new and glistening from Germany and America" during her visit to the Soviet factories.[150] The Soviet workers in these factories, which were built with prewar U.S. aid and were later supplied with Lend-Lease aluminum, steel, and machine tools during the war, helped produce the weapons by which Hitler's hordes tasted decisive defeat at the hands of the red warriors wielding them in battle.[151]

On 16 November 1933, newly-elected President Franklin Roosevelt extended official U.S. recognition to the Soviet regime, ending the period of mutual hostility that followed Wilson's brief intervention in the Russian Civil War.[152] Like his later attempts to prevent a separate peace between Stalin and Hitler, Roosevelt's initial diplomatic overtures to the Soviet premier appear to have been influenced by his growing apprehension at the rise to power of the Nazis in Germany in January of that same year.[153] Appreciating Stalin's assurances that he had abandoned Trotsky's aggressive endeavors, the president sought to lay the groundwork for cooperation with Moscow in the event of renewed belligerency from a militant, reinvigorated Germany. As later indicated by his refusal to attach conditions to Soviet Lend-Lease aid, his underestimation of Stalin's duplicitous character, and his overestimation of his own ability to charm the red ruler, Roosevelt's foresight regarding Hitler's aggression does not appear to have extended to his perception of the Soviet premier.[154]

Following this formal diplomatic recognition of Stalin's regime, American businessmen, attracted to the idea of industrializing a nation while earning a profit, could continue conducting business with the Soviets free of federal scrutiny, limited though such scrutiny appears to have been in the first place.[155] These financial investments and the technical expertise of many American men, including prominent individuals such as Stettinius, Ford, and Kahn, continued to help build massive factories in the Ural Mountains and around Stalingrad.[156] In 1937, the Electric Boat Company of Groton, Connecticut, received the Roosevelt administration's approval to build submarines and ordnance for the Soviet Red Fleet as a result of the president's desire to provide U.S. Navy men with work.[157]

On 26 January 1934, Stalin forecasted, "a new [global] war" on the horizon in a report to the 17th Congress of the Communist Party of the Soviet Union and, after claiming that he sought only peaceful coexistence, stated that the Red Army could spare no effort in its military preparations.[158] Assigning inevitable blame for such a potential future conflict to the Western powers, Germany, and Japan, Stalin then told his Party comrades that the Soviet Union had made great strides in strengthening its industrial capacity. Rightly commending Soviet industrial workers while omitting to mention the numerically miniscule, but still technically helpful, U.S. engineers and industrialists that contributed to his massive program, Stalin praised the Red Army's military achievements and predicted that it could rely on the support of faithful Communists throughout the world in the event of a second global conflict.[159]

Enabled by Roosevelt's establishment of diplomatic relations with the Soviets, U.S. observers also appear to have taken notice of Stalin's successful expansion of Soviet heavy industry and the Red Army's war potential throughout the 1930s. While many Western leaders initially dismissed the Red Army as a primitive force incapable of withstanding the perceived invincibility of Hitler's army, some U.S. officials later provided key support for the Soviet Lend-Lease program. Chief among these individuals, Colonel Faymonville recognized the Red Army's potential and later played an important early role in arguing for the necessity of supplying the Soviets in the fight against the Axis Powers.[160]

According to scholars James S. Herndon and Joseph O. Baylen, Faymonville served as a U.S. military observer under Roosevelt's personal friend and his first U.S. ambassador to the Soviet Union, William C. Bullitt, beginning in January 1934.[161] A veteran of AEF-Siberia, Faymonville established an excellent rapport with many local Russians and mastered their language during the U.S. intervention.[162] After observing Soviet training maneuvers in 1935 and 1936, Faymonville authored a report commending the Red Army's soldiers and officers as being physically fit, politically committed, and capable of extraordinary military exploits. Rebutting the early 1937 claims by some exiled tsarist officers, Faymonville concluded that the Red Army possessed "excellent" military capabilities.[163]

Famous for shamefully referring to Stalin's mass starvation of Ukrainian peasants between 1932 and 1933 as, "a big scare story in the American press about famine in the Soviet Union," British-American journalist Walter Duranty also contributed to early U.S. perceptions of the Red Army.[164] In a February 1934 report for *The New York Times*, Duranty quoted Marshal Kliment Voroshilov, Stalin's close comrade and Defense Commissar, as boasting that, "[the] Red Army is up to or above western levels" during an enormous military parade in Moscow.[165] In his report the following year, Duranty appears to have further concurred with Faymonville's conclusions regarding the Red Army's improved mechanization under Stalin.[166]

While other U.S. military officials are said to have criticized Faymonville's findings as being suspiciously pro-Soviet, a reputation that he reportedly began acquiring during his service in AEF-Siberia, his arguments fell on the sympathetic ears of U.S. Commerce Secretary Harry Hopkins.[167] Frustrated by the pessimistic views of other U.S. officials in Moscow following Hitler's 1941 attack, Hopkins is said to have enthusiastically embraced Faymonville's opinion that Stalin's Red Army merited U.S. aid. According to Admiral William Standley, Hopkins ordered Faymonville promoted to Brigadier General during his 1941 visit to the Soviet Union, and he continued serving zealously in his virtually autonomous role, defying the ambassador while unquestioningly agreeing to Stalin's demands.[168]

In 1938, Hopkins, the architect of Roosevelt's New Deal program, left his position as the Administrator of the Works Progress Administration (WPA) and became the U.S. Secretary of Commerce, a position in which he served only until late 1940 due to severe health issues.[169] Nevertheless, Hopkins appears to have displayed a dogged determination in serving his friend Roosevelt, often staying the night at the White House at the president's insistence, and he later became a key assistant to Stettinius, managing many aspects of Lend-Lease between 1941 and 1945. Hopkins's support for Soviet Lend-Lease aid proved crucial for Stalin following Hitler's attack, and the zealous enthusiasm with which he oversaw the shipment of massive quantities of material to the Red Army helped ensure the Nazi tyrant's defeat. While not a Soviet spy, Hopkins also voiced strong admiration for Stalin's leadership and the Red Army's determined defense and, in an indefensible decision that, unlike Soviet Lend-Lease, cannot be said to have served U.S. security interests, he appears to have played a key part in supplying the wartime Soviet Union with uranium, thorium, and other materials related to atomic research.[170]

In 1934, Roosevelt's Secretary of the Treasury, Henry Morgenthau, appointed a respected economist named Harry Dexter White to work as one of his assistants.[171] Throughout the decade, White gradually expanded his reputation, earning the trust of Roosevelt and Morgenthau, and working as a spy for Stalin's NKVD and military intelligence (GRU).[172] In his position as a key Treasury Department official, White exerted a strong influence on Morgenthau's economic policies, and he appears to have used this authority to push the administration's increasingly confrontational economic sanctions on Japan, angering Tokyo. As argued by historians John Koster, Ben Steil, and Sean McMeekin, White's boldness in his proposals for economic sanctions on Japan was motivated by his mission to strategically aid Stalin by provoking tensions between Tokyo and Washington, helping to shorten the path to war even if a conflict between Japan and the United States may be inevitable.[173]

According to the testimonies of two confessed former Communist spies and defectors to the FBI, Elizabeth Bentley and Whittaker "Carl" Chambers, Alger Hiss, a U.S. State Department assistant, also aided Stalin's espionage efforts beginning in the 1930s.[174] In his postwar congressional testimonies, U.S. Army Major George Racey Jordan, a key Lend-Lease expeditor, stated that he recalled his Soviet counterparts receiving copies of State Department documents.[175] Describing his wartime interactions to the House Un-American Activities

Committee (HUAC) in 1949 and 1950, Jordan recalled observing Hiss's signature on the copies held by the Soviets during the war, and former NKVD agent Pavel Sudoplatov later recalled his superiors' assessment of the State Department attorney as, "highly sympathetic to the Soviet Union."[176]

In May 1937, a Soviet aircrew made U.S. headlines by flying over the North Pole in a successful flight to San Jacinto, California, in a demonstration of Moscow's growing aerial capabilities.[177] After landing in the United States, the aviators were invited as guests into the home of First World War fighter ace Captain Eddie Rickenbacker, with whom Soviet copilot Andrei Yumachev established a friendly and solid personal rapport. Rickenbacker enthusiastically entertained Yumachev and the Soviet aircrew at his New York home, and the Soviet copilot later became a general during the Second World War and recalled the kind treatment that the American fighter pilot had provided him after the First World War ace visited Moscow. Before Rickenbacker's 1943 volunteer mission to the Soviet capital, Yumachev had been appointed to command, "one of the most sensitive military operations in Russia" regarding the role of U.S. P-39 "Airacobra" aircraft in Moscow's defense, and he proudly gave a demonstration of the planes' contribution to his American former host.[178]

Between 1936 and 1938, Joseph E. Davies served as the U.S. Ambassador to the Soviet Union, replacing Roosevelt's personal friend and first U.S. ambassador, William Bullitt, in Moscow.[179] According to U.S. diplomat Charles E. "Chip" Bohlen, then serving as an assistant to Davies in Moscow, the new U.S. ambassador displayed a positive opinion of Stalin and echoed the "pro-Soviet line" attributed to some of Roosevelt's chief advisers on Soviet affairs.[180] Davies appears to have largely accepted without question Stalin's explanations that those executed during the Great Purge show trials of the late 1930s in Moscow were Trotskyist intellectuals collaborating with Germany and Japan to plot an attack on the Soviet Union. Like the Allied leaders in 1918, Davies associated Trotsky and his followers with pro-German plots, a view that Stalin encouraged, and this later played a key part in shaping his support for the Red Army as he served as an assistant to Secretary of State Cordell Hull beginning in 1939.[181]

Despite the U.S.-Soviet diplomatic hostility that began with Wilson's reluctant and limited intervention in the Russian Civil War and the subsequent Red Scare, Stalin appears to have secured the support of several key U.S. industrialists by the 1930s. His portrayal of the Soviet regime as having abandoned Trotsky's aggressive calls for Communist expansion appears to have been met with a warm reception by top Roosevelt administration officials. Had Roosevelt and his senior advisers not adopted a fresh approach and unwittingly hired several influential Soviet agents into key governmental posts, Stalin may not have succeeded in influencing U.S. policy to the extent that he eventually did, even as he secured considerable wartime aid from American Lend-Lease officials. Inadvertently aided by Roosevelt's desire to forge political relations, conduct business, and confront Axis belligerency, Stalin ended the 1930s with a key diplomatic foothold in Washington that endured his 1939 pact with Hitler and the subsequent global war that it helped ignite.[182]

U.S. perceptions of Hitler's haughty hordes, Stalin's struggling soldiers, and the Red Army's rising resistance to the Nazis

Despite Roosevelt's success in establishing relations with the Soviet Union, tensions in Europe led to a temporary reversal of the president's fortunes in altering U.S.-Soviet relations to the perceived benefit of U.S. national interests. Stalin's non-aggression pact with Hitler, the subsequent Nazi invasion of Poland (followed by the Red Army's attack two weeks later) and the Nazi-Soviet division of that country, and the Red Army's attack on Finland reignited anti-Communist fervor in the United States, prompting Roosevelt to declare a "moral embargo" on the Soviet Union. Yet as this chapter demonstrates, Roosevelt's anger at Stalin's perceived duplicity in suddenly and unexpectedly concluding a pact with Hitler appears to have faded quickly and did not alter his chief advisers' readiness to aid the Red Army once the Nazi tyrant betrayed the Soviet premier.[1]

This work's second chapter explores how U.S. public opinion gradually shifted in the Soviet Union's favor by the time of the Pearl Harbor attacks, reversing the sour attitudes towards Stalin's regime that occurred following his pact with Hitler.[2] The chapter also demonstrates the careful ways in which Roosevelt, inadvertently aided by Hitler's growing submarine attacks, contributed to this shift in public perceptions of the Red Army as a force worthy of Lend-Lease aid as the Nazi menace gradually overtook Stalin as the perceived greater threat to U.S. national interests and security by late 1941. It also discusses the initially slow, but increasingly rapid, expansion of Soviet Lend-Lease in the immediate aftermath of Pearl Harbor, as well as Roosevelt's preparations for an eventual U.S. entry into the war and the psychological conditioning of Americans in identifying the Axis threat.

As German, Italian, and Japanese aggression increased throughout the late 1930s, Roosevelt delivered a series of speeches identifying the three major Axis Powers as the foremost threat to U.S. security.[3] By recognizing the Soviet Union and denouncing Axis expansion, Roosevelt appears to have believed that he could persuade Stalin to help the West contain the Nazi and fascist regimes in Europe and Asia, as discussed in the previous chapter.[4] Following Stalin's non-aggression pact with Hitler and his invasion of Finland in late 1939, Roosevelt declared a "moral embargo" on the Soviet Union.[5] Yet in his private conversations with Hopkins, Roosevelt repeatedly expressed his hopes that Stalin could be persuaded to recognize the danger posed by Hitler's expansionist policies and turn against his Nazi strategic partner.[6]

As Nazi forces advanced throughout Western Europe, North Africa, and the Balkans with the help of Soviet raw materials between May 1940 and June 1941, Roosevelt desperately sought to assist British Prime Minister Winston Churchill with material aid.[7] The Nazi defeat of the Anglo-French forces and subsequent occupation of France in May 1940 appears to have greatly alarmed Washington, and on the night of Hitler's infamous Paris visit, Roosevelt invited Commerce Secretary Hopkins to stay at the White House, and the two men began discussing the need to arm Great Britain. In a 17 December 1940 "Fireside Chat" address to the American people, Roosevelt proposed the Lend-Lease program to support Great Britain and China against Axis aggression.[8] Emphasizing the unexpected collapse of the French Army, previously perceived as one of Europe's finest, if not *the* finest in Europe, by many U.S. officials, Roosevelt repeatedly asked his listeners if Americans could afford to watch as Churchill's soldiers struggled alone against the rising tide of tyranny.[9]

Against strong opposition from congressional isolationists led by Senator Robert Taft (R-OH), the U.S. Congress passed H.R. 1776, the Lend-Lease bill proposed by Roosevelt and his supporters and largely developed with Hopkins's help, on 11 March 1941.[10] The new policy authorized the president to provide material assistance to any country resisting aggression if he deemed that country's national security vital to the defense of the United States. Senator Taft's opposition to H.R. 1776 lay rooted in the vast powers that it entrusted to the president, yet his arguments ultimately failed as Nazi tanks and bombers continued to menace British armies and independent countries in the Balkans and North Africa in the spring of 1941, while Stalin's Soviet resources poured literal fuel onto Hitler's rapidly spreading fire. Hoping to mask Hopkins's influence on the new U.S. policy and appease congressional southern Democrats and Republicans, Roosevelt appointed industrialist Edward Stettinius as Administrator of the Office of Lend-Lease Administration, and U.S. trade vessels carrying bacon, eggs, arms, and other goods requested by Churchill began sailing for Great Britain.[11]

As a result of the Red Army's attack on Finland in November 1939, Stalin initially could not have been considered a beneficiary of Lend-Lease upon its inception, and such a suggestion may have been loudly condemned in Congress had Roosevelt advised it at the time due to the Soviet premier's pact with Hitler, although the power that the program granted to the president gave him the sole authority to designate recipients of U.S. aid. After Finnish leaders

Kyoesti Kallio and Carl Gustav Mannerheim refused Stalin's demands for a strip of territory stretching across the Karelian Isthmus and several Gulf of Finland islands, Soviet troops invaded Finland and, after facing a determined resistance executed by Finnish snipers and ski infantry, the "Winter War" ended in March 1940 with the Red Army capturing the desired areas.[12] The Finns' tenacious resistance and the Red Army's eventual success in seizing the territories demanded by Stalin, reportedly at a cost of more than 200,000 Soviet casualties, influenced the perceptions of many Americans against Moscow and temporarily disrupted Roosevelt's diplomatic efforts at drawing Stalin away from Hitler. Yet as Nazi forces subsequently invaded and occupied Norway, Denmark, the Low Countries, and France, Hitler gradually replaced Stalin as the main face of aggression and threat to democratic governments, especially after his bombers mercilessly struck London and other British cities in "The Blitz" between September 1940 and May 1941.[13]

Despite his anger at Stalin's aggression against Finland, Roosevelt's "moral embargo" on the Soviet Union appears to have lasted only until October 1940, at which point the president resumed his efforts to engage with Stalin, rendering export licenses the only remaining obstacles for U.S. companies willing to accept Soviet orders.[14] According to U.S. Treasury Secretary Henry Morgenthau's diary entry for 1 March 1941, Stalin's purchasing company, Amtorg, had placed a total of 19,403 orders for machine tools, 167 orders for various, "aircraft products," and 1,798 orders for motor vehicles from U.S. companies by 15 February 1941.[15] Apparently, the Soviet premier anticipated a pressing need for improved production efforts at his factories and felt confident enough in Roosevelt's conciliatory approach towards him to order a large number of American-manufactured products even before the conception of Lend-Lease. According to Morgenthau's records, most of the companies, including Bellis Heat-Treating Company, Babcock and Wilcox, Acme Well Supply Company, and Gardner-Denver Company accepted Amtorg's orders and agreed to fulfill them between March and July 1941.[16]

Acting on his long-held, genocidal plans to annihilate Eastern Europe's Jewish and Slavic peoples, Hitler broke his non-aggression pact with Stalin and launched a massive, three-pronged surprise offensive code-named Operation *Barbarossa* against the Soviet Union on 22 June 1941.[17] Because Hitler's generals perceived the Red Army as weak due to its considerable losses in the war with Finland, they did not prepare for a winter campaign that required warm uniforms and frost-resistant fuel, causing Stalin to dismiss prior reports from Churchill and others warning of an imminent Nazi invasion despite his expectations of an eventual war.[18] Sharing their overoptimistic expectations of a quick victory, Hitler reportedly boasted of his alleged goal to station German troops, "from Vladivostok to Gibraltar" according to Berlin-based U.S.

commercial official Sam E. Woods in a report to Secretary of State Cordell Hull.[19] The attack surprised Stalin, and German bombers quickly destroyed thousands of Soviet aircraft on the ground, allowing the Nazi ground forces to quickly encircle and overwhelm the Red Army's forward operating bases, many of which were unprepared for conducting immediate defensive operations as emphasized by David Glantz, Mark Harrison, and other top scholars of the Eastern Front.[20]

Almost immediately, Roosevelt and his senior officials grasped the strategic importance of exploiting Hitler's sudden betrayal of the Nazi-Soviet pact and began signaling to Soviet diplomats their eagerness to supply the Red Army in its moment of urgent need on 24 June 1941.[21] On 25 June, Stalin appointed Anastas Mikoyan, with whom Lend-Lease Administrator Stettinius had been acquainted in the 1930s, as previously discussed, to the position of Soviet Trade Commissar to place orders for war material from the United States as the German troops advanced quickly while capturing key Soviet airbases, factories, and farms.[22] Churchill immediately offered Great Britain's support to the suddenly-besieged Red Army, and Roosevelt, quietly and unofficially at first due to American public opinion, began discussions with Stettinius to officially include the Soviet Union as a recipient of U.S. Lend-Lease aid.[23]

While going largely unopposed due to Great Britain's ongoing state of war with Nazi Germany, Churchill's pledge to immediately provide all possible aid to the Red Army nevertheless met with little enthusiasm from senior British officials such as Lieutenant General Sir Henry Pownall. Expressing his reservations in a 29 June 1941 diary entry, Pownall denounced both Hitler and Stalin as, "the two biggest cut-throats in Europe," adding that, "I only hope Stalin will make a deep gash in Hitler's throat" before estimating the conquest of Soviet Europe to take no longer than three months.[24] Identifying the most important issue for Great Britain as the Red Army's continued resistance to Hitler beyond the Ural Mountains, Pownall recorded his hope that even after losing Moscow, Stalin could, "still maintain a front somewhere – even in the Urals."[25]

Roosevelt sought to provide immediate support to the Red Army but also feared that Stalin might seek a compromise with Hitler or that Soviet forces may be defeated before help could arrive. Like many of his senior officials, the president appears to have based his fears on Lenin and Trotsky's Brest-Litovsk Treaty with Berlin in 1918, and despite the risks that supplying Stalin inevitably involved, many of his top advisers quickly concluded that it remained the best available option as it provided an unprecedented opportunity to harm Germany.[26] Echoing General Pownall's sentiments in Great Britain, many of Roosevelt's cabinet members and congressional Republicans alike initially urged him to remain strictly neutral and allow the two totalitarian tyrants to settle their affairs as violently as they wished.[27] Yet many bipartisan U.S.

lawmakers gradually changed their views over time as the United States edged closer to war, and by the end of 1941, much of the American public, despite its deep-rooted distrust of Moscow, had somewhat altered its perception of Stalin's Red Army.[28]

Although ill and recovering at home at the time of the Nazi assault, Secretary of State Hull called Roosevelt from his bedside telephone and insisted to the president that the United States must, "give Russia all aid to the hilt."[29] While recovering, Hull remained in daily contact with Roosevelt and Under Secretary of State Sumner Welles, insisting that Stalin must not be allowed to falter and should receive constant assurances of U.S. material aid to prevent the Red Army from collapsing. After returning to Washington on 4 August, Hull began regularly receiving Soviet Ambassador Konstantin Umansky and GRU General Filipp I. Golikov to obtain regular reports on the Red Army's immediate needs and assure them of incoming aid while dismissing the pessimistic views of some U.S. military observers predicting Stalin's defeat.[30]

Most senior American officials, like many of their British counterparts, appear to have quickly concluded that the sudden outbreak of war between Hitler and Stalin offered a critical opportunity to maintain a two-front war in Europe by ensuring the Red Army's survival while attaching no conditions to Soviet aid. According to Herbert Feis, Roosevelt's Economic Advisor for International Affairs, the president ordered Soviet aid requests to be reviewed without delay on 21 July 1941 and emphatically explained that the Red Army's continued resistance to Hitler served as the sole condition that he sought to impose on Stalin.[31] While fearing that the Red Army could not indefinitely withstand the Nazi assault, U.S. Secretary of the Navy Frank Knox, a Republican, told Roosevelt on the day after the German invasion that he could not afford to squander the opportunity provided by Hitler's sudden attack. While concurring with some of his U.S. Armed Forces colleagues that Stalin's soldiers could only resist, "from six weeks to two months," before their supposedly inevitable defeat, Knox nevertheless urged the president to give the Red Army the material aid needed to hand Hitler a pyrrhic victory.[32]

Barely a month after Hitler's troops surged across the Soviet frontier, Edward C. Carter, the former head and founder of the Institute of Pacific Relations, presided over a New York meeting at which he and others from his former non-governmental organization (NGO) formed a new group to support Stalin's beleaguered Red Army.[33] After being officially incorporated in New York State as the Russian War Relief Fund but popularly known as Russian War Relief (RWR), Carter's new organization officially began operating in support of the Red Army on 12 September 1941.[34] Throughout the war, the RWR raised funds and shipped medical supplies to Stalin's soldiers, with its first U.S. $35,000 load of operating equipment being shipped to the Soviets on 3 October 1941.

According to Carter in an August 1944 article, the organization held an "immensely successful" rally to raise U.S. $1,000,000 to "Help Russia – Hasten Victory" in New York on 27 October 1941, the first of many such wartime occasions.[35]

As the German Army initially advanced quickly into Soviet territory and inflicted staggering losses on the unprepared Red Army, the shadow of Brest-Litovsk appears to have occupied the thoughts of U.S. officials seeking to use the opportunity to weaken Hitler by aiding Stalin.[36] Two weeks after Hitler's attack, former Ambassador Davies, then a key assistant to Hull, authored a memorandum for Harry Hopkins, strongly implying that U.S. policy should focus on avoiding such a scenario at all costs, raising the frightening specter early on in the war's initial stages.[37] Davies's memorandum further strengthened Roosevelt's arguments favoring the inclusion of the Soviet Union in Lend-Lease, stating that the Red Army's defeat could lead to, "a Trotzkyite [sic] pro-German" seizing power from Stalin and concluding a separate peace, following Lenin and Trotsky's 1918 example.[38] Reflecting the 1918 Allied perceptions of Trotsky and Lenin as pro-German agents, Davies stated that even if Stalin preempted a coup, the Soviet premier could himself be forced to conclude peace with Hitler and give him unrestricted access to the vast resources of Ukraine and European Russia.[39]

In such a situation, Davies argued, Churchill's Great Britain might not only be facing the European Axis alone as before, but a Germany further strengthened by its army's full, unhindered domination and exploitation of Soviet Europe's great industrial and agricultural capacity.[40] While acknowledging that many Americans remained staunchly anti-Communist and alleging that this somehow amounted to many of them automatically wishing for a Nazi victory, Davies stated that by no means could Washington afford to provide Stalin's Red Army with anything less than maximum aid.[41] Falling on already-sympathetic ears, Davies's analysis strongly influenced the administration's management of Soviet Lend-Lease as he urged Hopkins and Roosevelt, for good measure, to resist any temptation to demand concessions from Stalin, dismissing the notion that Communism could threaten either Europe or the United States even in the event of a Soviet victory. Rather than attach conditions to Soviet aid, Davies argued, Washington must follow London's example by assuring Stalin of, "all out" U.S. support to keep the Red Army fully supplied to ensure Hitler's total defeat.[42]

Davies's memorandum appears to have proven decisive in amplifying the fears of a second Brest-Litovsk in Washington and bolstering Roosevelt and Hopkins's determination to prevent a repeat of the perceived disaster of March 1918 by assuring Stalin that he could expect them to spare no effort in aiding him. While somewhat understandable considering the seemingly invincible

Nazi advance that the administration and the world faced in the turbulent atmosphere of summer 1941, Davies's assurances that aggressive Soviet Communism could not pose a postwar threat, "for many years" proved horribly naïve, however understandable they may have appeared at the time.[43] Yet his arguments in favor of avoiding the past's perceived mistakes were perfectly sensible given the contemporary wartime atmosphere faced by the administration, and they helped to galvanize the U.S. aid effort as Roosevelt carefully prepared the groundwork for Soviet Lend-Lease, first dispatching Hopkins to Great Britain before later authorizing him to approach Stalin. For Roosevelt, Davies's use of the phrase "all out" meant that all resources, with no exceptions, must be utilized in ensuring total victory over Germany's perceived military might, including arming Stalin's forces to the maximum possible extent, to wage the traditional American, total way of war described by historian Russell Weigley.[44]

In *The American Way of War: A History of United States Military Strategy and Policy*, Weigley states that the U.S. government adopted a total war approach or, "strategy of annihilation" developed by General Grant during the Civil War and applied again in the Plains' Indian Wars and the European Theater of the Second World War as mentioned in an earlier section of this book.[45] This strategy requires the full mobilization of the military, civilian sector, and industry in the prosecution of all-out war to ensure the complete, unquestioned defeat and overthrow of the enemy's military forces, civilian support structure, and political system. Roosevelt is said to have adopted this approach after the Pearl Harbor attack, yet his foresight in countering the threat posed by the Axis led him to begin preparing for an inevitable war by supporting the Allies to the maximum possible extent in the hope of wearing Germany down before U.S. forces could take the field. The possibility of a second Brest-Litovsk appeared frightful to many U.S. observers until much later in the war, and Roosevelt and his aides sought to prevent such a development from undermining their total war approach to defeating Hitler, especially as Davies predicted that the Red Army could prevail with sufficient U.S. aid.[46]

Arguing that Stalin's regime could remain in power in Soviet Asia even if Hitler's forces managed to reach the Ural Mountains, Davies pointed out that German troops could be further weakened in their occupation of Soviet Europe through partisan raids and civilian resentment of the occupiers.[47] These arguments appear to have resonated deeply and profoundly with Hopkins and Roosevelt as the Red Army continued resisting the merciless Nazi offensive into the late summer and early fall of 1941, despite suffering staggering casualties. While Stalin remained in power and the Red Army persevered in the field, the opportunity to ensure a two-front war for Hitler remained too enticing a prospect for Roosevelt to ignore in his total war approach that gathered greater momentum and public support after the U.S. entry into the war. Following

Davies's and his own instincts, he sought to provide Stalin with enough aid to thwart any potential Trotskyite coup and maintain the Red Army's resistance to the invader, while keeping it supplied to eventually carry the battle to Hitler and ensure his total defeat.[48]

While staying in London to discuss Lend-Lease matters with Churchill, Hopkins expressed his belief to Roosevelt that despite the Soviets' ongoing battlefield defeats, Stalin must be provided with the means to, "maintain a permanent front" at all costs.[49] Volunteering to travel to Moscow from London and serve as Roosevelt's, "personal envoy" to Stalin and assess his character and the Red Army's military needs and capabilities, Hopkins proceeded to emphasize his conviction that while the situation appeared temporarily bleak, no effort should be spared in prolonging the Red Army's survival. Roosevelt quickly agreed to his friend's proposal, and on 30 July 1941, Hopkins departed London for Moscow to meet with Stalin, analyze the situation, and report his findings to the president accordingly.[50]

After arriving in the Soviet capital, Hopkins immediately sought the perceptions of other U.S. officials in the city to obtain an initial report of the situation developing at the front before beginning his discussions with Stalin. He displayed frustration at the pessimistic mood of military observers such as Major Ivan D. Yeaton, whose reports predicted the Red Army's swift collapse and Stalin's inability to remain in power in the face of the rapid Nazi advance.[51] Only four days after Hitler's assault, Major Yeaton had requested U.S. Ambassador Laurence Steinhardt to obtain instructions from Washington regarding the need to evacuate in the event of a Nazi advance upon Moscow. Yeaton initially sought to accompany Steinhardt in the event of such an evacuation, while inquiring whether his assistant, Major Joseph A. Michela, should remain in the city, "until the [seemingly inevitable] entry of German troops," and his fear of the Red Army's imminent doom angered Hopkins.[52]

While visiting Moscow, Hopkins expressed great appreciation for the more optimistic views of Colonel Faymonville regarding the Red Army's military potential and its ability to resist the Nazi invasion, and he recommended the former ordnance officer for promotion to Brigadier General, as mentioned previously. Described as an "asset" of the Soviets by Sean McMeekin, Faymonville subsequently played a key part in transmitting Stalin's demands directly to Hopkins, an action that offended his official superior, Admiral Standley, with whom Roosevelt replaced Ambassador Steinhardt in the spring of 1942 due to Soviet complaints.[53] At Hopkins's urging, Faymonville subsequently replaced Yeaton in his key role as an adviser to the U.S. War Supply Mission in Moscow due to his insistence that the Red Army could triumph over the odds and merited unrestrained, unquestioned, and unconditional U.S. Lend-Lease aid.[54]

During Hopkins's visit to Moscow, photographer Margaret Bourke-White received permission to visit the Soviet capital to photograph Stalin and the anticipated Nazi bombing raids on the city that Soviet and U.S. officials expected the German Air Force to execute to coincide with the former Commerce Secretary's visit.[55] As Hopkins arrived in late July and the Nazi bombers struck Moscow as expected, Bourke-White captured for U.S. public consumption numerous photographs of the struggle between the city's defiant defenders and their brutal assailants. The images that she captured were subsequently published in *Life* magazine and helped portray to American audiences the bold efforts of Stalin's Red Army, Red Army Air Forces, and the Soviet people in their anti-Nazi struggle.[56]

Her photographs of Stalin and Hopkins standing together confidently in the Kremlin conveyed the message that the Soviet premier and his people were reliable allies against Axis aggression and that the American people should come to the aid of their Soviet comrades resisting Berlin's brazen assault.[57] Upon meeting Stalin, Bourke-White appears to have been initially unimpressed by the Soviet premier's pock-marked face and his small physical stature at less than five-feet, five-inches tall. Recalling that "My own height is five feet five, and Stalin was shorter than I am," Bourke-White states that she quickly realized her error in judgment as the Soviet premier's "granite face" exuded an admirable determination and his supreme, unchallenged authority.[58] Far from appearing as a weak and frightened peasant cowering behind a primitive country and army on the brink of collapse, Stalin impressed both Hopkins and Bourke-White with his stolid, unshakable firmness, convincing them both of his commitment to Hitler's defeat and his need for U.S. arms and aid.[59]

In a chance episode that appears to have made a strong and deep impression on Hopkins, Stalin quickly ushered his American guest to his personal car as German bombers attempted five times to breach Moscow's air defenses that night.[60] Escorted by his NKVD chief and fellow Georgian-born Communist, Lavrenti Beria, the Soviet premier paused for a moment and called Hopkins's attention to the distant sky as Soviet anti-aircraft gunners suddenly struck two Ju 88 bombers sweeping over the city.[61] Pointing to the planes as they stalled, sputtered, and fell to the earth, the Soviet leader boldly declared to Hopkins that such a fate inevitably awaited all enemies of Soviet power, according to Stalin biographer Oleg Khlevniuk.[62]

Combined with reports of Red Army tenacity and local success in slowing the German advance, this show of confidence made a powerful impression on Hopkins and contributed heavily to his and Roosevelt's increasingly firm conviction regarding the pressing need to effectively arm Stalin's soldiers.[63] After returning to Washington, Hopkins convinced Roosevelt that Stalin's unbending resolve and the Red Army's tenacity served as a lethal combination and key factor in halting Hitler's armies and corroborated the views of Hull, Knox, Davies, and others that the Soviet Union must be included in Lend-Lease.[64] Deeply impressed by Hopkins's report, Roosevelt immediately authorized him to arrange the details of full Lend-Lease support to the Red Army, while temporarily remaining silent on the matter in his public speeches, and to provide Stalin with any material that he requested.[65]

Following Roosevelt's decision, Hopkins and Stettinius immediately began working to arrange the delivery of war material to the Soviet Union. Perceiving Stalin to be a crucial ally in the fight against Hitler, the two men embraced their task zealously, displaying a determination described as fanatical and overzealous by their associates.[66] Naturally, the program also received the firm support of the previously mentioned Soviet spy Harry Dexter White, an increasingly influential Treasury Department official whose influence over Secretary Morgenthau further ensured that Stalin's perceived needs were prioritized, which, to be fair, debatably may not have been a treasonous act in and of itself as it temporarily served U.S. wartime strategic interests in contrast to his documented anti-American espionage activities.[67]

Despite Hopkins's positive appraisal of Stalin, Roosevelt understood that the American public generally had little appreciation for the Soviet regime, even though major industrialists such as Henry Ford, Albert Kahn, and Edward Stettinius had previously conducted business in the Soviet Union.[68] Hoping to generate broader public support, Roosevelt began a campaign to win the approval of wartime isolationists in the Congress and the American public by emphasizing the greater threat to the country posed by Hitler. Throughout the summer and fall of 1941, a series of violent confrontations between German submarines and U.S. ships provided the president with the crucial rhetorical ammunition that he required to argue his position.[69]

Even before Hitler broke his pact with Stalin, the Nazi tyrant's submarines had been increasingly inflicting damage on U.S.-German relations by striking U.S. merchant ships, especially after the birth of Lend-Lease in March 1941 as a tool for aiding London's war effort. On 21 May 1941, a German submarine torpedoed and sank the SS *Robin Moor*, a U.S. merchant vessel in the South Atlantic, and Roosevelt subsequently emphasized the Nazi naval raid in his Fireside Chats to the American people.[70] On 4 September, the German submarine *U-652* fired at the USS *Greer*, narrowly missing the destroyer operating out of Iceland in support of British convoys carrying war material to North Russia. The next day, a German bomber sank the U.S. merchant ship SS *Steel Seafarer* during its voyage to an Egyptian Red Sea port operated by British forces, providing the president with more legitimate grievances against Berlin to emphasize in his speeches.[71]

In addition to overcoming the American public's initial reluctance to support the Soviet Union, Roosevelt had to address congressional concerns that the Red

Army may collapse as Kerensky's army had done in 1917. In August and September 1941, the Red Army suffered a series of staggering defeats as German troops encircled and captured large Soviet forces defending the cities of Kiev and Smolensk.[72] Reportedly resulting in the loss of 975,000 Soviet soldiers and officers, these defeats presented a challenge for Roosevelt as he sought to persuade Congress of the need for a Soviet Lend-Lease program, while quietly approving of Churchill's diversion of U.S. arms to the Red Army and accepting Ambassador Umansky's orders for aid.[73]

While reeling from the recent death of his mother, Roosevelt addressed the American people on 11 September 1941, denouncing the *Greer* incident as piracy and issuing a "shoot on sight" order to all U.S. Navy and Coast Guard commanders.[74] Describing the German attacks as unprovoked, he denounced the Nazi regime, emphasizing the importance of freedom of the seas to U.S. trade and arguing that Hitler's actions posed the greatest threat to the American economy and way of life. Drawing parallels with the plundering of U.S. trade ships by the Barbary Pirates during Thomas Jefferson's presidency, Roosevelt urged his listeners to support Lend-Lease for all the European Allies, including the Soviet Union, as the Red Army fought fiercely against the Nazi aggressors.[75]

On 29 September 1941, Stalin and Foreign Commissar Vyacheslav Molotov met with American and British officials Averell Harriman, Admiral Standley, and Lord Beaverbrook in Moscow at the Three Powers Conference to discuss the Red Army's long-term needs in the war against Germany.[76] The men discussed specific details, including the transportation of tanks, planes, and trucks to strengthen the Red Army's striking capabilities, paving the way for the Soviet Lend-Lease program.[77] Acknowledging the Red Army's setbacks at the front and repeating the verbal list of needs that he had presented to Hopkins, Stalin emphasized the importance of ammunition, small arms, fighter aircraft, aluminum, and tanks as the items that he needed the most urgently for the Soviet war effort.[78] Three days later, the U.S. diplomats returned home to discuss with Roosevelt a blueprint for the First Protocol of Lend-Lease aid to the Soviet Union, committing the United States to fulfilling Stalin's orders before 30 June 1942, after which point Congress could renew the successive Second, Third, and Fourth Protocols if the president deemed it necessary.[79]

Despite Stalin's record of military aggression and in accordance with orthodox Communist political ideology, his suppression of religious freedoms in the Soviet Union, Roosevelt, in a desperate, clumsy effort to generate public support for combatting the greater contemporary threat to Americans, attempted to portray the Soviet Constitution as permitting both religion and the freedom to oppose it in a 30 September 1941 press conference.[80] His comments provoked swift condemnation from Congressman Hamilton Fish (R-NY), and the New York lawmaker confidently stated that more than 90 percent of U.S. church leaders disagreed with the president's claim in a 6 October opinion piece for *The New York Times*.[81] Acting on the advice of Hopkins, the president then employed a new tactic by emphasizing the anti-religious policies of the Nazi regime as he repeatedly denounced Hitler's blatant aggression and offered praise for the brave fight being waged by the Red Army.[82]

In their 2008 book *The Myth of the Eastern Front: The Nazi-Soviet War in American Popular Culture*, Professors Ronald Smelser and Edward J. Davies II argue that by late 1941, many Americans had begun viewing the Red Army in a more positive light than its Nazi foe due in part to the tenacious resistance that many Soviet units displayed in battle.[83] Smelser and Davies identify the beginning of this shift in the American public's mood as the opening days of *Barbarossa* as the deceitful nature of Hitler's attack on the Soviet Union inadvertently helped Stalin win the psychological war for Americans' sympathy early on.[84] By the time of the Pearl Harbor attack and Hitler's subsequent declaration of war on the United States, the hostility of many U.S. lawmakers to Roosevelt's Soviet Lend-Lease proposals had begun to evaporate, and the two hostile acts of the Axis partners appear to have dried it up completely. As emphasized by Smelser and Davies, Stalin's 1942 revival of the Russian Orthodox Church appeared to many contemporary Americans as a sign of his regime's moderation in comparison to Hitler's, and the Soviet premier's early upbringing as a Georgian Orthodox Church seminarian and his alleged confession to a British diplomat that, "he too believed in God" won him much praise in U.S. news articles.[85]

During these critical months in late 1941, German submarines continued to sink merchant ships in the North Atlantic and exchanged fire with a U.S. Navy destroyer, further exacerbating tensions and generating more sympathy for Roosevelt's arguments. In the weeks after Congressman Fish's criticism of the president's speech, U.S. public opinion continued to shift in favor of supporting Hitler's enemies as a practical measure to safeguard U.S. interests and national security.[86] Congressional isolationists gradually began to view Lend-Lease as a measure to avoid deploying U.S. troops into another European war, and an opinion poll of 17 October 1941 revealed that 51 percent of Americans supported aiding the Red Army.[87]

On 16 October 1941, German submarines struck the USS *Kearny* docked at Reykjavik, Iceland, killing 11 American sailors during a Nazi raid against a British convoy gathering nearby. Combined with the previous German attacks denounced by Roosevelt, the *Kearny* incident reinforced public outrage and support for Lend-Lease aid to the Soviet Union.[88] Two weeks later, German submarines torpedoed the USS *Reuben James*, escorting merchant ships to Iceland, killing 100 sailors and solidifying support for Roosevelt's increasingly assertive approach.[89] As Smelser and Davies point out, the Nazi invasion had already, "made the Soviet Union appear as a victim rather than as a victimizer," and by late 1941, Moscow had replaced Berlin as the lesser evil in the eyes of many Americans fearing, in their words, "that if Hitler conquered Russia, he might be unstoppable."[90]

As emphasized by George Herring, Jr. and Raymond Dawson, while Roosevelt and Hopkins's rhetorical attempts to silence congressional opposition to aiding the Red Army achieved some limited successes, congressional infighting enabled the president's supporters to include Stalin as a Lend-Lease recipient.[91] The most potent wartime challenge to Roosevelt's decision to add the Soviet Union to his aid program appears to have occurred in October 1941 after Congressman Robert F. Rich (D-PA) proposed an amendment to exclude the Red Army from Lend-Lease. Even as his attention remained focused on events at the front, Stalin may have also been observing domestic developments in the United States that could potentially undermine U.S. officials' attempts to aid the Red Army, and the Soviet premier appears, perhaps, to have grasped the urgency of Roosevelt's emphasis on Hitler's anti-religious policies as he subsequently began introducing the rhetoric of faith into his speeches.[92] To be sure, Stalin had other motives for appealing to the faith of Soviet citizens besides helping Roosevelt to make his case for aiding the Soviet Union, such as his urgent need to boost morale and patriotism in the Red Army's ranks and combat Hitler's attempts to undermine the Soviet regime by falsely portraying the German Army as a liberating force that tolerated religious freedom. Yet Stalin's sudden inclusion of religion in his rhetoric helped Roosevelt and Hopkins to argue in favor of supporting the Red Army, even though the Soviet premier had other, equally pressing reasons for appealing to faith as he sought desperately to reverse the ongoing massive losses at the front and counterattack the invaders.[93]

As Representative Rich's supporters and opponents debated in the House in October 1941, Stalin issued a broadcast in which he called on the Soviet people to flock to the Red Army's ranks to defend "Holy Russia" from the invading Nazi hordes, and Roosevelt subsequently cited the Soviet premier's seemingly desperate tactical appeal to religion in conversations with congressional isolationists.[94] To further defang the proposed "Rich amendment" to Lend-Lease, Roosevelt is also said to have obtained and emphasized a statement from Pope Pius XII in which the Roman Catholic pontiff differentiated between arming and feeding Stalin's soldiers and giving aid to global Communism.[95] As mentioned, to mask Hopkins's influence in his aid program and appeal to congressional conservatives, Roosevelt had already appointed former industrialist Edward Stettinius, Jr. as Lend-Lease Administrator in March 1941, and he later repeated this tactic to again appease his critics by replacing Stettinius with Leo Crowley in late 1943. Crucially, Roosevelt carefully concealed his plan to attach no conditions to Soviet Lend-Lease aid, save for Stalin's continued prosecution of the war against Hitler, and strongly implied that he and Stettinius intended to use the program as a bargaining chip to compel the Soviet premier to both repay U.S. aid and moderate his regime's policies.[96]

In arguing his case to Congress, Roosevelt insisted that while he, Morgenthau, and Stettinius could effectively manage the aid program and prevent Stalin from essentially stealing U.S. war aid without repaying it, timing remained crucial. Implying that the restoration of a single Nazi front in the west against Churchill remained a dangerous possibility even as the lawmakers debated, Roosevelt argued that his hands should not be, "tied in any way" in determining Lend-Lease recipients as such a move could disastrously impact Soviet morale.[97] A combination of Roosevelt's arguments and Hitler's continued advances into Soviet territory appears to have convinced several key congressional isolationists to participate in voting down the Rich amendment, as even Congressman Fish declined to vote in favor of amending Lend-Lease to prevent the president from designating aid recipients.[98]

Congressman John Taber (R-NY), Chairman of the House Appropriations Committee, then delivered a fatal blow to the Rich amendment. Arguing that while he detested the Soviet Union's Communist political system, Taber expressed his conviction that he thought it highly unwise to obstruct the president, as Commander-in-Chief, from exercising his judgment in arming those that he and his advisers deemed worthy of U.S. aid.[99] On 20 October 1941, a vote of 328 to 67 crushed the Rich amendment in the House, and, despite their professed distaste for Stalinism, neither Rich, Taber, nor Fish appear to have again attempted to amend Lend-Lease to exclude Stalin's Red Army after the United States entered the war that December.[100]

In addition to Rich's efforts, Congresswoman Edith Rogers (R-MA) led a brief, defiant effort in the House of Representatives to attach an amendment to Soviet Lend-Lease aid. Emphasizing Stalin's record of ruthlessly suppressing religious freedoms in the Soviet Union and the Red Army's record of aggression against neighboring countries such as Finland, the Massachusetts representative urged her House colleagues to consider her proposal as a serious effort for U.S. leaders to take a bold stand for religious freedom.[101] Stating, "This is an opportunity after all, however, for us to make an effort to fight for religious freedom, and to stop the flow of communism that has emanated from [Soviet] Russia to the United States," Congresswoman Rogers concluded her argument as the House debate began on 6 October 1941. Her proposed amendment subsequently suffered a staggering defeat on the House floor as even her few supporters, such as Representative James F. O'Connor (D-MT) who voiced his disgust with, "Joe Stalin…. [who is] as big a brute and human monster as the man he is fighting – Hitler," feared such legislation to be a moot point as they could not guarantee or enforce the Soviet premier's cooperation.[102]

In a somewhat heated 27 October 1941 U.S. Senate debate, Roosevelt's supporters and opponents discussed the matter of appropriations for a supplemental Lend-Lease bill intended to more effectively ensure the shipment of the materials requested by Churchill, Chiang Kai-shek, and Stalin.[103] Senator Burton Wheeler (D-MT) voiced strong support for Roosevelt's proposal to supply all of the food, arms, and raw materials requested by the Allied Powers, including Stalin's Soviet Union, to help them halt Axis aggression.[104] Senator Taft quickly rose in opposition but conceded defeat after several of his colleagues provided a detailed briefing of Nazi resources in occupied Europe and the desperate struggle faced by London and Moscow, summoning memories of Brest-Litovsk by emphasizing the danger of Soviet resources falling to Berlin.[105]

On 28 October 1941, the Senate passed the supplemental bill authorizing an additional $5,980,000,000 in appropriations to finance Lend-Lease operations.[106] Watching with satisfaction and already armed with the immense presidential authority that Congress had earlier given him in designating which countries qualified for Lend-Lease aid, Roosevelt prepared to officially announce the Soviet Lend-Lease program on 7 November after already opening up a $1,000,000,000 credit line for Soviet war material purchases free of interest.[107] Although the Red Army continued suffering major setbacks as Nazi forces pushed closer to Moscow and besieged Leningrad that fall, Stalin's soldiers had already begun receiving small quantities of U.S. arms even as Roosevelt maintained his public silence on the matter, and the Japanese attack on Pearl Harbor soon guaranteed an even greater flow of aid.[108]

A major obstacle to Roosevelt's efforts to effectively supply the Red Army lay in the difficulties involved in the supply routes to the Soviet Union. U.S. supplies transported by Great Britain's Royal Navy had been reaching the Soviet Arctic ports since the late summer of 1941, and Stalin and his top diplomats continued expressing their preference for this northern route throughout the war.[109] In October 1941, small numbers of U.S. ships also began transporting supplies to Soviet East Asia, and Stettinius began advocating for a supply route to be opened in Iran as American and British engineers slowly began the badly-needed work needed to improve that country's road networks.[110] Despite initial difficulties, Anglo-American officials eventually managed to transform each of these routes into potent pipelines flowing with arms and ordnance to the Red Army's fighting men and women.[111]

As the fighting on the Eastern Front continued into late 1941, with German troops advancing closer to Moscow despite the Red Army's dogged defense, Roosevelt, Hopkins, and their supporters in the administration hastened to provide Stalin with the war material that he requested.[112] Stalin's demands for American aircraft intensified as the fierce fighting raged into the fall, and Major

Yeaton declined to comment on the situation at the front to inquiring journalists, as reported in *The Daily Iowan* on 30 October 1941.[113] Yeaton had previously repeated his earlier view that the Red Army could not continue to resist the Germans and expressed concern that U.S. material shipped to the Soviet Arctic ports as demanded by Stalin may be captured by the Nazi invaders, prompting a swift rebuke from Hopkins.[114]

Upon her return from the Soviet Union, photographer Margaret Bourke-White and her husband Erskine Caldwell publicly called on Americans to relinquish their fears of aiding the Red Army in its hour of need, praising Stalin's leadership in a 3 November 1941 statement to *The New York Times*.[115] The celebrity couple argued that without official, immediate, and substantial U.S. aid, the Soviet forces may crumble in the face of Hitler's brutal offensives, leaving the Nazi *Fuehrer* with unchallenged access to Soviet Europe's vast resources. The report quoted Bourke-White and Caldwell as stating bluntly to their compatriots that, "we will all be helling' [sic, heiling] Hitler within the next eighteen months" unless Americans rallied around Roosevelt's proposals to provide, "all-out aid" to Stalin's beleaguered Red Army.[116]

Initially, Great Britain supplied the bulk of the material as Royal Navy warships and Merchant Navy transport vessels braved the hazardous northern seas and Nazi submarines operating out of Norway on their route to Archangel and Murmansk.[117] The Nazi submarine and aerial menace to these Allied "Arctic convoys" did not fully materialize as a major threat to Stalin's supplies from the West until after the route captured Hitler's attention in December 1941 however, and the first few convoys of August and September that year managed to safely supply the Soviets. On the day of Hitler's attack on the Soviet Union, Prime Minister Churchill, as mentioned, immediately pledged Great Britain's full support of the Red Army's struggle against the invaders, and on 8 July, he initiated the first of his and Roosevelt's many telegram exchanges with Stalin.[118]

In one such telegram on 3 September 1941, the Soviet premier thanked the British prime minister for promising to send a further 200 aircraft in addition to 200 others that he had previously pledged to ship, using the term "sell" to shame Churchill into attaching no conditions to the aid by implying that London sought to make a profit at Moscow's expense.[119] Stalin then strongly emphasized the heavy losses suffered by Soviet industry after Hitler's recent reinforcing of his invasion force with an estimated 30 to 34 more infantry divisions backed by armor, airpower, and 46 fresh Romanian and Finnish divisions. He then emphasized the importance to the Soviet war effort of aluminum, steel, and iron, and urged Churchill to begin shipping, "30,000 tons of aluminum by the beginning of October" along with, "a minimum *monthly* aid of 400 aeroplanes and 500 tanks (of small or medium size)."[120] These specific raw materials and weapons were more urgently needed, Stalin added, due to the Red Army's loss to the Germans of the largest Soviet aluminum plants in Tikhvin near Leningrad and Zaporozhia on the Dnieper River, three motor production plants, and four aircraft factories in Ukraine and Leningrad.[121]

Stalin's emphasis to Churchill that Hitler's capture of these key facilities represented a "mortal danger" to the Soviet war effort and the Red Army's ability to continue fighting seems to at least somewhat justify Sean McMeekin's claim that without Western aluminum shipments after the fall of Tikhvin and Zaporozhia, Soviet resistance may have crumbled and collapsed.[122] The Soviet premier's urging of Churchill to commit to supplying his forces with a combined monthly minimum total of 900 aircraft and "small or medium" tanks also appears to lend support both to Alexander Hill's argument that Lend-Lease armor played a considerable part in Moscow's 1941 defense and Mark Harrison's statement that initial Anglo-American arms shipments contributed, "over 20 per cent of newly available combat aircraft and tanks" to the Red Army in 1942, not an insignificant amount of early wartime aid.[123] While Anglo-American aid shipments may have provided only a small amount of material overall in 1941, Churchill and Roosevelt acted swiftly, boldly, and decisively in quickly responding to Stalin's pleas for help even before the attack on Pearl Harbor led to Washington's official entry into the war.[124]

From the time of his first telegram exchanges with Churchill and Roosevelt, the Soviet premier appears to have sensed their desire to prevent a second Brest-Litovsk and, while he may not have considered forging a separate peace with Hitler, began playing on their fears to obtain crucial aid. Claiming that the Red Army, "will be defeated or weakened" to the point of passivity in the field without the specific supplies that he requested, along with the launching of a, "second front" against the Nazis in either France or Norway, Stalin immediately raised over Churchill the specter of a separate peace.[125] Expressing regret at having to inform Churchill of the dire circumstances that Hitler's capture of half of Ukraine and advance on Leningrad had inflicted on the Red Army's defensive struggle, Stalin deployed the implicit diplomatic threat of a second Brest-Litovsk in his 3 September 1941 correspondence with the British prime minister.[126]

Stalin's implied threat appears to have spurred Churchill into taking urgent action as the British prime minister replied on the following day with a promise to send from Great Britain's domestic production half of the weaponry requested by the Soviet premier.[127] Expressing hope that the United States could supply the remainder of the Red Army's pressing needs, Churchill hastened to inform Stalin that he had cabled Roosevelt to request the swift arrival in London of Averell Harriman and the initiation of a discussion on supplying the Soviets.[128] While stating that he could not yet open a second front against Germany in Europe, even as British troops faced Hitler and Mussolini's armies in Libya, Churchill praised the Red Army's tenacious resistance and committed to opening a new supply route to the Soviet Union through Iran, which had been jointly seized by British and Soviet troops in August. Seeking to assure Stalin of his total commitment to Hitler's defeat, Churchill vowed to attach no conditions to aid in the same spirit, "as the American Lend-Lease Bill, of which no formal account is kept in money" and to threaten Finland with war if Helsinki's troops advanced past its original borders.[129]

In a diary entry two days after Stalin's 3 September telegram to Churchill, General Pownall recorded his perception that while the Red Army faced an arduous struggle, the Soviet premier appeared to be "blackmailing" London into aiding Moscow's fight by dangling the prospect of a separate peace.[130] After criticizing Harriman and Roosevelt for their eagerness to supply the Soviets, Pownall lamented that Beaverbrook, despite London's other global naval commitments, seemed ready, "to say 'yes' to anything that the Russians may ask – prepared to offer them the Earth."[131] According to Alexander Hill, by the end of 1941, 2,010 field telephones were delivered to the Red Army instead of the original 6,000 requested by Stalin, prompting complaints from the Soviet premier even as the Royal Navy struggled in the Atlantic, Mediterranean, and Pacific.[132] Facing the threat of German forces in North Africa and across the English Channel, Churchill informed his Soviet counterpart that Great Britain could not yet provide the Spitfire aircraft that he desired, shipping Hurricane fighters instead while expressing hope that U.S. industry could soon accommodate the Kremlin's pressing needs.[133]

The entrance of the United States into the war as a member of the Allies largely stifled isolationist sentiments, gradually created a vigorous wartime economy, and guaranteed a far greater flow of Lend-Lease material to the Red Army. Initially, major difficulties arose regarding Lend-Lease shipments to the Soviet ports in East Asia, forcing Stalin's generals to fight without some of the desired military items he and they had requested by the end of 1941.[134] Yet Churchill's decisiveness and Roosevelt's determination to provide aid to Stalin's struggling soldiers resulted in urgently needed arms deliveries before the year ended, despite these initial shipments being much smaller than either Moscow or Washington desired. Four days after the Pearl Harbor attack, Hitler and his Italian fascist ally Benito Mussolini declared war on the United States, and German submarines launched operations along the Atlantic seaboard in an act that further rallied Americans to their country's war effort and ultimately doomed the Axis to defeat.[135]

While Hitler's aggression may have eventually rendered the U.S. entry into the Second World War inevitable, Stalin's loyal agents working within Roosevelt's administration appear to have helped hasten the president's increasingly belligerent stance toward the Axis Powers.[136] Despite the considerable influence of some key administration officials now known to have served as Soviet spies, Stalin could not have hoped for success in executing this careful strategic maneuver had Roosevelt not refocused the American public and government on preparing to face the Axis.[137] Inadvertently aided by Hitler's submarine attacks and his sudden, frightening advances in Europe, Roosevelt managed to gradually shift the attention of many Americans, including many congressional critics, away from Communism and toward the more immediate Axis threat. Roosevelt's foresight in combating Axis expansion, while commendable and proper, appears in some ways to have helped paved the way for Stalin's agents to influence U.S. policy to further the Soviet Union's strategic interests. In calling the American public's attention to the more immediate enemy while ignoring the subversive threat posed by another, the president and his senior aides unwittingly deflected Americans' attention away from Stalin's malevolent tendencies, inadvertently allowing his agents in key governmental posts to execute their espionage missions more effectively.[138]

Of particular importance to Stalin's successful manipulation of Roosevelt's foreign policy, an endeavor that may have failed had the president not underestimated the Soviet leader so greatly while rightly and understandably focusing on the Axis, is the influence of Treasury Department official Harry Dexter White.[139] As previously mentioned, White joined Roosevelt's Treasury Department under the president's close friend Henry Morgenthau in 1934 and, according to several confessed former spies, including Whittaker Chambers and Elizabeth Bentley, began aiding Moscow later in the decade.[140] By the time of the Second World War's outbreak in 1939, White had proven himself to be a reliable economist and had become a close friend of Morgenthau, on whom the Treasury Secretary depended heavily. Historians John Koster, Ben Steil, and Sean McMeekin point out that by 1941, White's importance to Morgenthau had captured the interest of Soviet officials, and, after answering a fateful phone call with an intriguing, "White here" in May 1941, he is said to have met with Soviet GRU agent Vitali Pavlov to discuss exacerbating U.S.-Japanese tensions through hostile economic measures.[141]

Initially recruited by his first GRU agent, Ishkak "Bill" Akhmerov, in the 1930s, White appears to have zealously embraced the task that Pavlov assigned to him, and he began laboring to help make Stalin's alleged dream of igniting a war between the United States and Japan a reality almost immediately after discussing Operation *Snow* over lunch at Washington's Old Ebbitt Grill with his new Soviet handler.[142] As emphasized by Koster, McMeekin, and Steil, Operation *Snow's* objectives carried tremendous importance from Stalin's perspective regarding the Soviet Union's strategic global interests.[143] Relations between Washington and Tokyo had continued to sour following Roosevelt's denunciation of Japan's partnership with Berlin and its invasions of China, Manchuria, and former French Indochina after Hitler's June 1940 occupation of France. In the event of a U.S.-Japanese war, Stalin could avoid waging a two-front war in Europe and Asia and focus on arming his troops to resist Hitler, as his non-aggression pact appeared to be crumbling by early 1941, and he hoped to buy precious time to sufficiently strengthen the Red Army.[144]

On 6 June 1941, just weeks after his lunch meeting with Pavlov, White authored a Treasury Department memorandum in which he argued for the importance of a stronger position against further Japanese expansion in East Asia while advocating economic overtures that were highly favorable to the Soviet Union.[145] Apparently attracting little suspicion from Morgenthau and Roosevelt due to the administration's already deep focus on opposing the Axis through limited but increasingly strong means while attempting to lure Stalin away from Hitler, White's 6 June memorandum laid the groundwork for several key elements of Soviet Lend-Lease.[146] After ridiculing the supposedly tepid and weak response of the U.S. State Department to Axis aggression, White painted a grim picture of the United States facing Berlin, Rome, and Tokyo alone, playing on Morgenthau and Roosevelt's fears.[147] Cleverly feigning hope that hostilities with Japan could be avoided, White brazenly advised that the United States should offer the withdrawal of all naval forces from the Pacific and a 10-year non-aggression pact with Tokyo on the strict condition that Hirohito remove his forces from all occupied territories and conclude financial agreements with Washington.[148]

White proceeded to state that to avoid economic penalties as punishment for its record of aggression, Tokyo must agree to finance, at two percent, a 1,000,000,000-yen loan to the Chinese government, grant most-favored-nation status to the United States and China, and lend the Americans 50 percent of Japan's naval and air forces for three years.[149] Further insisting that U.S. officials be given sole authority to designate exactly which Japanese ships and aircraft should be loaned, he then stated that Tokyo must also replace its yen currency at a rate subject to the joint approval of the United States, Great Britain, and China. Should Hirohito reject these terms and conditions and thereby refuse such a "peaceful solution," White argued, the United States must immediately enact, "a complete embargo on imports from Japan" as a crucial economic, "first step."[150] White deliberately designed this memorandum to offend Tokyo, and eventually succeeded in this quest, later influencing his superior Morgenthau to pressure Roosevelt to enact a somewhat different but equally forceful approach in a 26 July oil embargo against Japan.[151]

Significantly, at the time of White's 6 June memorandum to Morgenthau, Hitler had not yet attacked the Soviet Union, yet the Molotov-Ribbentrop Pact had slowly been coming apart, and, as previously shown, Roosevelt's "moral embargo" against Stalin seemed to have lasted in practice only until October 1940.[152] This factor appears to have emboldened White to propose that the administration further coax Stalin into forging friendlier relations with the West while providing the Soviet premier with easier access to U.S. war material, at a period in which neither the United States nor the Soviet Union had yet gone to war with Germany. Implying that Moscow expected war, a factor that is said to have motivated Stalin's GRU to reconnect with him in the spring of 1941, White's memorandum advocated the delivery of any arms or raw materials requested and purchased by the Kremlin to Soviet ports, "In the event of war between Russia and any major power."[153] In such a situation, White stated, the U.S. government must immediately embargo the imports of any country that may go to war with the Soviet Union and permit Stalin to purchase U.S. $2,000,000,000 in material per year while concluding a five-year "Mutual Economic Assistance Pact."[154] White also advised that the Soviet Union should receive most-favored-nation status and immediately place an embargo on all exports from Germany and countries under Nazi occupation.[155]

While White's initial recommendations were not immediately embraced by Morgenthau and Roosevelt in June, he later revised its more aggressive elements that were approved and incorporated into the infamous "Hull note" handed to Japanese Ambassador Kichiasaburo Nomura and peace envoy Saburo Kurusu by Secretary of State Hull on 26 November 1941.[156] White's audacious proposals, with which Morgenthau, Hull, and Roosevelt appear to have largely agreed, amounted to an outrageous threat from the perspective of Hirohito's war cabinet, claiming that Japan could avoid, "certain defeat" and have, "peace at once" but on terms dictated solely by Washington.[157] As emphasized by Koster, White's deliberately aggressive proposals received not only Morgenthau's approval but Hull's, as the Secretary of State later handed them personally to Japanese officials with Roosevelt's authorization.[158]

Although ascribed to Secretary Hull, the document's contents had been authored by a desperate White at a time in which it appeared, frightfully from his perspective, that Hirohito and Prime Minister Hideki Tojo's diplomats were making limited progress with U.S. officials in the middle of November 1941. Tojo, then a new prime minister known as *kamisori* or "the razor" due to his reputed personal modesty and his razor-sharp, clear focus on international diplomacy, appears to have been prepared to agree to some of Roosevelt's demands that Japanese forces withdraw from many of the occupied territories.[159] He refused, however, to withdraw Tokyo's troops from occupied Manchuria and Korea, hoping to forestall the popular domestic resentment that such action could generate and to keep the areas as strong military bases from which Japanese troops could resist potential future Soviet incursions. Although Stalin had concluded an April 1941 non-aggression pact with Hirohito, Japanese anti-Communism, motivated by the tsar's murder in 1918 and Tokyo's subsequent military intervention in Siberia, remained potent, and while the Japanese leadership maintained its neutrality in the Soviet premier's anti-Hitler struggle, it remained wary of potential future aggression by Moscow.[160]

On 17 November 1941, White delivered another memorandum to Morgenthau that included many of his previous proposals as well as others that he appears to have designed to help push U.S.-Japanese relations to the breaking point, although, unknown to White at the time, Tojo's admirals had already embarked for the Pearl Harbor operation.[161] Described as a "hysterical missive" by John Koster, White's "November Memorandum," like his introductory speech as U.S. Chairman at the 1944 Bretton Woods Conference, fully revealed his conviction that economic attrition served as a vital war weapon at least as important as battlefield victories.[162] Combining praise of Morgenthau and Roosevelt with the specter of the Red Army's potential collapse and, by implication, a second Brest-Litovsk at a time in which the Nazis appeared poised to storm into Moscow, White argued for the application of stronger penalties on Japan. Comparing the administration's recent attempts to continue discussions with Japanese officials to the alleged Anglo-French betrayal of Czechoslovakia to Hitler at the 1938 Munich Conference, White stated, "We must cut loose from that outdated and decayed pattern of diplomacy [appeasement]."[163]

Without knowing that the Japanese leadership had already deployed its fleet to strike Pearl Harbor, White then proposed a series of demands that he hoped might be deemed unacceptable, offensive, and threatening by Hirohito, urging that Secretary Hull demand the full withdrawal of Japanese military, political, and financial support for any non-nationalist Chinese government, including Tokyo's puppet regime in Manchuria. Another of White's conditions required Japan to sell the United States three-fourths of its armaments, "including naval, air, ordnance and commercial ships" at an exact price to be determined solely by Washington rather than Tokyo.[164] Emphasizing that he sought to help end the current "uncertain status" and tensions between the administration and the Japanese leadership, White cleverly played on Roosevelt's emotions at the possibility of being seen as presiding over a "Far East Munich."[165] By entertaining Japanese counterproposals and not insisting on Tokyo's full troop withdrawal from all parts of China, White argued, Roosevelt risked playing the part of Judas Iscariot in the betrayal of Christ, "over thirty blood-stained coins of gold [sic, silver]."[166]

After approving much of White's new, more forceful memorandum the following day, Morgenthau forwarded it to Roosevelt and Hull, and the president ordered the Secretary of State to deliver it to his Japanese counterparts after reportedly becoming enraged at reports of Japanese reinforcements arriving in Indochina from occupied Chinese territory.[167] White followed up his 17 November memorandum, the core demands of which were included by Hull in his 26 November meeting with Nomura and Kurusu with Roosevelt's approval, with an invitation for RWR Chair Edward Carter to come to Washington. According to historian Ben Steil, White audaciously asked

Carter, known for his staunchly pro-Soviet positions, to join him in Washington in lobbying against any further diplomatic overtures to the Japanese.[168]

Even before rejecting Hull's conditions as aggressive, insulting, and unacceptable demands, conceived of and authored by White, Tojo and his cabinet had already begun preparations to launch their fleet against the U.S. naval base at Pearl Harbor, Hawaii, and White's desperate, last-ditch attempt to help provoke a war appears to have been unnecessary in this regard.[169] Yet White's authorship of the "Hull note" reveals his fanatical determination to serve Stalin's Pacific strategy in a somewhat stealthy manner by using his influential government position in helping to ensure that Washington and Tokyo did not arrive at an understanding before the outbreak of hostilities and, in taking this desperate action, he helped to guarantee that Tojo and Hirohito did not abandon their plan of attack by heaping insults on their pride as the leaders of a great, imperial East Asian power and further provoking their anger.[170]

On 8 December 1941, Stalin officially gained a powerful new ally as Japan's sudden, surprise strike on Pearl Harbor on the previous day triggered the U.S. entry into the war and a gradual but crucial and tremendous increase in Soviet Lend-Lease aid.[171] The U.S. entry into the war galvanized Stettinius, Hopkins, and other American officials to prioritize Lend-Lease shipments to the Soviet Union as anti-Japanese prejudice combined with patriotic resentment of the Axis Powers and temporarily overshadowed public fears of Communism as mentioned.[172] White's success at provoking war with Tokyo, even if his actions alone cannot be said to have triggered Tojo's aggression against the U.S. fleet at Pearl Harbor, continued to pay dividends and temporarily allowed him and other Soviet agents to cover their tracks while capitalizing on the anti-Japanese hysteria that that their actions had helped enable after Roosevelt issued Executive Order 9066 on 19 February 1942. This act led to the forced internment of 112,000 Japanese-Americans during the war, allowing White and others to become more brazen, cocky, and open in their pro-Soviet positions as Americans were advised to embrace the Red Army's supposed fight for freedom.[173]

Acting further on the orders that he received from his GRU handler Pavlov, White also played a part in advising the administration on the diversion of financial resources to the acquisition of many of the specific items desired by Stalin, although again, this specific action also served as a confluence of interests with U.S. wartime strategy at the time in helping the then-desperate Red Army.[174] Yet White's open emphasis on aiding Stalin's struggle naturally fell on sympathetic ears during the war as Morgenthau, Hopkins, and Stettinius readily agreed to provide anything to Washington's newfound Soviet ally, and removed any obstacles to the Soviet leader's aid orders. Enabled by the administration's zeal for arming the red warriors, White's influence in the Treasury Department appears to have eventually aided in the shipment of 1,465 pounds of U.S. uranium chemicals and one kilogram of uranium metal to the

Soviet Union, reportedly with Hopkins's approval, an indefensible and counterproductive act that cannot, in any way, be excused even if Roosevelt's administration authorized it at the time.[175]

White's treason and pro-Soviet espionage efforts, together with those of Alger Hiss and others in Roosevelt's administration, created almost limitless opportunities for Stalin to influence and, to a certain extent, hijack through his agents certain aspects of U.S. foreign policy during the war.[176] Yet this could not have happened without Roosevelt's warm embracing of the Red Army's cause and his naivete in underestimating Stalin's character and Communism's appeal among some in his administration, an attitude enhanced by his fears that battlefield events could force the Soviet premier into signing a separate peace with Hitler. Determined to preside over Germany's total, unquestioned, and final defeat and prevent a second Brest-Litovsk from blemishing his record and wrecking Washington's strategy, Roosevelt worked to avoid repeating the perceived errors that occurred on Wilson's watch and zealously embraced the Red Army's struggle as vital to achieving an Allied victory. In full agreement with the president in this regard, Hull, Hopkins, Stettinius, Feis, Standley, and Knox, none of whom are known to have been Soviet agents, zealously and wisely executed the supplying of Stalin's forces to permanently defeat Berlin's genocidal National Socialists, while foolishly overestimating their own ability to charm and permanently win over the red warrior in Moscow and convert him to Washington's semi-capitalist vision for a peaceful postwar world.[177]

The triumphs and tragedies of the early Arctic convoys crews and the strategic expansion of the Persian Corridor and ALSIB

Following the Pearl Harbor attack and Hitler and Mussolini's declarations of war on the United States four days later, Roosevelt began to rapidly strengthen Washington's Soviet Lend-Lease program as the remaining congressional opposition, having already somewhat diminished by late 1941, as discussed in this work's previous chapter, largely collapsed. With the United States officially involved in the war as a full belligerent power in the Allied ranks, the mission of supplying Stalin's soldiers rapidly gained momentum.[1] While Pearl Harbor's immediate aftermath led to a highly urgent prioritization of equipping the U.S. military for a modern, mobile military conflict and led to a brief decrease in Lend-Lease exports in December 1941, Roosevelt quickly refocused Washington's attention to arming the Soviets in March 1942. Yet how could the administration accomplish this task to Stalin's satisfaction with the Pacific supply route now closed to U.S. vessels by the Japanese?[2] This third chapter seeks to answer this question while focusing on the hurdles and advantages within each supply route that Roosevelt and Churchill faced as they sought to keep Stalin's Red Army in the war and actively fighting Hitler's forces to avoid a repeat of the March 1918 Brest-Litovsk fiasco.[3]

The three major Lend-Lease supply routes to the Soviet Union ran from Great Britain's Loch Ewe to the Soviet Arctic ports of Archangel and Murmansk, from the respective Iranian and Iraqi ports of Abadan, Bushehr, and Basra to the Soviet Caucasus region, and from Fairbanks, Alaska to the Siberian cities of Krasnoyarsk and Uelkel.[4] Many historians have correctly emphasized the political aspect of the Arctic route's importance by pointing to the need for Roosevelt and Churchill to demonstrate their commitment to aiding Stalin's war effort, yet few, until now, appear to have identified Anglo-American efforts in this regard as being motivated and influenced by the precedent of Brest-Litovsk in the First World War. While rightly commending the courage of the crews braving the fierce Arctic gales, ice, and enemy attacks, scholars such as

David Wragg and Michael Walling have also emphasized the route's role in the Soviet Union's defense as being unappreciated by Stalin and therefore not worth the Western leaders' efforts.[5] Yet Stalin's emphasis on the convoys' importance and the frustration that he expressed in telegrams following their brief suspension indicates otherwise, somewhat suggesting, perhaps, that the North Russian route proved more vital to the Red Army's war effort in a practical sense than has often been assumed.[6]

As briefly mentioned in the previous chapter, British vessels initially transported the bulk of equipment to Stalin's beleaguered forces as Churchill vowed to supply all forms of aid to his newfound and, perhaps somewhat understandably, suspicious Soviet ally.[7] On Churchill's orders, British naval forces launched the first of many Arctic convoys carrying supplies to the Soviet northern ports on 21 August 1941 in a small, successful convoy simply dubbed "Dervish."[8] The next month, a second convoy code-named PQ-1 embarked on its Arctic journey, and the subsequent convoys sailed largely unopposed until the Nazi submarine *U-454* sank the destroyer HMS *Matabele* on 17 January 1942, killing 209 sailors as the British vessel escorted the eight merchant ships of Convoy PQ-8 on its otherwise successful voyage to North Russia.[9] With Great Britain's vaunted but hard-pressed Royal Navy already stretched thin across the globe by Hitler's submarines and even more so by his Japanese comrades after December 1941, Churchill's government grew increasingly reliant on the Merchant Navy to execute its task of supplying Stalin.[10]

As U.S. war production soared to increasingly higher levels following the Pearl Harbor attack, Roosevelt, Hopkins, and Stettinius labored zealously to ensure that their military arms buildup did not detrimentally impact Soviet Lend-Lease aid.[11] Even as U.S. Army Chief of Staff Marshall and Navy Secretary Knox scrambled to upgrade and supply the U.S. Armed Forces' equipment and prepare young Americans to fight a modern, mobile war, the administration demanded that Stalin's war effort receive top priority. As pointed out by Sean McMeekin, Roosevelt's approach to Germany's total defeat appears to have played a central part in the president's emphasis on keeping Stalin well-supplied to carry on the war throughout 1942.[12] German forces resumed their offensive operations on the Eastern Front early in the year and it appeared vital to Roosevelt, Churchill, and their respective advisers that a repeat of March 1918 be avoided and that Stalin remain in the war and in control of the Red Army and Soviet people as they faced merciless Nazi attacks.[13]

Beginning in August 1941, shortly after Hopkins's return to Washington from Moscow and his glowing report on Stalin to Roosevelt, American and British military officials started working to improve the port facilities in Anglo-Soviet-occupied Iran to increase the flow of material through the country. The Iranian ports of Abadan and Bushehr, together with the nearby port of Basra in British-occupied Iraq, eventually grew into massive delivery centers for Lend-Lease material destined for Stalin's soldiers.[14] Together with the ALSIB air route and, to a lesser extent, the Soviet naval transportation of material across the North Pacific, the Persian Corridor increased in importance to the Soviet Lend-Lease program from 1943 forward.[15]

These U.S.-British efforts to improve Iran's port facilities, U.S.-Soviet efforts at organizing the ALSIB air route, and Soviet-Japanese diplomacy to agree on terms acceptable to Tokyo regarding the transportation of material across the Pacific increased after Pearl Harbor but also took crucial time for development.[16] Despite Stalin's strict neutrality or, as McMeekin controversially argues, his unofficial collaboration with Hirohito in the Pacific Theater, the Japanese leadership remained suspicious of Moscow's motives, as mentioned previously and initially refused to permit Allied arms to travel through Tokyo's territorial waters. The Americans could, therefore, initially only ship non-military items, such as food and raw materials, to Vladivostok and only in Soviet ships flying the Red Fleet's banner, influencing Roosevelt's transfer of 63 U.S. ships to Stalin's control by the summer of 1943 as Moscow had few transport vessels in the Pacific.[17]

Likewise, U.S. and Soviet officials did not fully establish the ALSIB route, by which roughly half of the Lend-Lease aircraft ultimately supplied to the Soviets are said to have been delivered, until late 1942 due to Stalin's consistent rejections of Roosevelt's offer to have U.S. pilots fly the planes to Siberia. The agreement finally reached in late 1942 essentially placed Soviet pilots in charge of the entire route, providing them with a base located in Fairbanks, Alaska from which they could take control of the planes and fly them to Siberia.[18] Until Allied personnel significantly improved Iran's Persian Gulf ports and desert and mountain roads by which they delivered trucks, jeeps, and other vehicles crucial to Stalin's war effort in the late spring of 1943, the Persian Corridor could supply only small quantities of Lend-Lease goods.[19]

Before the inherent problems of the ALSIB route and the Persian Corridor were largely resolved by the middle of 1943, the bulk of material aid provided to Stalin's beleaguered Red Army appears to have been successfully delivered by the Arctic convoys to North Russia's ports.[20] This route, while very dangerous for the Allied sailors involved and the precious cargo that they transported to arm the Red Army's anti-Nazi struggle and feed its foot soldiers, also served as the geographically shortest, most practical, and direct route to the Soviet Union. For this reason, Churchill established the route and ordered Great Britain's Royal Navy and Merchant Navy to begin convoying supplies to Stalin's soldiers in the late summer of 1941, and the Soviet premier insisted that the convoys be continued in his telegrams to his Anglo-American counterparts well into late 1943.[21] Yet due to the constant perils to which the Arctic convoys were subjected, such as facing the arduous sea conditions and Hitler's forces, and the overall smaller volume of supplies that they delivered to the Red Army, this supply route has often been unfavorably portrayed in comparison to its Iranian and Siberian-Pacific counterparts.[22]

While the two other major Soviet Lend-Lease routes have long been known to scholars as having supplied a larger total amount of material aid to Stalin's war effort, the question of the Arctic convoys' practical contributions to the goal of keeping the Red Army killing German troops in the east appears to have received less attention. Roosevelt's initial success in selling Lend-Lease to the American public and Congress resulted in many ways from his definition of the program as a defensive effort to serve U.S. interests by arming and feeding others already resisting Axis aggression. Yet the president and his closest associates, in their foresight as they adhered to Grant's annihilation strategy, appear to have had a much broader definition of "defense" than merely helping the Red Army fight back, viewing the unconditional supplying of Stalin as a crucial part of their strategic approach to Hitler's total defeat while saving American lives and hoping to win him over to their views of peaceful coexistence after victory.[23] Despite facing daunting obstacles and suffering some tragic losses, the Arctic convoys that delivered between 1,530,000 and 1,630,000 tons of Lend-Lease material between 1942 and 1943 alone played an important part in achieving this strategic objective.[24]

The Arctic convoys to the Soviet Union's northern European ports at Archangel and Murmansk that Churchill launched in August 1941 with the successful "Dervish" voyage quickly increased in importance and gained momentum as larger convoys began sailing following the U.S. entry into the war.[25] According to Alexander Hill and Steven Zaloga, while initial British aid shipments may have supplied the Red Army with little equipment overall, London's naval forces managed to deliver enough tanks and aircraft to help contribute to Moscow's defense in late 1941.[26]

British Matilda and Valentine tanks and U.S. M3 Stuart tanks also began to arrive at the Arctic ports late in the year to help in some small but important way to replenish the Red Army's tank losses at Stalin's request.[27] While these vehicles alone, like the U.S. P-40s and British Hurricane fighter planes, cannot be said to have won the Battle of Moscow, they certainly appear to have been of at least some value to the Red Army's tank park, as indicated by Stalin's insistence to Churchill that he receive these urgently-needed vehicles, somewhat justifying Hill's conclusions regarding their importance that year.[28] According to Hill and Steven Zaloga in their respective works on the subject, Soviet tank crews manning their British tanks appear to have contributed to some of the crucial actions in the fighting as the Battle of Moscow raged in the first weeks of December 1941, suffering a loss of 77 of these vehicles from a total of 182.[29]

In early 1942, the crucial year in which Stalin's soldiers began irreversibly repulsing the Nazi invaders, according to Robert Citino in *Death of the Wehrmacht: The German Campaigns of 1942*, Roosevelt acted decisively to ensure that Soviet Lend-Lease received top priority.[30] Alleging that Soviet needs were not being met by U.S. war production, the president scoldingly wrote to his war agency directors on 7 March ordering that all aid requested by Stalin for the First Protocol period be prepared and shipped immediately, "regardless of the effect of these shipments on any other part of our war program."[31] Roosevelt thereby created a situation in which Lend-Lease officials had only to mention his order to their subordinates to ensure that Soviet aid shipments received immediate prioritization, and between April and June 1942, 44 U.S. Liberty ships delivered 300,000 tons of material to North Russia.[32]

On 16 March 1942, Roosevelt informed Stalin of the desperate action that he and his senior Lend-Lease advisers had taken to prioritize the Red Army's battlefield needs and fulfill the Soviet premier's First Protocol orders of war material. Seeking to assure the Soviet dictator that his requests were not going unanswered in Washington and thereby not risk jeopardizing the crucial wartime alliance, Roosevelt promised Stalin that, "we are going to bend every possible effort to move these supplies to your battle lines."[33] After receiving no reply from his Soviet counterpart, perhaps an intentional move by Stalin to keep Roosevelt guessing and concerned, the American president again wrote to the Kremlin leader on 12 April, lamenting the fact that they had not yet met in person and describing such a meeting as being, "of the utmost military importance."[34] Perhaps detecting Roosevelt's desperation to keep the Red Army fighting and avoid a repeat of March 1918, Stalin briefly replied on 20 April with an offer to send Molotov to Washington in May, thus refusing to meet him as an equal and somewhat fueling his fears.[35]

On 4 May, Roosevelt expressed to Stalin his regret at the difficulties faced by the Arctic convoys as Hitler's admirals, upon discovering the potential dangers to Berlin's eastern campaign being posed by the Allied ships sailing supplies to North Russia, had begun targeting them.[36] Nevertheless, he promised his Soviet ally, "that no effort will be spared to get as many ships off as possible," before thanking him for warmly receiving Admiral William Standley as U.S. Ambassador in Moscow and vowing to fully accommodate Molotov at the White House.[37] Apparently seeking to ensure the continued flow of unconditional U.S. aid by keeping Roosevelt concerned that he may forge a separate peace with Hitler, Stalin replied only on 15 May, the latest date by which he had promised Molotov's departure, blaming inclement weather for the Foreign Commissar's delayed journey to Washington and urging the Anglo-American leaders to maintain the convoys despite the dangers.[38] Despite Ambassador Standley's proposals to open a Lend-Lease air route between Alaska and Siberia and the efforts of Roosevelt and Churchill to expand the Persian Corridor's capacity,

Stalin repeatedly insisted on the vital necessity of maintaining the Arctic route to North Russia, and his Western Allies, haunted by Brest-Litovsk's shadow, obliged to keep the Red Army fighting.[39]

As more U.S. and Panamanian merchant vessels arrived to participate in delivering Lend-Lease material to North Russia in January and February 1942, British Commander-in-Chief, Home Fleet Admiral Sir John Tovey, to whom Churchill had entrusted the protection of the Arctic convoys, labored to provide enough naval forces for their defense. On 12 March 1942, the 15 merchant ships and one oiler of Convoy PQ-12 arrived safely in Murmansk after narrowly avoiding an encounter with the feared German battleship *Tirpitz* that Hitler had ordered to Trondheim, Norway.[40] Shortly after the success of PQ-12 and the 15 homebound ships of QP-8, with the lone exception of, "the straggler *Ijora*" being sunk by the Nazi destroyer *Friedrich Ihn* according to the British Naval Staff's history, the Arctic convoys faced growing dangers beginning in March 1942.[41]

Yet despite Allied fears of raids by Hitler's surface vessels, the German Navy remained limited in its northern operations due to Grand Admiral Erich Raeder and Vice Admiral Otto Ciliax's concerns that deploying *Tirpitz* and their other precious, rare surface vessels exposed them to great dangers for little gain.[42] Following PQ-12's success, the two men advocated for the continued use of *Tirpitz* and other surface ships in their primary role of coastal defense in the event of an Allied invasion of Norway, and Hitler subsequently ordered further interdiction raids against the Arctic convoys to be executed primarily by submarines and aircraft. Nazi *Reichsmarschall* Hermann Goering subsequently deployed more of the German Air Force's He 111 and Ju 88 bombers and torpedo planes to occupied Norway to target the Allied vessels, and Hitler demanded that construction on the planned aircraft carrier *Graf Zeppelin* be intensified, the latter task ending in a futile, vain effort.[43]

Laboring to prioritize Soviet Lend-Lease deliveries and keep the Red Army armed and fighting as Stalin's soldiers continued clashing with the Nazi invaders during the fierce spring engagements, Roosevelt and Navy Secretary Knox deployed Task Force 99 for Arctic convoy escort duty in April 1942.[44] Consisting of the cruiser USS *Tuscaloosa* and the destroyers USS *Emmons*, USS *Rodman*, HMS *Onslaught*, HMS *Martin*, and HMS *Marne*, Task Force 99 executed key support operations for the convoys. Admiral Tovey later lamented the *Tuscaloosa's* return to the United States and the subsequent cancelation of Task Force 99, recalling, "This force had provided a welcome reinforcement to the Home Fleet at a time when its strength was much reduced."[45] Describing U.S. Vice Admiral Robert C. Giffen as, "a loyal and enthusiastic colleague," Tovey assessed the force's men as, "admirable" in their tenacity, their sinking of the Nazi minelayer *Ulm* on 24 August, and their successful delivery of two squadrons of Hampden fighter aircraft to Archangel in support of Convoy PQ-18.[46]

While many convoys successfully repulsed the Germans with depth charges, carrier-based aircraft, and deck cannon fire during the winter, the constant daylight during the Arctic summer months enabled the Nazi attackers to strike for more prolonged periods.[47] In the late spring of 1942, Nazi bombers hammered Convoy PQ-16 for five days, sinking eight ships while the remaining 24 arrived and unloaded safely at Murmansk and Archangel on 30 May.[48] Between 4 and 9 July, Convoy PQ-17 under Captain Jack Broome suffered a loss of 23 ships carrying 57,176 tons of cargo during another five days of Nazi submarine and air assaults. The cargo lost totaled 430 tanks, 3,350 trucks, jeeps, and other transport vehicles, and 210 aircraft, in addition to 153 men killed at a time in which every vehicle mattered as the Red Army struggled against Hitler's ongoing offensive aimed at Stalingrad and the Caucasus.[49]

PQ-17's massive losses appear to have resulted in many ways from a communication in which Admiralty officials in London mistakenly stated that the convoy faced imminent attack from the Nazi battleship *Tirpitz* and its potent cruiser and destroyer escort forces and ordered the convoy to, "scatter."[50] Following the naval procedure and in full compliance with London's orders, Captain Broome obediently and bravely prepared his men to face the perceived oncoming threat from *Tirpitz* and its destroyer escorts while ordering the merchantmen to proceed to North Russia. The Admiralty's order for Broome to scatter the convoy, conceived in an atmosphere of uncertainty and nervousness due to the *Tirpitz's* mere presence in Norwegian waters and London's fear of losing too many U.S. vessels, inadvertently exposed the merchant ships to the real danger of air and submarine attack.[51] Due to *Tirpitz's* brief, earlier action against PQ-12, the Admiralty does not appear to have been aware of Hitler's subsequent reluctance to again expose his few surface ships, and as Broome's men courageously prepared to face the German battleship, Nazi submarines and aircraft struck the exposed merchantmen.[52]

Writing in his war diary about three weeks after PQ-17's disastrous journey, Soviet Northern Fleet Admiral Arseni Golovko stated that London had alerted Moscow on 4 July that the *Tirpitz* and the cruiser *Admiral Hipper* had left their base at Trondheim, Norway, after Nazi reconnaissance aircraft had discovered the convoy.[53] While both Nazi warships and their accompanying escort destroyers are said to have had initially been assigned to attacking PQ-17, somewhat justifying the concerns of Churchill's admirals both in London and at sea, they were quickly redirected to Altenfjord, Norway. This fact, initially unknown either to the Admiralty or to Hero of the Soviet Union Captain Nikolai Lunin, whose submarine *K-21* bravely set out to intercept the Nazi warships, appears to have influenced the Admiralty's decision to scatter the convoy.[54] After firing four torpedoes in a daring but unsuccessful attack on the *Tirpitz*, Lunin observed that the German battleship and its escort force of two cruisers and seven destroyers appeared to be changing course away from PQ-17 on 5 July, by which point Broome and his comrades had received London's order.[55]

The heavy losses incurred during the relentless German attacks on PQ-17 forced Churchill, at the British Admiralty's urging and against Roosevelt's wishes, to temporarily halt all further Arctic convoys in the remaining summer months of 1942.[56] Churchill's decision angered Stalin, and the Soviet premier immediately expressed his frustration, ridiculing the Royal Navy's performance and minimizing its sacrifices in delivering the material in comparison to the Red Army's suffering.[57] In the late summer, Roosevelt began urging Churchill and Field Marshal Lord Alanbrooke, the latter man having always taken a rather dim view of the Arctic route, to accept the likelihood of further losses and to resume the convoys to North Russia. While the Anglo-American Allies diplomatically wrangled with Stalin's constant complaints about the Royal Navy, U.S. tank quality, and his need for aluminum, food, trucks, and "pursuit planes," Soviet General Vasili Chuikov's 62nd Army fought tenaciously as the Nazi troops and tanks of General Friedrich von Paulus's 6th Army stormed into Stalingrad.[58]

Despite Berlin's attempts at interdiction, the vast majority of Lend-Lease convoys operating along the Arctic route successfully reached Murmansk, Molotovsk, and Archangel, delivering thousands of tanks, planes, trucks, and jeeps to the Red Army and Red Army Air Forces.[59] In 1944, Edward Stettinius proudly reported that many U.S. Liberty ships carrying Lend-Lease supplies had arrived safely alongside their British and Canadian counterparts, stating that, "Enough supplies did get to [North] Russia, however, to be of real value in the summer fighting of 1942" including 2,000 tanks and 1,300 planes delivered by June.[60] In addition to weaponry, the ships delivered food and raw materials such as eggs, meat, wheat, steel, aluminum, and machine tools produced in American farms and factories as U.S. war production soared and Roosevelt and Hopkins spared no effort to aid Stalin while preventing a separate peace between Moscow and Berlin, however remote such a possibility may have, in fact, been at the time.[61]

Despite PQ-17's massive losses and Churchill's agreement with the Admiralty's decision to immediately suspend the Arctic convoys, Roosevelt and Hopkins came to Stalin's aid as the Red Army faced Hitler's most merciless offensives in the Nazi drive on Stalingrad in late summer and fall 1942.[62] Fretting over Brest-Litovsk's shadow as Stalin's demands for either a resumption of, "the northern [convoy] route" or the opening of a second front grew in desperation, the American president began urging the British prime minister to resume the convoys, stating, "the Russians are today killing more Germans and destroying more equipment than you and I put together."[63] The two great Western leaders also redoubled their efforts to improve the supply flow through Iran and Alaska, yet Stalin's insistence that neither route could substitute for the deliveries to North Russia soon led them to resume the convoys as the Stalingrad bloodbath raged daily.[64] Their determination to prevent Stalin's overthrow or a Nazi-Soviet peace, and in doing so, ensure Hitler's ultimate defeat, led the U.S. and British leaders to launch a convoy even larger than PQ-17 in August 1942.[65]

In an indication of the Anglo-American leadership's respective desire to assure Stalin of their commitment and keep him and the Red Army persevering in the war, Churchill flew to Moscow for a meeting with the Soviet leader on 14 August 1942 in a show of Allied solidarity as Red Army General Georgi Zhukov, General Chuikov, and their subordinates faced Hitler's Stalingrad offensive.[66] Despite this public, political display of support, tensions ran deep between the two leaders as Churchill informed Stalin that he and Roosevelt could not open a "second front" in Europe at any point in 1942.[67] The Soviet premier angrily reminded the prime minister of Roosevelt's promise of a second front in 1942 to Molotov during the Foreign Commissar's White House visit in May, yet he carefully neglected to mention that Moscow had declined the offer after the president stated that such an effort required a reduction in Soviet Lend-Lease aid.[68] After delivering the news of the Arctic convoys' planned resumption and the planning of Operation *Torch* in North Africa, Churchill enjoyed an impromptu Kremlin dinner with Stalin and his daughter Svetlana before departing for London and privately and angrily denouncing the Soviet premier to his bodyguards.[69]

Under the command of Rear Admiral Edye K. Boddam-Whetham, the 40 merchant ships and four naval auxiliaries of Convoy PQ-18 departed from Loch Ewe on 2 September 1942 and joined with several Fighting Escort Groups totaling 76 British warships sailing from Reykjavik, Iceland.[70] As described by Michael Walling in *Forgotten Sacrifice: The Arctic Convoys of World War II*, Admiral Tovey called Churchill's attention to the irony in PQ-18's freighters carrying the most advanced Hurricane fighters to Stalin while its lone aircraft carrier *Avenger* boasted only twelve older models and three Swordfish planes for defense.[71] On 12 September, eight Nazi submarines struck but quickly withdrew after 9:00 p.m. under fire from the *Avenger's* aircraft and after the sinking of *U-88* by HMS *Faulknor*, as recalled by Royal Navy veteran Charlie Erswell in his 2021 memoir.[72]

The enemy submarines struck the next day again and sank the Soviet freighter *Stalingrad* and the U.S. oil tanker *Oliver Ellsworth*, and a swarm of 85 Ju 88 and He 111 torpedo aircraft emptied their lethal loads in a fanatical attack at close range that proved suicidal for several bombers as flames spewed by the destroyers' guns danced across the sky.[73] As the courageous crews of HMS *Offa* and HMT *St. Kenen* struggled to rescue as many survivors as possible from the sinking Allied ships, the attackers regrouped to refocus their efforts on striking the convoy's escort vessels. On the following day at 12:35 p.m., two groups totaling more than 20 German torpedo bombers focused their respective assaults against the *Avenger* and the cruiser HMS *Scylla* in an unsuccessful attack resulting in eleven Nazi aircraft downed and no Allied losses. The crews of HMS *Ulster Queen*, HMS *Wheatland*, and HMS *Wilton* executed a tenacious defense alongside the *Avenger's* pilots that managed to quickly scramble into the sky and repulse many Nazi aircraft despite the enemy's successful avoidance of radar detection by sweeping in low.[74]

According to the British Naval Staff's postwar report, Allied radar, having improved since the PQ-17 disaster, quickly warned of another bombing raid by a squadron of twelve Ju 88s shortly after 1:00 p.m., narrowly saving the *Avenger's* crew from a direct hit.[75] A subsequent attack by 25 torpedo aircraft resulted in the sinking of SS *Mary Luckenbach* and the loss of three Hurricanes whose pilots were quickly rescued from the frigid Arctic waters by destroyer crews. Beginning at 12:45 p.m. on 15 September, roughly 50 Nazi aircraft repeatedly swept over PQ-18 for about three hours, menacing the convoy with bombs but failing to strike any ships as the escort gunners and fighter pilots mounted an effective, defiant defense, downing three German planes.[76] The Nazis also lost the submarine *U-457* to fire from HMS *Impulsive* that day, prompting German Group Command North to withdraw and refocus its eleven remaining submarines in the area on the homebound convoy QP-14 that suffered a loss of several ships and a Catalina aircraft.[77]

Two days after the Soviet destroyers *Gremyashchi* and *Sokrushitelni* relieved Rear Admiral Burnett of escort duty as he withdrew the *Scylla*, HMS *Alynbank*, *Avenger*, and the submarines *P-614* and *P-615* to assist QP-14 on the afternoon of 16 September, Nazi forces made a desperate, final effort to deprive Stalin's Red Army of PQ-18's precious cargo.[78] At 8:20 a.m. on the morning of 18 September 1942, twelve Nazi torpedo bombers and several Ju 88s struck at the convoy's flanks for slightly more than two hours, eventually sinking the U.S. Liberty ship SS *Kentucky* and retreating after suffering a loss of four aircraft. Two days later, twelve Ju 88s launched an unsuccessful hour-long assault as PQ-18, despite losing one-third of its ships, neared Archangel that afternoon with vast amounts of material. Despite the best efforts of Hitler's admirals to repeat their brutal assault on PQ-17, the men of PQ-18 persevered and repulsed repeated enemy air and submarine assaults and docked safely at Archangel's harbor on 21 September 1942.[79]

The 28 surviving freighters of PQ-18 delivered a crucial amount of the specific materials that Stalin had urged Roosevelt to prioritize in Anglo-American aid shipments, ranging from attack aircraft and trucks to food, machine tools, and raw materials.[80] British sailor Leonard H. Thomas marveled in his diary at the colossal crates of food being brought ashore from the U.S. Liberty ship SS *Patrick Henry*, stating, "every time we looked at her, she seemed to be unloading food from the endless stocks she had in her."[81] In his diary, British merchant mariner Alfred Grossmith Mason also recorded his amazement as Soviet stevedores and crane drivers unloaded an army's worth of weaponry from the SS *Empire Baffin* alone, the vessel on which he served. Recalling the sight of, "Bren carriers, large and small tanks, troop carriers, and heavy-duty wagons" emerging from the ship alongside carefully-crated aircraft, Mason described the ship as, "a huge, floating Pandora's box" from which an endless stream of arms and ordnance flowed.[82]

In late December, Hitler's forces suffered another humiliating setback at the Battle of the Barents' Sea that appears to have significantly salted the wounds inflicted by their Stalingrad debacle and PQ-18's successful voyage to North Russia.[83] Anxious to keep Stalin's soldiers supplied, Roosevelt and Churchill launched Convoys JW-51A and JW-51B, with the former docking safely at Murmansk and Molotovsk on 25 December undetected and unmolested by the Nazis as Goering redeployed many aircraft from Norway to face Operation *Torch*, the Anglo-American landings in North Africa.[84] As JW-51B entered the Barents' Sea near Norway's northern coast at 8:00 a.m. on 31 December, Vice Admiral Oskar Kummetz launched Operation *Regenbogen* (Rainbow) against the convoy's main body of ships on orders from the German Naval Staff, having learned of its existence from Nazi patrol pilots a week earlier. After spotting Kummetz's force, Captain Robert Sherbrooke of HMS *Onslow*, aided by the captains of HMS *Obdurate*, HMS *Obedient*, and HMS *Orwell* prepared to face the enemy while ordering HMS *Achates* to proceed ahead with the merchant ships.[85]

In a bold, calculating move, Sherbrooke and his comrades feigned a torpedo attack on the German warships, and Kummetz, fearing Hitler's wrath as the Nazi dictator had ordered him not to risk Germany's prized surface ships unnecessarily, swallowed the bait and ordered his *Admiral Hipper* to withdraw.[86] After executing this cautionary maneuver, *Admiral Hipper's* crew resumed the attack on *Onslow*, damaging the ship, wounding Sherbrooke, and killing 17 British sailors. Emboldened by this success, Kummetz then sent *Admiral Hipper* and the Nazi destroyer *Friedrich Eckholdt* north, sinking the British minesweeper *Bramble*, which they had mistaken for a destroyer, and the *Achates*.[87] These attacks quickly caught the attention of the crews of HMS *Sheffield* and HMS *Jamaica*, and both cruisers then badly damaged *Admiral Hipper* in a surprise attack, forcing the Nazi warship into a desperate retreat.[88]

Mistaking the *Sheffield* for the *Admiral Hipper*, the German captains of *Friedrich Eckholdt* and *Richard Beitzen* attempted to get into formation with the British cruiser, only to find themselves being fired upon, with the former of the two Nazi vessels sinking.[89] Attempting to strike JW-51B from the east and link up with *Admiral Hipper*, the Nazi destroyer *Luetzow* unexpectedly encountered the *Jamaica* and *Sheffield* before returning to base while its British foes rejoined their convoy and sailed with its 14 merchant ships safely to North Russia.[90] Enraged by his admirals' failure to intercept another important Arctic convoy as the Soviet bear's claws slashed von Paulus's encircled 6th Army at Stalingrad, Hitler threatened to enact an order to scrap Germany's surface fleet and force the German Navy to focus strictly on submarine operations. In a further indication of the Arctic convoys' contribution to Moscow's war effort, he also accepted the resignation of Grand Admiral Raeder and replaced him with

Grand Admiral Karl Doenitz following the battle, angered at his admirals' inability to prevent the flow of vital goods from reaching Stalin's Red Army.[91]

On 17 January 1943, as Red Army Generals Zhukov and Chuikov continued squeezing von Paulus's encircled 6th Army in Stalingrad, the crews of the 43 total ships of Convoy JW-52 began their journey to Murmansk to deliver more Lend-Lease aid to the Red Army as Churchill and Roosevelt spared no effort to ensure a crippling defeat for Hitler.[92] According to U.S. merchant mariner Herman Melton, then serving on the Liberty ship SS *Cornelius Harnett*, a Nazi BV 138 reconnaissance aircraft appeared on 23 January and escaped to report the convoy's position after attracting Allied anti-aircraft fire.[93] Three He 115 torpedo bombers struck at the *Harnett* the next day and received a resounding rebuff at the hands of the ship's tenacious anti-aircraft gunners under the courageous leadership of Lieutenant Richard Stone boldly directing the men in firing their newly-installed 5"/38 caliber deck guns added in Philadelphia.[94]

JW-52's safe arrival in Murmansk on 27 January, followed by the success of Convoy JW-53 the following month, appears to demonstrate the Allies' ability to repulse Nazi air and naval assaults and deliver enough material to North Russia in 1943 to help the Red Army counterattack the invaders.[95] Contemporary documents housed at the British National Archives, Kew, reveal that preparations for JW-52 began on 14 December 1942 as Churchill emphasized the need to maintain a steady flow of supplies to Stalin's forces in a note to First Sea Lord Sir Dudley Pound.[96] After commending the Red Army's splendid and ongoing successes at Stalingrad in a 29 December telegram, Churchill excitedly informed Stalin that he intended to, "send a full convoy of thirty or more ships in January," while cautioning that the vessels could potentially sail in two separate convoys depending on naval developments.[97]

Implicitly dangling the threat of a second Brest-Litovsk over Churchill's head during this period, Stalin's top diplomats in London faithfully maintained their barrage of accusations alleging that the Western Allies were somehow attempting to remain on the sidelines while Soviet soldiers fought, bled, and died defending their homeland. In early January 1943, Admiral Pound informed Churchill that Soviet Ambassador Ivan Maisky had complained about London's decision to divide the planned convoy into two groups, alleging that the prime minister had promised a 30-ship convoy, "in January and February [each]."[98] In his reply to Pound, Foreign Secretary Anthony Eden, and First Lord of the Admiralty Sir Alfred V. Alexander on 9 January, Churchill fumed that Maisky had misquoted him, stating that he had promised Stalin nothing of the sort and had rather cautioned him that a single convoy may be divided into two separate convoys. Already burdened by Stalin and Roosevelt's demands to maintain the convoys to North Russia no matter the cost, Churchill sniped in exasperation that, "Maisky should be told that I am getting to the end of my tether with these repeated Russian naggings and that it is not the slightest use trying to knock me about any more."[99]

The documents contained in the British National Archives, Kew provide a key window into Churchill's strenuous efforts to organize and sail more Arctic convoys even as the Soviet victory at Stalingrad appeared imminent, attesting to his and Roosevelt's determination to keep Stalin satisfied and fighting Hitler.[100] Determined to preempt even the slightest possibility of a separate peace, the British prime minister and American president had undertaken every effort, at the latter's stubborn insistence, to resume the Arctic convoys after the PQ-17 tragedy and keep them sailing as the Stalingrad fighting raged.[101] Ambassador Maisky's pointed complaints, including a 2 January note to Foreign Secretary Eden alleging British "arrears" regarding Second Protocol deliveries and insisting that London immediately double its proposed shipment of 100 Hurricane fighters, enhanced these fears and frustrations.[102] Dictated in an almost disinterested and apathetic tone, Stalin's very brief 15 January reply to Churchill's detailed message from five days earlier informing him of JW-52's progress had the same effect and served to exacerbate the prime minister's (and the president's) concerns.[103]

Reflecting his exasperation with Stalin's implied dissatisfaction and the strategic ramifications that he and Roosevelt feared could potentially result from this situation, Churchill simply replied, "Lamentable" after receiving Admiral Pound's report that four of the 20 merchant ships planned for JW-52 could not sail for various reasons.[104] Subsequently expressing his concerns to Eden, Churchill lamented that, "This will make our position with the [Soviet] bear even worse than it is now" in a further indication of his perception that Stalin could be tempted to forge a separate peace.[105] As strongly suggested by the documentary record of the time, Brest-Litovsk's shadow continued to impact Churchill and Roosevelt's execution of Soviet Lend-Lease aid, at least until Tehran in November 1943, as they labored to keep Stalin's Red Army in the war and resisting Berlin's brazen attacks.[106]

Further feeding into Churchill and Roosevelt's fears and frustrations and Stalin's rhetorical ammunition that he fired at his Western allies, the British Admiralty reported on 20 January that while JW-52 had embarked on schedule three days earlier, two more ships had failed to join the convoy. The Admiralty's report listed the six total vessels that could not sail for a host of reasons ranging from "boiler defects" to shifted cargo as the British freighters *Dover Hill*, *Llandaf*, *Empire Kinsman*, and *Atlantic*, the British oil tanker *Marathon*, and the American Liberty ship *Israel Putnam*.[107] While such setbacks annoyed Churchill, Eden, and their chief subordinates, they do not appear to have diminished the overall positive impact made by the Arctic convoys that arrived safely at the North Russian ports, and the ships that could not sail on 17 January were simply repaired, reorganized, and sent with the next successful convoy, JW-53.[108]

After JW-52's safe arrival and unloading at Murmansk on 27 January 1943, Herman Melton witnessed firsthand the value to the Red Army Air Forces of Lend-Lease U.S. P-39 aircraft as German bombers based in nearby Petsamo, Finland, struck the city on 19 and 20 February, losing 10 planes to the Soviet shoreline artillerists.[109] Having completed their mission in Murmansk, the convoy crews reassembled in their ships and prepared for their return voyage as RA-53 on 28 February, and the Nazi attackers returned shortly after 12:00 p.m. to target the ships in a brutal bombing raid. As the homebound Westerners returned fire, Soviet fighter pilots based at nearby Vaenga bravely struck the screaming swarm of Ju 87 dive bombers, known as *Stukas*, soaring into the sky in their prized P-39 aircraft.[110]

Unable to hear Lieutenant Stone's order to cease firing their ship's Philadelphia-built gun in the chaotic fighting that ensued, one of the *Harnett's* men tragically erred in striking a Soviet P-39 as the plane's pilot doggedly pursued a Nazi Ju 87 attempting to escape. In an earlier episode in December 1942, Soviet officials had complained bitterly to Rear Admiral Douglas Fisher, the Senior British Naval Officer (SBNO), North Russia, about the inadvertent loss of a Soviet airman and his Lend-Lease *Kobrushka* or "little cobra," as the Soviet pilots affectionately called their P-39s, to Allied fire.[111] As JW-53 delivered its cargo to Molotovsk on 27 February with the *Israel Putnam, City of Omaha, Francis Scott Key*, and other U.S. Liberty ships accompanied by their British, Panamanian, and Soviet counterparts, SBNO Fisher recorded another instance in which three Allied vessels opened fire on a Soviet aircraft. According to Fisher, the Soviet airman had failed to, "carry out recognition procedure" and flew too close to JW-53 as the Allied gunners and other Soviet fighter pilots repulsed a mixed squadron of between 22 and 24 Ju 88s and Bf 109s sweeping over the convoy.[112]

Armed and delivered to the Soviets with a 37mm nose cannon and four machine guns, the P-39Q, an advanced version of the U.S. aircraft that constituted the bulk of the 4,700 P-39s supplied to the Red Army Air Forces, appears to have made a crucial difference in the steady hands of Soviet fighter pilots in North Russia's skies by 1943.[113] Stalin had consistently voiced a favorable opinion of this American attack aircraft and repeatedly emphasized its importance to the Soviet war effort in his telegrams to Roosevelt, along with Lend-Lease trucks, aluminum, and food.[114] By the time of JW-52's arrival in Murmansk in January 1943, the aircraft had become a favorite of the Soviet aces in whose hands it served as a formidable weapon, saving countless Allied ships, lives, and the precious cargo that the men brought for Stalin's Red Army. Recalling his time ashore at Murmansk as Nazi bombers twice attempted to breach the city's air defenses in late February 1943, U.S. merchant mariner Melton states that Soviet fighter pilots spoke fondly of their beloved P-39s and rated their speed, maneuverability, and firepower favorably in comparison to the enemy's Finland-based Fw 190s and Bf 109s.[115]

While the successes of PQ-18, JW-52, JW-53, and many other Arctic convoys docked safely at North Russia's ports and delivered considerable war material to the Red Army, Roosevelt remained determined to do more.[116] Along with Churchill, the president labored to keep Stalin in the war as the Soviet premier continued refusing their proposals for a, "very essential meeting between our three governmental heads," until very late in 1943, keeping them guessing as to his motives regarding Germany's total defeat.[117] In an effort to prevent themselves from repeating the First World War's perceived errors that continued haunting their minds until Stalin's long-awaited arrival at the Tehran Conference, Roosevelt and many U.S. officials and lawmakers worked to increase the supply flow to the Red Army by improving the Persian Corridor and ALSIB to ensure a stinging and permanent defeat for Hitler and Germany.[118]

In the summer of 1943, veteran fighter pilot Eddie Rickenbacker voluntarily traveled to Iran and witnessed the improvements that the U.S. Army's efforts had made to the route, ensuring more effective aid deliveries to the Red Army.[119] By the end of the spring, the uncompromising approach of Major General Donald Connolly in recruiting and training many local Iranian drivers and focusing U.S. efforts on clearing and expanding railroads and the Army's truck assembly plants had resulted in improved delivery routes through Iran's arid southern deserts and icy northern mountains. Beginning with Connolly's promotion in the spring of 1943 and continuing until early 1945, thousands of planes and trucks and many tons of food and raw materials began flowing through Iran into the Soviet Union's Caucasus republics.[120]

In April 1942, Roosevelt appointed Admiral William Standley as the U.S. ambassador and chief representative of the U.S. War Supply Mission to the Soviet Union based in Moscow following Stalin's complaints alleging Ambassador Steinhardt to be a defeatist.[121] Over time, Standley began clashing with Hopkins's favorite observer, General Faymonville, over his eagerness to supply the Red Army without obtaining any concessions from the Soviet government, eventually leading him to resign his official post in late 1943. Perhaps intentionally, Stalin and Molotov often aggravated Standley by directing their aid requests directly to Roosevelt and Hopkins through Faymonville, bypassing the U.S. Ambassador and Chief of the War Supply Mission.[122] In response, Ambassador Standley requested several personal meetings with Stalin, during which the Soviet leader repeatedly accused Washington of trickery and secretly planning to discontinue the Arctic convoys as the ambassador, echoing Roosevelt's telegrams, sought to emphasize the importance of expanding the ALSIB and Iranian routes.[123]

Following his visit to Iran, Rickenbacker traveled to Moscow to meet with Stalin's Foreign Commissar Molotov and, if possible, to assess the impact of U.S. P-39 fighters, now manned by Soviet fighter pilots, on the Eastern Front.[124] In his memoir, Rickenbacker states that he questioned Soviet General Andrei

Yumachev, the copilot of the first Soviet polar flight whom he had met, befriended, and entertained at home in 1937, on the reluctance of Nazi bombers to attack Moscow despite executing raids on cities more than 500 miles behind the Soviet capital. Yumachev motioned to Rickenbacker before activating an air raid siren and opening an underground airbase, revealing more than 100 P-39 fighters, which Rickenbacker claims to have counted within 39 seconds.[125] Recalling his surprise at witnessing the planes rush into the sky, Rickenbacker states in his memoir that, from his contemporary perspective, by the summer of 1943, Lend-Lease aircraft had apparently begun playing a key defensive role in the skies over Moscow, helping the Soviets to contest Nazi air superiority.[126]

According to Rickenbacker, Brest-Litovsk's shadow continued hanging over U.S. Ambassador Standley and his assistant General Michela, Roosevelt, Generals Arnold and Marshall, and the U.S. War Department as Congress prepared to vote overwhelmingly to renew Lend-Lease in spring 1943.[127] Pointing out that Nazi forces remained 500 miles deep inside Soviet Europe and lethally dangerous from the prevailing, contemporary U.S. perspective in June 1943, Rickenbacker recalls the grim view that administration officials expressed to him as they feared the Red Army's potential collapse and emphasized the perceived need to prioritize and increase Soviet Lend-Lease aid. Stating that "forthright reports" on the Red Army's use of U.S. Lend-Lease material were not forthcoming from Stalin, Zhukov, or their subordinates, Rickenbacker emphasized that, "The War Department could not be positive of any action the Russians might take [in June 1943]."[128] Stalin's silence on the issue and his continued refusal to meet with Roosevelt until that November seems to have added greatly to these concerns, spurring the administration's efforts to expand the Persian Corridor and ALSIB, while transferring many U.S. Pacific Ocean ships to Soviet control.[129]

Crucially, Rickenbacker sums up the shared attitude of the War Department officials in Washington and Standley's diplomats in Moscow as one of desperation to keep Soviet soldiers fed and fighting in the field, indicating that Stalin's questionable commitment to Germany's unconditional surrender (from the contemporary American perspective) motivated their desire to not only renew, but increase, Lend-Lease aid to the Red Army.[130] Referring to the prevailing perception of the U.S. leadership regarding Stalin and the Red Army's war effort at the time, Rickenbacker recalled, "If they [the Soviets] collapsed, as in 1917, or signed a separate peace, several German armies would be released to resist us in the west. Or did the Russians [Soviets] have the capability and the determination to carry the war on to Germany?"[131] Seeking to prevent the first two possibilities at all costs, Roosevelt and his senior officials worked to help Stalin's soldiers remain in the war and eventually bring it to Hitler's doorstep, and their success at sending more U.S. material through Iran and from Alaska in the Third Protocol helped to accomplish this mission.[132]

In a strong endorsement of the Arctic convoys' importance to the Soviet war effort, Stalin voiced staunch opposition to Roosevelt and Churchill's postponement of further deliveries to North Russia in the spring of 1943 as the Western leaders concentrated their efforts on increasing the Persian Corridor's volume, the latter action being a decision that he ridiculed ruthlessly. In a 2 April telegram reply to the British prime minister, the Soviet premier decried the Anglo-American decision as causing a, "catastrophic cut in the delivery of strategic raw materials and munitions to the Soviet Union by Great Britain and the U.S.A."[133] Stalin proceeded to lament that, "the Pacific route is limited in shipping and none too reliable, and the southern [Iranian] route has small clearance capacity, which means that those two routes cannot make up for the cessation of deliveries by the northern [Arctic] route" before concluding, "this circumstance cannot but [adversely] affect the position of the Soviet troops."[134] Yet the Soviet leader appears to have severely miscalculated and underestimated the quantity and quality of the aid that he subsequently received through these two routes over which his Allies delivered a flood of material, totaling roughly 75 percent of U.S. Lend-Lease aid to the Red Army, from 1943 forward.[135]

Following the strategy on which they had agreed after PQ-17's disastrous voyage and PQ-18's comparatively striking success, Roosevelt and Churchill halted the Arctic convoys until the middle of November 1943, shortly before meeting Stalin at Tehran, Iran, and resumed them at the Soviet premier's insistence only during the winter months until 1945.[136] By this point, however, the Arctic convoys' deliveries to the Soviet war effort had already been greatly surpassed by the Anglo-American leaders' efforts to keep the Red Army fighting by expanding the Persian Corridor and the ALSIB air route. From the summer of 1943 forward, larger volumes of Lend-Lease material began flowing to Stalin's soldiers over the greatly improved Iranian railroads to the Soviet Caucasus region and by air from Great Falls, Montana, to Fairbanks, Alaska, to Krasnoyarsk and Uelkel in Soviet Siberia.[137] In addition, Roosevelt's transfer that summer of many West Coast U.S. Liberty ships to Stalin's control also ensured that Soviet Lend-Lease aid grew from a steady North Russian stream into a Pacific tsunami.[138]

After the U.S. Congress renewed Roosevelt's Lend-Lease program for all the Allied Powers, including the Soviet Union, in spring 1943, Stalin again expressed anger at his Western counterparts' reluctance to open a "second front" in Europe and implicitly dangled the specter of Brest-Litovsk in a telegram to Churchill.[139] Earlier, in 1942, the British prime minister had been forced to intervene and object after Roosevelt, haunted by Moscow's separate peace with Berlin in 1918, appeared ready to send Anglo-American forces into Western Europe long before they were prepared, hoping to please Stalin as emphasized by Sean McMeekin.[140] Now, in the summer of 1943, the Soviet premier stated, "I must tell you that the point here is not just the disappointment of the Soviet Government, but the preservation of its confidence in its Allies, a confidence which is being subjected to severe stress."[141] Even though the Arctic convoy crews' perseverance had already served Lend-Lease's stated purpose by keeping the Red Army armed and fed well after the Stalingrad counterattack, Roosevelt and Churchill persisted in their efforts to expand the Persian Corridor and ALSIB in June 1943, unleashing an avalanche of aid to their red warrior.[142]

The origins of the Persian Corridor date to the Anglo-Soviet invasion and occupation of wartime Iran, codenamed Operation *Countenance*, in August 1941, a mission executed to overthrow the allegedly pro-Axis monarch Reza Shah Pahlavi and replace him with his son and heir Mohammad Reza Shah Pahlavi.[143] The Allies regarded the younger monarch as a trustworthy, pro-Allied leader and hoped to use their influence in his regime to begin building an effective supply route to the Soviet Union's Caucasus region through northern Iran.[144] Despite Stalin's consistent and rash dismissals of the Iranian route's potential value as a reliable supply line to the Red Army, Anglo-American officials continued working to develop the major roads and railroads of the country from late 1941 forward even as the Arctic convoys remained the major source of Lend-Lease supplies to the Soviets at the time. Under Colonel Don D. Shingler of the United States Military Iranian Mission, U.S. Army engineers began working alongside their British counterparts in southern Iran to develop the region's ports of Abadan and Bushehr, together with the neighboring Iraqi Shatt al-Arab River port of Basra, from November 1941 forward.[145]

After Pearl Harbor, Roosevelt, Hopkins, and Stettinius redoubled their efforts to improve the Iranian supply route to Soviet Azerbaijan and to surmount the obstacles posed by the slow progress by addressing the problems of Iran's sand-swept desert roads that damaged aircraft engines.[146] As the administration struggled to equip the U.S. Armed Forces to counterattack Tojo's Pacific tide, battle Hitler's submarines along the East and Gulf Coasts, and keep Stalin in the war by sailing the Arctic convoys, the Persian Corridor's progress commenced slowly. In late 1942, Roosevelt replaced Colonel Shingler with General Connolly and on 1 April 1943 the U.S. Army Air Corps officially assumed control of aircraft assembly efforts at Abadan, Iran, a responsibility previously entrusted under contract to Douglas Aircraft Company. In this way, Roosevelt, Hopkins, and General Marshall sought to fulfill Stalin's aid orders more effectively and quickly for aircraft deliveries in the Third Protocol period between July 1942 and June 1943, despite the Soviet premier's constant, rude dismissals of the route's potential.[147]

During the period of Douglas's aircraft assembly operations at Abadan between 20 November 1941 and 31 March 1943, American aircraft deliveries to Soviet pilots in Iran averaged about 75 planes per month, according to U.S. Army historian Thomas H. Vail Motter in his 1952 book *The Persian Corridor and Aid to Russia*.[148] After the Army's takeover of the Abadan facilities in April 1943, aircraft assembly operations steadily surged to unprecedented levels, resulting in the transfer of more than 182 planes per month for a total of 2,902 delivered through the Persian Corridor during the Third Protocol between 1 July 1943 and 30 June 1944. Between March 1942 and April 1945, nearly half of the 409,526 U.S. Lend-Lease trucks shipped to Stalin's Red Army arrived in the Soviet Caucasus through the Persian Corridor, with 88 percent of these being assembled by U.S. Army engineers based at the facilities in Andimeshk and Khorramshahr, Iran.[149] In January and February 1943, General Connolly opened two schools in Tehran and Andimeshk to train local Iranian drivers, interpreters, and instructors to increase the volume of trucks, particularly the US6 "Studebakers" that formed the bulk of American motor vehicle shipments, to be delivered to the Soviet forces.[150]

Stettinius and Hopkins generally viewed the supply route through Iran as the most effective and least dangerous route due to the small number of enemy submarines in the Indian Ocean and the presence of Soviet troops in northern Iran.[151] Believing this route to be ideal for supplying the Red Army, they worked to develop an effective road system in Iran for transporting U.S. military vehicles and aircraft. Major obstacles such as desert roads and violent dust storms created problems for driving the vehicles and, until Connolly's spring 1943 improvements, often damaged the aircraft engines, limiting the initial Anglo-American aid deliveries over the Persian Corridor to a trickle.[152]

Connolly's opening of the training schools for Iranian drivers and his significant expansion of the two major American truck production plants at Andimeshk and Khorramshahr ensured a tremendous increase in the mass deliveries of American trucks and other motor vehicles to the Red Army from 1943 forward.[153] In Stalin's War, Sean McMeekin states that General Zhukov's magnificent, "mobile flanking operation" at Stalingrad appears to have been aided "just in time" by the arrival of thousands of U.S. Studebaker trucks and Willys jeeps by late fall 1942, 27,000 of which are said to have boosted the counterattack.[154] This may very well have been the case, and, to be sure, it is far beyond the scope of this work to either concur or argue otherwise. Yet scholars must bear in mind that, as has been shown, most of the Lend-Lease vehicles supplied to the Red Army by the time of Operation *Uranus*, Zhukov's tide-turning counterattack at Stalingrad, had been delivered by the Arctic convoy crews as Connolly's efforts in Iran finally bore fruit only in late spring 1943.[155] The Red Army's victorious operation, in turn, increased U.S. officials'

confidence in its capabilities as they worked to increase the aid flow to Stalin'
forces over Iran's roads and Alaska's skies as Secretary Hull praised the Soviets'
fighting prowess in the pages of *The New York Times*.[156]

Yet Roosevelt, still unable to obtain a meeting with Stalin until late that year,
shared the fears of Standley, Rickenbacker, and other prominent Americans
that the Soviet premier could still be forced into making peace with the Axis
enemy and persisted in ensuring that the Red Army could take the offensive,
shorten the war, and reduce Allied casualties. Because of Connolly's successful
execution of the Iranian mission, 4,200,000 tons of Lend-Lease material arrived
in the Soviet Caucasus from Iran by the end of the war in 1945, a slightly higher
tonnage total than was delivered to North Russia in the same period.[157]
Washington's expansion of the Persian Corridor and the ALSIB air route,
therefore, appears to have helped to ensure that the Red Army could wrest the
strategic initiative from the Nazis, as emphasized by Alexander Hill and David
Glantz and drive them from Soviet soil, thereby obliterating any possibility of a
separate peace.[158]

As further stated by both Hill and Russian historian Boris Sokolov, the
thousands of P-39s and tons of Lend-Lease aluminum for aircraft armor and
tank motor production delivered to the Soviets helped the Red Army Air Forces
to challenge and ultimately break the German Air Force's air superiority over
the battlefields, while the tens of thousands of Studebakers and other American
trucks boosted the Red Army's mobile operations.[159] By placing the Soviet
infantry on wheels, Lend-Lease officials helped Stalin's soldiers to reconquer the
occupied territories and ultimately drive into Europe, a task that could not have
been achieved by aircraft alone. Before Connolly's improvements of spring 1943,
Lend-Lease shipments could only reach the Persian Corridor after traveling
halfway around the world from the U.S. East Coast around the southern tip of
Africa and into the Persian Gulf, keeping the flow of supplies to the Soviets over
the route at a bare minimum. Rather than following the pattern of 1942 and
continuing to rely primarily on the Arctic convoys to deliver Lend-Lease goods to
Stalin, U.S. officials began flooding the Red Army with trucks, jeeps, and planes
built in Iran, hastening the delivery of weaponry to the Soviets and tremendously
expanding the flow of aid.[160]

Frustrated by the inherent limitations in the Pacific supply route due to
Japanese expansion, Roosevelt ordered Army Air Corps General Arnold and
General Follett Bradley to develop an air route from Alaska to Siberia after Stalin
reluctantly agreed to Washington's proposal.[161] Between 1942 and 1945, the
Soviet leader repeatedly rejected General Arnold's offers to send American
pilots to deliver U.S. aircraft directly to the Siberian airfields and emphasized
the importance of the northern supply route from the U.S. East Coast to the
Soviet Arctic ports.[162] In August 1942, after their Soviet counterparts appeared

open to the idea, General Bradley established a supply center in Great Falls, Montana, to serve as a base for U.S. pilots to fly P-39 fighters, A-20 bombers, B-25 bombers, C-47 transport planes, and other U.S.-designed aircraft to the Ladd Field airbase in Fairbanks, Alaska. In Fairbanks, Soviet pilots were to acquire the aircraft and fly them across the Bering Strait to the Siberian cities of Uelkel and Krasnoyarsk once these cities' airports had been prepared to accommodate more air traffic.[163]

According to Otis Hays, Jr., Stalin's objections, expressed as late as 19 September 1942 through Soviet Purchasing Commission Chairman Major General Alexander Belyaev in Washington, again delayed the opening of the ALSIB air route until October that year.[164] Soviet officials appear to have had a change of opinion regarding the route's suitability as the Stalingrad fighting raged, and ALSIB operations began shortly after the arrival in Fairbanks of the 1st Ferrying Aviation Regiment under the command of Lieutenant Colonel Pavel Nedosekin on 24 September.[165] Deliveries were disappointingly small during the first several months after ALSIB's opening, with only 43 Lend-Lease aircraft transferred to the Soviet ferrying pilots in October 1942. Hazardous winter weather conditions along the route and the limited number of landing strips at many airbases between Great Falls and the Siberian airports also created problems that initially caused many crashes and limited the number of aircraft that could be delivered.[166]

Yet from April 1943 forward, Arnold and Bradley succeeded in addressing many of these issues as U.S., Canadian, and Soviet officials launched a joint effort to increase the number of landing strips at key airports located along the route, helping to exceed the monthly goal of 142 aircraft per month by the Second Protocol's expiration on 30 June 1943.[167] Working closely with Red Army Air Forces Colonel Anatoly Kotikov, Captain George Jordan served as a Lend-Lease control officer for the U.S. Army Air Corps at the Great Falls airbase between 1942 and 1944 after being transferred from the airbase at Newark, New Jersey. During this time, Jordan earned the praise of his Soviet counterparts due to his effective work in overseeing the transfer of thousands of U.S. planes to Soviet pilots and earned a promotion to Major on Kotikov's recommendation.[168] By the end of 1944, Jordan had helped oversee the transfer of 8,094 fighter planes, a large portion of the more than 14,000 total American combat aircraft eventually transferred into Soviet hands, over the air route from Great Falls to Krasnoyarsk, and, despite the problems posed by dangerous weather, the improved airport conditions along the route enabled the safe arrival of most of these aircraft.[169]

At roughly the same time that Arnold and Bradley worked to improve ALSIB by helping to coordinate the successful U.S., Canadian, and Soviet efforts to increase air traffic capacity, Roosevelt authorized the transfer of more U.S. Liberty ships in the Pacific to Soviet control. By the summer of 1943, Soviet merchant ships, built in the United States, were safely transporting enormous amounts of food, raw materials, machine tools, and transport vehicles through Japanese territorial waters as Stalin clung to his April 1941 non-aggression pact with Hirohito.[170] As emphasized by Sean McMeekin, the Soviet dictator also imprisoned U.S. bomber pilots from General James "Jimmy" Doolittle's famous Tokyo air raid in 1942 after some of the men were forced to crash land in Soviet territory. While Ambassador Standley received permission to visit the American POWs, the men were refused pardon as the Soviet leader continued placating Tokyo even as his newly acquired Liberty ships transported a total of 8,200,000 tons of material to Vladivostok by 1945 unmolested and free from interdiction by the Japanese Navy and Air Force.[171]

The increased amount of aid that Stalin received from the Western Allies over the Persian Corridor and through the ALSIB-Pacific route appears to have contributed significantly, from the contemporary U.S. perspective to the Allied strategic objective of keeping Stalin's forces supplied and in the war. Yet it must also be remembered that these routes were improved and capable of delivering such enormous tonnage of material only after early 1943.[172] Up until that point in time, and afterwards as well, the mariners of the Arctic convoys served the Allied cause admirably and responsibly braved the treacherous, icy seas while delivering arms, foodstuffs, and raw materials to Stalin's North Russian ports, and they continued their courageous efforts into 1945.[173]

As emphasized by historian Malcolm Llewelyn-Jones of the British Naval Historical Branch in his Preface to *The Royal Navy and the Arctic Convoys: A Naval Staff History*, scholars either dismiss the impact of the Arctic convoy deliveries or relegate their importance to one of mere inter-Allied politics have often been somewhat misled by the sheer totals of Lend-Lease equipment delivered to the Red Army over the various supply routes.[174] Llewelyn-Jones states that while the other routes delivered a larger amount of supplies, totaling more than 77 percent of all deliveries as stated by London's wartime Trade Division Director Brian B. Schofield, the nearly 23 percent delivered by the Arctic convoys nevertheless proved crucial.[175] Anglo-American naval personnel faithfully delivered this aid at a time in which Stalin's Red Army arguably faced its greatest challenges, and the 5,350 war weapons and 168,500 tons of explosives and other goods carried by PQ-18 alone, much of which arrived safely at Archangel, doubtlessly sustained many red warriors.[176] Such considerable deliveries of trucks, attack aircraft, aluminum, machine tools, and food to North Russia's ports at a point in time in which all aid mattered tremendously to the Red Army surely helped to boost Stalin's fortunes, and therefore those of all the Allied leaders, in crushing the Nazi invaders and shortening the path to victory.[177]

CHAPTER 4

About the late war Anglo-American Arctic convoys

Despite being overtaken and surpassed by the Persian Corridor and ALSIB in the arena of sheer volume and tonnage of U.S. war material being delivered to the Red Army, the men of the Arctic convoys did not cease their operations after the spring of 1943. Rather, in keeping with the British Admiralty's prudent recommendations, Churchill and Roosevelt resumed sailing their Anglo-American convoys to North Russia, during the winter months only, in the latter half of the war. The spectacular successes that the Allied merchant mariners achieved during this period between winter's onset in late 1943 and the late spring of 1945 attest to their continued strategic contribution to averting a second Brest-Litovsk. Their actions, therefore, succeeded in hastening the Allied victory while Roosevelt, Bradley, and Connolly expanded the Persian Corridor and ALSIB for good measure, even as Stalin ridiculed their efforts and urged them to merely maintain the North Russian convoys and open a second front in Western Europe.[1]

At Stalin and Molotov's insistence, Churchill's Royal Navy and Merchant Navy resumed Lend-Lease convoy deliveries to the Soviet Union's Arctic ports in late 1943 even as the Persian Corridor and ALSIB overtook the North Russian route as the primary Lend-Lease supply conduits to the Red Army.[2] Even though the two other routes had far surpassed the Arctic convoys in terms of the overall tonnage of war materials delivered to Stalin's fighting forces, the men of Churchill and Roosevelt's respective navies persisted on in their arduous journeys to North Russia's ports during the winter months. As explained by Michael Walling, the Allied mariners serving on these later Arctic convoys faced a somewhat enhanced threat from the Nazi naval menace as the German Navy's leaders had, by that time, equipped their submariners with newer, slightly improved armament.[3]

Although Allied forces did not encounter it until the voyage of Convoy JW-56A in January 1944, the Nazi leadership in late 1942 had introduced a new type of preprogrammed torpedo, known by the acronym FAT due to its German name, that could turn 180 degrees underwater after being fired rather than simply speeding through the sea in a straight line. In the fall of 1943, the Nazi naval command also introduced the "Wren," known as "GNAT" in Allied naval circles, a torpedo that could home in on and target the source emitting the loudest propeller sounds, an innovation that proved somewhat counterproductive as such sources often proved to be the Nazi submarines themselves as emphasized by Walling.[4] The snorkel appears to have been another clever and, perhaps, slightly more effective innovation as it proved barely visible to the naked eye and undetectable by radar despite the Allies' employment of improved radar in this period of the war, allowing the Nazi submarines to recharge their batteries while remaining submerged.[5]

On 15 November 1943, Convoy JW-54A sailed from Loch Ewe and embarked on its Arctic journey to North Russia's ports with 18 merchant vessels and an initial, local escort of four warships. A larger ocean escort force arrived to relieve the local vessels and safeguard JW-54A on 18 November, and the convoy ships docked and unloaded at Murmansk safely and intact six days later, undetected and unmolested by enemy forces.[6] The men of Convoy JW-54B and the Royal Navy's ocean escort that joined them three days after their voyage began on 22 November 1943 executed an equally successful mission, evading the Germany Navy's five-submarine task force or "wolf-pack," code-named *Eisenbart*, and docking safely at Archangel with all 14 merchant ships and their lethal, precious cargo on 3 December.[7]

Escorted by 11 warships, the 19 merchant vessels of Convoy JW-55A sailed from Loch Ewe on 12 December and safely arrived in two parts at Murmansk and Archangel on 21 and 22 December, respectively, despite some unconfirmed reports that German reconnaissance aircraft had spotted the carefully guarded convoy.[8] Determined not to incur Hitler's wrath by repeating the perceived failures of his predecessor Grand Admiral Raeder, Grand Admiral Doenitz attempted to persuade the Nazi ruler to sanction an interdiction raid by his remaining surface warships against the next Arctic convoy in late December 1943, even though he reportedly shared the tyrant's concerns of risking their precious few surface vessels. As the Murmansk-bound Convoy JW-55B and the homegoing Convoy RA-55A crossed paths near Norway's North Cape on 25 December, a Nazi force consisting of the battleship *Scharnhorst* under Captain Fritz Hintze and five accompanying destroyers sailed from Altenfjord in hopes of inflicting crippling losses on the intersecting Allied ships on the orders of Counter Admiral Erich Bey.[9]

German reconnaissance aircraft had reportedly spotted JW-55B and reported its location on the morning of 24 December while shadowing the convoy, presenting Bey with an enticing target. That afternoon, the eight German submarines of the *Eisenbart* wolf-pack stationed near Bear Island were ordered westward towards JW-55B, but most of the Nazi vessels lost contact with the convoy after 4:00 p.m. until a single submarine again located the Allied ships the next day.[10] British codebreakers quickly foiled the German Navy's plans, however, and alerted Admiral Sir Bruce Fraser and Vice Admiral Robert Burnett to the danger, each of whose respective naval task forces were escorting Convoys JW-55B and RA-55A. Rough seas and inclement weather also posed a threat to both the Allies and their Nazi opponents alike, prompting Bey to request Doenitz's permission to abort the mission out of concern for the five German destroyers.[11]

Doenitz reportedly refused Bey's request and ordered the mission to proceed with the *Scharnhorst* alone if Bey determined the destroyers to be incapable of remaining at sea, unaware of the size and battle readiness of the combined escort forces under Fraser and Burnett. Shortly before 9:30 a.m. on 26 December 1943, the first engagement of the Battle of North Cape began as Burnett's cruisers detected and surprised *Scharnhorst* with a series of potent salvos by the HMS *Norfolk's* gunners.[12] Four of Fraser's destroyers, HMS *Opportune*, HMS *Matchless*, HMS *Virago*, and HMS *Musketeer* quickly arrived to reinforce *Norfolk*, HMS *Belfast*, and Burnett's other cruisers, but the surprised *Scharnhorst* had disengaged and fled to the east by the time of their arrival. Burnett correctly calculated that the enemy intended to execute a desperate dash against the convoy, and at 12:05 p.m. the men of *Belfast* again detected *Scharnhorst* on their radar screen.[13]

The Allied force engaged the German battleship again about 25 minutes later in a 20-minute skirmish, and the frosty Arctic gloom that engulfed the surrounding sea flashed brightly with flames as the opposing ships belched forth vicious volleys of shells as each other. During the vicious fighting that ensued, the *Scharnhorst* retreated further away from JW-55B after twice striking *Norfolk* and inflicting "minor damage" on the *Sheffield*.[14] Throughout the day, Burnett's cruisers continued pursuing the Nazi battleship while Fraser's larger force approached from the southwest. At 4:50 p.m., the men of *Belfast* located and illuminated *Scharnhorst* with a star shell, rendering the German battleship an easier target for the gunners of HMS *Duke of York* and *Jamaica*. *Scharnhorst* attempted to flee to port with *Duke of York* in hot pursuit, nearly outrunning the Allied warship as the two ships exchanged fire during the late afternoon chase.[15]

At 6:20 p.m., the Scharnhorst began slowing to a halt as Captain Hinze reportedly sought to check his pursuers in a decisive duel on the seas. The *Scharnhorst's* radar room had been badly damaged by a British shell in one of the earlier engagements that day, however, and the heavy snowstorms on the high seas further exacerbated Hinze's problems as HMS *Scorpion*, HMS *Stord*, HMS *Savage*, and HMS *Saumarez* all arrived to assist *Duke of York*, *Belfast*, and *Jamaica* in vanquishing the feared Nazi battleship.[16] After another intense, 20-minute battle that began at 7:01 p.m., a series of daring torpedo barrages by the tenacious Allied gunners finally felled the *Scharnhorst*, sinking the German battleship beneath the icy Arctic waves along with Hitler and Doenitz's hopes of halting further convoys to North Russia with the help of their dwindling surface fleet.[17]

Following the Allied victory in the Battle of North Cape, Convoy RA-55A proceeded home safely and unmolested by the Axis enemy while all 19 merchant ships of Convoy JW-55B docked safely at Murmansk on 30 December and delivered their lethal loads for the Red Army, unhindered by Hitler's admirals.[18] On 12 January 1944, Convoy JW-56A embarked on its Arctic journey to North Russia with 20 merchant ships escorted by a force of seven destroyers and two corvettes. A savage storm forced the convoy to shelter for three days at Akureyri, Iceland, but on 21 January, all but five storm-damaged ships of the Allied force resumed their arduous trek. Doenitz's submariners had prepared a trap for the convoy, however, and on 25 January, the American Liberty ship SS *Penelope Barker* fell victim to the torpedoes of *U-278* with a loss of 16 killed and 56 survivors rescued by the crew of *Savage*. The following day, Nazi submarines sank the American Liberty ship SS *Andrew G. Curtin* and the British merchant ship SS *Fort Bellingham* and struck and badly damaged the *Obdurate* with a GNAT, forcing the British destroyer to return to port.[19]

The escorts of JW-56A successfully repulsed further enemy attacks throughout the day, however, and the convoy safely arrived at Murmansk with no further losses two days later, on 28 January 1944. Six days before JW-56A's arrival at Murmansk, Convoy JW-56B had begun its Arctic journey, sailing for North Russia from Loch Ewe on 22 January 1944. On 26 January, Nazi aircraft spotted and reported JW-56B as the convoy sailed past Iceland, and three days later, the *Whitehall* and HMS *Mahratta* repulsed and pursued two enemy submarines that appeared and attempted to shadow the Allied ships from a distance.[20] Other German submarines attempted occasionally to approach JW-56B throughout the next several days, and between 1:36 and 3:00 a.m. on 30 January, HMS *Offa*, HMS *Meteor*, and HMS *Inconstant* all executed a series of tenacious attacks on several of the six lurking submarines, sending several of them fleeing.[21]

At 4:04 a.m., however, the destroyer HMS *Hardy* fell victim to a GNAT, and the men of HMS *Virago*, HMS *Venus*, and HMS *Stord* rescued the surviving crew members from the frigid sea and struck the Nazi submarine with depth charges that forced it to the surface. Throughout the day, the Allied warships continued to engage their Nazi assailants in a series of deadly chases, repulsing the enemy and damaging or sinking several submarines, including *U-314*.[22] The Nazi wolf-pack reportedly withdrew from the fighting shortly after this series of rebuffs, and JW-56B reached Murmansk with most of its ships and cargo intact on 2 February 1944. During the North Russian journey of Convoy JW-57 that commenced on 20 February 1944, Allied forces struck several more deadly blows against Hitler's submariners. On 23 February, the pilot of an F6F aircraft based on the HMS *Chaser* located several enemy submarines lurking nearby after driving off a Nazi Fw 200 Condor reconnaissance plane.[23]

The 50 crew members of Nazi submarine *U-713* then fell to depth charges dropped by HMS Keppel under Commander Ismay J. Tyson, while a British PBY

Catalina aircraft sank U-601 and its 51-man crew beneath the icy waves on 25 February. At 8:55 p.m. that evening, an enemy GNAT struck and sank the *Mahratta*, yet the Nazi submarines failed to execute, and other successful attacks, and JW-57 docked at Murmansk with its 42 merchant ships intact and undamaged by the enemy.[24] On 27 March, another successful Arctic convoy, JW-58, sailed for North Russia under the command of Vice Admiral Frederick Dalrymple-Hamilton and inflicted further damage on Berlin's naval forces while transporting its precious cargo to Stalin's red warriors. Two days into JW-58's Arctic journey, HMS *Starling* and HMS *Magpie* depth-charged and destroyed *U-961*.[25]

Two days later, on 31 March, Doenitz's submariners approached the convoy and received a resounding rebuff, losing the submarines *U-288*, *U-355*, and *U-360* to the gunners of HMS *Beagle* and *Keppel* and the Swordfish aircraft of several other ships in an engagement on 3 April.[26] That same day, British Swordfish planes also executed an air raid code-named Operation *Tungsten* on the *Tirpitz*, badly damaging the dreaded German battleship then docked at Kaalfjord, Norway, and preventing it from again becoming operational for service against the Arctic convoys.[27] The next day, JW-58 sailed safely into Murmansk harbor, escorted by four Soviet destroyers with all its merchant ships and their material for Stalin's war chest fully accounted for, while Hitler's naval commanders had suffered a stinging setback. Following JW-58's successful voyage, Roosevelt and Churchill again paused the Arctic convoys until later in 1944 as they prepared to launch Operation *Overlord* and the long-awaited second front demanded by Stalin. They again resumed their courageous mariners' convoys to North Russia in the months immediately following the D-Day landings, however, and the successes of these later Arctic journeys remain no less crucial than those of their predecessor convoys in demonstrating the counterproductive futility of Roosevelt's opening of the Iranian and ALSIB supply routes.[28]

Royal Naval Volunteer Reserve (RNVR) Lieutenant Peter S. Cockrell served on board the HMS *Campania* in support of other warships performing escort duty for the Arctic convoys between September 1944 and February 1945.[29] While the Arctic treks of these late-war convoys to Murmansk and Archangel have received less attention overall than their early-war counterparts, their successes were no less spectacular and their Arctic journeys no less Spartan than those of their predecessors. Despite the Red Army's advances into Nazi-occupied Europe and the successful D-Day landings in the summer of 1944, Berlin's domination of Norway remained unchallenged until the war's end, rendering the formidable German naval and aerial units based there a constant threat to the Allied mariners persisting doggedly in their important work.[30]

On 29 November 1944, the 34 merchant ships and 34 escort vessels of Convoy JW-62 sailed from Loch Ewe while the Anglo-American and Soviet men and women warriors on the continent stubbornly persisted in fighting their way towards Hitler's doorstep from the west and the east, one bloody battle at a time. Nazi reconnaissance aircraft reportedly spotted JW-62 on 2 December, but Hitler's submariners failed to execute any attacks before the convoy docked safely in two parts at Murmansk and Archangel.[31] The Allied naval escorts detected and attacked the nearby Nazi naval force of seven submarines as JW-62 approached the Kola Peninsula, striking a deadly blow against their would-be assailants and helping to ensure the convoy's safe arrival on 7 December.[32]

The Arctic journey of Convoy JW-64 in February 1945 proved to be the last of the arduous Allied treks to North Russia in which the men involved endured and repulsed repeated enemy attacks as Hitler's admirals and Goering's pilots persisted in a final, desperate interdiction effort against the Anglo-American sea warriors and their lethal, Murmansk-bound cargo. Along with his comrades serving on board the HMS *Bellona* and HMS *Nairana*, RNVR Lieutenant Cockrell and the *Campania* sailed from Scapa Flow on 5 February 1945 and, together with other Allied warships the next day, "joined convoy [JW-64] of 30 [Liberty/merchant] ships (each carrying 30 trainloads of supplies for Russia) near Faeroe Islands," the merchant vessels having embarked from Greenock, Scotland three days earlier.[33]

That evening, a Ju 88 aircraft appeared and began shadowing the convoy before being shot down by two Grumman F4F "Wildcat" fighter planes based in *Campania*. Admiral of the Fleet Sir Rhoderick McGrigor credited the Royal Navy's recent employment of advanced Type 277 radar with alerting the warships of the approaching enemy aircraft and naval forces in a timely manner, correctly pointing out that the new and improved radar regularly proved reliable in detecting approaching enemy attackers.[34] At dawn the next day, 7 February 1945, a mixed squadron totaling about 12 Ju 88 and Ju 188 torpedo planes attempted to breach JW-64's defenses at 7:45 a.m. Allied radar quickly detected the approaching enemy squadron, which split into two groups that began stalking JW-64 from the northwest and southwest, respectively.[35]

Under the command of RNVR Lieutenant Commander Graham Butcher, the men of the corvette HMS *Denbigh Castle*, then sailing on its maiden voyage, quickly downed one of the enemy bombers, and the Nazi planes withdrew around 9:00 a.m.[36] Later that day, two Wildcat fighters based on the *Nairana* struck and set fire to a lone Nazi bomber that reappeared, but Goering's airmen failed to launch any further assaults as thick, heavy clouds and inclement weather on the frigid seas rendered operations impossible for both the attackers and defenders alike. The next day, Lieutenant Cockrell and his shipmates on board the *Campania* learned that more Nazi torpedo bombers, minus one which reportedly "crashed into a mountain," had been transferred from Trondheim to Bodo, Norway, in preparation for an interdiction raid against JW-64.[37] Throughout the day, BV 138 reconnaissance planes shadowed the convoy to report its position to Nazi submarines, and, despite the heavy snows and "pitch darkness," one British fighter pilot bravely struck at the enemy pursuers in his antiquated Fairey Fulmar night fighter, the only such aircraft allotted to JW-64's escorts, only to crash-land his plane into the *Campania's* bridge.[38]

The Nazi BV 138s persisted in their shadowing efforts throughout the next day, 9 February 1945, and managed to evade the Allied Wildcats that daringly executed a failed sortie against them in the increasingly frigid weather. The shadowing aircraft continued their pursuit into the morning of 10 February, and shortly before 10:00 a.m., the Royal Canadian Navy gunners of HMCS *Sioux* struck a deadly blow to the engine of an attacking Ju 88, initially mistaken for a Soviet plane.[39] Before retreating with its burning engine, the enemy aircraft dropped a torpedo that missed its target, prompting Admiral McGrigor to observe that, "it [the Ju 88's failed attack] was fortunate…as it gave the screens time to start moving into their anti-aircraft positions and brought everyone to the alert."[40]

At 10:19 a.m., Allied radar detected the main enemy squadron consisting of two separate groups with a combined total of 16 Ju 88s flying at sea level and approaching quickly. The anti-aircraft gunners of HMS *Whitehall* and HMS *Lark* quickly destroyed three enemy bombers, while the men of HMS *Orwell* and other warships and the fighter pilots of *Nairana* inflicted further casualties until the Nazi assailants withdrew at 11:10 a.m. Roughly 20 minutes later, however, a Nazi squadron consisting of about 25 Ju 88s launched another strike on the convoy. In the ensuing combat that raged, the Allied fighter pilots and deck gunners mounted a tenacious resistance and repulsed the Nazi attackers, inflicting heavy losses on the assailants and sending the seven surviving German aircraft fleeing at a cost of one Allied plane.[41]

The crew of the destroyer HMS *Opportune* quickly rescued the pilot of the downed Allied fighter aircraft, and the engagement ended in a German retreat with most of the Nazi planes either damaged or destroyed and no Allied ships or lethal Lend-Lease cargo damaged. According to Lieutenant Cockrell, JW-64 encountered heavy snowstorms and, "below freezing" weather conditions but no further enemy attacks throughout the next two days, and the convoy approached Kola Inlet on the evening of 12 February 1945.[42] That evening, as he reflected on the fierce fighting in which he had participated two days before, Cockrell observed that, "not since 1942 have the Germans paid such attention to a convoy."[43] Having surmounted the obstacles placed across its path, JW-64 sailed into Murmansk fully intact the next day in a further demonstration of the Arctic convoy crews' ability to consistently outwit their Nazi foes and deliver sufficient supplies of weaponry, raw materials, and food to the Red Army.[44]

In a brutal parting shot, a Nazi submarine struck *Denbigh Castle* with a torpedo, inflicting few losses but sinking the ship and ending its maiden voyage as it entered Vaenga Bay, prompting Cockrell to angrily note in his daily entry that evening, "Blast the Russians – they are quite incapable of clearing their own doorstep. Anchored in Vaenga Bay 1620. Ice floats around. Blue sky white hills – temperature 4 degrees."[45] Even though Cockrell had earlier opined in an 8 February entry that, "War by U-Boats in March [1945] will be the most intensive ever" as he marveled at the German Navy's recent technological innovations, such Allied concerns proved incorrect.[46] The Nazi leadership's failed assaults on JW-64 in February 1945 proved to be Berlin's last major attempts at interdicting the Arctic convoys despite the continued presence of German naval and air forces in occupied Norway until the end of the war.

Aside from the brutal Arctic weather conditions that Allied navy men and merchant mariners such as Peter Cockrell, Herman Melton, Alfred Goldsmith Mason, Charlie Erswell, and Leonard Thomas braved as they persevered in executing their Lend-Lease supply missions to North Russia, the voyages of the last Arctic convoys that continued into May 1945 appear to have been relatively uneventful.[47] The German Navy and Air Force had launched merciless attacks on the convoys, but the disaster inflicted on PQ-17 in July 1942 failed to deter the Anglo-American leaders, and Berlin's efforts bore little fruit as their mariners consistently outwitted and repulsed their adversaries, culminating in the victorious February 1945 Arctic journey of JW-64.[48] The successes achieved by the late war Arctic convoys appear to further attest to their ability to continue serving the Allied strategy of keeping the Red Army armed, fed, and fighting in the field during this period, thereby shortening the war and contributing to the Third Reich's demise.[49]

U.S. popular perceptions of Stalin's Red Army and the impact of Soviet espionage and disinformation agents in undermining postwar peace prospects

Following the previous chapter's examination of the key role of the Arctic convoys during the later years of the war, this fifth chapter discusses the U.S. popular media's portrayal of Stalin and the Red Army for American public consumption and the successes of Soviet spies and agents of influence in the West in aiding Moscow's espionage and disinformation efforts. While wisely acting to ensure a continued flow of war material to Washington's Soviet allies, Roosevelt, Hopkins, and their senior associates also foolishly and dangerously gambled that they could, through a combination of unconditional Lend-Lease and excessively generous gestures, convert Stalin into a moderate Communist leader and pave the way for postwar peace. U.S. leaders succeeded admirably in hastening Hitler's defeat by helping Stalin's soldiers to kill the enemy in the numbers sufficient for victory, as emphasized by Mark Harrison.[1] Yet while American Lend-Lease aid to the Red Army proved a prudent policy, Roosevelt and other U.S. leaders miscalculated in their estimation of the Soviet premier's character and their own ability to charm him into moderating his stance toward the "capitalist" West, failing in their secondary goal of winning a lasting peace and succeeding where they believed President Wilson had failed.[2]

As the U.S. wartime economy gathered strength through massive production throughout 1942, Stalin's diplomatic efforts bore fruit as Roosevelt and Hopkins gradually assumed greater responsibility and continued zealously supplying their Soviet ally, as previously discussed.[3] Alexander Hill states that while the Red Army alone had defended Moscow and won at Stalingrad, with the crucial help of some key Anglo-American Lend-Lease supplies, by the middle of 1943, U.S. trucks, jeeps, and railroad cars had begun helping Soviet forces transition to the strategic offensive.[4] During the desperate months of fighting to drive back the Nazi assault, Soviet factory workers had produced thousands of tanks and aircraft, according to both Hill and Albert Weeks, with the help of imported American aluminum in 1942 and 1943, while motorized transportation had been largely neglected.[5] As emphasized by Robert Jones, Walter Dunn, and Sean McMeekin, Lend-Lease deliveries seem to have helped to compensate, at least somewhat, for the Red Army's lack of trucks and helped enable Zhukov's powerful, mobile counteroffensive at Stalingrad.[6] Weeks concludes in his 2004 book *Russia's Life-Saver* that without Stalin's successful procurement of U.S. transport vehicles, the Red Army may have suffered even greater losses in driving the Germans out of Nazi-occupied Soviet territory, let alone bringing the war to Berlin.[7]

In the summer of 1943, Soviet forces followed up the Stalingrad victory by inflicting another resounding defeat on the Nazi invaders at the Battle of Kursk, as emphasized by David Glantz, while the Western Allies landed troops in Sicily, heralding a bloody campaign as the Anglo-American forces fought their way up the Italian Peninsula against well-entrenched German forces.[8] As both Glantz and Sean McMeekin point out, Generals Hermann "Papa" Hoth and Erich von Manstein had deployed many of Berlin's new Panther and Tiger tanks, the former of which should not have been built due to its multiple problems according to tank authority Steven Zaloga, for Operation *Citadel*, their Kursk offensive.[9] Yet Generals Zhukov and Konstantin Rokossovsky had cleverly prepared a series of anti-tank death traps for the Germans, and the Soviet T-34 crews successfully lured many of them into hidden land mines and lethal ambushes from concealed, entrenched Soviet tanks and artillery pieces. After achieving victory after several bloody months during the Battle of Kursk, Zhukov's armies continued racing ahead, recapturing Soviet territory and remaining on the offensive as their Anglo-American allies continued shipping an avalanche of Lend-Lease trucks, planes, and raw materials, and Hitler transferred several elite Nazi divisions to face the Allied advance in Italy.[10] Regarding motor vehicles in particular, American Lend-Lease shipments reportedly resulted in a combined total of 471,257 trucks and jeeps being delivered to the Red Army during the war, with U.S. Studebakers forming the largest portion of these vehicles.[11]

In addition to the overwhelming numbers of Studebakers delivered to the Soviet Union, several types of U.S. Army infantry support and armored fighting vehicles were also delivered in significant quantities. Produced in large numbers by the White Motor Company in Cleveland, Ohio, the M3A1 "White" armored scout is said to have served as another prized American contribution to Stalin's war arsenal.[12] In his memoir, Eddie Rickenbacker recalls his Soviet driver making positive comments about the performance of U.S.-delivered jeeps while escorting him in one to view Soviet P-39 fighters during his June 1943 visit to the Soviet Union.[13]

While junior Red Army commanders often rated the quality of British and U.S. tanks poorly, the vehicles bought crucial time for Soviet workers to produce domestic models in greater quantities and helped compensate for battlefield losses of Soviet models.[14] As previously noted, Hitler's forces had captured entire factories and industrial centers during their 1941 advance into Soviet Ukraine, and while Stalin's commissars had overseen the transportation of many factories to safety beyond the Ural Mountains, many others quickly fell into enemy hands.[15] Due to the loss of several enormous ammunition factories, Stalin's diplomats requested and began receiving large amounts of ammunition and Thompson submachine guns from the United States as the Lend-Lease program gained momentum in 1942.[16] Throughout 1942 and 1943, U.S. war workers produced more ammunition and small arms produced more for the Red Army as Roosevelt and Hopkins prioritized Stalin's perceived needs, and after the expansion of the Iranian supply route, guns and bullets flowed to the Red Army in the field at unprecedented levels.[17]

While the U.S. Sherman tanks lacked the sloped frontal armor and wide tracks of the Soviet T-34s, Second World War tank expert Steven Zaloga argues that many American vehicles were, nevertheless, welcomed by some Soviet commanders into the Red Army's temporarily depleted tank park in the war's first years despite their poorer overall designs and the complaints of many junior Red Army officers.[18] As discussed in a previous chapter, Alexander Hill points to the participation of many British Valentine and Matilda tanks in the Red Army's counterattack around Moscow on 6 December 1941, the day before Pearl Harbor. During the spring fighting of 1942, Sherman tanks reportedly began arriving in North Russia and Iran in growing numbers, and, according to both Hill and Robert Forczyk, by 1943, General Zhukov had organized entire tank battalions consisting of Lend-Lease vehicles.[19]

U.S. aluminum is also said to have helped the Soviet war industry to maintain air support for the Red Army by serving as a key component for the construction of aircraft armor.[20] Soviet aircraft engineers had designed aluminum armor for the I-16 and IL-2 *Sturmovik* fighters, and Stalin consistently requested the material in his telegrams to Churchill and Roosevelt throughout the war and in his meeting with Hopkins in the Kremlin in July 1941.[21] Ultimately, U.S. aluminum shipments reportedly provided more than 55 percent of the aluminum used in the Soviet wartime production of aircraft armor and tank motors, serving the Allied cause by helping keep Stalin's aerial warriors in the fight and covering the armored thrusts that felled the Nazi enemy.[22]

U.S. Lease-Lease officials also emphasized the importance of food deliveries to the Red Army, resulting in the delivery of more than 4,500,000 tons of food during the war and, as emphasized by Hill and Weeks.[23] U.S. leaders intended their deliveries of canned goods and other foodstuffs supplied through Lend-Lease to help the Red Army's commanders keep their men and women fed, fighting, and ready to take the battle to their hated enemy while the Lend-Lease aluminum and machine tools that Stalin emphasized as crucial were, from the American wartime perspective, shipped in growing amounts to help keep Soviet workers producing the armaments needed for the task.[24] One of the first historians to emphasize the importance of food to the Red Army, Weeks concludes that without the bacon, canned beef, eggs, soup, and vegetables supplied by Lend-Lease, mass starvation may have either forced Stalin to the bargaining table or forced him into a desperate situation comparable to that of the tsar and Kerensky.[25] In their respective memoirs, Soviet General Secretary Nikita Khrushchev and Red Army solider Nikolai Litvin, the latter being a Second World War veteran, U.S. canned goods and other food items helped to feed Stalin's Red Army throughout the war despite the German occupation of much of wheat-abundant Ukraine until late in the wat.[26]

For all their martial talents, it seems that Stalin's commanders may have sustained much heavier losses and been greatly delayed first in executing their tide-turning counterattacks and later switching to the strategic offensive had they been denied their regular, reliable shipments of Lend-Lease trucks, aircraft, aluminum, machine tools, and food.[27] Equally, had Roosevelt and Churchill not endeavored to keep Stalin in the war as a member of the Allies, the U.S., British, Canadian, Australian, Polish, Free French, and other Allied armies that stormed Nazi-occupied Normandy on 6 June 1944 may have been driven back into the sea. Ultimately, as Mark Harrison concludes, it was this combined Allied effort that stymied Hitler's attempt to dominate Eurasia, an outcome that may not have occurred had the Anglo-American leaders not ensured and increased the flow of arms and aid to Stalin's soldiers in a valiant effort that saved Allied lives and contributed to the Nazi tyrant's defeat.[28] Yet had Roosevelt, Hopkins, and other U.S. officials not simultaneously underestimated Stalin's character and his commitment to spreading Communism at gunpoint while overestimating their own abilities to charm him or, in a sense, purchase his loyalty through their unconditional aid, they may have realized that the Soviet leader could not be "bought" and, for example, refrained from supplying him with atomic bomb materials.[29]

The naivete of some American officials towards Stalin appears in some ways to have been influenced by the reports of several major U.S. journalists, such as Henry Cassidy and Leland Stowe.[30] Just as Roosevelt, Hull, Hopkins, Knox, and other leading U.S. officials seem to have readily and rightly embraced the need to supply Stalin's Red Army almost from the moment that Hitler attacked his former strategic partner, popular news reports began extolling the bold efforts by the Soviet soldiers resisting Berlin's aggression, painting them and Stalin as defenders of freedom. Margaret Bourke-White's photographs of the German bombing of Moscow in the summer of 1941, that were subsequently published in *Life* magazine, humanized the Soviet struggle for many American readers, and her praise of Stalin's leadership appeared in *The New York Times* even before the Pearl Harbor attack.[31]

As the fighting on the Eastern Front raged in early 1942, Americans were increasingly subjected to portrayals of Stalin as a courageous war chief leading a bold, defiant people against freedom's greatest enemies in Berlin. Ronald Smelser and Edward Davies point out that even the most traditionally "conservative" Americans began to express admiration for the characteristics of Red Army commanders such as Generals Zhukov and Semion Timoshenko as newspaper reports and popular magazine articles emphasized for American readers, both men's humble beginnings.[32] Throughout 1942 and 1943, these two Red Army generals, among others, were portrayed as rugged, freedom-loving outdoorsmen that preferred family time, fishing, and horseback riding to waging war or praising Communism. Such reports appear to have contributed to a popular wartime perception of Stalin and his senior military commanders as essentially being Communists in name only and men that were merely fighting to defend their families, culture, and even faith from Teutonic barbarity and, therefore, merited nothing less than the maximum support that Americans could provide.[33]

While Smelser and Davies emphasize the fact that these perceptions evaporated rapidly after the Allied victory in 1945, they certainly appear to have remained the prevailing American views of Stalin's military leadership and the Red Army, while Berlin and Tokyo remained the most immediate threats to free men and women.[34] Moreover, as prominent Americans met with Stalin, a wartime image of the Soviet premier as a rational, businesslike leader emerged as popular American media portrayed him as a moderate Communist that readily embraced Western capitalists, an inaccurate image that appears to have contributed to Roosevelt's misjudgment of the Kremlin leader.[35] On 5 October 1942, former Republican presidential candidate Wendell Willkie, then serving as a special envoy for Roosevelt, published a gushing report on Stalin in *Life* magazine about his recent visit to the Soviet premier in Moscow, praising the Red Army's "great fight" against the Nazis.[36] Enhanced by several accompanying photographs of Soviet combat units, Willkie's article proceeded to emphasize Stalin's commitment to defending Soviet soil at all costs, regardless of the losses of Ukrainian farmland, before turning to his visit with the Soviet leader.[37]

In a 5 September 1942 *Indianapolis Times* article, war correspondent Leland Stowe, whose reports sometimes quoted Stalin's ridicule of U.S. tanks and demands for a second front, painted a vivid picture of the Red Army's valiant defensive efforts for his readers, discussing the clothing of local villagers and the daily struggle they faced as the fighting raged near Rzhev.[38] While the horrors of the Holocaust were still virtually unknown, many Americans, including their president, were familiar with the German Army's reputation for cruelty during the First World War, and Stowe's report emphasized the brutality of Nazi soldiers in starving locals and reportedly striking Soviet babies crying in hunger according to claims by local eyewitnesses.[39] News articles such as Stowe's appear to have led a growing number of Americans to sympathize with the Soviet people and admire "Uncle Joe" Stalin and the Red Army's determined struggle, and the enormous amount of metal scrap that Americans contributed in numerous "scrap drives" across the country continued to fuel U.S. war production, boosting Lend-Lease aid to all the Allied Powers.[40]

As the war progressed, Americans continued to receive regular reports on the Red Army's efforts even as U.S. soldiers and Marines fought doggedly against their Japanese adversaries in the Pacific Theater and the Nazi enemy in North Africa and the Mediterranean.[41] In addition to major newspapers such as *The New York Times*, newspaper reports regularly appeared in the *Evening Star*, *Indianapolis Times*, and others commending the Red Army's stubborn defiance of the merciless Nazi war machine.[42] In addition to regular media reporting in newspapers and popular magazines in the civilian sector, U.S. military publications sometimes featured stories on the Soviet war effort and kept American servicemen and servicewomen informed of events on the Eastern Front.[43]

Edward Carter's RWR continued holding mass rallies in support of donating medical supplies to the Red Army in Madison Square Garden, and on one such occasion in 1942, Hopkins and Soviet Ambassador Maxim Litvinov attended to voice their staunch support for the Soviet cause and RWR's efforts, with Hopkins publicly committing the United States to, "A second front? Yes, and if necessary, a third and a fourth front."[44] At this 22 June 1942 event marking the first anniversary of the Nazi invasion of the Soviet Union, Hopkins publicly vowed to Litvinov that, "nothing shall stop us from sharing with you all that we have and are in this conflict" after lauding the Red Army's effective anti-Nazi efforts for providing, "all humanity a service that can never be repaid."[45] The former Commerce Secretary and Lend-Lease architect labored to make good on his public promise that he made in Litvinov's presence and reportedly proceeded to authorize the transfer of highly sensitive atomic bomb ingredients to satisfy Stalin and keep him in the war against Hitler, an unfortunate decision that, even considering the need to supply the Red Army with conventional aid at the time, later proved fatal to world peace.[46]

A 6 October 1942 report for *The Tampa Tribune* emphasized recent statements by Soviet Ambassador Litvinov in Washington telling Under Secretary Sumner Welles that the Red Army required more material aid. The report further alleged that deliveries up to that point were not enough considering the Soviet Union's immense sacrifices, essentially parroting the Kremlin's claims.[47] The article concluded by echoing Litvinov's complaint about Welles's alleged unwillingness to discuss the urgent need for "a second front," while quoting Stalin's claim that the Red Army continued facing, "the main force of the German Fascist" with "little effective" aid from the West, the latter statement surely being a highly propagandized assertion meant to dimmish the importance of Lend-Lease's contribution to the Allied cause.[48]

Upon returning to the United States from the Soviet Union in February 1943, American war correspondent Cassidy stated that "the Russian people" were in full agreement with the Soviet premier's recently voiced satisfaction with the ongoing Anglo-American efforts in North Africa.[49] In an interview with Clark Lee of *Evening Star*, Cassidy stated that Stalin had gleefully referred to the Operation *Torch* landings as a "prelude" to a second front and believed that the Red Army could take the offensive in 1944 with the help of more Lend-Lease aid.[50] On 4 January 1943, *TIME* magazine named Stalin "Man of the Year" and published a glowing article about the Soviet premier. Playing on American perceptions of the Red Army as the underdog in its anti-Nazi struggle, the *TIME* report hailed Stalin's military leadership as the key factor in repelling the Nazis at Moscow and Stalingrad while openly praising Cassidy's reports, portraying Stalin as a non-revolutionary, moderate Communist in contrast to Lenin and Trotsky, for example, and blaming American, "prejudice" for previous tensions.[51]

In a 28 June 1944 article for *The New York Times*, William H. Lawrence trumpeted Stalin's recent meeting with U.S. Chamber of Commerce President Eric Johnston in Moscow in the presence of Ambassador Harriman. In keeping with wartime media tradition and Washington's prevailing perceptions at the time, Lawrence's report included for his readers an appraisal of the Soviet premier as pro-business and open to moderation, citing his "high praise to the job done by American business, labor and agriculture and by the United States government in aiding the Soviet Union's victorious war effort."[52] On 9 July, the Soviet newspaper *Izvestia* published a letter from Johnston to Stalin in which the U.S. Chamber of Commerce official praised the massive leaps in Soviet industry and commended the Soviet premier's ongoing efforts to lead the Red Army to victory. Ambassador Harriman forwarded the letter to Secretary Hull and, summing up the administration's official, prevailing views, Johnston subsequently authored an article in *Reader's Digest* echoing its contents, praising Stalin's, "inspiring" leadership and wishing him, "good health for many years and [a] speedy victory over our common enemy."[53]

Reports such as these that praised Stalin in various ways and portrayed him as a moderate Communist leader with capitalistic tendencies appear to have helped contribute to Roosevelt's naivete regarding the Soviet ruler and fueled his perception that extravagant U.S. aid could, he hoped, motivate him to turn away from orthodox Communism. The earlier experience of industrialists like Stettinius, Henry Ford, Albert Kahn, and other leading American businessmen that Stalin welcomed to conduct business in the 1930s doubtlessly contributed to Roosevelt's false sense of security in believing that the Kremlin could not enforce its totalitarian rule for much longer.[54] As discussed previously, the earlier experiences of these men, several of whom either worked in Roosevelt's administration or contributed to Soviet Lend-Lease in other ways, appear to have played a part in the president's official recognition of Stalin's regime in 1933. As his friend William Bullitt discovered after trying to persuade him to obtain concessions from Stalin, Roosevelt had long before fallen for the Soviet premier's clever ruse that masked his adherence to Communist orthodoxy, and his portrayal in wartime U.S. media further reinforced this view.[55]

In a summer 1944 visit to the Soviet Union, U.S. war correspondent William White experienced a guided tour to a major Soviet aircraft factory involved in the production of IL-2 *Sturmovik* attack planes. White expressed shock that the Soviet Union's aluminum supply, on which the country's production of aircraft armor for the IL-2s depended heavily, appeared to remain desperately low even at the time of his visit to the country.[56] His account of the deficiencies in Soviet wartime domestic production appears to indicate that U.S. aluminum shipments helped Soviet war workers, to an extent, in the manufacturing of these excellent combat aircraft. White also spoke to many Soviet fighter pilots that expressed deep appreciation for the American P-39s and indicated that these planes helped the Red Army Air Forces to somewhat supplement the otherwise superior IL-2, contributing to the contemporary American perspective that these planes were helping Stalin's airmen to continue countering Nazi attempts to regain air superiority over the battlefield even at times of low IL-2 production.[57]

Regardless of Stalin's later betrayal of Washington's good faith, American Lend-Lease aid to the Red Army doubtlessly helped render the war shorter, less bloody, and less costly overall, and on 1 March 1943, the U.S. Senate Committee on Foreign Relations invited Lend-Lease Administrator Stettinius and Navy Secretary Knox to discuss the renewal of the program to the Allies during the first session of the 78th U.S. Congress. Titled S.813, the proposed bill contained the power, "to extend for one year the provisions of an act to promote the defense of the United States, approved March 11, 1941," renewing Roosevelt's authority to continue designating the countries he deemed worthy of Lend-Lease aid for the next year.[58] During his presentation, Stettinius emphasized the perceived impact (from the American perspective) of Lend-Lease trucks, munitions, and food on the Soviet victory at Stalingrad, stating that the Red Army still required much more to keep Stalin's soldiers fed and fighting as, "The food situation in the Soviet Union is now critical. It will grow increasingly critical for some time to come."[59] Senator Alben Barkley (D-KY) questioned the effectiveness of Lend-Lease aid on the Eastern Front, and Stettinius replied that U.S. aluminum and machine tools remained vital to Soviet aircraft and tank production.[60]

Stettinius then gave the senators a detailed description of the goods provided to the Red Army's war effort up to 1 January 1943, citing a "dollar value" of U.S. $1,300,000,000 consisting of 130,000 submachine guns, 174,000 pounds of brass and copper, 98,000 pounds of toluol and TNT, 6,200 U.S. and British tanks and 5,600 aircraft, "and 85,000 other military motor vehicles."[61] Emphasizing the administration's position that aluminum and nourishment remained crucial to the Soviet war effort, Stettinius then explained to Senator Barkley that, "other munitions, raw materials, and food" amounted to a large percentage of the Lend-Lease aid delivered to the Soviet Union in 1942.[62] Insisting that Lend-Lease be renewed to guarantee Stalin's continued prosecution of the war, Stettinius implied that the Western Allies could not afford to risk the possibility of repeating the perceived Allied errors of the First World War.[63]

Following Stettinius's presentation, Navy Secretary Knox advocated for the need to increase the flow of attack aircraft to the Soviet Union and highlighted the administration's efforts to improve the Persian Corridor and ALSIB the next day. Senator Barkley and Senator Wallace H. White (R-ME) then asked Knox to confirm whether he agreed with the need, "to send all the airplanes we can send to Russia" to offset the German Air Force's alleged numerical superiority that Stalin had continued to emphasize in his telegrams to Roosevelt.[64] Knox confirmed his view on the matter and the senators continued to debate the issue.[65]

As Congress debated the need to renew Lend-Lease to the Allies, including the Soviet Union, U.S. Ambassador Standley in Moscow voiced frustration that the Soviet people were not being informed about the American people's generosity by their government.[66] Standley had recently returned after consulting with Roosevelt and, in addition to being angered by Stalin's perceived indifference to the dangers to which the Arctic convoys were subjected, grew increasingly frustrated by General Faymonville's zeal in unquestioningly agreeing to anything the Kremlin requested. After failing to obtain public praise from any top Soviet officials for the U.S. Lend-Lease contribution to the Red Army's struggle, Standley held a press conference at which he voiced his frustration in a desperate attempt to force Moscow's hand as he expressed fear that Congress's decision could be delayed if it seemed that Stalin cared little for the aid he received. Standley's wife and daughters were also heavily involved in Carter's RWR, and the ambassador, reflecting Roosevelt's views, had long advocated for improving the Iranian and Alaskan supply routes to keep Stalin in the war by providing much more war material, yet his comments appear to have angered many congressmen that viewed them as counterproductive.[67]

On 9 March 1943, the day before deciding on the renewal of Lend-Lease for the next year, the U.S. Senate and House of Representatives debated Ambassador Standley's comments and the need for the Allies to maintain a united front against the Axis by renewing Lend-Lease aid. Senator Tom Connally (D-TX) assailed Standley's comments as divisive and unnecessary, pointing to Stettinius's detailed report of, "a great variety of items of a distinctly American type" and criticizing the U.S. ambassador in Moscow for his perceived "ineptness."[68] Pointing out that, "Two-thirds of all shipments from the United States have been made in American ships," Senator Connally argued that the Soviet fighting men and women had little choice but to know the origin of the, "2,900,000 tons of war supplies" that they had received by March 1943.[69]

In the House of Representatives, Foreign Affairs Committee Chairman Sol Bloom (D-NY) likewise characterized Standley's complaint as ridiculous, citing a 6 March 1943 article by U.S. war correspondent Cassidy that emphasized the "American trucks and jeeps" that Red Army soldiers and commanders rode to the battlefield in.[70] After further quoting Cassidy's article on the quantity and quality of American food and aircraft delivered to the red warriors, Bloom's comments triggered a brief debate as Congressman Fish challenged his fellow New York representative to seriously consider Standley's complaint. The debate ended with most of the congressmen present arguing for the need to maintain amity and close cooperation with all the "United Nations" in their shared strategic approach to resisting the Axis.[71]

Echoing Chairman Bloom's conclusions and those of most of his House colleagues, Congressman John Kee (D-WV) called attention to the immediate crisis, stating, "In less than 20 years, Germany, a nation we [the Allied Powers collectively] had beaten to her knees, rose to undreamed of power and soon plunged the world into the bloodiest war in human history."[72] Asking his House colleagues, "Are we going to repeat our mistakes of 25 years ago?" Congressman Kee challenged Fish and others advocating on Standley's behalf to prove whether they cared more for ensuring Hitler's defeat by renewing Lend-Lease or bickering over allegedly trivial matters.[73] Kee's comments and the subsequent congressional renewal of Lend-Lease appear to mirror Roosevelt's perception that in early 1943 a second Brest-Litovsk remained a disturbing possibility as Nazi occupation forces remained on Soviet soil and Stalin had not yet agreed to meet Roosevelt in person. Determined to avoid repeating past errors during a global war, leading U.S. lawmakers renewed Roosevelt's Allied aid program that automatically included the Soviet Union as Lend-Lease uniquely gave the president sole authority to designate countries that he deemed meriting aid, as pointed out by Sean McMeekin.[74]

Following the October 1941 defeat of Congressman Rich's proposed amendment to Lend-Lease in the House, even Congressman Fish, despite expressing his distaste for Stalin's regime and briefly challenging Chairman Bloom to consider Standley's complaints, declined to mount a serious effort at amending Roosevelt's program.[75] As repugnant as these men rightly determined Stalin's Communist regime to be, they understandably found it unwise during a second global war to remove Roosevelt's authority, granted to him by Congress in 1941, to designate recipients of U.S. war aid. The unique nature of the Lend-Lease Act meant that while Congress continued to execute its constitutional duty of authorizing and appropriating funds for the war effort, the president, as Commander-in-Chief, bore the responsibility of determining the recipients of the war material that congressional funding produced.[76] Following the Rich Amendment's defeat, no serious challenges emerged as the war raged in March 1943 because many congressmen, including Fish and Taber, concluded that removing Roosevelt's authority required them to repeal H. R. 1776 to produce and approve new legislation to limit his ability to designate aid recipients.[77]

Fish and others appear to have feared that repealing Lend-Lease to revise it and limit Roosevelt's authority, essentially crafting an entirely new piece of legislation, may have endangered their ongoing efforts to aid Great Britain and China, a possibility made even more frightful by the prevailing U.S. perception of Hitler's army as a potentially unbeatable opponent in spring 1943.[78] They also seem to have agreed with the administration's staunch congressional allies that such action could potentially damage Allied morale by leading Churchill and Chiang Kai-shek to fear for their own support and question the long-term reliability of Washington to continue supplying their troops until the defeat of the Axis.[79] Once the Soviet Union had been added to Lend-Lease after the Rich Amendment's defeat in late 1941, removing it became impractical as drafting and passing new legislation with more limits on Roosevelt's role could have jeopardized aid to the British and Chinese forces, even if temporarily, a risk that most lawmakers opted not to take in 1943.[80]

In late 1943, Senator Connally of Texas, a staunch supporter of Lend-Lease, further ensured that no serious attempts to repeal and revise the program to exclude Stalin's forces could be mounted as he sponsored Senate Resolution 192 in a public display of Allied solidarity in prosecuting the war.[81] A propaganda measure that further committed Congress to supporting the president's wartime policies, Connally's resolution passed the Senate vote virtually unopposed, effectively framing opposition to aiding any of the Allied Powers as tantamount to inviting defeat.[82] Senator Connally's success that November appears to have been an unnecessary effort, however, as the president's few wartime critics in Congress declined to launch an effort to remove his Lend-Lease powers in March, and Standley's criticism of the Kremlin's attitude failed to negatively impact the program's renewal in spring 1943.[83]

Congress subsequently proceeded to vote overwhelmingly to renew Lend-Lease aid to all 44 countries at war with the Axis Powers, with the Senate voting 82 to zero in favor of continuing the program, and Roosevelt gladly signed off on the bill on 12 March 1943.[84] Seeking, perhaps, to further ensure that Ambassador Standley's complaints continued to be ignored in Washington, Soviet Ambassador Litvinov, for good measure, immediately expressed deep gratitude for Lend-Lease aid to the Red Army on behalf of the Soviet government and people in the pages of *The New York Times*.[85] Roosevelt proceeded to hail his program as the key to defeating the Axis, emphasizing the recent Soviet victories and the need to deliver even more aid to Moscow as Generals Connolly, Arnold, and Bradley labored to increase the flow of aid to the Red Army from Iran and Alaska.[86]

According to Ambassador Standley and Roosevelt's former presidential aide and speechwriter Robert Sherwood, the president remained desperate and determined in his attempts to obtain a personal meeting with Stalin to discuss the war's continued prosecution well into 1943.[87] In a further strong indication that the fear of a second Brest-Litovsk continued to haunt Roosevelt's mind even after the Stalingrad victory as Stalin kept him at arm's length and repeatedly put off a personal meeting, the president dispatched former Ambassador Joseph Davies to Moscow in early May 1943. Standley and Sherwood's respective accounts indicate that Roosevelt, aware that Churchill's August 1942 meeting with Stalin had ended poorly and that tensions remained chilly between London and Moscow, sought to "break the ice" with the Soviet premier and ensure his continued prosecution of the war against Hitler.[88] As noted previously, Davies had been among the first U.S. officials to warn Roosevelt and Hopkins of the need to prevent a separate peace at all costs in summer 1941, and the former U.S. ambassador agreed to serve as the "Special Representative of the President."[89] According to authors Martin Weil and Sean McMeekin, Roosevelt is said to have decided in either March or April 1943 to send Davies to Moscow due to, "rumors" circulating in contemporary wartime Washington that Stalin's representatives were allegedly holding secret peace talks with their Nazi counterparts.[90]

This desperate diplomatic overture by Roosevelt in spring 1943 met with initial failure as Stalin warmly welcomed the pro-Soviet advocate Davies but continued putting off a meeting with the president, keeping him guessing until finally agreeing early that fall to go to Tehran in November. Offended by yet another perceived slight from Washington that enabled further insubordination of his authority as U.S. Ambassador in Moscow, Admiral Standley offered his resignation in a letter to Roosevelt on 3 May 1943, and the president replaced him that October with Averell Harriman.[91] Harriman had led Standley and other U.S. delegates at the Harriman-Beaverbrook Conference with British and Soviet officials, that resulted in the birth of the Soviet Lend-Lease program's First Protocol that began in late 1941. Roosevelt hoped that Stalin would discern and appreciate this warm gesture and reciprocate by remaining in the war until Germany's total defeat, the goal that the president had identified early on as the sole condition that he intended to attach to Soviet Lend-Lease aid.[92]

In a 1 November 1943 congressional debate, Senator Richard Russell (D-GA) characterized Roosevelt's handling of Lend-Lease affairs as a "prodigal hand" that placed U.S. interests behind those of the other Allied countries and subsequently launched an investigation of the program.[93] While publicly ridiculing this rare wartime senatorial probe, Roosevelt acted quickly in a public compromise with his conservative southern Democrat critics by firing Under Secretary Sumner Welles and further masking Hopkins's influence on Lend-Lease by incorporating the program into the newly formed Foreign Economic Administration (FEA). Headed by Leo Crowley, a businessman that the president's opponents viewed favorably in comparison to Hopkins and Stettinius, the latter man having become known to many congressmen as a friend of the New Deal architect by late 1943, the FEA incorporated Lend-Lease into its program and the senatorial investigators subsequently canceled their probe.[94]

On 26 April 1944, Senator Connally chaired a session of the Senate Committee on Foreign Relations as he and other lawmakers discussed the need to again renew Lend-Lease to all Allied countries, including Stalin's Soviet Union, until 30 June 1945 through H. R. 4254.[95] The gathering of United States senators listened in rapt attention as FEA Head Crowley gave a detailed account of the enormous amount of aid that U.S. farmers and factory workers had delivered to the Allied Powers through their strenuous war production efforts. Stating, "Every dollar's worth of war supplies we and the British Commonwealth send to Russia enables the Red Army to strike harder blows at our common enemy," Crowley emphasized the need to continue Lend-Lease in the interest of hastening victory.[96]

Continuing, Crowley stated emphatically that "Already the Red Army has put out of action millions of Nazi soldiers and tens of thousands of Nazi planes, tanks, and guns," before concluding, "And every Nazi soldier killed and every German plane, tank, or gun destroyed by the Red Army means less opposition for American and British forces when the western invasions are launched."[97] Crowley's arguments before the Senate summarized the administration's strategic approach to Nazi Germany's defeat in a way that many congressmen could appreciate. Reflecting Washington's desire to avert a second Brest-Litovsk, he emphasized the crucial role of Lend-Lease food, stating, "The Ukraine is the Soviet Union's bread basket. Just now liberated, it has been under the Nazi heel for 2 years. The resulting food shortage in Russia has been acute."[98] Congress proceeded to pass H. R. 4254, renewing Lend-Lease for the remainder of the war, and guaranteeing that the Red Army continued to sweep onward to victory as Stalin continued receiving more aid than he required for the Soviet Union's defense from the U.S. supply bases in Iran and Alaska.[99]

At the Allies' November 1943 Tehran Conference held in the Iranian capital, Stalin praised Roosevelt and credited U.S. industry with supplying the Soviet war effort with an enormous amount of material that had proved invaluable to the Red Army's victories.[100] Echoing his earlier emphasis (through his telegrams) on the Red Army's need for U.S. combat aircraft such as the P-39, Stalin offered some long-awaited praise for Roosevelt's role in prioritizing Lend-Lease aircraft deliveries to the Soviet Union, stating, "Without the use of those machines, through Lend-Lease, we would lose this war."[101] After contrasting U.S. aircraft production with that of Great Britain and ridiculing London's focus on manufacturing, "principally heavy bombers" rather than the attack planes that he requested, Stalin openly acknowledged the crucial impact of Lend-Lease on the Soviet war effort in a rare public admission to his Allied counterparts.[102]

While some British leaders such as Pownall and Alanbrooke appear to have displayed a more realistic view of the Soviet premier's duplicitous tendencies, Roosevelt rejected their concerns, and London agreed that the aid flow to Moscow be continued even as Stalin questioned whether he could consider Churchill as, "my friend" at the Tehran Conference.[103] While later adding a note in his *War Diaries* that he may have misread U.S. intentions at the time of the Tehran Conference, Alanbrooke nevertheless recorded his contemporary perception that Roosevelt and Harriman sought to flatter Stalin at Great Britain's expense.[104] Roosevelt is said to have used the occasion, as well as others, to poke fun at Churchill after noticing that Stalin appeared to find it amusing and reportedly burst into laughter as the British prime minister turned red in embarrassment. Despite knowing of Stalin's past actions, Roosevelt appears to have largely dismissed the notion that his Red Army could pose a postwar threat to the West, and the Soviet premier's comments at Tehran chiding Alanbrooke for his allegedly negative view of the Soviet people appears to have been a rhetorical snipe at the British general's more cautious view of the Kremlin.[105]

Following Standley's resignation and return to the United States, Roosevelt also demoted Generals Faymonville and Michela due to the former ambassador's constant complaints about insubordination and sent General John Deane to serve as the new Chief of the U.S. Military Mission in Moscow.[106] Roosevelt appears to have hoped to simultaneously satisfy both Stalin and his critics, such as Standley and Bullitt, by sending Harriman as the new U.S. ambassador and replacing Faymonville with General Deane. Yet soon after assuming Faymonville's former post in late 1943, Deane strongly advised Roosevelt to somewhat reduce Lend-Lease aid to demonstrate U.S. economic leverage as a sign of strength to Stalin and expressed his concern that the Red Army had begun receiving more than it required.[107]

Replying that he perceived himself and Hopkins as perfectly capable of judging Stalin's character, Roosevelt stubbornly insisted that by providing unconditional aid, he could later secure Soviet participation against Japan while preventing the Soviet leader from striking another deal with Hitler or pursuing an aggressive postwar path.[108] Despite the Red Army's outstanding victories at Stalingrad and Kursk, Roosevelt appears to have assumed that so long as Soviet forces had not reached German soil, the possibility that Stalin could conclude a separate peace remained a legitimate concern and continued to cite the Soviet premier's continued participation in the war as the only condition that he sought to impose. While the fears in Washington of a second Brest-Litovsk may have been greatly diminished after Roosevelt's long-sought and important personal meeting with Stalin in Tehran in November 1943, the president's reaction to Deane's advice indicates that he remained concerned over such a possibility so long as the Red Army had not advanced into Nazi territory.[109]

Roosevelt's old friend and the first U.S. ambassador to the Soviet Union, William Bullitt, also wrote to the president repeatedly during this period, urging him to consider attaching conditions to further Soviet Lend-Lease deliveries and cautioning him on Stalin's duplicitous character and quiet desire for expansion.[110] Preferring the advice of Davies and Hopkins, Roosevelt repeatedly rejected Bullitt's advice on obtaining concessions from Stalin as counterproductive to ensuring Germany's total defeat and unconditional surrender. The president appears to have correctly regarded the Red Army's rapid advance from 1944 forward as critical to hastening Germany's defeat, yet he erred in continuing to foolishly view Stalin as being open and susceptible to moderation that could be purchased, in a sense, through unconditional American aid.[111]

Roosevelt's insistence on hastening Germany's collapse by unconditionally supplying Stalin's forces during the war appears to have been connected to his desire to ensure a crushing defeat for Berlin to keep it from rising again as a major European power that could disturb the peace a third time. Although Bullitt persisted in his attempts to convince Roosevelt to either attach conditions to Soviet Lend-Lease, open a second front in the Balkans in 1943, or obtain concessions from Stalin, the president adhered to his strategy of unconditionally aiding the Red Army.[112] Roosevelt's staunch commitment to his generals', "strategy of annihilation" against Germany, described by Russell Weigley, appears to have been inextricably connected to his prioritization of Lend-Lease aid to the Red Army and his rejection of peace offers by anti-Nazi German officials that he dismissed as scheming, "East German Junkers."[113]

On several occasions after Roosevelt's January 1943 unconditional surrender declaration, the president reportedly rebuffed offers by German intelligence (*Abwehr*) Director Admiral Wilhelm Canaris, Baron Kurt von Lernser of distant

Jewish heritage, and the devoutly Catholic Baron Franz von Papen.[114] These men had secretly initiated several meetings in neutral Istanbul, Turkey, with U.S. naval observer and former Pennsylvania Governor George H. Earle and proposed to lead an anti-Hitler coup if Roosevelt could renounce his unconditional surrender policy and allow the German Army to resist Soviet expansion. After repeatedly ignoring Earle's initial reports, Roosevelt received the American diplomat at the White House in May 1944 and listened to his concerns before brushing them aside. Roosevelt listened as Earle urged action and stated that the anti-Nazi plotters could not execute their coup as many German officers remained loyal to Hitler due to the unconditional surrender policy that they perceived as hatefully anti-German.[115]

After Earle attempted to persuade him that, "the real menace is not Germany. It is Russia," Roosevelt replied, "George, Russia is a nation of 180 million people speaking 120 different dialects. When the war is over, she will fly to pieces like a cracked centrifugal machine at high speed."[116] In reflecting on the experience of the First World War, Roosevelt appears to have distrusted all German officials, even those proposing Hitler's overthrow, and clung to his total war strategy to crush Germany rather than negotiate peace with a post-Nazi regime. Ascribing the outbreak of war to Germany's aristocratic "Junkers" rather than a solely Nazi plot, the president sought the country's total and unquestioned defeat to ensure that it could not rise again as a major European power.[117] Roosevelt's comments reveal that as late as May 1944, he regarded Stalin's forces as incapable of dominating Europe and believed that continuing to arm and feed them remained essential to defeating ethnically and linguistically homogeneous Germany and temporarily prolonging the Soviet Union's national survival.[118]

Roosevelt casually acknowledged the concerns of Earle and Bullitt and Stalin's record of aggression but stated his firm belief that he and Hopkins had a "hunch" that Hitler's duplicity and the West's eagerness to help unconditionally had convinced the Soviet leader to abandon such thinking.[119] Stubbornly insisting that his discussions with Hopkins and Stalin at Tehran had convinced him that Hitler's attack had somehow redirected the Soviet premier's motives, Roosevelt, even if his motives made sense during wartime, downplayed the potential threat that could be posed by a reinvigorated Red Army. His responses to the concerns voiced by Standley, Deane, Bullitt, and Earle indicate that he severely underestimated Stalin's cunning character while overestimating his ability to charm the Soviet leader through his unconditional support of the Red Army.[120]

Basing his views of the situation on the Allied experience in the First World War, he appears to have much preferred a Red Army presence in Eastern Europe over a German military presence, even a non-Nazi one, and refused to allow Berlin the chance to regain power once again and potentially unleash a third world war. Vastly underestimating the Red Army's long-term occupation capabilities, Roosevelt appears to have simply believed that Stalin's armies could not enforce Moscow's political ideology outside of Soviet borders for long. He appears to have concluded that Lend-Lease inherently gave the United States enough leverage to tempt Stalin into accepting some form of capitalism or coax him into moderating his policies by causing him to rely on further U.S. aid to help rebuild the territories that Hitler's attack had ravaged and assumed that subsidizing Moscow guaranteed postwar peace.[121]

Regardless of their intentions, and irrespective of their correct decision to supply all forms of conventional military aid to the Red Army and thereby hasten victory, Roosevelt and his senior Lend-Lease advisers all but ensured that a third world war could be launched, not by Berlin, but by Moscow, as they supplied Stalin with key secret ingredients for atomic bomb construction in the naïve belief that the Soviet atomic program could not become effective for many years. The most current research indicates that after Soviet officials requested thorium, cadmium, heavy water, and uranium, their U.S. counterparts dangerously concluded that refusing to ship such sensitive material may have indicated its true importance and potential to Stalin's scientists.[122] Gambling on the importance of not offending Stalin and keeping the Red Army in the war, Roosevelt and Hopkins opted to keep their unfortunate 1942 pledge to share everything in Washington's arsenal with Stalin. Their gamble boomeranged harmfully against U.S. security interests and global stability in the postwar years and virtually guaranteed that tyrannical aggressors could intimidate, invade, and occupy other nations with virtual impunity and threaten the nuclear destruction of those that resisted them.[123]

On three occasions between April 1943 and June 1944, Soviet officials reportedly managed to secure U.S. uranium through the Lend-Lease supply center in Great Falls. In an early 1943 telephone conversation, Hopkins ordered Major Jordan to expect and approve in advance a shipment of "special priority" material that arrived several days after their conversation.[124] Unaware of uranium's atomic potential at that time, Jordan expressed his concern that Soviet officials were undermining Lend-Lease by procuring materials omitted from the official records.[125] Following a visit with Jordan after returning to the United States from his visit to Moscow and other Allied capitals, Eddie Rickenbacker relayed the information to General Marshall in Washington and later noted his confusion at the general's lack of concern.[126]

In a 1944 report to Stalin, Mikoyan assessed the quantities of Lend-Lease munitions, food, and raw materials provided by the United States and Great Britain. His report also alludes to the unofficial acquisition of U.S. uranium by briefly stating that several important "additional items" of American origin were intentionally omitted from the report.[127] Mikoyan's 1944 report appears to offer strong supporting evidence of Major Jordan's diary entries recording the shipments of aluminum, thorium, and other sensitive materials to the Soviets in 1943 and 1944. Mikoyan's emphasis to Stalin that his report did not include some important items shipped from the United States appears to lend further supporting evidence to Jordan's recollections and congressional testimony that Hopkins had specifically ordered that all such material, "is not to go on the records."[128]

Pouring such extravagant and ultimately counterproductive aid into Stalin's war effort, in contrast to the decision to simply supply the Red Army with all conventional forms of Lend-Lease aid, does not seem to have been necessary to defeating Hitler and may have undermined Roosevelt and Hopkins's desire to coax Stalin into adopting a more moderate Communism and commit to postwar peace with the democratic Western powers.[129] In contrast to the furnishing of conventional Lend-Lease aid, overdoing Roosevelt's efforts to woo Stalin through such excessive and unnecessary gestures appears to have ultimately been a self-defeating act on the part of the American wartime leadership. Yet the excess did not end with the supplying of atomic bomb materials, and, as Albert Weeks points out, "FDR wanted to do all he could to keep the Red Army juggernaut rolling westward," a process that began with the Stalingrad victory in February 1943, and, therefore, he attempted yet another "stunning personal gesture" in a vain effort to woo the Soviet premier and keep him in the war.[130]

According to John Beasant, Roosevelt decided to ship to Stalin a load of silver bullion ingots worth U.S. $26,000,000 and weighing more than 2,000 pounds between the Tehran Conference and the next "Big Three" meeting at Yalta on the Soviet Union's Crimean Peninsula in February 1945. Determined to "purchase" Stalin's loyalty, so to speak, and reverse Woodrow Wilson's perceived failures to secure world peace after the first global war against Germany and its allies, Roosevelt opted to send his silver gift to through the Persian Corridor that Lend-Lease officials favored over the Arctic route as comparatively safer.[131] On 19 July 1944, the men of the U.S. Liberty ship *John Barry* sailed around South Africa's Cape of Good Hope and into the Indian Ocean bound for the Iranian port of Abadan with their precious cargo that Roosevelt sought to offer as a gift to Stalin as further confirmation that no conditions were attached to his support in the apparent hope that such a gesture could, at least essentially, buy the Soviet premier.[132] As the *Barry* neared Oman's Arabian Sea coast on 28 August, the Nazi submarine *U-859* struck the vessel, and while most of its crew members were rescued by a nearby Dutch trawler, the ship's treasure sank to a depth of 8,500 feet below the surface.[133] The *Barry's* contents largely remained a mystery to the world's public until a French research group assisted by the Oman-based British journalist Beasant, Captain Brian Shoemaker, California businessman Jay Fiondella, and a Florida-based U.S. deep-sea diving team explored the shipwreck in fall 1994.[134]

Known as the Ocean Group Consortium, the research group also received aid from the German government and Captain Jan Jebsen, the former captain of *U-859*, in locating the wreck, along with the financial backing of the Omani government in an effort led by Yemeni-born Omani businessman *Shaykh* Ahmed Farid al-Awlaki.[135] The Yemeni government of General Ali Abdullah Saleh, whose forces had just emerged victoriously in a vicious civil war with the key help of al-Qaeda leader Osama bin Laden and his guerrilla comrades from the Soviet-Afghan War, also financed the expedition.[136] On investigating the wreckage, the salvage team discovered that the *Barry's* cargo also included more than U.S. $1,000,000 in 3,000 silver Saudi riyal coins that were reportedly intended for Saudi Arabia's King Abdul Aziz Ibn Saud, with the bulk of the ship's silver being meant for Stalin.[137] Contemporary reports from the *Barry's* discovery indicate that the divers discovered and brought back to the surface only a portion of the material loaded onto the Liberty ship, providing just one example of Roosevelt's desperation to keep Stalin's Red Army in the war and demonstrate U.S. generosity in the hopes of courting his friendship.[138]

In his 1945 book *Report on the Russians*, a firsthand account of his travels to the Soviet Union during the previous summer, U.S. war correspondent White recalls witnessing a strange machine described by his Soviet guide as a cyclotron used for splitting atoms during a 1944 visit to Leningrad.[139] Without knowing the significance of such a scientific process at the time, White noted that his Soviet guides stated that the machine, "was made to the order of the great Russian physicist, [Abram] Joffe, who has been engaged in splitting the atom."[140] The guides then proceeded to degrade the device as outdated, while boasting that the Soviet Union possessed far more advanced machines for splitting atoms behind the Ural Mountains, indicating that Soviet atomic research capabilities had grown considerably during the war.[141]

Throughout the war, Roosevelt continued reminding the American people and Congress, correctly, of the important contributions made by the Lend-Lease program to the Allies in Great Britain, the Soviet Union, and China.[142] On 27 August 1943, he stated that more than U.S. $13,900,000,000 in supplies had been delivered to the Allies as of 31 July, accurately portraying the aid as a necessary contribution to defending democracy from a common foe, while naively expressing his view that this amounted to ensuring peace with Stalin after victory.[143] After dispatching Harriman to Moscow to replace Admiral Standley as U.S. Ambassador to the Soviet Union that December, the president continued to emphasize the Red Army's inflicting of massive losses on the Nazi enemy at an enormous cost in Soviet lives, stating, "Hitler will not be able to use these men on the western front."[144] Even as he continued to insist upon Great Britain's repayment of Lend-Lease aid, Roosevelt consistently defended his refusal to attach conditions to Stalin's arms deliveries, portraying the Red

Army's operations as, "Reverse Lend-Lease" in his 23 August 1944 report to Congress in a further indication of his belief that his cordial approach to the Soviet leader amounted to purchasing his goodwill and ensuring peace.[145]

Harriman's role in the First Moscow Protocol meetings of September 1941 had earned him the reputation as a strong proponent of aid to the Soviet Union and, as previously mentioned, Roosevelt hoped in vain that Stalin might perceive the new ambassador's appointment as a signal of friendship.[146] In 1944, Roosevelt enlisted the help of Air Corps General Arnold in persuading Stalin to permit a U.S. Army Air Corps base in the recaptured Poltava region to allow U.S. bombers to attack the Romanian oilfields.[147] Stalin accepted, enabling the Americans to strike the Ploesti oilfields critical to the Nazi war effort, and Roosevelt interpreted the agreement as a diplomatic success and a reciprocal gesture of trust.[148]

In his November 1943 and August 1944 reports to Congress on Lend-Lease operations, Roosevelt again emphasized the role of the Red Army in repulsing Hitler's most powerful offensives. While the president's report focused on materials delivered to Great Britain and Churchill's financial reimbursement efforts, he also referenced the Red Army's performance and the need to maintain support for the Soviet Union.[149] Describing Allied successes on all fronts as, "Reverse Lend-Lease," Roosevelt portrayed Stalin's victories as a contribution to ending the war at a comparably smaller cost in American lives, a worthy and noble goal that, in fact, rendered the war less bloody and devastating.[150]

Yet as the president and his senior aides persisted in boldly supplying all forms of conventional Lend-Lease aid to Stalin's Red Army, Soviet spies in powerful administration posts, such as Harry Dexter White and Alger Hiss, continued their espionage activities to ensure that Stalin's expansionist goals were not obstructed, undermining wartime Washington's efforts at promoting mutual goodwill.[151] As discussed in this work's second chapter, White had played a part in helping to push U.S.-Japanese relations to the breaking point and triggering a war between Tokyo and Washington in 1941, perhaps somewhat earlier than it may have otherwise occurred, thereby helping Stalin's strategic maneuvering in several ways. Emboldened by Washington's intense wartime focus on fighting the Axis, White advised his superiors to refocus U.S. machine tool production to favor Stalin's aid requests barely two weeks after the Pearl Harbor attack, according to Sean McMeekin.[152]

White's advantageous position as a trusted Treasury Department economist on whom Roosevelt's close friend Secretary Morgenthau relied heavily allowed him to exert even greater influence on U.S. policy on Stalin's behalf, and in 1942, he authored a document titled L-208 that quickly became wartime law.[153] According to Major Jordan, White's authorship of L-208 further served Stalin's interests by shutting down 4,000 gold mines across the United States and allowing the Roosevelt administration to ship the equipment to the Soviet Union.[154] Much of this equipment reportedly passed through the Great Falls, Montana Lend-Lease base during Jordan's time as Hopkins's supply expeditor there in 1943 and 1944 and is said to have been shipped to the Soviet merchant ships sailing from the West Coast.[155]

White's action appears to have helped equip Soviet gold mining operations in Siberia at the expense of the U.S. gold industry, and, according to historians John Koster and Ben Steil, he is also said to have become more brazen and arrogant throughout the war, authoring the infamous "Morgenthau Plan" that proposed turning Germany into a permanent agrarian state.[156] Roosevelt initially went along with this proposal before various protestations within his administration forced a change of policy, and, as emphasized by McMeekin, U.S. troops were expected to follow JCS 1067, also authored by White, to permanently destroy German economic potential, as they advanced into Germany in 1945.[157] The contents of JCS 1067 expressly forbade U.S. commanders and their troops from in any way contributing to the revitalization of the German economy once the country had been defeated, divided, and occupied by the Allies.[158]

Such punitive measures, originating in White's desire to serve Stalin's long-term strategic interests by ensuring that Germany remained permanently crippled after Hitler's defeat and therefore incapable of challenging Soviet expansion, angered General Marshall after German units began fighting the Allied advance fanatically.[159] White's proposals, which were briefly adopted as the planned U.S. policies for a defeated Germany, reportedly spurred German commanders to fight harder and led to Marshall's heated complaints to Morgenthau, eventually contributing to a more conciliatory occupation approach. Going by his espionage pseudonym "Jurist," the increasingly arrogant and cocky White boasted to a Soviet agent identified only as, "Koltsov" in a 4 August 1944 correspondence that he and his wife were fully prepared, "for any self-sacrifice" in his ongoing efforts to influence U.S. policy in a pro-Soviet direction.[160] According to John Koster, Stalin's NKVD agreed to pay for White's daughter to attend college as a reward for his espionage activities and his success in helping to further aggravate U.S.-Japanese tensions to the point of no return in 1941.[161]

As White persisted in his pro-Stalin espionage during the war, Hiss continued aiding the Soviet premier's agents in various ways in his key role as a State Department attorney and played a part in arguing in favor of the Soviet Union's geostrategic interests at the 1945 Yalta Conference.[162] At this crucial meeting of the "Big Three" Allied leaders and their senior military and diplomatic aides in the coastal Crimean Peninsula town between 4 and 11 February, Hiss is said to have assisted in convincing Roosevelt to insist on an alliance between Chiang Kai-shek's nationalists and Mao Zedong's Communists in the postwar Chinese government. Hiss also worked closely with Stalin's GRU before and during the war, according to Communist defectors Elizabeth Bentley and Whittaker Chambers, and, as described by Major Jordan in his postwar congressional testimony, appears to have played a part in supplying State Department documents to the Soviets.[163]

Stalin's wartime espionage campaign could not have succeeded without the willing and eager participation of agents such as White and Hiss, neither of whom appear to have been official members of the U.S. Communist Party but were rather drawn by their ideological convictions to serve the Soviet cause.[164] Nor could the effort have succeeded had it not been for the tremendous naivete of Roosevelt, Hopkins, and others such as former U.S. Vice President Henry Wallace, whose 1944 visit to the Soviet Union led to his subsequent authorship of the book *Soviet Asia Mission* in 1946. In his glowing firsthand account of his time in Siberia and other parts of Soviet Asia, Wallace characterized the towns of the Kolyma region of northeastern Siberia and, particularly, its major urban center, Magadan, as having, "wonderful air" and strong, healthy inhabitants.[165] Soviet officials carefully guided Wallace's tour of the region, showing him young, healthy men hard at work, leading him to accept his host Commissar Ivan Nikishov's claim that the local people were, "big, husky young men who came out to the Far East from European Russia" and only a handful of women.[166]

Nikishov had treated the U.S. vice president to an elaborately disguised fiction, however, as Kolyma's true inhabitants were not the young, strong NKVD men engaged in sham construction work, but were men and women that their colleagues had arrested and sentenced to a cruel and torturous prison camp existence. According to forced labor camp survivor Elinor Lipper, a Jewish Lithuanian woman arrested by Stalin's NKVD and imprisoned in Kolyma, the Magadan location housed about 300,000 prisoners, many of them starving and constantly subjected to Nikishov's physical and verbal abuse, at the time of Wallace's visit.[167] Stating that the former vice president neglected to mention half of Kolyma's actual population, Lipper recalls that many inhabitants were, in fact, Jewish, Christian, and other women, including many former nuns, arrested for their faith and enslaved in female-only parts of the prison camp system. Male and female prisoners alike in the Kolyma region worked in the hills outside of the various towns that Wallace described mining for gold with very little food under horrendous conditions that virtually guaranteed a death sentence for many of them.[168]

Some of these tortured, hungry women and men from all parts of the Soviet Union may have been forced to labor in the appalling, freezing Siberian winter conditions of Kolyma while using the U.S. gold-mining equipment that White appears to have played a part in obtaining for Stalin's labor camp commandants through L-208.[169] In her 1950 memoir *Eleven Years in Soviet Prison Camps*, Lipper recalls that gold mining and the construction of more regional towns to hold many more prisoners served as the main functions of Kolyma's inmates during her time there between 1937 and 1948. Guided by his watchful Soviet hosts, Wallace understandably could not see the horrific realities of life at Magadan and other prison towns in Kolyma and seems to have accepted Nikishov's claim that, "Magadan has 40,000 inhabitants and all are well housed."[170]

Like Roosevelt and Hopkins in their dealings with Stalin, Litvinov, and other Soviet officials, Wallace had been duped by Soviet disinformation tactics that obscured and distorted the truth behind the deceptive picture presented to him by Nikishov and his NKVD hosts. Throughout the war, the Kremlin maintained a steady barrage of disinformation through Stalin's diplomats and agents as the Soviet premier sought to accuse both his opponents and wartime allies of conspiring to commit deeds that he and his henchmen had either plotted or committed themselves.[171] Stalin's response to the discovery of a mass grave in Nazi-occupied Soviet territory filled with the corpses of thousands of Polish POWs that were later confirmed as having been executed by the NKVD in the Katyn Massacre serves as another example of Soviet wartime disinformation. After the exiled Polish leadership in London demanded an independent investigation into the matter by the International Red Cross in the spring of 1943, Stalin responded by breaking off diplomatic relations with the exiled Poles and denouncing their supporters as Hitler's "helpmates," as emphasized by McMeekin.[172]

German troops had discovered the mass grave, and the fact that the site lay in Nazi-occupied Soviet territory played into Stalin's hands, allowing him to temporarily dupe Churchill and Roosevelt, the latter of whom required little persuasion, into publicly agreeing with his claim that the slain Poles were more of the many victims of Nazi terror.[173] The atrocity's location also allowed the Soviet premier to effectively claim that because of Nazi control over the occupied area, no wartime investigation could be conducted independently and free of manipulation by Hitler's propagandists. In this instance, the Soviet secret police, rather than their Nazi counterparts, were responsible for the carnage, yet Roosevelt swallowed Stalin's lies unquestioningly, reportedly telling George Earle, "George, this is entirely German propaganda and a German plot. I am convinced the Russians did not do this."[174] By ascribing his war crime to Hitler, Stalin obscured the facts surrounding the killings, and U.S. officials did not recognize the Katyn Massacre as a Soviet atrocity until well after the war.[175]

In addition to their espionage activities, Stalin's agents in Washington also engaged in disinformation in their portrayals to Roosevelt of non-Communist

Allied heads of state and other world leaders. According to former Romanian Communist intelligence director General Ion Mihai Pacepa and Professor Ronald J. Rychlak, Soviet agents began spreading slanderous rumors through a 1945 *Radio Moscow* broadcast that Pope Pius XII had served as, "Hitler's Pope" during the war and had done nothing to prevent Berlin from perpetrating the Holocaust.[176] Pius is said to have abhorred Hitler's genocidal anti-Semitism and provided shelter in the Vatican for many Jews fleeing Nazi persecution, yet Stalin's slander campaign proved to be an effective disinformation tactic that triggered considerable controversy and, to an extent, tarnished the papacy's reputation.[177]

University of Cambridge Professor Christopher Andrew and former KGB operative Oleg Gordievsky state in their 1990 book *KGB: The Inside Story of its Foreign Operations from Lenin to Gorbachev* that Soviet officials informed Ambassador Harriman late in the war that numerous Soviet citizens were residing in Germany, France, and elsewhere in Nazi-occupied Western Europe.[178] Many of these individuals had, in fact, never been Soviet subjects but were Russian refugees that had fled Communist rule after Lenin and Trotsky's victory in the Russian Civil War, yet Roosevelt and Churchill, with the prodding of Stalin's agent Hiss and his unwitting dupe Hopkins, agreed at Yalta to the Soviet premier's request that these people be repatriated. In a tragic example of Stalin's successful disinformation campaign, the White House ordered Operation *Keelhaul*, forcibly deporting roughly 2,000,000 Russian exiles and Soviet POWs seeking refuge in Western Europe to the Soviet Union.[179]

Knowing that they faced certain execution by the NKVD as the Kremlin accused many former White Army tsarist exiles and Red Army POWs alike of being Nazi sympathizers, many of these people attempted to escape, take their own lives, or provoke the Allied soldiers sent to round them up into shooting them.[180] In one gruesome episode, a group of 400 liberated Red Army POWs in Dachau, Germany, whose only crime appears to have been being captured by the Nazis while fighting for their country, wept bitterly and begged the U.S. troops to execute them rather than forcibly repatriate them to face Stalin's accusations of cowardice and treason.[181] After refusing to harm the former captives, the American servicemen watched in horror and tried to intervene as the Soviet POWs raced around the room, with some attempting to hang themselves or find a steep location from which to jump to their fate. In a desperate attempt to avoid being sent to Stalin's hangmen, one soldier reportedly rammed his head through a closed window and repeatedly raked his throat over the shards of broken glass.[182]

In addition to his disinformation victories over the Polish exile government, Pius XII, and numerous Soviet POWs and tsarist exiles in Western Europe, Stalin, with the help of his agents such as Hiss at the Yalta Conference, gradually succeeded in turning Roosevelt and Churchill against non-Communist Allied resistance leaders and heads of state.[183] As emphasized by Sean McMeekin, Stalin's targets of disinformation included the Yugoslav *Chetnik* commander, General Dragoljub "Draza" Mihailovic, and Chinese Nationalist Premier Chiang Kai-shek.[184] In late 1943, Harry Dexter White and Solomon Adler, another Treasury Department economist now known to have been a Soviet agent, authored several reports alleging that Chiang had misused and embezzled funds while collaborating with Japanese occupation forces in China, abandoning Mao Zedong's Communists to fight the invaders by themselves. Adhering to Moscow's classic disinformation technique, White and Adler had ascribed Mao's duplicitous actions to Chiang, as the Chinese Communist leader had, in fact, benefited from Stalin's neutrality pact with Tokyo.[185]

Since October 1940, Stalin had secretly negotiated a series of truces with Hirohito by which Japanese commanders and Mao's guerrillas refused to attack each other, giving the Chinese Communists crucial time to refit, regroup, and recruit while the invaders focused their fury on Chiang's army.[186] Adler had served as the U.S. Treasury Department representative in Chiang's headquarters in Chungking, and his distortion of the truth influenced Roosevelt's decision to gradually reduce the non-Communist Chinese leader's already meager Lend-Lease aid allotment to a mere trickle in comparison to U.S. deliveries to Stalin and Churchill. Ruthlessly wielding his authority to designate Lend-Lease recipients, Roosevelt threatened Chiang's aid program in the way that Bullitt, Deane, and Standley advised him to handle support to Stalin by attaching conditions to further U.S. aid after White and Adler's late 1943 reports. While firmly rejecting the advice of anyone seeking to obtain concessions from Stalin, Roosevelt began curtailing Lend-Lease shipments to Chiang's forces, insisting that the Chinese premier, "democratize" his government and establish a "united government with the Communists at Yenan" as emphasized by McMeekin.[187]

Once Treasury Secretary Morgenthau discovered that U.S. $200,000,000.00 in aid to China's armies had been delayed, White, Adler, and Frank Coe, another confirmed Soviet agent serving in the Treasury Department, promptly explained that Chiang, who they portrayed as collaborating with Tokyo, could no longer be allowed to embezzle or misuse the aid that Roosevelt promised him. In his memoir, Lieutenant Colonel Frank Dorn recalls that his wartime superior in the China Burma India Theater, General Joseph Stilwell, backed Roosevelt's reduction of aid to Chiang and received orders from Washington to prepare the Chinese Nationalist leader's assassination after Japanese troops captured the city of Changsha in a brutal 1944 offensive.[188] While Dorn later expressed his relief that Stilwell never ordered Chiang's assassination, despite preparing for it, the picture of the Chinese premier that White, Adler, and Coe had painted by 1944 destroyed his image, leading Roosevelt to commend the supposedly noble fight being waged by Mao's Communists in a conversation with his son, Elliott.[189] Through his faithful agents in Washington, Stalin had executed a victorious disinformation war against Chiang while helping to plant the seeds of Mao's later rise to power as the Chinese Nationalists gradually lost the favor of the White House.[190]

Like White and his Treasury Department and State Department-based associates in their influence on Roosevelt's abandonment of Chiang's armies, Stalin's disinformation agents in Great Britain also appear to have played a part in turning Churchill against Yugoslav *Chetnik* leader Mihailovic. After Nazi forces invaded and occupied Yugoslavia in response to an anti-Axis coup that seized control in Belgrade in March 1941, Mihailovic affirmed his allegiance to the country's exiled monarchy and launched his resistance movement against the invaders from bases in Serbia.[191] Following Hitler's invasion of the Soviet Union in June, Communist politician Josip Broz Tito began leading the Yugoslav Partisans in a separate struggle in his group's Croatian and Bosnian strongholds.[192]

In July 1942, Soviet disinformation agent James Klugmann, a British intelligence officer working for London's MO4 intelligence agency based in Cairo, Egypt, spearheaded the Kremlin's disinformation war against the *Chetniks* by alleging that Mihailovic had been cooperating with the Nazi troops and crediting Tito's fighters with more victories than they had achieved. Tito also benefited from the efforts of another of Stalin's loyal agents, Guy Burgess, a *BBC* reporter whose broadcasts portrayed the Yugoslav Communist leader as a heroic, legendary figure on whom the Allies could depend to strike the enemy relentlessly. Simultaneously, Tito personally transmitted a barrage of disinformation to Churchill's hand-picked representative to the Yugoslav Partisans, Major General Fitzroy Maclean. Maclean visited and remained with Tito's insurgents for nearly a month in late 1943 before issuing a report to his superiors that October urging London to switch its support to the Communists.[193]

Maclean does not appear to have witnessed the battles that Tito and his lieutenants claimed to have won against the Germans during his stay, but rather foolishly parroted their accounts of resounding victories over the occupiers in his report to Churchill. By late 1944, Churchill had entirely redirected his Cairo-based intelligence unit's support from Mihailovic to Tito, airlifting nearly 27,000 tons of supplies to the Yugoslav Communists in comparison to a total of 272 tons delivered to the *Chetniks* before London abandoned them.[194] A 9 October 1944 *TIME* article subsequently portrayed Tito to American readers as a preferable choice to Mihailovic as a Yugoslav leader worthy of Allied support.[195]

To be sure, Tito's adherence to Communism did not render him either an automatic or willing puppet of Stalin, and the independent, neutral-minded Yugoslav Communist leader later proved to be somewhat of a thorn in the Soviet dictator's side as they reportedly broke with and threatened assassinations of each other as the Cold War dawned. Supplying Tito's insurgents, therefore, did not necessarily undermine Western interests any more than supporting the Red Army did, and may have been equally essential to furthering the Allied strategy of hastening victory. Yet surely both Tito and Mihailovic merited Allied aid if both were, in fact, involved in killing Nazi troops, the goal that should have received priority in both wartime London and Washington regardless of the ideology of the aid recipients. Klugmann and Burgess's wartime support for Tito, however, and their success in undermining London's support for Mihailovic indicates that the two agents, or, perhaps, their Kremlin superiors, nevertheless smiled upon the Yugoslav Communists with sufficient camaraderie as to help furnish them with British aid, to the detriment of the anti-Communist and anti-Nazi *Chetniks*. Parroting Maclean's perception of Tito, the *TIME* article proceeded to champion the Communist leader, portraying him for Americans as an outstanding war hero and a, "a man of decision" whose forces had, "struck the Germans at every chance, captured their supplies and arms."[196]

Stalin's smear campaigns against Chiang and Mihailovic could not have been effective without the help of agents of influence such as Adler, Klugmann, Burgess, White, and others. Nor could these men have succeeded in their quest to serve the Kremlin's interests without Roosevelt's gullibility towards Stalin (and, to an extent, Mao) and Churchill's truly followed a policy of, "even-handedness" in supplying the Yugoslav resistance.[197] Yet in each respective case, their disinformation campaigns were unwittingly aided by key non-Communist dupes such as Generals Stilwell and Maclean, whose negative perceptions of Chiang and Mihailovic influenced their leaders' policies that ultimately benefited the Communists in China and Yugoslavia.

Lend-Lease aid, therefore, served Allied and U.S. interests as intended and played no part in undermining postwar peace. It appears, however, that the actions of influential English-speaking Western officials serving in key governmental positions of power and acting as Stalin's agents contributed to a situation that helped undermine postwar peace by strengthening the Soviet Union's global strategic position, actions that had little to do with the Soviet Lend-Lease program and much to do with the ideological loyalties of some American and British officials. As previously noted, Vice President Wallace shared Roosevelt's desire to aid the Red Army and his underestimation of Stalin and preferred the advice of those with similar views, and he reportedly planned to promote Harry Dexter White to Treasury Secretary upon assuming the presidency.[198]

Due to a fortunate change in the Democratic Party ticket during the 1944 presidential election, Wallace did not remain vice president, and Harry S. Truman, a former United States senator from Missouri that had expressed his desire to see Hitler and Stalin destroy each other in 1941, rose to the position.[199] Yet Roosevelt, in increasingly ill health, continued to rely on those that shared his underestimation of Stalin's duplicitous nature and the Red Army's potential to occupy Eastern Europe into 1945, and during the Yalta Conference, he agreed to the likewise increasingly ill Hopkins's argument that "I don't think we should let them [the Soviets] down."[200] Suffering from his physical ailments like Hopkins, with only a short time left to live as Roosevelt nevertheless acted wisely in prosecuting the war and hastening its end by supplying Stalin's armies, even as he unfortunately (and perhaps unnecessarily?) conceded to a Soviet sphere of influence in Manchuria and Korea in the hopes of eventually obtaining Soviet participation against Japan.[201]

Roosevelt had already agreed to Stalin's demands regarding a pro-Soviet government in Poland at the November 1943 Tehran Conference, and at Yalta, he quickly agreed to the Soviet premier's offer to break his non-aggression pact with Hirohito and seize Japanese conquests in exchange for more Lend-Lease aid. Sensing success in obtaining Stalin's commitment to betraying his pact with Tokyo, Roosevelt hastily agreed to the Soviet leader's conditions, and he promptly gave General Deane a list of supplies sufficient to equip an army of 1,500,000 men by the Fourth Protocol's 30 June 1945 expiration. With no fear of interdiction by the Japanese Navy and Air Force, Stalin's U.S.-built Pacific merchant fleet transferred much of this material, totaling 1,066,140 tons, to Vladivostok in preparation for the assault that brought Soviet forces to the gates of two key East Asian capitals.[202]

After Roosevelt's death in April 1945, U.S. leaders continued to focus their efforts on ensuring Stalin's eventual participation in the war against Japan as Hitler and his mistress Eva Braun committed suicide in his Berlin bunker with Red Army troops only a short distance away and his genocidal Third Reich collapsing around them.[203] In July 1945, U.S. Secretary of State James F. Byrnes accompanied President Truman as Allied leaders gathered in the Berlin suburb of Potsdam to discuss postwar Europe and Soviet entry into the war against Japan. Byrnes noted Stalin's lack of concern after the president informed him of the atomic bomb's existence, a factor likely resulting from the Soviet atomic advances enabled by Hopkins's apparent authorization of extra-Lend-Lease uranium shipments and other materials.[204]

Following the Potsdam Conference, Stalin broke his pact with Emperor Hirohito and began deploying the Red Army to the borders of countries under Japanese occupation. On 9 August 1945, Soviet troops delivered a crushing surprise attack on the Japanese occupation forces in Manchuria, China, and

Korea, rapidly encircling entire Japanese armies, bypassing strongholds, and quickly capturing major cities.[205] Stalin annexed the Japanese territories of southern Sakhalin and the Kuril Islands and transferred excess war material acquired through Lend-Lease to Communist guerrillas in China and North Korea, enabling the rise of Mao Zedong and Kim Il Sung.[206]

Although American leaders, through their Lend-Lease program, had succeeded remarkably in helping remove the threat to the democratic Western world posed by Hitler and his Axis partners, they had failed in their attempts to inculcate in Stalin a more moderate, peaceful Soviet ruler. The more dangerous world that emerged in 1949 as Mao's Communists rose to power in mainland China and Stalin's scientists successfully tested the Soviet Union's first atomic bomb guaranteed the continuation of aggression and ushered in a new world full of horrifying new possibilities in the event of a third world war.[207] Despite Roosevelt and Hopkins's foresight and their noble attempts to prevent such a scenario, the global Cold War nevertheless began with Stalin's demands for more territorial concessions in Asia, Africa, and Latin America, the rise of powerful Communist Parties in Italy and France, and the exposure of Soviet agents in Washington.

While the trials of some prominent Soviet spies such as Alger Hiss captured national attention, Assistant Treasury Secretary Harry Dexter White opted to avoid such a fate by committing suicide after outliving his usefulness to Stalin after nearly physically assaulting, over lunch, Morgenthau's speechwriter Jonathan Mitchell as described in detail by John Koster.[208] After reportedly jumping to his feet, swinging his fists angrily, and nearly attacking Mitchell, whose sole lunchtime offense appears to have been not sharing White's positive views of Harold Laski's recently published, pro-Communist work *Faith, Reason, and Civilization*, White unwittingly exposed himself by openly bragging that he personally knew and admired several known Soviet agents and that he admired Stalin's successes in creating, "a new faith that would replace capitalism and Christianity" according to Koster.[209] White's, "towering rage" is said to have been contained only after, "three to four minutes" thanks to the intervention of another present colleague, Herbert Gaston, whose efforts to wrap his arms around and essentially dance with the Assistant Treasury Secretary and Soviet spy managed to restore an uneasy calm to the then-uncomfortable lunch meeting.[210] White subsequently and fatally overdosed on prescription digitalis on 16 August 1948 after incriminating himself three days earlier before an August 1948 HUAC hearing (that he arrogantly demanded) in which the young Congressman Richard Nixon (R-CA) played a key part in questioning the former Treasury Department economist.[211]

At a 21 February 1946 U.S. Senate session, Senator Styles Bridges (R-NH) called attention to recent reports of Soviet espionage in the United States and

Canada and expressed deep concern over Stalin's apparent success at subverting U.S. government officials and obtaining crucial secrets from them. Bridges quoted the statements made by former Ambassador Davies in which he said that Stalin's regime had the "moral" right to obtain military secrets, including atomic secrets, from its former allies in the West by any means, including theft.[212] The United States senator proceeded to cite three articles from the *Times-Herald*, the *Washington Daily News*, and the *New York Daily Mirror* discussing Davies's verbal defense of Moscow's espionage efforts and Canadian Prime Minister Mackenzie King's speech announcing the capture of several Soviet spies.[213]

Bridges then pointed to the case of an agent identified by the name of Shimishenko, who had been caught while attempting to purchase the blueprints for a new U.S.-designed jet aircraft. The New Hampshire senator then stated that while the FBI had sought to have Shimishenko arrested and charged, the State Department had intervened on the Soviet spy's behalf and allowed him to sail home with his wife on 6 January without the blueprints.[214] Bridges then emphasized the case of a second Soviet spy briefly detained in Bremerton, Washington who "not only had plans of the atomic bomb, but samples of the metal from which the bomb is made."[215] After stating that, "The agent had sailed for Russia," with atomic secrets on board and the State Department's approval despite various U.S. law enforcement agencies' attempts to charge him, Bridges concluded by assessing some Washington officials' desire to placate Stalin as a horrendous betrayal of U.S. national security tantamount to treason.[216]

In a 16 April 1946 House of Commons session, MP Colonel Sir Oliver Crosthwaite-Eyre asked Prime Minister Clement Attlee to provide Parliament with, "a comprehensive statement" of the material aid with which the British Empire had furnished the Soviet war effort, along with the financial cost of the aid, from 1 October 1941 until the Allied victory.[217] Calling attention to London's Official Report, Attlee proceeded to cite the figures of 5,218 tanks, including 1,388 Canadian vehicles and 7,411 aircraft, including 3,129 U.S. Lend-Lease planes, along with raw materials, machinery, medical equipment, and other items. Listing a financial sum of 428,000,000 British pounds' worth of cargo delivered to North Russia, a figure also cited in the British Naval Staff's report on the Arctic convoys, Attlee clarified that the official figures did not take into account the additional costs incurred by the Royal and Merchant Navies delivering the aid.[218] Stating that Nazi submarines, aircraft, and surface ships had menaced the mariners relentlessly, "especially on the route followed by the Northern Convoys," Attlee emphasized the "fortitude and endurance" of those whose efforts had ensured a steady stream of priceless aid to the Red Army totaling nearly 4,000,000 tons.[219]

In increasing aid to the Red Army's soldiers from the Third and Fourth Lend-Lease Protocols forward, U.S. Lend-Lease officials helped to hasten Hitler's defeat in Europe and liberate Hirohito's East Asian conquests, succeeding brilliantly in this regard.[220] Washington's successful 1943 expansion of ALSIB and the Persian Corridor had greatly helped in ensuring, from the American leadership's perspective, that Stalin's troops could continue to persevere, thereby greatly strengthening the Allied cause and sealing the doom of the Axis aggressors for the better of millions of innocent people in Europe, Asia, and elsewhere. In overestimating their own ability to charm Stalin and, in a sense, purchase his goodwill through unconditional Lend-Lease aid and several excessive non-Lend-Lease gestures, however, U.S. officials erred in assuming that their efforts sowed the seeds of postwar peace as their red warrior proceeded to act aggressively, betraying Roosevelt's wartime goodwill and sowing the seeds of later wars.[221]

CONCLUSION.
A comparative analysis of Roosevelt's Soviet Lend-Lease program and Reagan's Operation Cyclone and the rebirth of Lend-Lease for Ukraine's war effort

This work's five preceding chapters focus on U.S. perceptions of Stalin, wartime Washington's motives for prioritizing his and the Red Army's perceived needs, and the often-overlooked late-war contributions of the Arctic convoys in delivering Lend-Lease aid to North Russia. As also discussed in the previous chapter, Stalin (and his assets in Roosevelt's administration), acting on his own independent motives, appears to have found ways by which to acquire extra-Lend-Lease aid that further strengthened the Soviet Union in the form of materials needed for the construction of atomic bombs. He and his henchmen could not have achieved this without the carelessness of the non-Communists Roosevelt, Hopkins, and other American capitalists whose zeal for arming the Red Army furthered U.S. national interests by defeating the Axis while, other the other hand, leading them to jeopardize U.S. security by dangerously underestimating Stalin's capabilities and supplying him with non-conventional lethal aid that he did not require in order to defeat Hitler.[1]

As previously explained, the Soviet Lend-Lease program, reinforced by Roosevelt's determination to avoid a second Brest-Litovsk and keep the Red Army supplied and capable of bringing the war directly to Hitler's Reich, greatly hastened Nazi Germany's defeat. Without the program, including its 1943 and 1944 renewals by Congress that have been criticized by Sean McMeekin, the Allied Powers may have experienced a far longer and much bloodier war by depriving Stalin's soldiers and workers of the tools required for victory, ranging from American food, steel, and aluminum to Studebakers and Airacobras as argued by Lend-Lease experts such as Robert Jones, Mark Harrison, and Albert Weeks.[2] From the contemporary perspectives of Roosevelt, Hopkins, Stettinius, Standley, Deane, Hull, Rickenbacker, and other leading Americans, such a situation may have rendered a second Brest-Litovsk more likely and increased Nazi Germany's strength, leaving the Western Allies to face Berlin's wrath with no Red Army to sustain Hitler's fiercest attacks.[3]

While the U.S. wartime leadership cannot and must not be faulted for supporting Stalin's Red Army during the war, less overestimation of Washington's ability to buy his loyalty and goodwill may have reduced the effect of the Soviet espionage campaign conducted by White, Hiss, and other agents had Roosevelt considered his wartime Soviet ally's duplicitous tendencies. Yet the president does not appear to have considered this and, as indicated in his May 1944 conversation with George Earle, he continued underestimating Stalin's ability to keep the Red Army together and fighting even as he and Churchill prepared to launch Operation *Overlord* and open the long-awaited second front that Stalin, Molotov, Litvinov, and Maisky had consistently demanded.[4] Even as his administration continued to supply the Red Army in the hopes that doing so could contribute to its counterattacks on Hitler's forces and bring the battle to Berlin, Roosevelt seems to have believed that Stalin had abandoned aggression, and preferred to trust his own instincts in coaxing the Soviet premier to moderate his rule through the offer of unconditional aid and excessively generous, non-Lend-Lease gestures, instincts that proved incorrect in contrast to his foresight in defeating the Axis.[5]

As emphasized by Harrison and Weeks, the Soviet Lend-Lease program helped to significantly speed the Red Army's victories, and therefore, the ultimate Allied victory, over German and Japanese occupation forces in Eastern Europe and Northeast Asia.[6] This achievement cannot be denied, and it also set a precedent for later U.S. support programs for those resisting Soviet expansion as the Cold War proceeded to engulf the world and Roosevelt's White House successors confronted the Kremlin's rulers, with each superpower financing and arming their respective allies or proxies for much of the late twentieth century. In the 1980s, U.S. President Ronald Reagan faced a volatile international situation not unlike the one that Roosevelt had encountered, and he applied the earlier success of Soviet Lend-Lease in arming those resisting Soviet occupation most tenaciously, the Afghan resistance fighters.[7] This Conclusion discusses the Soviet Lend-Lease program's key similarities with and differences from Reagan's support for the Afghan insurgents before proceeding to briefly assess Washington's recent revival of Lend-Lease to support the Ukrainian military.[8] Readers who wish only to learn about U.S. perceptions of Stalin's strategic wartime role and who regard a comparison of American Lend-Lease aid to the Red Army with Reagan's covert action aid program for the Afghan insurgents as a mere side alley may prefer to skip this section, which I, the author, regard as very important, and skip ahead to this book's Epilogue, while those seeking to understand and appreciate an important and relevant lesson from history are encouraged to proceed into this Conclusion.

Anticipating Stalin's refusal to repay Lend-Lease aid in full as the global Cold War began, President Truman initially requested that the Soviet Union only reimburse the U.S. government for U.S. $2,500,000,000 to cover civilian supply costs.[9] In 1960, Nikita Khrushchev angrily refused an offer from the Eisenhower administration to pay $300,000,000 in exchange for the U.S. government writing off the remaining official $11,000,000,000.[10] Echoing Stalin's arguments for refusing to pay in 1945, Khrushchev stated that while Lend-Lease played a vital role, the Red Army had already paid its fair share by absorbing the bulk of Hitler's attacks.[11] More than two decades after Khrushchev's parroting of Stalin's well-worn excuse, President Ronald Reagan began negotiations with General Secretary Mikhail Gorbachev, and Reagan's White House successor George H. W. Bush later concluded an agreement with the Soviet leader to pay $300,000,000 within 30 years, a deadline finally reached by the Russian government in August 2006.[12]

Reagan had taken office in 1981 and, in a break with previous Cold War U.S. presidential administrations, quietly and calculatingly revisited the issue of Soviet Lend-Lease as he simultaneously sought to weaken Moscow's political and military influence in Asia, Africa, and Latin America while preparing the groundwork to negotiate an end to the global Cold War from a position of strength.[13] In the early 1980s, the new U.S. president, who is said to have remained vigorous and athletic throughout much of his presidency despite being the oldest man elected to serve in the Oval Office at that time, also faced a tense and dangerous international situation not unlike the era in which Roosevelt sought to counter Axis expansion by seeking out potential alliances, even with Stalin's totalitarian dictatorship. Between the time of Stalin's March 1953 death and Reagan's landslide election to the U.S. presidency in November 1980, the Kremlin's rulers, while not outwardly declaring an intent to conquer the globe, nevertheless undertook policies that appeared threatening to consecutive U.S. presidents and many Americans.[14] From geographically distant Pyongyang, North Korea to nearby Havana, Cuba, Soviet-backed tyrants from Kim Il Sung to Fidel Castro loudly spewed forth rage, hatred, and profanities against Washington's capitalist "Yankees" and, "imperialists" while singing Moscow's praises.[15]

From the contemporary U.S. perspective, totalitarianism appeared again to be alive, aggressive, and on the march just as it had been in the 1930s as Kremlin-backed politicians assumed the roles formerly occupied by fascists like Italy's Mussolini and Spain's Francisco Franco in aligning their regimes with one that many Americans rightly regarded as the greatest threat to their free, democratic way of life. In contrast to Roosevelt, however, Reagan, like other Cold War U.S. presidents, bore on his shoulders the responsibility of either carefully avoiding a nuclear exchange with the Kremlin or facing the possibility of unleashing a nuclear holocaust as the threat of war remained ever-present.[16] Like Roosevelt, Reagan clearly identified for the American public the potential enemy that remained the greatest threat to U.S. freedoms and national security, and, while avoiding nuclear war with Leonid Brezhnev's Soviet Union, he opted to expand his presidential predecessors' policies in arming those already resisting Moscow's aggression.[17]

Reagan's White House predecessor, U.S. President Jimmy Carter, had already begun a program of limited support for the Afghan guerrilla fighters resisting their country's Communist government.[18] In support of the besieged, brutal central government, which had come to power in an April 1978 coup, Soviet forces invaded and occupied Afghanistan in December 1979 in Operation *Storm-333*, an act that ultimately exacerbated Moscow's problems by galvanizing the growing resistance movement.[19] For many devout Muslims, the conflict constituted a just war of resistance against the Communist infidel occupiers and their apostate agents in the Afghan capital, Kabul, and Carter's administration began working with the government of neighboring Pakistan to furnish aid to the rebels.[20]

Initial aid deliveries to the Afghan fighters were, however, considerably small and were mocked and derided as insignificant by Pakistani President and military dictator General Muhammad Zia ul-Haq, himself the product of a successful 1977 military coup.[21] Yet while Carter and his National Security Advisor Zbigniew Brzezinski are sometimes said to have welcomed the Soviet military intervention in Afghanistan as a means by which to create mischief for the Kremlin, much as Roosevelt had sought to lure Stalin away from his pact with Hitler even before *Barbarossa*, the CIA's covert action aid program, called Operation *Cyclone*, received little support until after the first years of Reagan's presidency.[22] While hoping that the Soviet 40th Army could be bruised and, perhaps, somewhat bloodied by its Afghan military venture, many U.S. officials initially viewed the Afghan *mujahedin*, or "holy warriors," as hopelessly doomed, a position that they maintained well into the mid-1980s.[23] Moscow's mechanized military might in 1979, like Berlin's in 1941, appeared invincible to many U.S. officials, and as the Afghan fighters doggedly resisted the Soviet occupiers with comparatively far greater material disadvantages than the Red Army had fought the Nazi invaders with, many Western observers initially predicted their swift defeat.[24]

Just as some Americans, such as Congressmen Fish and Rich and Congresswoman Rogers, were initially uncertain about, or even opposed to, aiding the Red Army in its anti-Nazi struggle, so, too, were some Western observers, such as the Irish-American political journalist Alexander Cockburn, opposed to aiding the Afghan resistance in the early 1980s. After Soviet forces invaded Afghanistan, Cockburn is said to have voiced support for the Soviet 40th Army's occupation of the country, reportedly stating that, "We all have to go one day, but pray God let it not be over Afghanistan."[25] Cockburn reportedly proceeded to characterize Afghanistan as a primitive, backwards society that merited Soviet intervention and enlightenment, calling it, "An unspeakable country filled with unspeakable people, sheepshaggers and smugglers, who have furnished in their leisure hours some of the worst arts and crafts ever to penetrate the occidental world."[26] For good measure, Cockburn expressed sympathy for other people's suffering behind the Iron Curtain, concluding that, "I yield to none in my sympathy to those prostrate beneath the Russian [sic, Soviet] jackboot, but if ever a country deserved rape it's Afghanistan."[27]

Yet just as the news reports and photographs produced by Henry Cassidy, Margaret Bourke-White, Joseph Davies, and Leland Stowe portrayed the Red Army's soldiers as fighting, "for freedom" 40 years earlier, Debra Denker, Steve McCurry, Edward Girardet, Radek Sikorski, and Robert Kaplan echoed Reagan's assessment of the Afghan insurgents as, "freedom fighters."[28] Like their Second World War predecessors in Soviet territory, these journalists braved the war-torn Afghan frontier and, due to the Kremlin's alleged threat to kill Western journalists covering the resistance fighters and the constant aerial presence of Soviet attack helicopters, they arguably faced greater dangers in their war reporting.[29] McCurry's famous "Afghan girl" photograph of Sharbat Gula, whose bright green eyes stared hauntingly from the cover of the June 1985 *National Geographic* issue, combined with Denker's firsthand account of her conversations with insurgent commanders such as Ishaq Gailani to captivate readers.[30] Girardet's reporting from 1983 forward likewise told the story of Afghanistan's suffering under Soviet occupation and the war of resistance being waged by the various nationalistic, monarchist, and Islamist insurgent groups.[31]

Robert Kaplan's courageous coverage of the Afghan fighters in action, including their dogged defiance of a massive Soviet armored offensive against the rebel strongholds near Kandahar and the Soviet Air Force's merciless bombing of the region in 1987, also captured their tenacity for American readers.[32] Yet Moscow's hostility and constant campaign the seal off the Afghan-Pakistani border with relentless airpower and Special Forces interdiction raids endangered Denker, Kaplan, and their colleagues while their journalistic predecessors four decades before, except for Bourke-White's presence in the Kremlin during a Nazi bombing raid, faced no such threats.[33] As discussed previously, much of the war reporting by Stowe and Cassidy occurred in the immediate aftermath of battles once local Red Army commanders approved the Americans' presence, while the Afghan warriors escorting Sikorski, Denker, and Kaplan were constantly at risk. Despite the inherent obstacles to their frontline reporting, the few U.S. journalists covering the Afghan battlefields in the 1980s managed to bring home for their audiences a story of the Afghans' defiance of the odds in the same way that Soviet soldiers were once lauded by Americans as heroes, and, by 1988, films such as *Rambo III* appear to have begun applying this same heroic image to the rebels.[34]

Just as Roosevelt had immediately worked to prioritize and increase Soviet Lend-Lease aid in early 1942, Reagan managed to increase the flow of CIA-purchased ordnance and weaponry gradually and massively to the Afghan fighters from 1983 forward.[35] As pointed out by George Crile in *Charlie Wilson's War: The Extraordinary Story of How the Wildest Man in Congress and a Rogue CIA Agent Changed the History of Our Times*, other than Congressman Charles "Charlie" Wilson (D-TX), few U.S. officials expressed confidence in the Afghan resistance.[36] Yet Wilson's decisive action and his key position on the House Subcommittee for Defense Appropriations enabled him to gradually persuade his congressional colleagues to double the amount of aid being appropriated for the CIA's program. Despite his fierce public criticism of the CIA, Senator Gordon J. Humphrey (R-NH) also became a staunch supporter of the Afghan resistance as he and Wilson led a small but potent group of congressional activists that promoted their cause on the House and Senate floors.[37]

Yet due to the limitations placed on CIA operations following the agency's alleged role in the Watergate scandal of the early 1970s, Reagan and CIA Director William J. "Bill" Casey could not operate as quickly as Roosevelt and Hopkins had done 40 years earlier in support of Stalin's Red Army.[38] Nor could the president adopt the same blank check approach and immediately begin shipping the Afghan guerrillas countless tons of U.S. war material as Roosevelt had done for the Red Army through Soviet Lend-Lease. Rather, circumstances such as the always pressing need to avoid a nuclear war or a Soviet invasion of Pakistan forced Reagan and Casey to proceed with caution, despite both men being at least as zealous in their approach to repulsing aggressive Soviet Communism as Roosevelt and Hopkins had been in reversing the Axis tide.[39] Reagan's National Security Decision Directive Number Seventy-Five (NSDD-75) that he issued on 17 January 1983 enabled Casey's CIA to greatly increase the aid delivered to the Afghan fighters through Pakistan's military intelligence agency Inter-Services-Intelligence (ISI).[40]

In compliance with congressional concerns and oversight, however, NSDD-75 continued the Carter policy by permitting the CIA to supply only Soviet-designed arms to the Afghan fighters, weaponry reportedly purchased from the Egyptian and Chinese governments, to maintain a level of U.S. deniability if the rebels managed to kill a Soviet general.[41] Unlike Stalin's soldiers, the Afghan warriors fighting in the ranks of the Sunni Islamist insurgent groups led by men such as Gulbuddin Hekmatyar, Abdul Rasul Sayyaf, Jalaluddin Haqqani, and *Mawlawi* Muhammad Yunis Khalis could not expect to freely receive, with no strings attached, Washington's latest war technology.[42] Senator Humphrey remained a strong supporter of Operation *Cyclone*, but unlike Congressman Wilson, he reportedly maintained a largely critical public stance on the CIA's activities and ensured the agency's cooperation with the post-Watergate senatorial oversight. While the Reagan administration managed to deliver a limited number of heat-seeking FIM-92 "Stinger" anti-aircraft missiles from September 1986 forward, thanks to Wilson and Humphrey's persuading of many of their key congressional and senatorial colleagues, the rebels mainly fought with Soviet weaponry.[43]

While a potent morale-boosting weapon that certainly helped the Afghan guerrillas to inflict greater losses on Soviet jet aircraft and attack helicopters, the Stinger ultimately did little to force Moscow's retreat from Afghanistan. As pointed out by Professors Mark Galeotti, Rodric Braithwaite, and Artemy Kalinovsky, Gorbachev had already decided in late 1985, albeit after escalating the campaign, to eventually withdraw the 40th Army after attempting to sufficiently cripple the insurgency, nearly a year before the Stinger's battlefield introduction, due to the determined resistance of the Afghan fighters.[44] By contrast, the Red Army Air Forces' pilots in the Second World War could consistently count on huge deliveries of U.S. fighter planes, particularly the thousands of prized P-39s that Roosevelt dutifully shipped to Stalin, and American aluminum shipments contributed to the continued production of attack aircraft. The Afghan resistance fighters, by contrast, faced a constant uphill battle as the Stinger inflicted losses but could not diminish the Soviet Air Force's air supremacy over their embattled, occupied country, whereas the immense authority granted to Roosevelt by Lend-Lease helped ensure that Stalin's airmen remained capable of constantly contesting Hitler's air superiority.[45]

The senatorial oversight of CIA operations that prevailed after Watergate, in addition to the vitally important need to prevent an escalation and potential nuclear confrontation with Moscow, forced Reagan and Casey's CIA to work closely with, and rely heavily on, Pakistan's ISI in arming the Afghan resistance fighters.[46] As pointed out by Geoffrey Wawro in *Quicksand: America's Pursuit of Power in the Middle East*, the Pakistani military leadership had long regarded Afghanistan as the key location on which they could rely for, "strategic depth" in the event of a conventional invasion by their main and most hated regional rival, New Delhi's Indian Army.[47] The presence of Soviet occupation forces on Afghan soil denied the Pakistan Army access to this large, crucial rear area from which its soldiers could have otherwise been able to regroup and refit in such a scenario.[48]

Just as Roosevelt had emphasized to Churchill and others the need to arm and feed Stalin's soldiers without question and attach no conditions to Soviet Lend-Lease aid as the Red Army appeared to be the most ruthless and effective anti-Nazi force, President Zia and ISI General Akhtar Abdul Rahman Khan regarded the four fundamentalist Afghan resistance factions as indispensable allies.[49] General Akhtar, an ethnic Pashtun like most of the Afghan Islamist insurgent commanders, reportedly viewed the four major fundamentalist guerrilla factions as the most determined, dedicated, and ruthless in fighting the Soviet occupiers and their Afghan puppet rulers. His and Zia's underestimation of the motivations and capabilities of the most militant Afghan Islamist factions appears to have ultimately boomeranged harmfully on their successors in Islamabad as recently as November 2022, with the Pakistani Taleban (*Tehrik-e-Taleban Pakistan* or TTP) leadership renouncing its truce with the government and renewing its insurgency in Baluchistan Province and elsewhere.[50]

For his part, Zia appears to have concluded that by implementing some components of the Islamic laws, or *Shariah*, that he could satisfy the demands of the Afghan and Pakistani Sunni Islamist groups and keep them focused on fighting infidels, rather than the Islamabad government, after the Soviet-Afghan War.[51] Like Roosevelt in his underestimation of Stalin's duplicity and rigid ideological commitment to enforcing and spreading Communism, Zia seems to have erred in his miscalculation in assuming that the Islamist insurgents could, in essence, be "bought" with unconditional wartime support. Yet just as with Roosevelt's limited options four decades earlier, to the Pakistani military leadership of the 1980s – surrounded at the time on all sides by hostile governments in New Delhi, Tehran, and Kabul, as has very often been the case for much of Pakistan's tumultuous history – there appeared to be few acceptable alternatives at the time in ousting the Kabul regime and its Soviet protectors and enablers, a mission on which the ISI reportedly embarked after the Communist coup in 1978 in the goal of serving Islamabad's immediate national interests and most pressing needs.[52] In 1983, the ethnic Tajik commander Ahmed Shah Massoud, described as moderate by many scholars, concluded a temporary truce with the Soviets, allowing the 40th Army's commanders to refocus their efforts in an ultimately unsuccessful but nevertheless brutal and destructive offensive against the Pashtun-led Afghan Islamist insurgents.[53]

From General Akhtar's perspective, Massoud's action understandably rendered him an unreliable asset and unfit to receive further CIA-ISI aid as it temporarily endangered Pakistan's most pressing contemporary national interests and regional strategy by freeing more Soviet forces to attack the Islamist strongholds in rural southern and eastern Afghanistan and across the Pakistani border.[54] Somewhat constrained by congressional oversight, the constant threat of nuclear escalation, and Islamabad's concerns over a potential full-scale Soviet invasion of Pakistan, Reagan and Casey naturally deferred to the ISI regarding which Afghan groups merited the most aid.[55] The Pakistani leadership tended to regard the more hardline Islamist factions as those fielding the most tenacious fighters that were fully committed to defeating the atheist infidels occupying a traditional Muslim country. Like the Red Army's soldiers in the Second World War, these zealous men sought no compromise and remained firmly focused on driving the perceived threat to their faith, families, and mosques from Afghan soil no matter the cost, and fought doggedly and ruthlessly despite facing overwhelming Soviet air supremacy, armor, and Special Forces.[56]

Just as Roosevelt and Hopkins had relied upon Joseph Davies's advice to attach no conditions to Soviet Lend-Lease aid and were influenced from the beginning by his warnings of a second Brest-Litovsk if Stalin were overthrown or forced to negotiate with Hitler, Reagan administration officials made the decision they felt best served U.S. strategic interests.[57] By deferring to, rather than interfering with, their Pakistani counterparts in supplying the Afghan factions that they deemed the most dependable and deserving aid recipients, Casey's officers allowed ISI's small, 200-man logistical unit to move the ordnance and arms more effectively to the fighters based in Peshawar.[58] Many key congressional supporters of Operation *Cyclone* are also said to have regarded the decision as a necessary means by which Washington could claim some limited deniability and prevent tensions with Moscow from escalating to an even more dangerous, nuclear-level degree.[59] While Wilson and Humphrey remained staunch congressional supporters of the Afghan cause, they nevertheless thought it wise to compromise somewhat, at least officially, in debates on the need to supply the insurgents with Soviet-designed small arms while allowing ISI to prioritize its preferred aid recipients.[60]

According to General Akhtar's former wartime head of ISI's "Afghan Bureau," Brigadier Mohammad Yousaf, the Pakistan Army deployed into forward positions along the Afghan border in 1983 due to Islamabad's fears of an imminent Soviet invasion as the Kremlin leadership under General Secretary and former KGB Chairman Yuri Andropov escalated its campaign.[61] Soviet forces increasingly conducted interdiction raids against insurgent supply caravans crossing the Hindu Kush mountains with arms, ordnance, and food for the fighters, causing the frequent bombing and strafing of Pakistani border villages by the Soviet Air Force.[62] In this tense and dangerous international atmosphere that U.S. and Pakistani leaders viewed as potentially leading to a third world war inevitably accompanied by nuclear horrors, a reality that Roosevelt did not have to confront, Reagan and Casey, along with many U.S. congressmen, logically concluded that ISI should be granted unhindered authority to distribute aid to the fighters.[63]

Much of this aid is said to have traveled to the Pakistani port city of Karachi in CIA cargo ships, while some weaponry occasionally arrived via U.S., Saudi, and Chinese Air Force planes to Islamabad, and it took time for ISI's small logistical department to transport and distribute the arms and ordnance to the rebel organizations based in Peshawar on the Afghan border.[64] It therefore appeared to Casey as more practical not to interfere and increase tensions with the Pakistani leadership at the local level as Akhtar's ISI ruthlessly forbade the CIA from contact with the insurgents, likely knowing of the anti-Western outlook of the Islamists. Just as Hopkins feared that attaching conditions to Lend-Lease aid could offend Stalin and wreck the alliance, Casey opted to keep tensions with Akhtar's ISI to a minimum as the Pakistani people and their leaders were the ones bearing the risk of receiving Moscow's full fury if the Kremlin chose to launch an invasion of their country.[65]

As with Roosevelt's total war approach to Nazi Germany's defeat, Reagan and Casey sought to arm those that they regarded as most effective in fighting the greater immediate threat to U.S. interests at the time. In their approach to Soviet-occupied Afghanistan, they walked a deadly tightrope as they balanced the need to aid those already resisting Soviet aggression in wearing down the occupiers while preventing an escalation that could, from their contemporary perspective, trigger a nuclear holocaust.[66] Like Roosevelt's praise for the Red Army, Reagan offered rhetorical support for the Afghan cause, acknowledging the insurgents' struggle in yearly "Afghanistan Day" declarations while U.S. Undersecretary of State for Political Affairs Michael H. Armacost persistently engaged in diplomatic efforts to affect a Soviet withdrawal.[67] Beginning with a 16 November 1983 letter to the Presidium of the Supreme Soviet, Reagan also prepared the groundwork for discussing Soviet Lend-Lease repayments, and, after many negotiations with Gorbachev later in the decade, the president's White House successor, George H. W. Bush, eventually won Moscow's commitment to pay $300,000,000 and settle the issue.[68]

Perhaps most crucial to a comparison with Soviet Lend-Lease is the fact that while the Afghan insurgent factions received a tremendous amount of U.S. and Saudi governmental aid through Pakistan's ISI, whether hailing from nationalist, monarchist, or Islamist resistance parties, they, as with the Red Army and Soviet Lend-Lease, do not appear to have been oversupplied and turned into a threat to Western security interests through Operation *Cyclone*. The U.S., Saudi, and Pakistani governments contributed a truly considerable amount of aid to the Afghan insurgents during the Soviet-Afghan War that helped the guerrillas to inflict a painful lesson on their opponents.[69] Yet this aid did not enable the Islamist fighters of Hekmatyar, Sayyaf, Khalis, or Haqqani to flood into Soviet Central Asia to liberate their oppressed Muslim brethren as their militant Sunni Islamist ideologies mandated.[70] Instead, the various Afghan insurgent factions turned on each other as the Soviet troops retreated, even as they fought against and eventually overthrew the Communist regime in 1992. While the Taleban leadership later aided Sunni Islamist groups in the former Soviet republics between 1996 and 2001, they lacked the same level of Washington-produced-and-supplied weaponry that had gradually made a difference in the Red Army's earlier wartime struggle, all for the better.[71]

Limited congressional controls and President Reagan's promotion of, "peace through strength," with his emphasis on the latter being a key means by which to attain the more desirable former, appear to have guided the CIA in arming the Afghan fighters to resist and oust the Soviet occupiers, serving *Cyclone's* purpose just as Soviet Lend-Lease had done earlier.[72] Had Roosevelt operated in a similarly restrained atmosphere 40 years earlier in wartime Washington, however, U.S. officials may have had a more difficult time in arming Stalin, and the Second World War may have dragged on considerably longer. Yet wartime Washington had granted Roosevelt immense authority through Lend-Lease, and once U.S. forces were attacked at Pearl Harbor and Congress declared war on the Axis, restraint became a non-issue, and the White House could dramatically increase its Soviet aid program, paving the way for the hastening of the Allied victory.[73] The fears of U.S. officials that Stalin could be forced to conclude a separate peace with Berlin led to the expansion of Lend-Lease deliveries through the Persian Corridor and ALSIB, even as the Arctic convoys persisted in their North Russian journeys, hastening Hitler's defeat as required by Washington's total war strategy.[74]

With a large but more limited amount of Western material aid than that delivered to the Red Army four decades earlier, the Afghan insurgents nevertheless managed to resist, outfight, and wear down the Soviet 40th Army of occupation and thereby contributed somewhat to Moscow's economic woes and the Soviet Union's subsequent collapse in 1991.[75] While ISI's arming of the Afghan fundamentalists with CIA-purchased weaponry is sometimes alleged to have boomeranged to Washington and Islamabad's detriment later, this assertion, like the idea that Soviet Lend-Lease aid turned the Red Army into an anti-Western threat, seems far-fetched. Reagan and Zia's wartime support for the Islamic guerrillas proved limited enough to keep Taleban fighters from later overrunning and raising their white flag over their Central Asian neighbors to the north and, moreover, the Afghan Sunni Islamist leaders, like Stalin earlier, exercised their own independent agency in pursuing their ultimate military aims and ideological objectives in furthering the perceived interests of their people.[76] The Red Army, in contrast to the Afghan Islamists, proved capable of not only counterattacking the Nazis but eventually driving into Europe and Asia to bring the battle to the Axis heartlands. Accordingly, just as most scholars seem to agree that it cannot be said that U.S. Lend-Lease aid "created" the Soviet threat, it seems at least as unlikely that Reagan and Casey's *Cyclone* somehow birthed the Afghan and Pakistani Deobandi Islamist militancy which, like Soviet Communism before the 1941 Nazi attack, already existed locally long before the Soviet invasion and the White House's subsequent response.[77]

Motivated by their militant, fundamentalist Deobandi and Salafist interpretations of Sunni Islamic law, the major Afghan Islamist insurgent leaders such as Hekmatyar, Sayyaf, and Haqqani also desired to eventually liberate their beleaguered Muslim brethren in former Soviet Central Asia after driving the Soviet occupiers from Afghan soil.[78] Due to the limitations that Cold War realities imposed on contemporary Washington's 1980s' covert action aid program, however, the Afghan rebels – nationalists, royalists, and Islamists alike – could not hope to receive the same massive degree of U.S. material support that Cordell Hull had demanded the Red Army be furnished with following Hitler's invasion and which Roosevelt, Hopkins, and their subordinates promptly began providing to Stalin, their ruthless red warrior, in his country's hour of need.[79] Yet the considerable arms and ordnance that Reagan's officials delivered to the Afghan warriors, even as they carefully balanced their aid program with the perceived necessity of not provoking nuclear-armed Moscow too greatly, proved both sufficient and effective in bloodying the 40th Army and hastening the Kremlin's retreat from Afghanistan. The Islamic guerrillas, like the Red Army of the 1940s, fought doggedly to defend their homes, faith, families, and brethren regardless of whether Washington intended to provide a nickel in support of their wartime resistance to the Soviet invasion and occupation.[80] Yet, as with Lend-Lease aid to the Red Army earlier, CIA-ISI support for the Afghan fighters via Operation *Cyclone* helped the defending side to exact a more painful price on the aggressors, rendering the struggle less costly overall in terms of blood and destruction than it otherwise may have been.[81]

To be sure, there are key differences between Reagan and Casey's increased support for Operation *Cyclone* and Roosevelt and Hopkins's prioritization of Soviet Lend-Lease aid. A difference in historical eras is perhaps the most obvious case in point here, and the fact that Roosevelt's administration faced a raging, fast-paced global war may, at first glance, cause a comparison of the Soviet Lend-Lease program with *Cyclone* to appear somewhat superficial in places. Yet it must also be remembered, however, that Reagan's administration, too, faced a threatening global menace, even if in the form of a Cold War rather than a hot, shooting war with the militarily vaunted, nuclear Soviet superpower, and in some ways, the threat in the 1980s appears to have been even more frightening in the sense that one false move could potentially trigger horrific, global destruction. As mentioned previously, Reagan's presidential predecessors in the 1970s had overseen an era in which Brezhnev's Soviet regime had shored up Communist governments and insurgencies across Asia, Africa, and Latin America, with a Soviet combat brigade discovered training in neighboring Cuba in September 1979.[82] From the 1980s' U.S. leadership's contemporary perspective, Moscow's invasion and occupation of Afghanistan that commenced in December 1979 appeared as earth-shattering as Hitler's invasion of Stalin's Soviet Union had in June 1941 and provided a similar, critical opportunity to aid resistance fighters that were already persevering in the field in weakening a global aggressor that understandably appeared at the time to many U.S. officials as the greatest threat to both their nation's security and that of their international allies.[83]

By February 1987, Casey's CIA Directorate of Intelligence (DI) could rightly and proudly state in a now-declassified report that Soviet forces, while remaining merciless and brutal in conducting their counterinsurgency operations, had suffered significant casualties at the hands of the insurgents, an outcome hastened by Reagan's increased support for the Afghan fighters via his authorship of NSDD-166 in 1985. The DI's assessment prepared for Casey proceeded to emphasize the need to maintain support for the rebels as their tenacity and refusal to stop fighting had proved lethal to the Soviet economy as well as the 40th Army's operations by rendering the Kremlin's war more financially costly.[84] Like the Red Army's defeat of the Nazi invaders, the Afghan fighters achieved a hard-fought victory over the Soviet occupiers, and they arguably did so against even greater odds and with comparably more limited help overall from Washington's leadership.[85]

The necessity of avoiding a potential Soviet invasion of Pakistan or even a nuclear exchange by limiting CIA-supplied weaponry to Soviet designs, at least until the Soviet-Afghan War's final stages, served as a control mechanism of sorts on the Reagan administration's efforts to manage its covert action aid program.[86] Even the Stinger missiles shipped to the Afghan rebels, first supplied to Commander Mohammad Afzal's guerrillas on 25 September 1986, are said to have totaled only 1,000 by the end of the war, not all of which were delivered into rebel hands.[87] Yet while limited in scope compared to Soviet Lend-Lease, Operation *Cyclone* served its purpose in upgrading the Afghan warriors' small arms arsenal to include AK-47 assault rifles in addition to their antiquated Lee Enfields while avoiding, sometimes barely, a much more deadly and open confrontation with Moscow. The Afghan fighters, including many zealots hailing from the four major militant Islamist factions that, like Stalin's Red Army, were later identified by U.S. leaders as implacable anti-Western foes, ensured that the CIA could report a major success story on the Soviet 40th Army's growing casualties by February 1987.[88]

As the senior Reagan administration officials sought to avoid a full confrontation with the Kremlin while simultaneously acting to reverse its political and military advances in South Asia and the Middle East and undermine its outposts there, they could not rely on the full, unbridled war production of U.S. industry to supply the Afghan fighters persevering despite the odds.[89] Tiptoeing carefully, they nevertheless provided significant aid from their purchases of Soviet-manufactured weaponry in various countries, inherently limiting the amount of material that the rebels could receive until late in the war, while the Afghan rebels fought, bled, and waged a victorious insurgency.[90] By contrast, U.S. leaders during the Second World War were able to ship to Stalin's forces thousands of combat planes, including the almost 5,000 P-39s alone, and nearly 500,000 transport vehicles, along with thousands of tanks and millions of pounds of food, fuel, and raw materials that U.S. war production workers supplied to the Soviet Lend-Lease program.[91]

Supplying the Afghan resistance, while a tremendous and successful task, did not result in the Islamist fighters of Sayyaf, Haqqani, or Hekmatyar reaching, capturing, and flying their black banners over Dushanbe, Tashkent, Bishkek, Astana, or other Central Asian capitals in the name of liberating their beleaguered, oppressed Muslim brethren there.[92] In contrast to Reagan, Casey, Wilson, Humphrey, Zia, and Akhtar, Roosevelt, Hopkins, and Stettinius enjoyed the full and virtually unrestrained authority given to the president and his aides by wartime Washington and could fully back Stalin's armies, "to the hilt" as demanded by Secretary Hull as early as summer 1941.[93] The U.S. war effort and public backing of many officials served the admirable purpose of boosting the Allied cause in ensuring that Stalin's soldiers, like the Afghan fighters four decades later, could continue killing the greater contemporary enemies of the free world in the numbers needed to hasten victory. Arming the Soviets with conventional American-made material helped to achieve the Allied victory in the Second World War, while Roosevelt and Hopkins's inexplicable decision to also supply Stalin with atomic bomb-building materials contributed to a more dangerous postwar world. This second, seemingly indefensible action doubtlessly strengthened the Soviet premier's atomic program and may have emboldened his decision to keep the red flags flying over the Eurasian capitals into which his troops and tanks advanced rather than allowing the free elections that he had promised Roosevelt at Yalta.[94]

Occurring roughly four decades apart, the twentieth-century experiences of the U.S. presidential administrations of Roosevelt and Reagan in supplying the forces that each respective president and his top advisers perceived as most actively and effectively resisting those they deemed the greater threat to U.S. national interests offer crucial lessons for today's leaders. Roughly 40 years after the Reagan White House began increasing the flow of CIA aid to the Afghan rebels in their anti-Soviet struggle, Russian troops invaded Ukraine ostensibly to support the Russian-speaking separatist groups resisting the Kiev government in the country's eastern regions.[95] Western powers led by the administration of U.S. President Joe Biden launched an immediate effort to support the Ukrainian forces resisting Moscow's military incursion, and the war has since grown in ferocity with no apparent end in sight.[96]

While an extremely recent and current event at the time of writing, the ongoing war in Ukraine has, thus far, demonstrated many parallels with Roosevelt's approach to Soviet Lend-Lease in the Second World War, and although it remains far too early to determine the ways in which events may unfold, today's decision-makers must keep history's lessons in mind. U.S. officials reportedly predicted the Kremlin's operation in Ukraine shortly before it occurred on 24 February 2022 and, like their distant predecessors in the early 1940s and early 1980s, respectively, they grimly expected the invaders to achieve a swift conventional victory. In the weeks before the invasion, the Biden administration and its NATO allies appear to have expected to begin arming a Ukrainian insurgency that could resist the Russian Army in much the same way that Reagan had increased U.S. support for the Afghan rebels.[97] Yet the government of Ukrainian President Volodymir Zelensky did not fall as Russian President Vladimir Putin's forces advanced, and U.S. officials unexpectedly and quickly found themselves supplying a conventional army, navy, and air force in the manner of Roosevelt's Soviet Lend-Lease program.[98]

Like Reagan and his senior advisers, however, Biden and the Washington leadership of the early 2020s must carefully walk a fine line as they nevertheless seek to strengthen Zelensky's military capabilities and supply Kiev's war effort and thereby weaken a potential adversary that they have identified as such and reverse its perceived geostrategic gains.[99] Russia's conventional and nuclear arsenal remains a massive, vaunted, and potentially destructive force in the modern world, and, on several occasions since the war's outbreak in 2022, President Putin's occasional allusions to nuclear war have trigged alarm bells in Washington and elsewhere. The Russian leader reportedly made such statements in response to the West's ongoing and increasing aid to Zelensky, and, at the time of writing, tensions continue to rise to frightening levels reminiscent of the 1962 Cuban Missile Crisis or the 1983 Operation *Able Archer '83* escalation.[100]

While Biden's officials, like Reagan's four decades ago, grapple with the realities imposed on them by a nuclear-armed menace, one that is said to mutually perceive Washington's actions as aggressive and threatening acts, they also face a situation that is strikingly like Roosevelt's as they attempt to sufficiently equip a conventional military to repulse aggression.[101] The tremendous authority granted by Congress to the Roosevelt White House in 1941 allowed the administration to begin producing and delivering massive war aid to the Red Army, while post-Watergate congressional oversight and Moscow's nuclear arsenal prevented Reagan and his team from flooding the Afghan fighters with the same level of U.S.-designed arms and ordnance. Regardless, Operation *Cyclone* achieved its purpose many times over by contributing somewhat to the Soviet Union's defeat in Afghanistan and subsequent demise, as Reagan, Casey, and their congressional allies hoped, while Soviet Lend-Lease helped render the Second World War less costly in Allied lives and material.[102]

Evoking memories of Roosevelt's support program for Stalin's Red Army more than 80 years ago, the U.S. Congress reportedly granted similar authority to President Biden in summer 2022 and dubbed it Lend-Lease in support of the

Ukrainian war effort.[103] Like their historical predecessors, Biden and his aides now face the choice of how to best execute their mission of supplying Zelensky's military forces as they face a powerful foe whose capabilities and resources appear to remain abundant. As with Reagan's calculated approach to Afghan rebel aid between 1981 and 1989, they must also do so while weighing the risks of provoking Moscow too greatly and inadvertently pushing the Kremlin's anger to dangerous, irrational levels while arming those actively resisting its advances.[104]

Biden's team, however, does not currently face the need to arm a Ukrainian insurgency as many officials appear to have initially expected during the first weeks of Russia's intervention, but rather must determine how to supply Zelensky's conventional military forces more effectively as his government remains in power and fighting.[105] The newly revived Lend-Lease program, like its 1940s' predecessor, appears to grant Biden the authority to do so if the president determines the defense of Ukraine to be vital to the defense of the United States. Mirroring Roosevelt's view of Stalin's Soviet Union, the Biden administration currently appears to consider support for Kiev as crucially important to U.S. security, and, according to an earlier statement by U.S. Secretary of Defense General Lloyd Austin, hopes to "weaken" Putin's government in the process.[106]

Yet the lengths to which today's Washington is willing to go in arming Zelensky's anti-Putin struggle is uncertain and, like the outcome and continued prosecution of the war itself, is likely to remain unpredictable for quite some time. It seems apparent, however, that in applying the term "Lend-Lease" to Washington's current military aid program for Ukraine, U.S. lawmakers are sufficiently aware of the connotations that such labels convey, and today's Kremlin leadership, like its predecessors, is doubtlessly aware of the program's role in defeating Hitler.[107] While they may no longer wish to contradict the former Stalinist line and admit it publicly, the Kremlin's post-Soviet leaders are likely aware of the effectiveness of American Lend-Lease on the Eastern Front in the Second World War. Congress's recent revival of the program is likely a signal to Moscow as much as to Kiev and NATO capitals that the current administration intends to follow in the footsteps of Roosevelt's legacy in fighting perceived threats to U.S. national interests.[108]

Yet the question remains as to how far most of today's Americans and their leaders are prepared or willing to go in such a total, all-out effort short of a third world war in arming Zelensky's government and armed forces. Deep partisan political divides in the country and within the government currently seem to have many Americans supporting Washington's Ukraine policy, with many others advocating a more cautious approach.[109] Some U.S. lawmakers, such as Senator Rand Paul (R-KY), have resisted the administration's efforts to arm

Ukraine as far too costly to American taxpayers, particularly at a time of economic inflation, rising energy costs, and increasing scarcity of consumer commodities. On 12 May 2022, Senator Paul temporarily delayed a U.S. Senate bill to rush a U.S. $40,000,000,000 aid package to Ukraine by proposing the inclusion of an inspector general to monitor the program's spending efforts, angering congressional supporters of the administration's policy.[110]

Reportedly declaring, "My oath is to the U.S. Constitution, not to any foreign nation," Paul concluded his arguments against his senatorial colleagues' decision to send the aid package as urgent and thereby bypass standard, non-emergency congressional procedure by declaring, "We cannot save Ukraine by dooming the U.S. economy."[111] Both long before and since the time of Paul's speech on the U.S. Senate floor, many Americans have remained deeply divided over a range of political and social issues, including the need to support Ukraine's struggle. As the war continues to ravage parts of the large Eastern European country each day, reportedly resulting in mass power outages, food shortages, and civilian deaths, few Americans can deny that horrors continue to be inflicted on countless innocents as in other ongoing conflicts.[112]

The level to which the Biden administration is willing to fuel Zelensky's war effort, however, remains elusive as U.S. and NATO leaders continue to balance their support for the Ukrainian struggle with the need to prevent an escalation with Moscow and the potential destruction of large parts of Eurasia and North America. Just as the horrifying prospects of nuclear war or an invasion of Pakistan forced the Reagan administration to remain cautious yet steady in its support for the Afghan resistance, so, too, must Biden's aides balance the need to keep the war in Ukraine from spreading into NATO countries.[113] Roosevelt did not face such frightening realities in supplying Stalin's war effort and, blissfully free of the fear that one dangerous move could radiate and virtually destroy the world, his officials could move unrestrained in their efforts and began doing so very shorty after Hitler's invasion.[114]

Yet, as they continue working to arm Ukraine's military for a potentially protracted struggle ahead in the absence of peace terms deemed acceptable to both Kiev and Moscow, U.S. leaders must decide on the ultimate objective of their new Lend-Lease program of the early 2020s. Considering the latest developments, it may be fair and proper for U.S. officials to ask the question of how long they intend to maintain their flow of weaponry to Zelensky's soldiers.[115] Is Washington's strategic objective the ultimate defeat of the Russian Army by Ukrainian hands, or do U.S. leaders simply hope to damage Putin's image at home and abroad by making the war somewhat costlier on his government and reducing the perceived threat from today's Moscow? Clear and complete answers to these questions presently appear to be far from forthcoming, yet the fact remains that Washington has revived Lend-Lease in support of a leader whose country continues resisting its powerful adversary.[116]

In arming Ukraine, are U.S. officials seeking to protect the growing number of NATO countries in Europe by reversing Russia's advances, like Roosevelt and Reagan in their respective aid programs, or are Western leaders simply hoping, like some officials in each previously mentioned president's administration, to hand the perceived assailants a pyrrhic victory at best? While it is hoped that U.S. officials have the best interests of the American people and other innocents on their minds as they consider all possibilities, these questions merit their daily consideration. Like Roosevelt and Reagan, they must clearly define decisive victory and what constitutes success for U.S. national interests in the current crisis and have, perhaps, already done so. If Biden's administration determines the unquestioned, total defeat of Russia's army to be its objective in aiding Ukraine's forces, then it will likely supply an enormous amount of material to ensure to the best of its ability that Kiev can accomplish the task.[117]

The congressional lawmakers whose efforts have resulted in a new Lend-Lease program for Zelensky's Ukraine must also decide on the level of oversight that they wish to apply in executing the president's aid program, and the war's progress, for better or worse, is likely to influence such decisions to an extent.[118] Whether the program proceeds in the same way that it has thus far in 2022, 2023, and 2024 (that is, up to the time of writing), with some officials risking Putin's ire in their proposals to ship Ukraine even more deadly U.S. missiles capable of reaching military targets on Russian soil and others expressing a growing weariness with Washington's involvement, remains to be seen, as do the depths to which they are prepared to go in arming Zelensky's war effort.[119]

While today's realities appear far removed from those of the increasingly distant past, military aggression and warfare remain a key part of daily life for millions of people throughout the world, and U.S. leaders are, perhaps, more committed than ever to undermining potential adversaries by supporting those currently resisting them. As in the past, today's leaders must balance the risks and dangers involved in such endeavors that they execute in the apparent belief that such policies continue to serve U.S. national interests.[120] Yet, with history's lessons as their guides, decision-makers can likewise endeavor to both replicate the successes of their predecessors and simultaneously work to avoid repeating their counterproductive mistakes and assumptions.[121]

The respective lessons of Roosevelt's Soviet Lend-Lease program and Reagan's increased support for Operation *Cyclone* appear to demonstrate that a steady stream of effective material aid, even if somewhat limited, can potentially alter situations to Washington's strategic advantage by ensuring that those under attack or occupation can resist and outfight their oppressors and hasten victory. Both historical examples likewise demonstrate that U.S. leaders cannot, however, expect that their support can, in any way, buy the friendship and allegiance of foreign fighting forces once they have defeated their oppressors.[122] A Soviet propaganda poster from the 1980s insensitively depicted a bearded Afghan fighter's turban as being formed by an endless stream of U.S. dollar bills, a portrayal that seems at least as applicable, perhaps, to an image of a Second World War Red Army soldier's battle helmet. Keeping the Soviets well-supplied during the Second World War helped the Allies to shorten the path to victory, and, in this sense, Soviet Lend-Lease appears to have foreshadowed Reagan's 1980s' success with Operation *Cyclone* as each respective aid program helped those then resisting the greater threat to the West to emerge triumphantly over their foes.[123]

As seen in the case of *Cyclone*, reasonable, lawful limits on aiding foreign forces do not necessarily prevent steady streams of weaponry from reaching those resisting aggression abroad in a manner just as effective as Soviet Lend-Lease aid. Such efforts can help in weakening anti-American, anti-democratic adversaries abroad while sufficiently arming those fighting current aggressors to wear down their assailants and serving both their own and U.S. interests. Yet U.S. leaders can also learn from Roosevelt and Zia's apparent mistakes by recognizing that their respective aid recipients remain independent actors capable of acting on their own agency and cannot necessarily be bought in the sense of mercenary forces. Those manning the Arctic convoys, driving through the Persian Corridor, and flying the ALSIB combat aircraft all executed their Lend-Lease mission to the Red Army admirably, as did Casey's CIA and Akhtar's ISI in their covert action 1980s' Afghan program for the Islamic guerrillas.[124] Yet the positive, hard-fought achievements of the Allied Arctic warriors in the first instance, like those of Casey and Akhtar in the second, were not fully appreciated at the time and were inadvertently undermined as Roosevelt and Hopkins foolishly opted to furnish their supposedly noble red warrior in Moscow with atomic bomb materials while persisting in the belief that their actions amounted to purchasing his permanent peaceful intentions toward the Western capitalists.[125]

While it may appear unlikely to many Western observers in 2024 that the U.S. leadership could somehow err in making such assumptions regarding Ukraine's ongoing struggle and the rebirth of Lend-Lease, American planners and strategists must bear in mind that the situation appeared much the same to Roosevelt's advisers until well into 1943.[126] During the period of Roosevelt's original Lend-Lease program, U.S. leaders could not imagine a greater threat to their country's national interests than the one then in Berlin, and they underestimated Stalin's true motives as they wisely armed his forces to fight the greater threat from Hitler while unwisely seeking to flatter and, essentially, buy a more peaceful Stalin through a combination of unconditional Lend-Lease aid and several overly generous, non-Lend-Lease gifts. It therefore appears paramount that current policymakers refuse to ignore the lessons of the past, however unrelated they may appear at first glance, in serving U.S. interests in the present, thereby potentially saving countless lives in the future. In doing so, today's leaders can attempt to avoid repeating Roosevelt's misjudgment of Stalin's character, capabilities, and disinterest in contributing to a more peaceful world, while hoping to replicate his and Reagan's respective successes in rolling back the totalitarian tides once flowing from Berlin and Moscow during each of their respective historical eras.[127]

EPILOGUE.
Uncle Sam's arsenal of Stalinism – for better or worse

"I want to tell you, from the Russian [sic, Soviet] point of view, what the [American] President and the United States have done to win the war. The most important things in this war are machines…. The United States, therefore, is a country of machines. Without the use of those machines [American attack aircraft], through Lend-Lease, we would lose this war."- Joseph Stalin at the Tehran Conference, 30 November 1943[1]

A potent alliance of American industry, British bravery, and Soviet stubbornness on the battlefield combined to crush the Axis Powers in the Second World War in a truly Allied endeavor that would not have succeeded without such an awesome, all-out effort on the part of each respective country's people and leaders.[2] Stalin's determination to avoid the fates of the tsar and Kerensky, the Red Army's willingness to fight Hitler to the finish, and Roosevelt and Churchill's combined efforts to prevent a repeat of Brest-Litovsk led to Berlin's fall in 1945. Yet had U.S. officials not prioritized Soviet Lend-Lease and had their British counterparts not sacrificed many crucial resources of their own, the Red Army's survival would not have been assured. Stalin's soldiers may have been defeated and forced to surrender the Soviet Union's vast resources to Hitler's genocidal Reich. Stalin alone bears full responsibility for his decision to further his own country's perceived strategic interests and betray Roosevelt's good faith and misplaced trust by denying free elections and forcing the regimes of his choice on the peoples of Eastern Europe and Northeast Asia, and his blood-stained actions cannot, therefore, in any way, shape, or form, be blamed on his wartime allies helping the Red Army in its hour of need.[3]

The American wartime leaders' acted wisely, boldly, and decisively in helping to strengthen the then-struggling Red Army by opening the Persian Corridor and ALSIB in 1943 and by continuing, along with their British counterparts, to sail the Arctic convoys until the end of the war.[4] As emphasized by Mark Harrison, Albert Weeks, and others, U.S. Lend-Lease aid provided much-needed assistance to Stalin's soldiers and helped render the Second World War shorter and less bloody and destructive than it otherwise might have been, a thought that overwhelms the mind when one considers the mass destruction and death that did, indeed, occur.[5] Yet while the Soviet Lend-Lease program helped tremendously in crushing the Axis and winning the war, U.S. officials, particularly Roosevelt and Hopkins, must be criticized for providing Stalin's representatives with key ingredients for atomic bomb construction and for seemingly assuming that such excessively generous (and, ultimately, self-defeating) gifts, combined with unconditional Lend-Lease aid, could somehow "buy" the loyalty and friendship of a terrorist and former bank robber with a record not unlike Hitler's in murdering millions of innocents.[6]

To be sure, and as discussed throughout the preceding chapters of this work, Stalin unquestionably and, perhaps understandably, appeared to be the "lesser of two evils" to wartime Americans and their leaders, and aiding the Red Army doubtlessly saved untold Allied military and civilian lives in the long run. As pointed out by Harrison, van Tuyll, and other leading experts in Soviet Lend-Lease, the war could not have been won without the Red Army's fighting strength, and U.S. officials had no decent alternatives to prevent the risk of a separate peace between Moscow and Berlin and preempt a mechanized repeat of March 1918.[7] As I have argued in this work, the memories of the earlier Brest-Litovsk fiasco appear to have had a nearly traumatic effect on Roosevelt's team and other leading Americans and, correctly viewing Stalin's continued prosecution of the war in the east as crucial to victory, they regarded Lend-Lease aid to the Red Army as an absolute necessity to preventing a repeat of the past's errors.

Yet it cannot be said that U.S. leaders acted wisely in supplying Stalin's government with atomic bomb ingredients, as well as believing that such foolish and excessive gestures, in addition to unconditional Lend-Lease aid, would convince the Soviet leader to keep his word on allowing postwar free elections in Eastern Europe and softening his stance toward the capitalist world.[8] Perhaps a question might arise at this point asking if Roosevelt, Hopkins, and others in the U.S. wartime administration felt it necessary to keep their unfortunate, even if subjectively understandable, 1942 promise to share "all that we have and are" with Stalin in the most literal sense?[9] After all, considering this work's revelation of the key role of Brest-Litovsk in their motivations to supply the Red Army sufficiently, would it not have only made sense to keep Stalin as happy as possible and preempt even the remotest possibility of him again striking a deal with Hitler behind the backs of the Western Allies, as in August 1939? Perhaps, but even if this were the case, Roosevelt and Hopkins must have surely understood the risks and dangers involved. They appear to have underestimated Stalin's self-serving tendencies and overestimated their own ability to charm him into truly rejecting the path of, "might makes right" and contributing to world peace after achieving victory over Hitler.

Regardless, the mounting evidence discussed in this work appears to suggest that U.S. leaders, weighed down by the perceived failures of their First World

War predecessors, opted to take such risks in the hopes of keeping Stalin in the war and thereby minimizing casualties of all the Allied Powers and shortening the journey to victory. American Lend-Lease officials succeeded remarkably in this first effort of most urgent priority yet failed in their secondary goal of persuading Stalin to keep the peace and abandon his authoritarian impulses following the victory. Yet U.S. officials had few acceptable alternatives at the time and rightly regarded Stalin's Red Army as necessary to the Allied war effort. As has been shown, while Roosevelt's White House successors had to face decades of danger from a nuclear-armed Kremlin, Reagan's actions in the 1980s, with the combined help of Moscow's unwise Afghan overreach and key international allies such as Pakistani President Zia, replicated the earlier success of Lend-Lease in again dealing a death blow to the most immediate and merciless totalitarian threat.[10]

To be sure, Stalin's agents in the West also exploited the wartime atmosphere and, by working to promote Soviet interests through U.S. policy, took advantage of the desperate position in which U.S. officials found themselves as they worked feverishly to keep Stalin's soldiers armed and attacking the Nazi menace throughout the war. As revealed by the U.S. Army's VENONA decrypts and emphasized by scholars such as John Koster, Ben Steil, and Sean McMeekin, the role of Soviet spies and disinformation agents such as Harry Dexter White and Alger Hiss did, in fact, aid Stalin's quest to serve Soviet interests through U.S. diplomacy, such as, for example, Hiss's advice to Roosevelt and Hopkins to agree to Stalin's demands at Yalta and thereby allow him to betray his promise to oversee fair and free elections in the countries that the Red Army liberated.[11] In this regard, these scholars' claims that the naivete of Roosevelt, Hopkins, Wallace, and other top administration officials towards Stalin's adherence to aggressive, rigid Communist orthodoxy also contributed, even if inadvertently, to the Soviet Union's rise as a military superpower seem somewhat justified, although it should be clarified here that this resulted from these American officials' misreading of "Uncle Joe" rather than their provision of Lend-Lease aid for the Red Army.[12] While it is not possible to determine the extent to which the president may have continued trying to placate and, in a nonliteral sense, "purchase" Stalin after Hitler's defeat, when Lend-Lease was no longer necessary, his wartime policies indicate that he vastly underestimated the Soviet premier's duplicitous nature and his refusal to be "bought."[13]

Yet while this appears to be verifiably accurate, based on Roosevelt's wartime correspondence with Stalin, his refusal to attach conditions to Soviet Lend-Lease, and his comments to Hopkins and others, it is equally crucial to recall the global environment in which he and other U.S. officials lived and worked.[14] Based on his statements relating to Soviet Lend-Lease, Roosevelt, like many of his advisers and U.S. congressmen, greatly underestimated Stalin's character even as they rightly sought to keep him in the war. The prevailing perception among U.S. leaders that Stalin could be forced into suing for peace with Hitler presented a terrifying possibility in the form of a Nazi victory in the East and all its devastating ramifications.[15]

For Roosevelt and many of his associates, the risk of arming Stalin appeared to be far less than the strategic horror of a Nazi conquest of Soviet Europe and Berlin's successful exploitation of its land and people. Were Stalin's Red Army to mutiny or collapse on the battlefield, as had the armies of both Nicholas II and Kerensky in the First World War, Hitler could have been virtually assured of triumph in what would have been a genuine nightmare scenario with terrifying results.[16] Without Stalin's uncompromising ruthlessness in prosecuting the war and the soldiers of the Red Army remaining in the field and fighting tenaciously for their homeland, Hitler's forces may have achieved much more than the second Brest-Litovsk seemingly feared by Roosevelt and Churchill.[17]

During the tumultuous period in which they served as Americans' public servants, Roosevelt, Hopkins, Stettinius, Hull, and others could not escape the image of Germany and any powers allied with Berlin as the greatest potential adversaries of the United States. Basing their perceptions of the Soviet Union on Tsarist Russia's poor performance in the First World War, they, like Hitler and his generals in 1941, failed to comprehend Stalin's ruthlessness and ability to reorganize the Red Army into an effective and deadly military machine rivaling the Nazi opponent that they feared to be virtually indestructible and, more importantly, miscalculated in their efforts to inculcate a moderate attitude in him while wisely arming his fighting men and women to kill German troops in enormous numbers.[18] Fearing a repeat of Brest-Litovsk, a potentiality rendered more frightful by Hitler's genocidal goals and Nazi Germany's reputed mastery of armored warfare and airpower, they sought to keep Stalin sufficiently motivated and fully equipped to bring the war to Berlin, and succeeded admirably in this endeavor.[19]

The memoirs of Standley, Deane, Arnold, and Rickenbacker, and Roosevelt's interactions with Hopkins, Churchill, and others seem to indicate that for U.S. leaders, a repeat of the First World War had to be avoided at all costs and the final defeat of Germany assured. While exuding naïveté and foolishness in their assessments of Stalin's military capabilities and aggressive tendencies, these men appear to have genuinely sought to serve U.S. national interests through the annihilation strategy adopted and successfully applied first in the 1860s by General Grant as emphasized by Russell Weigley.[20] From their perspective, that manner of overthrowing the enemy's entire political system and utterly breaking its will to defy the United States ensured the defeat of the Axis and arming the Soviets seemed to them the most effective means by which to secure total victory.[21] These American leaders correctly concluded that Stalin's forces fighting Hitler's hordes in the east served as indispensable assets in the Allied cause, and they therefore worked, via Soviet Lend-Lease, to make Berlin's permanent downfall a reality.

Again, however, Hopkins's authorization of shipments to Moscow of uranium, thorium, and other materials necessary to produce atomic bombs serves as a testament to his and Roosevelt's inexcusable refusal to recognize the dangers in enhancing Stalin's non-conventional capabilities.[22] Perhaps fearing the possibility that Hitler's and Hirohito's scientists could potentially develop atomic capabilities of their own, U.S. Lend-Lease officials may have decided that by speeding Stalin's atomic research they could ensure an Allied nuclear edge. However, in their underestimation of Stalin's duplicity and adherence to spreading Communism at gunpoint, they failed to consider that such actions sowed the seeds of a more dangerous reality, a reality that conventional Lend-Lease aid did not, in and of itself, create.[23]

These fears of the Axis potentially developing atomic capabilities may, however, provide at least a partial explanation of Hopkins's authorizing of uranium and other vital atomic bomb components to be shipped to the Soviets. According to Major Jordan's diary entries and subsequent congressional testimony, Hopkins's first order for such material to be supplied to Soviet officials and kept out of official Lend-Lease records came shortly after Roosevelt's order for all Soviet aid to be prioritized.[24] In supplying Stalin with the material for atomic bomb production, Roosevelt's advisers appear to have underestimated Soviet scientific potential just as they underestimated the Red Army's combat capabilities, ironically making the same mistake as Hitler's generals in 1941.[25]

It is crucial to recall that the years in which Stalin reportedly received the initial shipments of this material left out of official Lend-Lease records, between 1942 and early 1943 according to Major Jordan, were also the years that saw the Red Army appear on the verge of collapse before counterattacking the Nazis at Stalingrad and Kursk.[26] According to Jordan's wartime diary entry, the Soviets received 13,440 pounds of thorium in 1942 and another 11,912 pounds in 1943.[27] Jordan provided these figures during his postwar congressional testimony, and Chief Council Frank Tavenner of HUAC confirmed the 1943 shipment, immediately producing, "a shipper's export declaration showing the exact figure 11,912 pounds of thorium nitrate shipped January 30, 1943, from Philadelphia on the Steamship *John C. Fremont*, the exporter being Amtorg Trading Corp."[28] In his official capacity as Hopkins's Lend-Lease Expeditor to the Soviet Union, Jordan initially oversaw the shipment of materials from the Newark, New Jersey base to the various Lend-Lease supply routes, although it remains unclear whether the *John C. Fremont* sailed for the Persian Corridor or joined Convoy JW-53's journey to North Russia.[29] Regardless of the specific supply route over which the *Fremont's* cargo traveled, Tavenner's confirmation of both the exact amount of weight in thorium that the ship contained and the date of 30 January 1943 strongly supports Jordan's recollections.[30]

As mentioned previously, Stalin's decision to act on his political and ideological convictions and ruthlessly occupy Eastern Europe and Northeast Asia can only have originated with the Soviet premier himself, and his deceitful actions cannot be ascribed to his wartime Western Allies and the aid that they delivered to him during the Red Army's arduous struggle.[31] Yet Roosevelt, in full knowledge of Stalin's record of revolutionary violence, mass murder, and military aggression, displayed outstanding naivete in underestimating the Soviet premier's duplicitous character and expecting him to be charmed into moderating, even as he rightly armed the Red Army to ensure to the destruction of the genocidal and far greater Nazi threat at the time.[32] While much less naïve in his perception of Stalin than the increasingly and, tragically, infirm Roosevelt, Churchill had been forced to embrace his unlikely Soviet ally after Hitler's 1941 attack, and he, too, understood that aiding the Red Army remained vital to the Allied strategy and therefore wisely continued sailing the Arctic convoys to North Russia that continued achieving outstanding successes even late in the war as discussed in Chapter 4.[33]

In 1885, the same year in which Stalin's seventh birthday occurred, former Union Lieutenant General and U.S. President Ulysses S. Grant wrote insightfully in his autobiography that, "Up to the battle of Shiloh [in 1862] I, as well as thousands of other [U.S.] citizens, believed that the [American South's] rebellion against the Government would collapse suddenly and soon, if a decisive victory could be gained over any of its armies. [Forts] Donelson and Henry were such victories.... But when Confederate armies were collected which not only attempted to hold a line farther south, from Memphis to Chattanooga, Knoxville and on to the Atlantic, but assumed the offensive and made such a gallant effort to regain what had been lost, then, indeed, *I gave up all idea of saving the Union except by complete conquest.*"[34] As emphasized by Weigley, Grant's thinking appears in many ways to have guided and influenced Roosevelt and Eisenhower's strategic approach to Germany's defeat in the Second World War, and Soviet Lend-Lease played a crucial part in ensuring the Reich's total and lasting collapse.[35] Under Stalin's leadership, the fighting men and women of the Red Army undeniably achieved this goal many times over, and their courage, steadfastness, and tenacity broke the back of Hitler's brutal and merciless military machine. Yet while Soviet blood and armor served as the key factors in the destruction of Nazi Germany's armies, U.S. Lend-Lease also played a key part in supplying the Red Army's struggle and, as pointed out by Alexander Hill, Mark Harrison, and Albert Weeks, among others, rendered the war less costly in Allied blood, toil, and tears than it otherwise may have been.[36]

In addition to the courage of the mostly American Army technicians and airmen braving the arid Iranian deserts and treacherous, wintry Alaskan skies, the crucial deliveries to the Red Army executed by the often-uncredited Allied sailors serving on the Arctic convoys appear to have played a key part, even in their often overlooked efforts of 1944 and 1945, in sealing Hitler's fate.[37] Had Roosevelt and Churchill not resumed the convoys despite the severe losses suffered by PQ-17 and had the men of their respective merchant navies not braved the icy Arctic waters and Hitler's bombers and submarines, the Nazi tide may have been much harder to check even with Generals Connally, Arnold, and Bradley's successes in expanding the Persian Corridor and ALSIB. Despite the notorious, massive losses incurred by PQ-17 in 1942, the Anglo-American Arctic mariners continued to courageously defy the odds in executing their Lend-Lease supply voyages to North Russia into 1945, ensuring the success of Churchill and Roosevelt's mission to shorten the journey to victory by keeping Stalin in the war at all costs.[38]

While the Arctic convoys suffered losses inflicted by Nazi bombers and submarines, improved radar usage and tactics, such as sailing only during the winter months, greatly reduced these dangers, limiting total losses in tonnage to only slightly more than seven percent by the Second World War's end. The Arctic winter conditions along the Allied convoy route to North Russia's ports imposed severe restrictions on Hitler's admirals as Raeder and Doenitz feared risking both their few surface vessels and Goering's precious aircraft pilots in the seasonal fog and icy waters around northern Norway.[39] As mentioned in this work's third and fourth chapters, Roosevelt and Churchill's willingness to take such bold risks and continue sailing the Arctic convoys during the winter months, a time that greatly reduced their ships' visibility to the enemy, doubtlessly played a part in helping to fuel the Red Army's victorious but bloody drive to Berlin. Despite Stalin's doubts and constant criticisms, General Connolly's success in improving the U.S. Lend-Lease supply facilities in Iran and General Follett Bradley's opening of the ALSIB route ensured the delivery of more badly needed material to the Red Army, and, to the Soviet premier's great relief, the Arctic convoys continued to sail in the winter months only and remained largely successful in delivering more war material well into 1945.[40] As late as 21 September 1943, only days after agreeing to the Tehran Conference, Stalin, through Molotov, persistently urged Churchill to resume the remarkably helpful deliveries of Lend-Lease shipments to North Russia, and the Anglo-American wintertime convoys continued until 1945, serving the Allied strategy, from the U.S. perspective, of satisfying Stalin and keeping him in the war.[41] The Anglo-American ships sailing to North Russia's ports, after all, provided the Red Army with most of the 79,000 trucks and jeeps that it received in 1942 alone, as pointed out and emphasized by Walter Dunn.[42]

In continuing to unravel the remaining mysteries surrounding the overall impact of Soviet Lend-Lease aid, future scholars can, perhaps, seek to explore the Russian (or possibly other) archives that were gradually opened to Western researchers after the Soviet Union's 1991 collapse and that were subsequently consulted by experts such as Harrison, Weeks, Dunn, and McMeekin, in search of documentary evidence as to whether American leaders had substantive reasons to believe that Stalin might have considered forging a separate peace with Hitler.[43] As several of these previously mentioned scholars point out, these military archives, together with the Russian Naval Archives in Murmansk that Michael Walling consulted, likely contain much more important and interesting information.[44] The success of future researchers into this still-controversial subject will, of course, likely depend on whether such a document even exists and is even findable, whether in a archived physical or digital online copy, that conclusively proves that Stalin's diplomats met with their Nazi counterparts in neutral Sweden during the war as alleged by Heinz Hohne in his 1976 biography *Canaris: Hitler's Master Spy*, the source cited by McMeekin in his recent *Stalin's War*.[45] Citing Admiral Canaris's account of a talk with his subordinate Edgar Klaus, Hohne alleges that Soviet NKVD agent Boris Yartsev offered, "peace in a week" in exchange for a return, "to the 1939 frontiers" at a meeting supposedly initiated by the Kremlin in Stockholm, Sweden between April and August 1943, a period coinciding with Eddie Rickenbacker's visit to Moscow and the increased supply flow to the Red Army over the Persian Corridor.[46]

Canaris reportedly ordered Klaus's supposed talks with Yartsev to be ended due to, "Hitler's violent objections" on 29 August 1943, yet if researchers are able, at some point, to verify the German intelligence chief's seemingly bizarre claim (one must remember that both the Nazis and Soviets tended to lie through their teeth), they can then argue that U.S. officials had every reason to fear that Stalin may have considered concluding a separate peace as German troops were still deep inside Soviet territory, an academic investigation that lies beyond the scope of this work.[47] Did Nazi-Soviet peace talks occur in Stockholm or elsewhere in 1943, or at any other point in the Second World War? And, if so, did Stalin genuinely seek a separate peace with Berlin, or might the Soviet premier have had other motives for initiating the alleged meetings, such as, perhaps, attempting to stall Hitler and buy precious time without truly seeking actual peace with the Nazi dictator? Answers to these questions may not be forthcoming for many years, yet future scholars armed with the necessary language skills and travel access can contribute to a more complete, full-circle account of Soviet Lend-Lease from all relevant perspectives *if* documents describing the alleged meetings even exist and, moreover, become available.[48]

In no way, shape, or form whatsoever have I sought to portray either myself or the work I have produced here as being some sort of "end-all" authority on American Lend-Lease aid to the Red Army in the Second World War. Such a claim would not only be inaccurate at best, but it would stray dangerously far from the path of wisdom, the path to which all genuine scholars should seek to adhere rather than risk miseducating others. It is also the tragedy and, at the same time, the ultimate success and triumph of the scholar, that once he or she has produced the final draft of their work and published their findings, others will become motivated to research and write more complete and, perhaps, more well-received historical accounts on the same subject as his or her work.

Yet, for the reasons that are mentioned in this work's Introduction, this is a subject that I very reluctantly approached to begin with, with *much* hesitation for many good reasons, and while it may not include an in-depth dissection of the Lend-Lease program's impact on the Red Army's campaigns, for better or worse, I can only say here that I have done my very best to explain the motivations of U.S. leaders in keeping Stalin supplied. Through its focus on U.S. perceptions of Stalin's importance to the Allied strategy and the role of Soviet Lend-Lease therein, the work that I have produced here can hopefully serve as a helpful guide in revealing that the fear of a second Brest-Litovsk gripped U.S. officials and influenced their decision to help keep Stalin's Red Army armed and killing Nazis in the field.[49] Whether or not Stalin genuinely sought out a separate peace with Hitler, Roosevelt and other U.S. leaders certainly regarded this as a very frightful possibility and worked to preempt it as they armed the Red Army and increased their support from 1943 forward to hasten the defeat of the greater perceived threat to Americans.

While it may still be some time before scholars are able to fully complete the picture and determine if American leaders had solid, legitimate reasons to fear the possibility of a separate Nazi-Soviet peace, accessing the considerable amount of available material at present reveals several important points that have helped this work to contribute to the previous conclusions of the experts in our subject which are briefly recapitulated here. The precedent of Brest-Litovsk in 1918 spurred Roosevelt and other U.S. leaders to arm Stalin's soldiers and keep them well-supplied once Hitler launched his 1941 surprise attack, and the Soviet premier's implicit threats to conclude a separate peace combined with the presence of German troops on Soviet soil to galvanize the supply efforts of Lend-Lease officials. From the wartime American perspective, the Arctic convoys proved vital to the Allied strategy of keeping Stalin's forces in the war and fighting, and continued to contribute to the Allied victory even late in the war despite being surpassed by ALSIB and the Persian Corridor in terms of overall supply tonnages.[50] For his part, Stalin repeatedly delayed meeting Roosevelt, thereby contributing to U.S. concerns that he might be forced into forging a separate peace with Hitler if the Red Army mutinied or collapsed in a repeat of 1918 and feeding into the Americans' fears, for the subjective better or worse.[51]

The United States of America's Soviet Lend-Lease program served the Allied strategy well in ensuring the delivery of vital arms, raw materials, foodstuffs, and much more to the Red Army. American leaders early on identified the strategic importance of keeping Stalin in the war as a crucial asset in the anti-Axis struggle, and they succeeded admirably in helping to keep his Red Army fed and fighting, hastening victory, and rendering the Second World War less costly for the Allies. Although Roosevelt, Hopkins, and other U.S. leaders miscalculated in overestimating their ability to purchase a more moderate and peaceful Stalin through Lend-Lease, they correctly viewed him and their wartime alliance with him as the key to defeating the greater threat posed by Hitler. Having succeeded in keeping the Red Army armed and fed until the fall of Berlin, American leaders had set an important precedent for their late Cold War and early twenty-first-century successors to follow, each in their somewhat unique and independent ways, in arming others abroad in their efforts to resist aggression.

ABBREVIATIONS

Author's Note: I have not sought to make this list of abbreviations exhaustive but to include in it only the major terms encountered frequently in the main body of text relating to political/governmental organizations, military code names, and some of the weapons relating to our subject that readers may be unfamiliar with. It therefore does not include every term that the reader may encounter while reading this book.

AEF- American Expeditionary Force, the name given to the U.S. forces in Europe in the First World War under the command of General John J. "Blackjack" Pershing.

AEF-Siberia- American Expeditionary Force-Siberia, the name given to the U.S. troops contingent dispatched to Siberia between August 1918 and April 1920 during President Wilson's intervention in the Russian Civil War under the command of General William S. Graves.

ALSIB- The acronym for Alaska-Siberia, the Allied code name for the Lend-Lease air supply route that began in Great Falls, Montana, stretched on through Canada and into Fairbanks, Alaska, and ended at the Soviet airports in Krasnoyarsk and Uelkel, two Siberian cities to which Stalin's pilots flew thousands of U.S.-built combat and transport aircraft after taking control of the planes from the American pilots who flew them to Fairbanks.

BV 138- These Nazi reconnaissance aircraft served as patrol planes and were dreaded by the Allied merchant mariners serving on the Arctic convoys and the Anglo-American navy men who escorted them to North Russia's ports as they could alert German submarines and torpedo bombers as to the location of the Allied ships.

FAT- An acronym for the *Federapparat Torpedo*, a type of German torpedo that entered service in late 1942 but saw no action until Nazi submarines attempted to interdict Convoy JW-56A in January 1944. Capable of performing 180-degree turns in the ocean, these torpedoes followed a preprogrammed course towards an Allied naval target rather than adhering to a straight line in the manner of conventional torpedoes.

Fw 200- Dubbed the "Condor," and designed by the aircraft manufacturer Focke-Wulf, these long-range reconnaissance aircraft were employed in the German Air Force's efforts to assist the Germany Navy's efforts against the Arctic convoys by locating the Allied vessels and reporting their location to Nazi bombers and submarines. Originally intended to serve as a passenger airliner during the prewar period, it also served as a transport aircraft during the Second World War and was also nicknamed *Kurier* (courier) by the German pilots.

"GNAT"- The Allied code-name for the German *Zaunkoenig*, or "Wren," a type of Nazi torpedo that entered service in the fall of 1943. After speeding through the ocean more than 1,300 feet away from its home submarine, the GNAT could home in on the loudest nearby propeller sounds in search of enemy targets, an innovation that appears to have mostly proved to be a failure as the loudest noises were often those emitted by the Nazi submarines themselves rather than the Allied Arctic convoy escorts that the GNATs were specifically designed to target.

GRU- Main Intelligence Directorate of the General Staff of the Soviet Armed Forces. Now known as the Main Directorate of the General Staff of the Armed Forces of the Russian Federation, it reportedly uses the same acronym today and was/is the Soviet and modern Russian military intelligence agency.

Heinkel He 111/He 115- Designed by the aircraft manufacturing company Heinkel, these German Air Force bombers not only struck Allied cities but were also deployed against the Arctic convoys to North Russia, with the He-115 often being equipped with torpedoes for striking the Allied merchant vessels and warships.

H.R. 1776- The Lend-Lease Bill proposed by Roosevelt and designed in large part by Harry Hopkins. Congress passed the bill in March 1941, delivering immense power to Roosevelt by granting him the authority to designate recipients of U.S. wartime aid, paving the way for the Soviet Lend-Lease program that officially began later in the year.

IL-2- Built by the Soviet aircraft manufacturer and design bureau Ilyushin, these ground-attack planes, known as *Sturmoviks*, were a key part of Stalin's war arsenal and proved highly effective in battle. Lend-Lease aluminum deliveries reportedly proved vital to the Soviet Union's continued production of ILs as the plane's armor was made of aluminum, a crucial ingredient that became scarce after Hitler's capture of the Soviet Union's key aluminum production centers early in the war.

IS-2- Together with the medium T-34, this heavy Soviet tank, dubbed the "Stalin," proved an almost unbeatable armored opponent on the battlefield and could outfight most of the German tanks that Berlin could deploy against it. Its continued production, like the T-34's, is also said to have depended, to at least some extent, upon the reliable deliveries of U.S. Lend-Lease aluminum. Both the IS-2 and the T-34 relied on aluminum alloy motors, and Roosevelt's determination to fulfill and prioritize Stalin's aid orders enabled Soviet workers to continue producing these tanks in large numbers during the war.

Junkers Ju 87/Ju 88/Ju 188- Built by the Junkers aviation company, these Nazi aircraft served in various capacities as dive bombers, tank busters, night fighters, and torpedo bombers during the Second World War. While the Ju 87 *Stuka* became most notorious for its dive-bombing role in support of the

German Army's offensive operations early in the war, the Ju 88s and, somewhat later in the war, the Ju 188s, proved most effective at targeting the Allied Arctic convoys to North Russia, with both of these models being equipped with torpedoes as Hitler's admirals constantly struggled to interrupt the flow of supplies being delivered to the Soviet Union's Arc**tic ports.**

JW/RA- This second series of Arctic convoys from Great Britain to the Soviet ports in North Russia ran between December 1942 and May 1945. The Allied leadership dubbed the outbound convoys "JW," while the homebound convoys of this series were referred to as "RA."

KGB- Soviet intelligence agency, the Committee for State Security.

MO4- British intelligence agency, responsible for Home Defense and infiltrated by Stalin's agents during the Second World War.

Nazi- The shortened, abbreviated form of the *Nationalsozialistiche Deutsche Arbeiterpartei*, also abbreviated as NSDAP and translated as "National Socialist German Workers' Party," the ruling political party of Hitler's genocidal Third Reich in Germany between 1933 and 1945.

NKVD- People's Commissariat of Internal Affairs, the main intelligence agency of the Soviet government during much of Stalin's rule. The agency was initially called the *Cheka*, and it experienced several name changes as the GPU, OGPU, NKGB, NKVD, and MGB before eventually becoming the KGB in 1954.

P-39- While often disregarded as being of lesser value in comparison to other U.S. and Allied aircraft at the time, this American attack aircraft, known as the "Airacobra," proved effective in the hands of Red Army Air Forces pilots during the brutal dogfighting on the Eastern Front. Stalin's fighter pilots, who affectionately dubbed the plane the *Kobrushka* or "little cobra," reportedly received some 4,700 of these aircraft via Lend-Lease and found them effective at performing in the aerial combat conditions of the Eastern Front in which Nazi and Soviet airmen often dogfought at altitudes below 15,000 feet. The most advanced model which formed the bulk of the Airacobras delivered to the Soviets, the P-39Q, boasted four machine guns and a nose cannon that proved a lethal combination in the capable hands of seasoned Soviet fighter aces who often managed to outfight their German opponents in their Fw 190s and Bf 109s.

PQ/QP- This first series of Arctic convoys ran from September 1941 until September 1942. Outbound convoys transporting tons of Anglo-American war supplies to the North Russian ports destined for the then-besieged Red Army, including large amounts of U.S. Lend-Lease material, were dubbed "PQ," while homebound convoys were dubbed "QP" to sow confusion within the Nazi naval and air command.

RNVR- Royal Naval Volunteer Reserve.

RWR- Russian War Relief, the popular name for the Russian War Relief Fund, an organization established by Chairman Edward C. Carter of the Institute of Pacific Relations in September 1941 to raise money, purchase, and ship medical supplies to the Red Army.

SBNO- Senior British Naval Officer, North Russia.

T-34- These powerful Soviet medium tanks proved far superior in quality to most of the German tanks that they faced and have often been ranked among the best tanks of the Second World War. Originally designed with a 76-mm gun as its main armament, the T-34's later models were mounted with 85-mm guns. All versions of the tank were equipped with sloped frontal armor and wide tracks, a result of Soviet engineers' experiments with the revolutionary tank suspension system developed by American engineer John Walter Christie. Christie's design also proved instrumental in the Soviet Union's production of the high-speed, light BT-7 tank. U.S. Lend-Lease aluminum deliveries are often said to have played a part in helping Soviet war workers to continue producing the T-34s and IS-2s as both vehicles required aluminum for the production of their motors.

US6- Known as the "Studebaker," this American truck proved highly effective and transporting troops and supplies, and the Roosevelt administration delivered them in huge numbers to the Red Army via Lend-Lease. Studebakers reportedly formed the majority of the nearly 500,000 total American-made trucks and jeeps delivered to the Soviet Union during the Second World War/

AUTHOR'S NOTE

Readers will notice that, in contrast to the dissertation upon which this work is based, I have largely refrained, to the extent that I found possible, from commenting on or otherwise attempting to assess the overall impact of Lend-Lease aid on the Soviet war effort while discussing our topic throughout this book. This is primarily because our subject is closely focused on U.S. perceptions of Stalin's Red Army and the necessity of not only supplying it, but openly demonstrating wartime Washington's total commitment to victory while keeping the Soviets at war with the Nazis and preventing a separate peace between Moscow and Berlin at all costs. As it was, and is, my intention to tackle our subject from a primarily U.S. perspective, I must again emphasize here than readers should not interpret this book as an attempt on my part to portray myself as being any sort of "end-all" authority on U.S. Lend-Lease aid to the Soviet Union or even a true expert on the Second World War, the Eastern Front, or, for that matter, any part of Russian (or Soviet) history, but merely as a contribution from an imperfect, American scholar whose intellectual strengths and knowledge base lie elsewhere in the realm of World History. As I have mentioned in this work's Introduction, the subject of U.S. Lend-Lease aid to the Soviet Union was neither my first nor second choice of a historical topic to explore for my doctoral research. Yet with the moral support of my dearest loved ones, I tackled it to the best of my ability to earn my doctorate and I am deeply thankful for having had the chance to revise it into the current work now in the reader's hands. Accordingly, I must humbly ask for the reader's understanding for producing an account that, while perhaps somewhat less than ideal regarding the complete picture of Lend-Lease's overall impact on the Second World War's outcome, may nevertheless prove a valuable academic contribution regarding the contemporary American perceptions of Stalin's strategic importance to the Allied war effort, which is how most of the excellent professors who served on my dissertation committee felt about the original work from which this book is derived.

NOTES

PREFACE

[1] Peter G. Tsouras, *Civil War Quotations: In the Words of the Commanders* (New York: Sterling Publishing Co., Inc., 1998), 106.

[2] Russell F. Weigley, *The American Way of War: A History of United States Military Strategy and Policy* (New York: MacMillan Publishing Co., 1973), 128-129, 150-152, 162-163, 357-359.

[3] Dwight D. Eisenhower, *The Papers of Dwight David Eisenhower: The War Years*, Vol. 1, ed. Alfred D. Chandler, Jr. (Baltimore: Johns Hopkins Press, 1970), 66; Weigley, *The American Way of War*, 312, 529n1. First set of italics mine, second set of italics in the original.

[4] U.S. President, "Map Room Papers Box 8 Roosevelt to Stalin May–December 1942," *The White House*, Washington, D.C., 1942, *National Archives and Records Service Franklin D. Roosevelt Library*, http://www.fdrlibrary.marist.edu/_resources/images/mr/mr0051.pdf.

[5] Office, Chief of Finance War Department, "Lend-Lease Shipments World War II," 31 October 1946, http://ibiblio.org/hyperwar/USA/ref/LL-Ship/index.html; Pastorfield-Li, "An excerpt from an interview with a Soviet soldier,"; The Navy Department Library, "Lend-Lease Act, 11 March 1941," *Naval History and Heritage Command*, https://www.history.navy.mil/research/library/online-reading-room/title-list-alphbetically/l/lend-le ase-act-11-march-1941.html; U.S. Department of State, *Soviet Supply Protocols* (Washington, D.C.: Government Publishing Office, 1948), iii-iv.

[6] *Congressional Record – United States Senate and House of Representatives*, 78th Congress, 2nd Session (1944), pt. 6, https://www.govinfo.gov/content/pkg/GPO-CRECB-1944-pt6/pdf/GPO-CRECB-1944-pt6-7.pdf; U.S. President, "Report to Congress on Reverse Lend-Lease," *The White House*, Washington, D.C., 11 November 1943, *The American Presidency Project*, https://www.presidency.ucsb.edu/documents/report-congress-reverse-lend-lease ; U.S. President, "Lend-Lease Policy Toward the Soviet Union," *The White House*, Washington, D.C., 3 July 1945, *Harry S. Truman Presidential Library & Museum*, https://www.trumanlibrary.gov/node/401220; *Wilson Center Digital Archive, Collection 27*, "Cold War Origins," "Report from Mikoyan to Stalin and Molotov Regarding Lend-Lease Shipments from the United States From 1 October 1941 to 1 May 1944," 1 May 1944, https://digitalarchive.wilsoncenter.org/collection/27/cold-war-origins/3.

[7] Loza, *Commanding the Red Army's Sherman Tanks*, 57, 73.

[8] Litvin, *800 Days*, 9, 48-51; Pastorfield-Li, "An excerpt from an interview with a Soviet soldier,"; The Navy Department Library, "Lend-Lease Act."

[9] Field-Marshal Lord Alanbrooke, *War Diaries 1939-1945* (London: Phoenix Press, 2001), 416-417; Winston S. Churchill, *Memoirs of the Second World War* (Boston: Houghton Mifflin, 1987), 406-407; Pownall, *Chief of Staff*, 39-40, 41-42; *The National Archives of the UK*, "PREMIER 3 393/8," December 1942-February 1943, "First Sea Lord," 14 December 1942; Whitehall History Publishing – Ministry of Defence, *The Royal Navy and the Arctic Convoys: A Naval Staff History*, ed. Malcolm Llewelyn-Jones (London: Routledge, 2007), 5-7.

[10] Richard H. Dawson, *The Decision to Aid Russia, 1941* (Chapel Hill: The University of North Carolina Press, 1959), xii-xiii, 126-128, 162, 165-166, 227.

[11] Robert Huhn Jones, *The Roads to Russia*, 220-221, 257, 282.

[12] George C. Herring, Jr., *Aid to Russia, 1941-1946: Strategy, Diplomacy, the Origins of the Cold* War (New York: Columbia University Press, 1973), viii-ix, 235-237, 244.

[13] Van Tuyll, *Feeding the Bear*, xii, 3-4, 27, 71, 83-84, 122-124.

[14] Mark Harrison, *Accounting For War: Soviet Production, Employment, and the Defence Burden, 1940-1945* (Cambridge, UK: Cambridge University Press, 1996), 128-131, 149-152, 152-154.

[15] Dmitriy Loza, *Attack of the Airacobras: Soviet Aces, American P-39s, and the Air War Against Germany*, ed. and trans. James F. Gebhardt (Lawrence: University Press of Kansas, 2002), 39-42 78-79; Weeks, *Russia's Life-Saver*, 52-53, 122, 126-127.

[16] Sean McMeekin, *Stalin's War: A New History of World War II* (New York: Basic Books, 2021), 516-519, 536-537; Vojin Majstorovic, "H-Diplo Roundtable XXIV-5 on McMeekin, *Stalin's War*," Review of McMeekin, Sean, *Stalin's War: A New History of World War II* (2021), *H-War, H-Net Reviews*, 26 September 2022, https://networks.h-net.org/node/284 43/discussions/10685214/h-diplo-roundtable-xxiv-5 stalin%E2%80%99s/war#_Toc1116 72159; Geoffrey Roberts, "Stalin's War: Distorted history of a complex second World War," *The Irish Times*, 8 May 2021, https://www.irishtimes.com/culture/books/stalin-s-war-disorted-history-of-a-complex-second-world-war-1.4551057.

[17] See again, for example, Majstorovic, "H-Diplo Roundtable XXIV-5,"; and Roberts, "Stalin's War."

[18] Viktor Suvorov, *The Chief Culprit: Stalin's Grand Design to Start World War II* (Annapolis, MD: Naval Institute Press, 2013), ix-xi, vx-xii, 278-280, 281-285.

[19] Suvorov, *The Chief Culprit*, 251-252, 253-259.

[20] McMeekin, *Stalin's War*, 278-279. McMeekin elaborates further on his position here, stating that, "Any lingering notion, which one still sometimes encounters in general histories of the Second World War, that Stalin and his generals were asleep at the wheel as Hitler's generals prepared for Barbarossa, must be dismissed as absurd."

[21] Stettinius, Jr., *Lend-Lease*, 215; Van Tuyll, *Feeding the Bear*, 83.

[22] Alexander Hill, *The Great Patriotic War of the Soviet Union, 1941-45: A Documentary Reader* (New York: Routledge, 2010), 172-173, 174-176; McMeekin, *Stalin's War*, 371-373, 382-384; Steven J. Zaloga, *Soviet Lend-Lease Tanks of World War II* (Oxford: Osprey Publishing, 2017), 6-8; Jones, *The Roads to Russia*, 84, 122-126, 209; Edward V. Rickenbacker, *Rickenbacker* (New York: Fawcett Crest, 1969), 389; Thomas H. Vail Motter, *The Persian Corridor and Aid to Russia* (Washington, D.C.: The Office of the Chief of Military History, Department of the Army, 1952), 3-5, 124-127; Van Tuyll, *Feeding the Bear*, 87, 94-96, 101.

[23] Ministry of Foreign Affairs of the U.S.S.R., *Stalin's Correspondence*, "No. 10," 3 September 1941, 20-22; Pownall, Sir Henry, *Chief of Staff: The Diaries of Lieutenant-General Sir Henry Pownall*, Vol. 2, ed. Brian Bond (Hamden, CT: Archon Books, 1974), 39-40, 41-42; Reynolds and Pechatnov, *The Kremlin Letters*, 40-41; *The National Archives of the UK*, "PREMIER 3 393/8: Convoy JW 52," "First Sea Lord," 14 December 1942.

[24] Cordell Hull, *The Memoirs of Cordell Hull, Vol. II* (New York: The MacMillan Company, 1948), 1167-1168.

[25] Ibid., 1171-1173.

[26] Ibid., 1169, 1171-1173; Ministry of Foreign Affairs of the U.S.S.R., *Stalin's Correspondence*, "No. 103: For Marshal Stalin from President Roosevelt and Prime Minister Churchill," 19 August 1943, 83; Reynolds and Pechatnov, *The Kremlin Letters*, 287-288; U.S. President, "Map Room Papers Box 8 Roosevelt to Stalin January – June 1943."

[27] Eisenhower, *Crusade in Europe*, 69-70; Hull, *The Memoirs of Cordell Hull*, 1171-1173.

[28] William Averell Harriman and Elie Abel, *Special Envoy to Churchill and Stalin 1941-1946* (New York: Random House, 1975), 179; U.S. President, "Map Room Papers Box 8 Roosevelt to Stalin January – June 1943."

[29] Harriman and Abel, *Special Envoy*, 179; U.S. President, "Map Room Papers Box 8 Roosevelt to Stalin January – June 1943."

[30] Eisenhower, *Crusade in Europe*, 489-490; Harriman and Abel, *Special Envoy*, 179, 190, 192.

[31] Harriman and Abel, *Special Envoy*, 179, 190.

[32] Ibid., 190, 192.

[33] Ibid.

[34] Michael Curtis, "Lend-Lease: How U.S. Kept the Soviets Afloat in World War II," *American Thinker*, 13 June 2020, https://www.americanthinker.com/articles/2020/06/lendlease_how_the_us_kept_the_soviets_afloat_in_world_war_ii.html; *The National Archives of the UK*, "PREMIER 3 393/8," "Telescope No. 152. Following for Keenlyside for Ministry of War Transport," 20 January 1943.

INTRODUCTION

[1] Glantz, *Colossus Reborn*, 22, 27, 40-41, 43, 58; Chuikov, *The Battle for Stalingrad*, 215-217, 227-229; Clark, *Barbarossa*, 273, 278; Khrushchev, *Khrushchev Remembers*, 238-239.

[2] U.S. President, "Map Room Papers Box 8 Stalin to Roosevelt July – December 1942,"; U.S. President, "Map Room Papers Box 8 Roosevelt to Stalin January – June 1943."

[3] Orville H. Bullitt, *For the President – Personal and Secret: Correspondence Between Franklin D. Roosevelt and William C. Bullitt* (Boston: Houghton Mifflin, 1972), v-vi; Joseph E. Davies, *Mission to Moscow* (New York: Simon and Schuster, 1941), xiii-xiv; Standley and Ageton, *Admiral Ambassador to Russia*, 308-309, 312-313.

[4] Standley and Ageton, *Admiral Ambassador to Russia*, 308-309, 312-313.

[5] Rickenbacker, *Rickenbacker*, 400-401, 402-403; U.S. President, "Statement on Raw Materials, Munition Assignments, and Shipping Adjustment Boards," *The White House*, Washington, D.C., 26 January 1942, https://www.presidency.ucsb.edu/documents/statement-raw-materials-munition-assignments-and-shipping-adjustment-boards.

[6] Curtis, "Lend-Lease,"; Stettinius, Jr., *Lend-Lease*, 215; Van Tuyll, *Feeding the Bear*, 83.

[7] U.S. Department of State, "The Yalta Conference, 1945" https://history.state.gov/milestones/1937-1945/yalta-conf#:~:text=The%20Americans%20and%20the%20British,territoryes%20liberated%20from%20Nazi%20Germany

[8] The Navy Department Library, "Lend-Lease Act."

[9] Edvard Radzinsky, *Stalin: The First In-Depth Biography Based on New Documents from Russia's Secret Archives*, trans. Harry T. Willets (New York: Anchor Books, 1997), 47-49, 59-64; Donald Rayfield, *Stalin and His Hangmen: The Tyrant and Those Who Killed For Him* (New York: Random House, 2005), 25-32, 32-34; Suvorov, *The Chief Culprit*, 1-2, 58-59.

CHAPTER 1

[1] B. H. Liddell Hart, *The Real War 1914-1918* (New York: Little, Brown and Company), 75, 113, 116, 142, 313, 472, 473, 476; Cornell University Library, *Proceedings of the Brest-Litovsk Conference*, 30-34, 39-42.

[2] Sean McMeekin, *The Russian Revolution: A New History* (New York: Basic Books, 2017), 64-65, 73.

[3] U.S. President, "Letter from Theodore Roosevelt to John Hay," 25 May 1905, *Theodore Roosevelt Center at Dickinson State University*, https://www.theodorerooseveltcenter.org /AdvancedSearch?r=1&st1=5&t1=%22Pogroms%22&v=expanded.

[4] *Alpha History Authors*, "Russian Revolution Documents," "Conditions of Factory Workers in Late 19th Century Russia (1885)," https://alphahistory.com/russianrevolution /russian-revolution-documents/.

[5] Ibid.

[6] *Alpha History Authors*, "Manifestos on the Assassination of Alexander II,"; Edvard Radzinsky, *Alexander II: The Last Great Tsar*, trans. Antonina W. Bouis (New York: Free Press, 2006), 115-118, 125-128, 131-133. 134-135.

[7] Radzinsky, *Alexander II*, 391-393, 394-396, 412-414, 415-421.

[8] Edvard Radzinsky, *The Last Tsar: The Life and Death of Nicholas II*, trans. Marian Schwartz (New York: Anchor Books, 1993), 43-45, 46-50, 50-53, 56-57.

[9] Radzinsky, *The Last Tsar*, 121-126, 127-131, 169-174, 174-179, 180-184, 184-188.

[10] U.S. President, "Letter from Theodore Roosevelt to John Hay."

[11] Daniel Ruddy, *Theodore the Great: Conservative Crusader* (Washington, D.C.: Regnery History, 2016), 186-188, 192-194; U.S. President, "Theodore Roosevelt on His Mediation of the Russo-Japanese War, For Which He Received the Nobel Peace Prize," 31 August 1905, *RAAB Collection*, https://www.raabcollection.com/presidential-autographs/tr-robinson.

[12] *Alpha History Authors*, "The 'Bloody Sunday' Petition to the Tsar (1905)."

[13] Radzinsky, *The Last Tsar*, 68-70, 86-91, 91-93. 93-94.

[14] *Alpha History Authors*, "Lenin's view of 'Bloody Sunday,' Gapon and 1905 (1905),"; U.S. President, "Letter from Theodore Roosevelt to John Hay."

[15] Geoffrey Wawro, *A Mad Catastrophe: The Outbreak of World War I and the Collapse of the Habsburg Empire* (New York: Basic Books, 2015), 117-118.

[16] Christopher Clark, *The Sleepwalkers: How Europe Went to War in 1914* (New York: Harper Perennial, 2014), 49; Wawro, 129-130, 135-136.

[17] Vejas Gabriel Liulevicius, *War Land on the Eastern Front: Culture, National Identity and German Occupation in World War I* (Cambridge, UK: Cambridge University Press, 2005), 15, 20.

[18] McMeekin, *The Russian Revolution*, 73-74; Carl J. Richard, *When the United States Invaded Russia: Woodrow Wilson's Siberian Disaster* (Lanham, MD: 2013), 10-11.

[19] Liulevicius, *War Land on the Eastern Front*, 73-74; McMeekin, *The Russian Revolution*, 67-68; Wawro, *A Mad Catastrophe*, 281.

[20] Wawro, *A Mad Catastrophe*, 146-147, 186-187.

[21] McMeekin, *The Russian Revolution*, 65, 78-79; Alan Moorehead, *The Russian Revolution* (New York: Harper & Brothers, 1958), 93-94; Wawro, *A Mad Catastrophe*, 186-187.

[22] Moorehead, *The Russian Revolution*, 93-94; Richard, *When the United States Invaded Russia*, 10-11.

[23] Samuel Lyman Atwood Marshall, *World War I* (New York: Mariner Books, 2001), 263; Richard, *When the United States Invaded Russia*, 10-11; Wawro, *A Mad Catastrophe*, 295.

[24] McMeekin, *The Russian Revolution*, 67-68; Richard, *When the United States Invaded Russia*, 10-11.

[25] William Bruce Lincoln, *Red Victory: A History of the Russian Civil War 1918-1921* (Boston: Da Capo Press, 1999), 33.

[26] Marshall, *World War I*, 263; McMeekin, *The Russian Revolution*, 75-76.

[27] Marshall, *World War I*, 263; McMeekin, *The Russian Revolution*, 75-76; Richard, *When the United States Invaded Russia*, 10-11.

[28] McMeekin, *The Russian Revolution*, 73, 78-79; Wawro, *A Mad Catastrophe*, 284-285.

[29] Richard, *When the United States Invaded Russia*, 11-12.

[30] Moorehead, *The Russian Revolution*, 48-49; Richard, *When the United States Invaded Russia*, 11-12.

[31] McMeekin, *The Russian Revolution*, 121-122; Moorehead, *The Russian Revolution*, 149.

[32] Evan Mawdsley, *The Russian Civil War* (London: Pegasus Books, 2009), 5-6; McMeekin, *The Russian Revolution*, 101-102.

[33] *Alpha History Authors*, "The Abdication Decree of Tsar Nicholas II (1917),"; McMeekin, *The Russian Revolution*, 121-122; Mawdsley, *The Russian Civil War*, 16-17; McMeekin, *The Russian Revolution*, 108; McMeekin, *The Russian Revolution*, 73-74; Carl J. Richard, *When the United States Invaded Russia: Woodrow Wilson's Siberian Disaster* (Lanham, MD: 2013), 10-11.; *Seventeen Moments in Soviet History: An on-line archive of primary sources*, "February Revolution," Michigan State University, https://soviethistory.msu.edu/home.

[34] Mawdsley, *The Russian Civil War*, 105; McMeekin, *The Russian Revolution*, 121-122.

[35] *Alpha History Authors*, "Milyukov's Note to the Allies (1917),"; McMeekin, *The Russian Revolution*, 149, 152; Richard, *When the United States Invaded Russia*, 13.

[36] Martin Gilbert, *The First World War: A Complete History* (New York: Owl Books, 1996), 157; S. L. A. Marshall, *World War I* (New York: Mariner Books, 2001), 166; Theodore Roosevelt, "Theodore Roosevelt on the Sinking of the Lusitania, 1915," *The Gilder Lehman Institute of American History*, 23 June 1915, https://www.gilderlehrman.org/site s/default/files/inline-pdfs/t-08003.pdf; Herbert Temple, "LUSITANIA TORPEDOED: Sinking of Great Liner May Involve United States – Fate of Passengers and Crew Uncertain – Victim of Submarine Sinks off Irish Coast in Thirty Minutes," *The San Diego Union-Tribune*, 7 May 1915, https://www.sandiegouniontribune.com/news/150-years/sd-me-150-years-may-7-20180425-htmlstory.html; U.S. President, "President Woodrow Wilson's Proclamation of Neutrality," *Naval History and Heritage Command*, 4 August 1914, https://www.history.navy.mil/research/publications/documentary-histories/wwi/1914 /ttl-president-woodro.html.

[37] McMeekin, *The Russian Revolution*, 23-24, 26, 61; Geoffrey Wawro, *A Mad Catastrophe: The Outbreak of World War I and the Collapse of the Habsburg Empire* (New York: Basic Books, 2015), 192-193, 229; U.S. President, "President Wilson's Proclamation."

[38] U.S. President, "President Wilson's Proclamation,"; Wawro, *A Mad Catastrophe*, 192-193, 229.

[39] Gilbert, *The First World War*, 312; Marshall, *World War I*, 275; McMeekin, *The Russian Revolution*, 125-126; Richard, *When the United States Invaded Russia*, 10; U.S. Department of State, "Telegram with a Translation of the Zimmermann Telegram," 24 February 1917, *The National Archives*, https://www.archives.gov/education/lessons/zimmermann.

40 U.S. President, "April 19, 1916: Message Regarding German Actions," 19 April 1916, University of Virginia – Miller Center: Presidential Speeches – Woodrow Wilson Presidency, https://millercenter.org/the-presidency/presidential-speeches/april-19-19 16-message-regarding-german-actions.

41 Richard, *When the United States Invaded Russia*, 10; U.S. President, "April 2, 1917: Address to Congress Requesting a Declaration of War Against Germany," University of Virginia – Miller Center: "Presidential Speeches – Woodrow Wilson Presidency," https://millercenter.org/the-presidency/presidential-speeches/april-2-1917-address-congress-requesting-declaration-war.

42 McMeekin, *The Russian Revolution*, 125-126; U.S. President, "April 2, 1917,"; Robert L. Willett, *Russian Sideshow: America's Undeclared War* (McLean, VA: Potomac Books, 2006), xxix-xxxii.

43 U.S. President, "April 2, 1917."

44 McMeekin, *The Russian Revolution*, 125-126; U.S. President, "April 6, 1917: Proclamation 1364," 6 April 1917, University of Virginia – Miller Center: Presidential Speeches – Woodrow Wilson Presidency," https://millercenter.org/the-presidency/presidential-speeches/april-6-1917-proclamation-1364; U.S. President, "American troops in Siberia: Message from the President of the United States," *The White House*, Washington, D.C., 22 July 1919, https://babel.hathitrust.org/cgi/pt?id=loc.ark:/13960/t01z4q15t&view=1up&seq=1.

45 U.S. President, "April 6, 1917."

46 John Deml, "'Get the Rope!': Anti-German Violence in World War I-era Wisconsin," *Atlantic Monthly*, Vol. 11, No. 1 (January 1919), 101-102, http://historymatters.gmu.edu /d/1/; Mary J. Manning, "Being German, Being American: In World War I, They Faced Suspicion, Discrimination Here at Home," *Prologue* (Summer 2014), 14-22, https://www.archives.gov/files/publications/prologue/2014/summer/germans.pdf.

47 Manning, "Being German, Being American," 16-17.

48 U.S. President, "Executive Order 9066, February 19, 1942," *The White House*, Washington, D.C., 19 February 1942, *National Archives and Records Administration*, https://www.archives.gov/historical-docs/todays-doc/?dod-date=219.

49 McMeekin, *The Russian Revolution*, 128, 132.

50 John M. House, *Wolfhounds and Polar Bears: The American Expeditionary Force in Siberia, 1918-1920* (Tuscaloosa: The University of Alabama Press, 2016), 10-12; Vladimir I. Lenin, *Lenin Collected Works*, Vol. 41, trans. Yuri Sdobnikov (Moscow: Progress Publishers, 1977), 397-398; Marshall, *World War I*, 321; McMeekin, *The Russian Revolution*, 20, 46, 132, 165-166, 173; John Lukacs, "America and Russia, Americans and Russians," *American Heritage*, Vol. 43, No. 1 (February-March 1992), https://www.americanheritage.com/america-and-russia-americans-and-russians.

51 Lenin, *Lenin Collected Works*, Vol. 41; McMeekin, *The Russian Revolution*, 173, 176.

52 *Alpha History Authors*, "Lenin Calls for Revolution (1917),"; David R. Francis, *Russia From the American Embassy: April, 1916-November, 1918* (New York: Charles Scribner's Sons, 1921), 19, 31, 52-55, 57-59; House, *Wolfhounds and Polar Bears*, 19; Marshall, *World War I*, 324; McMeekin, *The Russian Revolution*, 173.

53 Francis, *Russia From the American Embassy*, 115-117, 128-130, 134; Sherwood, *Roosevelt and Hopkins*, 306-308.

54 McMeekin, *The Russian Revolution*, 212; Moorehead, *The Russian Revolution*, 245.

[55] *Alpha History Authors*, "Lenin Calls for an October Revolution (1917),"; McMeekin, *The Russian Revolution*, 215, 217.

[56] House, *Wolfhounds and Polar Bears*, 23; McMeekin, *The Russian Revolution*, 226-227; *Seventeen Moments in Soviet History*, "Vladimir Lenin, Proclamation to Soldiers and Sailors. November 22, 1917."

[57] *Alpha History Authors*, "Decree Establishing a Soviet Government (1917),"; Lenin, *Lenin Collected Works*, Vol. 41; *Seventeen Moments in Soviet History*, "Second All-Russian Congress of Soviets, Decree on Peace. November 8, 1917."

[58] *Seventeen Moments in Soviet History*, "The Socialist Fatherland is in Danger! Soviet of People's Commissars, Proclamation. February 21, 1918."

[59] Christopher Dobson and John Miller, *The Day They Almost Bombed Moscow: The Allied War in Russia 1918-1920* (New York: Simon & Schuster, 1986), 43-44; Gilbert, *The First World War*, 401-402; Marshall, *World War I*, 334; McMeekin, *The Russian Revolution*, 226-227; *Seventeen Moments in Soviet History*, "Treaty of Brest-Litovsk, March 3, 1918."

[60] Francis, *Russia From the American Embassy*, 223-227, 229; The German General Staff, "Erich Ludendorff on the Opening of the 1918 Spring Offensive, 21 March 1918," Charles F. Horne (ed.) *Source Records of the Great War, Vol. VI*, (New York: National Alumni, 1923), https://www.firstworldwar.com/source/kaiserbattle_ludendorff.htm.

[61] The German General Staff, "Erich Ludendorff."

[62] Geoffrey Wawro, *Sons of Freedom: The Forgotten American Soldiers Who Defeated Germany in World War I* (New York: Basic Books, 2018), viii, 122-124.

[63] General John J. Pershing, "MY EXPERIENCES IN THE WORLD WAR; Enemy Growing Exhausted. New Offensives Planned. Wearing Down the Germans. Artillery and Tanks Needed. Our Plans Badly Disrupted. 1,200,000 Yankee Soldiers in France. A Regiment Sent to Russia. Against Dissipating a Great Effort Force to Russia to Guard Stores. First American Army Ordered. Harbord Named to Head S.O.S.," *The New York Times*, 7 March 1931, https://www.nytimes.com/1931/03/07/archives/my-experiences-in-the-world-war-ene my-growing-exhausted-new.html; Wawro, *Sons of Freedom*, 129.

[64] Wawro, *Sons of Freedom*, 129.

[65] The German General Staff, "Erich Ludendorff."

[66] Cornell University Library, *Proceedings of the Brest-Litovsk Conference*, 47-49, 51-54, 56, 61-65; E. M. Halliday, *When Hell Froze Over: The Secret War Between the U.S. and Russia at the Top of the World* (New York: Simon & Schuster, 2000), 21-23; Field-Marshal Lord Ironside, *Archangel: 1918-1919* (Uckfield, East Sussex, UK: Naval & Military Press, 2007), 45-46, 51, 55-56; *Seventeen Moments in Soviet History*, "Treaty of Brest-Litovsk."

[67] Henry P. Beers, "U.S. Naval Forces in Northern Russia (Archangel and Murmansk) 1918-1919," *Office of Records Administration, Administrative Officer, Navy Department*, 1943, https://babel.hathitrust.org/cgi/pt?id=mdp.39015011359273&view=1up&seq=1; John Bradley, *Allied Intervention in Russia* (New York: Basic Books, 1984), 8-9, 15-16; Deutscher Reichsanzeiger, "Treaty of peace between Finland and Germany. Signed at Berlin, 7 March, 1918," *Deutscher Reichsanzeiger*, 8 March 1918, https://documentsdedro itinternational.fr/ressources/TdP/1918-03-07-TraitedeBerlin(Finlande)(enanglais).pdf; Francis, *Russia From the American Embassy*, 261-162, 264-265, 278, 296, 297, 301-304.

[68] Dobson and Miller, *The Day They Almost Bombed Moscow*, 43-44; Halliday, *When Hell Froze Over*, 21-23; Clifford Kinvig, *Churchill's Crusade: The British Invasion of Russia, 1918-1920* (London: Hambledon Continuum, 2007), 26-27.

[69] James Carl Nelson, *The Polar Bear Expedition: The Heroes of America's Forgotten Invasion of Russia 1918-1919* (New York: William Morrow, 2020), 13, 29; *Seventeen Moments in Soviet History,* "Soviet of People's Commissars, Formation of the Worker-Peasant Red Army. January 28, 1918."

[70] *Alpha History Authors,* "The Oath of the Red Warrior (1918),"; *Seventeen Moments in Soviet History,* "Solemn Oath on Induction into the Worker-Peasant Red Army. 1918."

[71] House, *Wolfhounds and Polar Bears,* 26-27; Joel R. Moore, Harry H. Meade, and Lewis E. Jahns, *History of the American Expedition Fighting the Bolsheviks: U.S. Military Intervention in Soviet Russia, 1918-1919* (Detroit: Polar Bear Publishing, 1920), 9, 49, 57; UK Prime Minister, "Papers of David Lloyd George, 1st East Lloyd George of Dwyfor (as filmed by the AJCP) [microfilm] : [M1124-1125], 1903-1944," Series F/File 2/01/1932, "L.S. Amery to Lloyd George," 24 December 1918.

[72] Dobson and Miller, *The Day They Almost Bombed Moscow,* 63, 70; Halliday, *When Hell Froze Over,* 26-27, 225; Kinvig, *Churchill's Crusade,* 20; *Seventeen Moments in Soviet History,* "Soviet of People's Commissars, An Appropriation for the Support of World Revolution. December 26, 1917."

[73] U.S. Department of State, "Papers Relating to the Foreign Relations of the United States, 1918, Russia, Volume I: The Acting Secretary of State to Consul General at Moscow, Washington, March 11, 1918," 11 March 1918, https://history.state.gov/historicaldocum ents/frus1918Russiav01/d398.

[74] Beers, "U.S. Naval Forces in Northern Russia,"; Francis, *Russia From the American Embassy,* 261-162, 264-265, 278, 296, 297, 301-304; Halliday, *When Hell Froze Over,* 26-27, 225; Ironside, *Archangel,* 47-49.

[75] Halliday, *When Hell Froze Over,* 26-27; Ironside, *Archangel,* 47-49; Richard, *When the United States Invaded Russia,* 37-38; Willett, *Russian Sideshow,* 22.

[76] House, *Wolfhounds and Polar Bears,* 9; Gibson Bell Smith, "Guarding the Railroad, Taming the Cossacks: The U.S. Army in Russia, 1918-1920," *Prologue,* Vol. 34, No. 4 (Winter 2002), *U.S. National Archives,* https://www.archives.gov/publications/prologue/ 2002/winter/us-army-in-russia-1.html; U.S. President, "American Troops in Siberia."

[77] Francis, *Russia From the American Embassy,* 261-162, 264-265, 278, 296, 297, 301-304; U.S. President, "American Troops in Siberia,"; Willett, *Russian Sideshow,* 28-29.

[78] *The National Archives of the UK,* "The Cabinet Papers: The Western Front," British War Cabinet, "Cabinet Conclusion 1. The Western Front. 27 May 1918," http://filestore.nation alarchives.gov.uk/pdfs/small/cab-23-6-wc-419-41.pdf.

[79] British War Cabinet, "Cabinet Conclusion 1,"; UK Prime Minister, "Papers of David Lloyd George," Series F/File 2/01/1932, "L.S. Amery to Lloyd George," 24 December 1918.

[80] George F. Kennan, *Soviet-American Relations, 1917-1920, Vol. II: The Decision to Intervene* (Princeton: Princeton University Press, 1958), 482-485; Kinvig, *Churchill's Crusade,* 20; Richard, *When the United States Invaded Russia,* 37-38; U.S. Department of State, "The Secretary of State to the Allied Ambassadors: Aide Memoire," 17 July 1918, http://pbma.grobbel.org/aide_memoire.htm.

[81] Beers, "U.S. Naval Forces in Northern Russia,"; Dobson and Miller, *The Day They Almost Bombed Moscow,* 66; Kennan, *Soviet-American Relations,* 482-485; Lukacs, "America and Russia,"; *The National Archives of the UK,* "Spotlights on history: Allied intervention in Russia, 1918-19 – Fighting the Bolsheviks in North Russia – Catalogue reference 30/71/4 (15 August 1919)," https://www.nationalarchives.gov.uk/pathways/firstworldwar/spotli ghts/allies.htm; U.S. Department of State, "The Secretary of State to the Allied Ambassadors."

[82] Richard, *When the United States Invaded Russia*, 43; John Swettenham, *Allied Intervention in Russia, 1918-1919* (Oxfordshire: Routledge, 2019), 64, 164-165; *The National Archives of the UK*, "Spotlights on history – Fighting the Bolsheviks,"; UK Prime Minister, "Papers of David Lloyd George," Series F/File 2/01/1932, "L.S. Amery to Lloyd George," 24 December 1918.

[83] Beers, "U.S. Naval Forces in Northern Russia,"; Bradley, *Allied Intervention*, 113; Richard, *When the United States Invaded Russia*, 45-47; Swettenham, *Allied Intervention*, 97.

[84] Bradley, *Allied Intervention*, 93-94; Marshall, *World War I*, 334; *The National Archives of the UK*, "Spotlights on history – Fighting the Bolsheviks."

[85] Stephen Kotkin, *Stalin: Paradoxes of Power, 1878-1928* (New York: Penguin Press, 2014), 103; Willett, *Russian Sideshow*, xxxii.

[86] Jason Dawsey, "Trotsky's Struggle Against Stalin: Joseph Stalin was a hangman whose noose could reach across oceans," The National World War II Museum – New Orleans, 12 September 2018, https://www.nationalww2museum.org/war/articles/trotskys-struggle-against-stalin; Kotkin, *Paradoxes of Power*, 103; Rayfield, *Stalin and His Hangmen*, 49, 89-90, 92; Richard, *When the United States Invaded Russia*, 45-47.

[87] Kotkin, *Paradoxes of Power*, 103; Richard, *When the United States Invaded Russia*, 45-47.

[88] Bradley, *Allied Intervention*, 94.

[89] Beers, "U.S. Naval Forces in Northern Russia."

[90] McMeekin, *The Russian Revolution*, 266-267.

[91] Chief of the Imperial General Staff, "Revolutionary Russia – A British View: Poole, F C," 1-37, 12 January 1919, "King's Collections: The Serving Soldier," King's College London, https://kingscollections.org/servingsoldier/collection/revolutionary-russia-a-british-view/; DeWitt Clinton Poole, *An American Diplomat in Bolshevik Russia*, ed. Lorraine M. Lees and William S. Rodner (Madison: The University of Wisconsin Press, 2014), 149-152.

[92] Chief of the Imperial General Staff, "Revolutionary Russia," 9-10.

[93] Pershing, "MY EXPERIENCES,"; Poole, *An American Diplomat*, 149-152; UK Prime Minister, "Papers of David Lloyd George," Series F/File 2/01/1932, "L.S. Amery to Lloyd George," 24 December 1918.

[94] Moore, Meade, and Jahns, *History of the American Expedition*, 49; U.S. President, "American Troops in Siberia."

[95] Kennan, *Soviet-American Relations*, 482-485; U.S. Department of State, "The Secretary of State to the Allied Ambassadors,"; Moore, Meade, and Jahns, *History of the American Expedition*, 52-53; Willett, *Russian Sideshow*, xxix-xxxii.

[96] John Cudahy, *Archangel: The American War with Russia, By a Chronicler* (Chicago: A. C. McClurg & Company, 1924), 19-21; Moore, Meade, and Jahns, *History of the American Expedition*, 57; Nelson, *The Polar Bear Expedition*, 11; The American Sentinel (Unattributed Report), "Still, One Never Knows his Allies up Here," *The American Sentinel*, No, 8, 1 February 1919, https://quod.lib.umich.edu/p/polar/3241550.0001.008/3?page=root;size=100;view=text.

[97] Deane, *The Strange Alliance*, 21; William S. Graves, *America's Siberian Adventure 1918-1920* (New York: Peter Smith Publishing, Inc., 1941), 4-5, 55-57; Nelson, *The Polar Bear Expedition*, 11; The New York Times (Unattributed Report), "GRAVES TO LEAD OUR SIBERIAN ARMY," *The New York Times*, 8 August 1918, https://www.nytimes.com/1918/08/08/archives/graves-to-lead-our-siberian-army-former-assistant-chief-of-general.html.

[98] James S. Herndon and Joseph O. Baylen, "Col. Philip R. Faymonville and the Red Army, 1934-43," *Slavic Review: Interdisciplinary Quarterly of Russian, Eurasian, and East European Studies* Vol. 34, Issue 3 (September 1975), 483-505, https://www.cambridge.org

/core/services/aop-cambridge-core/content/view/2473C57D215570C91E8F1F5B22587
6DD/S0037677900071722a.pdf/col_philip_r_faymonville_and_the_red_army_193443.pdf.
99 Cudahy, *Archangel*, 41-43; The American Sentinel, "Still, One Never Knows his Allies
up Here."
100 Cudahy, *Archangel*, 41-43; Halliday, *When Hell Froze Over*, 62-64, 124-125; The
American Sentinel, "Still, One Never Knows his Allies up Here."
101 Associated Press, "ALLIES PAY TRIBUTE TO YANKS OVERSEAS: Troop in Russia Feast
on Delicious Wild Turkey," *The Morning Oregonian*, 29 November 1918, https://oregonne
ws.uoregon.edu/lccn/sn83025138/1918-11-29/ed-1/seq-18/; Halliday, *When Hell Froze
Over*, 62-64, 124-125; Ironside, *Archangel*, 47-49; Moore, Meade, and Jahns, *History of the
American Expedition*, 117; *Parliamentary Record – House of Commons*, 1st Session (1918),
https://hansard.parliament.uk/Commons/1918-10-17/debates/8bea1019-0383-4875-9
914-7bf2dbde4f29/ArchangelGovernment; Pershing, "MY EXPERIENCES,"; The American
Sentinel, "Yanks Took Part in Big Fighting Here: Historians Will Find Americans Played
Important Role in Campaign in North Russia," *The American Sentinel*, No. 25, 31 May 1919,
https://quod.lib.umich.edu/p/polar/3241550.0001.025/1?page=root;rgn=full+text;size=
100;view=image; U.S. President, "Proclamation 1496 – Thanksgiving Day, 1918," *The
American Presidency Project*, 16 November 1918, https://www.presidency.ucsb.edu/docu
ments/proclamation-1496-thanksgiving-day-1918; UK Prime Minister, "Papers of David
Lloyd George," Series F/File 2/01/1932, "L.S. Amery to Lloyd George," 24 December 1918.
102 Associated Press, "ALLIES PAY TRIBUTE TO YANKS OVERSEAS,"; Cudahy, *Archangel*,
90-94; The American Sentinel, "Still, One Never Knows his Allies up Here,"; *Parl. Rec. –
House of Commons*, 1st Sess. (1918).
103 Moore, Meade, and Jahns, *History of the American Expedition*, 117; Nelson, *The Polar
Bear Expedition*, 107; *Parl. Rec. – House of Commons*, 1st Sess. (1918); *The National
Archives of the UK*, "Spotlights on history – Fighting the Bolsheviks."
104 Moore, Meade, and Jahns, *History of the American Expedition*, 278; *Parl. Rec. – House
of Commons*, 1st Sess. (1918); The American Sentinel, "Yanks Took Big Part in Fighting
Here,"; The New York Times (Unattributed Report), "ALLIES TO QUIT ARCHANGEL IN
EARLY SPRING; Baker Announces That All Our Forces in North Russia Will Be Withdrawn.
ORDERED BY PRESIDENT Secretary Baker Instructed to Give Reasons to Military
Committees of Congress. WARNING OF MASSACRE R.E. Simmons Tells Senate
Committee Slaughter Would Follow Withdrawal of Allies in North. ALLIES TO QUIT
ARCHANGEL SOON RED PROPAGANDISTS BUSY IN ARCHANGEL American Soldiers
Get Leaflets Urging Them to Demand That They Be Sent Home," *The New York Times*, 18
February 1919, https://www.nytimes.com/1919/02/18/archives/allies-to-quit-archange
l-in-early-spring-baker-announces-that-all.html.
105 *Congressional Record – United States Senate*, 65th Congress, 3rd Session (1918), pt. 1,
Government Publishing Office, https://babel.hathitrust.org/cgi/pt?id=uc1.31210026472
934&view=1up&seq=1; Ironside, *Archangel*, 52-53, 57; Richard, *When the United States
Invaded Russia*, 67; U.S. President, "Proclamation 1496."
106 *Cong. Rec. – United States Senate*, 65th Cong., 3rd Sess. (1918), pt. 1; Richard, *When the
United States Invaded Russia*, 67.
107 *Cong. Rec. – United States Senate*, 65th Cong., 3rd Sess. (1918) pt. 1.
108 House, *Wolfhounds and Polar Bears*, 180; Richard, *When the United States Invaded
Russia*, 67.
109 *Cong. Rec. – United States Senate*, 65th Cong., 3rd Sess. (1918) pt. 1.

[110] *Congressional Record – United States Senate*, 65th Congress, 3rd Session (1919), pt. 4, Government Publishing Office, https://babel.hathitrust.org/cgi/pt?id=uc1.31210023079 575&view=1up&seq=5.

[111] Associated Press, "ALLIES PAY TRIBUTE TO YANKS OVERSEAS,"; *Cong. Rec. – United States Senate*, 65th Cong., 3rd Sess. (1919) pt. 4; Richard, *When the United States Invaded Russia*, 67; The American Sentinel, "Yanks Took Big Part in Fighting Here,"; U.S. President, "Proclamation 1496."

[112] *Cong. Rec. United States Senate*, 65th Cong., 3rd Sess. (1919) pt. 4; House, *Wolfhounds and Polar Bears*, 154-155; The Alaska Daily Empire (Unattributed Report), "Yankees Back From Russia Deny Mutiny," *The Alaska Daily Empire*, 15 July 1919, https://chroniclingam erica.loc.gov/lccn/sn84020657/1919-07-15/ed-1/seq-1/.

[113] Nelson, *The Polar Bear Expedition*, 133; Pershing, "MY EXPERIENCES," Richard, *When the United States Invaded Russia*, 67; The American Sentinel, "Yanks Took Big Part in Fighting Here,"; U.S. Department of State, "Papers Relating to the Foreign Relations of the United States, 1919, Russia: The Acting Secretary of State to the **Chargé** in Russia (Poole)," 29 March 1919, https://history.state.gov/historicaldocuments/frus1919Russia/d685.

[114] Graves, *America's Siberian Adventure*, 349; The Alaska Daily Empire, "Yankees Back From Russia Deny Mutiny,"; The American Sentinel, "Yanks Took Big Part in Fighting Here,"; *The National Archives of the UK*, "Spotlights on history: British support for 'Whites' in Siberia – Catalogue reference WO 158/741 (18 January 1919),"; The New York Times, "ALLIES TO QUIT."

[115] Ironside, *Archangel*, 68-70; Pershing, "MY EXPERIENCES,"; *The National Archives of the UK*, "Spotlights on history: Fighting the Bolsheviks."

[116] Ironside, *Archangel*, 125, 126-128; Pershing, "MY EXPERIENCES,"; The Alaska Daily Empire, "Yankees Back From Russia Deny Mutiny,"; The American Sentinel, "Yanks Took Big Part in Fighting Here,"; U.S. President, "Proclamation 1496."

[117] British War Cabinet, "Cabinet Conclusion 1,"; Dobson and Miller, *The Day They Almost Bombed Moscow*, 63, 70; Halliday, *When Hell Froze Over*, 26-27, 225; Kinvig, *Churchill's Crusade*, 20; Poole, *An American Diplomat*, 149-152; *Seventeen Moments in Soviet History*, "Soviet of People's Commissars, An Appropriation for the Support of World Revolution. December 26, 1917,"; The Alaska Daily Empire, "Yankees Back From Russia Deny Mutiny,"; U.S. Department of State, "The Secretary of State to the Allied Ambassadors."

[118] Moore, Meade, and Jahns, *History of the American Expedition*, 120.

[119] Weeks, *Stalin's Other War: Soviet Grand Strategy, 1939-1941* (Lanham, MD: Rowman & Littlefield, 2003), 36-37.

[120] Malaika Adero, *Up South: Stories, Studies, and Letters of This Century's African-American Migrations* (New York: The New Press, 1993), 54-55.

[121] *Primary Sources: The 1920s*, "Red Scare," "Attorney General A. Mitchell Palmer Makes 'The Case against the Reds,'" 1920, Christopher Newport University, https://cnu.libguibd es.com/1920s/redscare.

[122] *Primary Sources: The 1920s*, "Red Scare," "Attorney General A. Mitchell Palmer."

[123] *Congressional Record – House of Representatives*, 66th Congress, 2nd Session (1920), pt. 1, Government Publishing Office, https://babel.hathitrust.org/cgi/pt?id=hvd.320440192 71584&view=1up&seq=7&skin=2021.

[124] U.S. Department of Justice, "Red Radicalism as Described by its own Leaders,"1920, Government Publishing Office, https://babel.hathitrust.org/cgi/pt?id=umn.3195100155 6727y&view=1up&seq=1&skin=2021.

[125] U.S. Department of Justice, "Red Radicalism."

[126] Ibid.

[127] Stephen Kotkin, *Stalin: Waiting for Hitler, 1929-1941* (New York: Penguin Press, 2017), 73.

[128] Rayfield, *Stalin and His Hangmen*, 136, 145-146; 457-458; Romerstein and Breindel, *The Venona Secrets*, 3-4.

[129] Kotkin, *Waiting for Hitler*, 113-115.

[130] Weeks, *Stalin's Other War*, 37-38.

[131] Margaret Bourke-White, *Eyes on Russia* (New York: Simon and Schuster, 1931), 118-119, 123-124; Irene Brisson, "How Albert Kahn helped the Soviet Union industrialize: exploring the little-known history of the Architect of Detroit's impactful relationship with the USSR," *Detroit Curbed*, 13 December 2019, https://detroit.curbed.com/2019/12/13/21012559/albert-kahn-russia-ussr-detroit-world-war-ii; Danielle Dreilinger, "Built in the U.S.S.R. (by Detroit)," *LSA Magazine* (Fall 2019), University of Michigan, https://lsa.umich.edu/lsa/news-events/all-news/search-news/built-in-the-u-s-s-r---by-detroit.html; Stateside Staff, "Detroit architect Albert Kahn helped pave the way for Soviet victory in WWII," *Michigan Radio*, 10 August 2018, https://www.michiganradio.org/arts-culture/2018-08-10/detroit-architect-albert-kahn-helped-pave-the-way-for-soviet-victory-in-wwii?_amp=true.

[132] Bourke-White, *Eyes on Russia*, 123-124; Christina E. Crawford, "Soviet Planning Praxis: From Tractors to Territory," *Centerpiece*, Vol. 29, No. 2 (Spring 2015), Weatherhead Center for International Affairs, Harvard University, https://wcfia.harvard.edu/publications/centerpiece/spring2015/feature-crawford.

[133] Architect Staff, "The USA, the USSR, and Architecture: An exhibition at the Canadian Centre for Architecture explores American influences on Soviet culture," *Architect*, 15 November 2019, https://www.architectmagazine.com/design/exhibits-books-etc/the-usa-the-ussr-and-architecture_o; Deane, *The Strange Alliance*, 100-103; Sonia Melnikova-Raich, "The Soviet Problem with Two 'Unknowns': How an American Architect and a Soviet Negotiator Jump-Started the Industrialization of Russia, Part I: Albert Kahn," *The Journal of the Society for Industrial Archaeology*, Vol. 36, No. 2 (January 2010), 57-80, https://www.researchgate.net/publication/262098142_The_Soviet_Problem_with_Two_Unknowns_How_an_American_Architect_and_a_Soviet_Negotiator_Jump-Started_the_Industrialization_of_Russia_Part_I_Albert_Kahn.

[134] Crawford, "Soviet Planning Praxis,"; Historic Detroit (Unattributed Report), "Albert Kahn (March 21, 1869-Dec 8, 1942)," *HistoricDetroit.org*, https://historicdetroit.org/architects/albert-kahn; Melnikova-Raich, "The Soviet Problem with Two 'Unknowns'," 67-73.

[135] Boris M. Shpotov, "The Ford Motor Company in the Soviet Union in the 1920s-1930s: Strategy, identity, performance, reception, adaptability," Institute of World History, Russian Academy of Sciences, 1-7 (n. d.), https://studylib.net/doc/8309060/the-ford-motor-company-in-the-soviet-union-in-the-1920s; Antony C. Sutton, *National Suicide: Military Aid to the Soviet Union* (Las Vegas, NV: Dauphin Publishing, 1973), 112-113.

[136] Bourke-White, *Eyes on Russia*, 123-124, 125-127; Shpotov, "The Ford Motor Company in the Soviet Union," 3-5.

[137] Sutton, *National Suicide*, 126; Steven J. Zaloga and James Grandsen, *Soviet Tanks and Combat Vehicles of World War Two* (London: Arms and Armour Press, 1984), 43, 94.

[138] Deane, *The Strange Alliance*, 100-103; Boris Egorov, "How the newborn Soviet state took capitalist help and hushed it up," *Russia Beyond*, 25 July 2018, https://www.rbth.com/history/328834-soviet-state-took-capitalist-help/amp; Anne O'Hare McCormick, "When Henry Ford Was the Hero of the Soviet Union," *The New York Times*, 9 April 1947,

https://www.nytimes.com/1947/04/09/archives/when-henry-ford-was-the-hero-of-the
-soviet-union.html; *Seventeen Moments in Soviet History*, "Cars for Comrades,"; Boris M.
Shpotov, "Business without Entrepreneurship: the Ford Motor Company and the Soviet
Industrialization, 1920s-1930s," Institute of World History, Russian Academy of Sciences,
1-13 (n. d.), https://ebha.org/ebha2007/pdf/Shpotov.pdf.

[139] Kotkin, *Waiting for Hitler*, 113-115.

[140] Sutton, *National Suicide*, 112-113; Alexander Vershinin, "Christie's chassis: An
American tank for the Soviets," *Russia Beyond*, 18 May 2015, https://www.rbth.com/defe
nce/2015/05/18/christies_chassis_an_american_tank_for_the_soviets_46135.html.

[141] Zaloga and Grandsen, *Soviet Tanks and Combat Vehicles*, 166; Sutton, *National Suicide*,
112-113; Vershinin, "Christie's chassis."

[142] Bourke-White, *Eyes on Russia*, 125-127; Sutton, *National Suicide*, 124; Weeks, *Russia's
Life-Saver*, 82-83.

[143] Peter Kenez, *The Birth of the Propaganda State* (New York: University of Cambridge
Press, 1985), 82-83, 85-86, 89-90, 93-94, 98, 100.

[144] Bourke-White, *Eyes on Russia*, 125-127; Robert Vincent Daniels, *The Stalin Revolution:
Foundations of the Totalitarian Era* (New York: Houghton Mifflin, 1965), 182; John Scott,
Behind the Urals: An American Worker in Russia's City of Steel (Bloomington: Indiana
University Press, 1973), 42, 137.

[145] Romerstein and Breindel, *The Venona Secrets*, 49-50, 137.

[146] Dawson, *The Decision to Aid Russia, 1941*, 65-66; John Kelly, *Saving Stalin: Roosevelt,
Churchill, and the Cost of Allied Victory in Europe* (New York: Hatchette Books, 2020), 16.

[147] Margaret Bourke-White, "SILK STOCKINGS IN THE FIVE-YEAR PLAN; Despite the
Soviet Drive and the New Order of Things, Russia's Women Are Still Feminine," *The New
York Times*, 14 February 1932, https://www.nytimes.com/1932/02/14/archives/silk-
stockings-in-the-fiveyear-plan-despite-the-soviet-drive-and.html.

[148] Bourke-White, *Eyes on Russia*, 22-23.

[149] Bourke-White, "SILK STOCKINGS IN THE FIVE-YEAR PLAN."

[150] Bourke-White, *Eyes on Russia*, 118-119.

[151] Ibid.; Sokolov, *The Role of the Soviet Union in the Second World War*, 53-55.

[152] *The National Security Archive, Vol. II*, "Episode 1 Cold War Documents: Roosevelt-
Litvinov – The White House, Washington, November 16, 1933," https://nsarchive2.gwu.e
du/coldwar/documents/episode-1/fdr-ml.htm; Weeks, *Russia's Life-Saver*, 82-83.

[153] *The National Security Archive, Vol. II*, "Episode 1 Cold War Documents."

[154] Ibid.

[155] Weeks, *Russia's Life-Saver*, 82-83.

[156] Kotkin, *Waiting for Hitler*, 44-45.

[157] Sutton, *National Suicide*, 153, 157.

[158] Joseph V. Stalin, *Selected Works* (Honolulu, HI: University Press of the Pacific, 2002), 393.

[159] Stalin, *Selected Works*, 399; Weeks, *Stalin's Other War*, 112-115, 116-117.

[160] Herndon and Baylen, "Col. Philip R. Faymonville," 483-484; McMeekin, *Stalin's War*,
358, 361, 369-370; Sherwood, *Roosevelt and Hopkins*, 385, 395, 496.

[161] Bullitt, *For the President*, 57-59, 62-65; Herndon and Baylen, "Col. Philip R.
Faymonville," 486-488; Kelly, *Saving Stalin*, 26-29.

[162] Herndon and Baylen, "Col. Philip R. Faymonville," 492-493.

[163] Ibid.

[164] Walter Duranty, "RUSSIANS HUNGRY, BUT NOT STARVING; Deaths From Diseases Due to Malnutrition High, Yet the Soviet is Entrenched. LARGER CITIES HAVE FOOD Ukraine, North Caucasus and Lower Volga Regions Suffer From Shortages. KREMLIN'S 'DOOM' DENIED Russians and Foreign Observers In Country See No Ground for Predictions of Disaster," *The New York Times*, 31 March 1933, https://www.nytimes.com/19 33/03/31/archives/russians-hungry-but-not-starving-deaths-from-diseases-due-to.html.

[165] Walter Duranty, "RUSSIAN REDS SEE MECHANIZED ARMY; 2,000 Delegates to Congress Review Great Parade in Moscow's Red Square. BIG NEW TANKS DISPLAYED Voroshiloff Says Bolsheviki Are Ready 'To Hold Every Inch of the Fatherland,'" *The New York Times*, 10 February 1934, https://www.nytimes.com/1934/02/10/archives/russian-reds-see-mechanized-army-2000-delegates-to-congress-review.html.

[166] Walter Duranty, "SOVIET WAR GAMES OPEN ON BIG SCALE; Manoeuvres in Kiev Region Said to Be the Largest Ever Held by Red Army," *The New York Times*, 15 September 1935, https://www.nytimes.com/1935/09/15/archives/soviet-war-games-open-on-big-scale-manoeuvres-in-kiev-region-said.html.

[167] McMeekin, *Stalin's War*, 358n, 361, 369-370; Sherwood, *Roosevelt and Hopkins*, xv, 385, 395, 496.

[168] Standley and Ageton, *Admiral Ambassador to Russia*, 62, 127, 235, 247, 285, 309-310.

[169] Sherwood, *Roosevelt and* Hopkins, 87-88; Pavel Sudoplatov and Anatoli Sudoplatov, *Special Tasks: The Memoirs of an Unwanted Witness – A Soviet Spymaster* (New York: Little, Brown & Company, 1995), 222, 226-227.

[170] *Congressional Record – House of Representatives*, 81st Congress, 1st and 2nd Sessions (1949-1950), pts.?, https://www.ibiblio.org/hyperwar/NHC/NewPDFs/USAAF/United%20States%20Strategic%20Bombing%20Survey/USSBS%20Shipment%20of%20Atomic%20Material%20to%20the%20Soviet%20Union%20during%20WWII.pdf; George Racey Jordan, *Major Jordan's Diaries* (New York: Harcourt, Brace, and Company, 1952), 39; U.S. Air Force, *Project Rand Research Memorandum: The Soviet Union and the Atom: The 'Secret' Phase* (Santa Monica, CA: The Rand Corporation, 1957), 27-34.

[171] Koster, *Operation Snow*, 15.

[172] M. Stanton Evans and Herbert Romerstein, *Stalin's Secret Agents: The Subversion of Roosevelt's Government* (New York: Threshold Editions, 2013), 185-187, 196.

[173] Koster, *Operation Snow*, 15.

[174] Whittaker Chambers, *Witness* (Southbend, IN: Regnery, 1952), 413-415, 415-417; *Congressional Record – House of Representatives*, 80th Congress, 2nd Session (1948), pt.? https://web.archive.org/web/20100721003156/http://www.law.umkc.edu/faculty/proje cts/ftrials/hiss/8-17testimony.html; VENONA Decrypts, "Silvermaster Folder NY 65-14603 'Alger Hiss,'" *Internet Archive Wayback Machine*, n. d., https://web.archive.org/we b/20120310003840/http://www.education-research.org/PDFs/splitfiles/splitprocessed/Silvermaster006_Folder/Silvermaster006_page106.pdf; William Fitzgibbon, "The Hiss-Chambers Case: A Chronology Since 1934," *The New York Times*, 12 June 1949, https://arc hive.nytimes.com/www.nytimes.com/books/97/03/09/reviews/chambers-chronology.html.

[175] *Cong. Rec. – House of Representatives*, 81st Cong. 1st and 2nd Sess. (1949-1950).

[176] Ibid.; Pavel Sudoplatov and Anatoli Sudoplatov, *Special Tasks: The Memoirs of an Unwanted Witness – A Soviet Spymaster* (New York: Little, Brown & Company, 1995), 222, 226-227, 227-229, 230.

[177] Harold Denny, "SOVIET FLIERS LAND PLANE AT NORTH POLE FOR A BASE FOR FLIGHTS TO AMERICA; CAMP MADE ON ICE, Party Begins Clearing of Field for

Permanent Scientific Station THREE PLANES TO FOLLOW Buildings Will Be Erected for Four Men Who Will Remain a Year Near Pole RADIO REPORTS TO STALIN Expedition Sends Regrets for Fear Caused by Failure of Wireless Before Landing Field Base at Pole Planned SOVIET FLIERS LAND NEAR NORTH POLE Dog Will Warn of Bears Climax to Years of Effort SOVIET FLIERS WHO LANDED NEAR NORTH POLE," *The New York Times*, 22 May 1937, https://www.nytimes.com/1937/05/22/archives/soviet-fliers-land-plane-at-north-pole-for-a-base-for-flights-to.html.

[178] Madera Tribune (Unattributed Report), "RUSSIANS REACH SAN JACINTO LACK OF GAS CAUSES HALT LONG FLIGHT Pole Vaulting Plane Made Forced Landing in Cow Pasture Near Town VILLAGE IN TURMOIL Flyers Were Unaware That March Field Is But 20 Miles Away," *Madera Tribune*, 14 July 1937, https://cdnc.ucr.edu/?a=d&d=MT1937071 4.2.18&e=-------en--20--1--txt-txIN-------; Rickenbacker, *Rickenbacker*, 399-400.

[179] Bullitt, *For the President*, xiii-xiv, 57-59, 62-65.

[180] Charles E. Bohlen, *Witness to History, 1929-1979* ed. Robert H. Phelps (New York: Norton, 1973), 51-52.

[181] Davies, *Mission to Moscow*, 275-277.

[182] Bohlen, *Witness to History*, 51-52; Bullitt, *For the President*, xiii-xiv, 57-59, 62-65; *Cong. Rec. – House of Representatives*, 81st Cong. 1st and 2nd Sess. (1949-1950); Davies, *Mission to Moscow*, 275-277; Fitzgibbon, "The Hiss-Chambers Case,"; David Kaiser, *No End Save Victory: How FDR Led the Nation into War* (New York: Basic Books 2015), 27, 54, 74; Koster, *Operation Snow*, 15; Kotkin, *Waiting for Hitler*, 685-686, 692-695; B. H. Liddell Hart, *History of the Second World War* (London: Pan Books, 2011), 33-35, 36-39; Rayfield, *Stalin and His Hangmen*, 370, 378, 393, 413.

CHAPTER 2

[1] Kaiser, *No End Save Victory*, 27, 54, 74; Sherwood, *Roosevelt and Hopkins*, 144, 291.

[2] Kaiser, *No End Save Victory*, 27, 54, 74.

[3] Burton W. Folsom, Jr., and Anita Folsom, *FDR Goes to War: How Expanded Executive Power, Spiraling National Debt, and Restricted Civil Liberties Shaped Wartime America* (New York: Threshold Editions, 2013), 222.

[4] Franklin Delano Roosevelt, *Great Speeches*, ed. John Grafton (Mineola, NY: Dover Publications, 1999), 64-65.

[5] Kaiser, *No End Save Victory*, 320; Roosevelt, *Great Speeches*, 73-74.

[6] Sherwood, *Roosevelt and Hopkins*, 137-138.

[7] Churchill, *Memoirs*, 406-407; Liddell Hart, History of the Second World War, 95-98, 107-109, 110-111.

[8] Kaiser, *No End Save Victory*, 13-14, 17, 20, 22-23, 25; Roosevelt, *Great Speeches*, 79-80.

[9] Roosevelt, *Great Speeches*, 90.

[10] The Navy Department Library, "Lend-Lease Act."

[11] Edward R. Stettinius, Jr., *Lend-Lease: Weapon for Victory* (New York: Pocket Books, 1944), 52.

[12] Kotkin, *Waiting for Hitler*, 268, 334, 406, 693, 720, 722, 726-727; Liddell Hart, *History of the Second World War*, 54-55, 55-59, 68, 736-737, 738, 750.

[13] Joachim C. Fest, *Hitler*, trans. Richard and Clara Winston (New York: Harcourt, 1974), 640-643.

[14] Kaiser, *No End Save Victory*, 320; U.S. Department of the Treasury, "Diaries of Henry Morgenthau, Jr., April 27, 1933-July 27, 1945," Series 2: Morgenthau Presidential Diaries, "Russian Clearance Problems Requiring Immediate Attention," 1 March 1941, *Franklin D. Roosevelt Presidential Library & Museum*, http://www.fdrlibrary.marist.edu/archives/collections/franklin/index.php?p=collections/findingaid&id=535&q=&rootcontentid=1 89777.

[15] U.S. Department of the Treasury, "Diaries of Henry Morgenthau, Jr.," Series 2, "Russian Clearance Problems."

[16] Ibid.

[17] Paul Carell, *Hitler Moves East 1941-1943*, trans. Ewald Osers (New York: Bantam Books, 1966), 5-7, 12-15; Clark, *Barbarossa*, 65-67; Frank Ellis, *Barbarossa 1941: Reframing Hitler's Invasion of Stalin's Soviet Empire* (Lawrence: University Press of Kansas, 2015), xi-xv, 41-43; Fest, *Hitler*, 648-649; Adolf Hitler, *Mein Kampf*, trans. Ralph Manheim (New York: Mariner Books, 1999), 15, 38, 93, 95, 109, 120, 129, 147, 157, 300-308, 327, 447, 454, 454, 626, 630, 637-640.

[18] David Glantz, *Colossus Reborn: The Red Army at War, 1941-1943* (Lawrence, KS: University Press of Kansas, 2005), 5-6; Oleg V. Khlevniuk, *Stalin: New Biography of a Dictator*, ed. and trans. Nora Seligman Favorov (New Haven, CT: Yale University Press, 2015), 143; Radzinsky, *Stalin*, 463-465, 466-474, 486-487; Boris Sokolov, *Marshal K. K. Rokossovsky: The Red Army's Gentleman Commander* (Warwick, UK: Helion & Company, 2015), 79-80; Georgy Zhukov, *Marshal of Victory Vol. 1: The WWII Memoirs of Georgy Zhukov through 1941*, ed. and trans. Geoffrey Roberts (Mechanicsburg, PA: Stackpole Books, 2015), 281-282.

[19] Hull, *The Memoirs of Cordell Hull*, 967. Hull explains here that Woods reported hearing of Hitler's alleged boast from, "a German friend who, though an enemy of the Nazis, was closely connected with the Reichs ministries, the Reichsbank and high Party members," at some point after the Nazi leadership began officially but secretly meeting to discuss the planned invasion beginning in August 1940.

[20] David M. Glantz, *Stumbling Colossus: The Red Army on the Eve of World War* (Lawrence: University Press of Kansas, 1998), 102-103; Mark Harrison, *Soviet Planning in Peace and War 1938-1945* (Cambridge, UK: Cambridge University Press, 1985), 110-113, 114-115; Suvorov, *The Chief Culprit*, 251-252, 253-259; Vyacheslav Molotov and Felix Chuev, *Molotov Remembers: Inside Kremlin Politics*, ed. and trans. Ivan R. Dee (Lanham, MD: Rowman & Littlefield, 1993), 12-15.

[21] Dawson, *The Decision to Aid Russia*, 65-66.

[22] Kelly, *Saving Stalin*, 16; Molotov and Chuev, *Molotov Remembers*, 37-39.

[23] George W. Baer, *One Hundred Years of Sea Power: The U.S. Navy, 1890-1990* (Stanford, CA: Stanford University Press, 1994), 152, 157; Churchill, *Memoirs*, 476-479.

[24] Pownall, *Chief of Staff*, 29; Zaloga, *Soviet Lend-Lease Tanks*, 4.

[25] Pownall, *Chief of Staff*, 29.

[26] Sherwood, *Roosevelt and Hopkins*, 306-308; Jones, *The Roads to Russia*, 23-24, 31.

[27] Jones, *The Roads to Russia*, 31; Herring, Jr., *Aid to Russia*, 53, 60.

[28] Dawson, *The Decision to Aid Russia*, 16, 32, 71-73, 87-88; Herring, Jr., *Aid to Russia*, 44-47, 49, 84-85, 103-105; Ronald Smelser and Edward J. Davies II, *The Myth of the Eastern Front: The Nazi-Soviet War in American Popular Culture* (Cambridge: Cambridge University Press, 2008), 28, 31-34.

[29] Hull, *The Memoirs of Cordell Hull*, 967.

[30] Ibid., 973-974.

[31] Herbert Feis, *Churchill, Roosevelt, Stalin: The War They Waged and the Peace They Sought* (Princeton: Princeton University Press, 1967), 9-12.

[32] Feis, *Churchill, Roosevelt, Stalin*, 9-12.

[33] Edward C. Carter, "Russian War Relief," *The Slavonic and East European Review: American Series*, Vol. 3, No. 2 (Aug. 1944), 61-74, https://www-jstor-org.libproxy.library.u nt.edu/stable/3020236?seq=7#metadata_info_tab_contents; Smelser and Davies II, *The Myth of the Eastern Front*, 31-34.

[34] Carter, "Russian War Relief," 67; Smelser and Davies II, *The Myth of the Eastern Front*, 31-34.

[35] Ibid; Columbia University Library Digital Collections, "Allen Wardwell, RWR Chairman, to Herbert H. Lehman," Russian War Relief, Inc., 14 October 1942, http://www.columbia.ed u/cu/lweb/digital/collections/rbml/lehman/pdfs/0941/ldpd_leh_0941_0014.pdf; Cornell University Library Digital Collections, "What Russia Means to Us: A Speech by Albert Einstein. English Version," Jewish Council for Russian War Relief, 25 October 1942, https://digital.library.cornell.edu/catalog/ss:21072652; The Harvard Crimson (Unattributed Report), "BENEFIT TUESDAY NIGHT FOR RUSSIAN WAR RELIEF," *The Harvard Crimson*, 18 February 1944, https://www.thecrimson.com/article/1944/2/18/benefit-tuesday-nig ht-for-russian-war/; The New York Times (Unattributed Report), "Addresses of Litvinoff, Hopkins and Green at Russian War Relief Rally in Madison Sq. Garden," *The New York Times*, 23 June 1942, https://www.nytimes.com/1942/06/23/archives/addresses-of-litvi noff-hopkins-and-green-at-russian-war-relief.html.

[36] Carell, *Hitler Moves East*, 38-43, 62-64, 73-77, 77-78; Clark, *Barbarossa*, 65, 67-69, 70-73; Sokolov, *Marshal K. K. Rokossovsky*, 137-140, 140-143; Zhukov, *Marshal of Victory Vol. 1*, 281-282.

[37] Jones, *The Roads to Russia*, 39; Sherwood, *Roosevelt and Hopkins*, 306-308.

[38] Kaiser, *No End Save Victory*, 260; Sherwood, *Roosevelt and Hopkins*, 306-308.

[39] Sherwood, *Roosevelt and Hopkins*, 306-308.

[40] Ibid.

[41] Jones, *The Roads to Russia*, 39; Sherwood, *Roosevelt and Hopkins*, 306-308.

[42] Jones, *The Roads to Russia*, 39; *National Archives and Records Administration*, "Letter from Joseph E. Davies to Samuel Rosenman, January 22, 1945," *Harry S. Truman Presidential Library & Museum*, https://www.trumanlibrary.gov/library/research-files/le tter-joseph-e-davies-samuel-rosenman; Sherwood, *Roosevelt and Hopkins*, 306-308.

[43] Davies, *Mission to Moscow*, 275-277, 278-280, 285-287; Kaiser, *No End Save Victory*, 260; Sherwood, *Roosevelt and Hopkins*, 306-308.

[44] Kaiser, *No End Save Victory*, 260; *National Archives and Records Administration*, "Letter from Joseph E. Davies,"; Sherwood, *Roosevelt and Hopkins*, 306-308; Weigley, *The American Way of War*, 316-317, 357-359.

[45] Weigley, *The American Way of War*, 128-129, 150-152, 162-163, 357-359.

[46] Eisenhower, *Crusade in Europe*, 69-70; Sherwood, *Roosevelt and Hopkins*, 306-308.

[47] Davies, *Mission to Moscow*, 475-476, 487-489, 490-494, 495-497; Kaiser, *No End Save Victory*, 260, 375n50; Sherwood, *Roosevelt and Hopkins*, 306-308.

[48] Davies, *Mission to Moscow*, 475-476, 487-489, 490-494, 495-497; Kaiser, *No End Save Victory*, 260, 375n50; Sherwood, *Roosevelt and Hopkins*, 306-308.

[49] Kaiser, *No End Save Victory*, 260, 375n50; *Sherwood, Roosevelt and Hopkins*, 317-318.

[50] Jones, *The Roads to Russia*, 37; Sherwood, *Roosevelt and Hopkins*, 317-318; Weeks, *Russia's Life-Saver*, 45-46.

51 Kelly, *Saving Stalin*, 26-29; Khlevniuk, *Stalin*, 213-215; Sherwood, *Roosevelt and Hopkins*, 327; U.S. Department of State, "Foreign Relations of the United States Diplomatic Papers, 1941, General, The Soviet Union, Volume I: The Ambassador in the Soviet Union (Steinhardt) to the Secretary of State," 26 June 1941, https://history.state.go v/historicaldocuments/frus1941v01/d839; Georgy Zhukov, *Marshal of Victory Vol. 2: The WWII Memoirs of General Georgy Zhukov, 1941-1945*, ed. and trans. Geoffrey Roberts (Mechanicsburg, PA: Stackpole Books, 2015), 12-13.

52 Jones, *The Roads to Russia*, 39; Sherwood, *Roosevelt and Hopkins*, 330; U.S. Department of State, "Foreign Relations of the United States Diplomatic Papers, 1941."

53 Jones, *The Roads to Russia*, 139-140; McMeekin, *Stalin's War*, 403-404.

54 Kelly, *Saving Stalin*, 26-29.

55 Ibid.; Margaret Bourke-White, *Portrait of Myself* (New York: Simon and Schuster, 1963), 176-177.

56 Bourke-White, *Portrait of Myself*, 186, 191; Kelly, *Saving Stalin*, 26-29; Smelser and Davies II, *The Myth of the Eastern Front*, 28.

57 Bourke-White, *Portrait of Myself*, 186, 191; Smelser and Davies II, *The Myth of the Eastern Front*, 28.

58 Kelly, *Saving Stalin*, 26-29; Bourke-White, *Portrait of Myself*, 183-184.

59 Bourke-White, *Portrait of Myself*, 187-188.

60 Khlevniuk, *Stalin*, 211-212.

61 Rayfield, *Stalin and His Hangmen*, 344, 349-353.

62 Khlevniuk, *Stalin*, 211-212.

63 David M. Glantz and Jonathan M. House, *When Titans Clashed: How the Red Army Stopped Hitler* (Lawrence: University Press of Kansas, 1995), 1-2; Kelly, *Saving Stalin*, 26-29; Catherine Merridale, *Ivan's War: Life and Death in the Red Army, 1939-1945* (New York: Metropolitan Books, 2006), 394-395; Sherwood, *Roosevelt and Hopkins*, 323.

64 Glantz and House, *When Titans Clashed*, 52-53; Khlevniuk, *Stalin*, 211-212; Merridale, *Ivan's War*, 128, 262, 264-265; Weeks, *Russia's Life-Saver*, 45-46.

65 Jones, *The Roads to Russia*, 37; 120-122; Herring, Jr., *Aid to Russia*, 53, 60.

66 Deane, *The Strange Alliance*, 87-89, 90-94; Standley and Ageton, *Admiral Ambassador to Russia*, 75, 118.

67 Koster, *Operation Snow*, 15, 132-135; McMeekin, *Stalin's War*, 43-44, 261-264; Steil, *The Battle of Bretton Woods*, 57-58.

68 Architect Staff, "The USA, the USSR, and Architecture,"; Bourke-White, *Eyes on Russia*, 123-124; Brisson, "How Albert Kahn helped the Soviet Union industrialize,"; Crawford, "Soviet Planning Praxis,"; Dawson, *The Decision to Aid Russia, 1941*, 65-66; Melnikova-Raich, "The Soviet Problem with Two 'Unknowns,'"; Shpotov, "The Ford Motor Company in the Soviet Union."

69 Dawson, *The Decision to Aid Russia*, 75-76, 77-79; Kaiser, *No End Save Victory*, 114, 143, 197, 207-209; Sherwood, *Roosevelt and Hopkins*, 320-322, 328-330, 332-334.

70 Dawson, *The Decision to Aid Russia*, 82-85; Roosevelt, *Great Speeches*, 106-107.

71 Kaiser, *No End Save Victory*, 114, 143, 197, 207-209; Roosevelt, *Great Speeches*, 106-107.

72 Clark, *Barbarossa*, 160-165; Ellis, *Barbarossa 1941*, 330-332, 335-337; Heinz Guderian, *Panzer Leader*, ed. and trans. Constantine Fitzgibbon (New York: Da Capo Press, 1996), 234-235; Weeks, *Stalin's Other War*, 132-133.

73 David M. Glantz, *Colossus Reborn: The Red Army at War, 1941-1943* (Lawrence: University Press of Kansas, 2005), 88-89; Guderian, *Panzer Leader*, 234-235; Suvorov, *The Chief Culprit*, 251-252, 253-259; Zhukov, *Marshal of Victory Vol. 1*, 284-285.

74 Kaiser, *No End Save Victory*, 114, 143, 197, 207-209; Roosevelt, *Great Speeches*, 106-107.

75 Kaiser, *No End Save Victory*, 114, 143, 197, 207-209; Roosevelt, *Great Speeches*, 109-110, 111-112; Weeks, *Russia's Life-Saver*, 110-111.

76 Churchill, *Memoirs*, 484; Standley and Ageton, *Admiral Ambassador*, 74; The New York Times (Unattributed Report), "THIRD TALK HELD BY STALIN ON AID; Harriman and Beaverbrook See Premier Again After a Long Parley Together PRIORITIES ARE DISCUSSED Biggest Task Is to Find Ships to Carry Arms and Supplies Diverted from Britain," *The New York Times*, 1 October 1941, https://www.nytimes.com/1941/10/01/archives/third-talk-held-by-stalin-on-aid-harriman-and-beaverbrook-see.html.

77 Weeks, *Russia's Life-Saver*, 111-112.

78 Churchill, *Memoirs*, 485-486; Khlevniuk, *Stalin*, 211-212; The New York Times, THIRD TALK HELD BY STALIN ON AID."

79 Churchill, *Memoirs*, 485-486; The New York Times, THIRD TALK HELD BY STALIN ON AID,"; U.S. Department of State, *Soviet Supply Protocols*, 1-3.

80 Dawson, *The Decision to Aid Russia*, 259; Office, Chief of Finance War Department, "Lend-Lease Shipments World War II."

81 Hamilton Fish, "Article 6," *The New York Times*, 6 October 1941, 3, https://www.nytimes.com/1941/10/06/archives/article-6-no-title.html.

82 Dawson, *The Decision to Aid Russia*, 265-269; McMeekin, *Stalin's War*, 353-354; Sherwood, *Roosevelt and Hopkins*, 396-398, 400-402.

83 Smelser and Davies II, *The Myth of the Eastern Front*, 9-11, 28.

84 Ibid.

85 Ibid., 18-20, 27, 31-34, 35-36.

86 Dawson, *The Decision to Aid Russia*, 285-287; Kaiser, *No End Save Victory*, 114, 143, 197, 207-209; Roosevelt, *Great Speeches*, 107-109, 110-112; Smelser and Davies II, *The Myth of the Eastern Front*, 18-20, 26-27, 28, 31-34, 35-36.

87 Dawson, *The Decision to Aid Russia*, 285-287; Smelser and Davies II, *The Myth of the Eastern Front*, 18-20, 26-27, 28, 31-34, 35-36.

88 Deane, *The Strange Alliance*, 62; Roosevelt, *Great Speeches*, 107-109, 110-112.

89 Dawson, *The Decision to Aid Russia*, 292; Smelser and Davies II, *The Myth of the Eastern Front*, 18-20, 26-27, 28, 31-34, 35-36.

90 Smelser and Davies II, *The Myth of the Eastern Front*, 9-11.

91 Dawson, *The Decision to Aid Russia*, 279-281; Herring, Jr., *Aid to Russia*, 20, 93.

92 *Congressional Record – House of Representatives*, 77th Congress, 1st Session (1941), pt. 7, Government Publishing Office, https://babel.hathitrust.org/cgi/pt?id=uc1.31210018789337&view=1up&seq=1&q1=rich%20amendment; Dawson, *The Decision to Aid Russia*, 279-281; Herring, Jr., *Aid to Russia*, 20, 93; Sherwood, *Roosevelt and Hopkins*, 791-793, 796, 802; Joseph Stalin, *The Great Patriotic War of the Soviet Union*, ed. and trans. Harry F. Ward (New York: International Publishers, 1945), 20-22, 23.

93 Stalin, *The Great Patriotic War of the Soviet Union*, 20, 22-23.

94 *Cong. Rec. – House of Representatives*, 77th Cong., 1st Sess. (1941) pt. 7; Herring, Jr., *Aid to Russia*, 20, 93, 112-117, 120-122, 124-128; McMeekin, *Stalin's War*, 349-350, 722n4; Sherwood, *Roosevelt and Hopkins*, 791-793, 796, 802; Stalin, *The Great Patriotic War of the Soviet Union*, 35-38.

[95] Dawson, *The Decision to Aid Russia*, 279-281; Herring, Jr., *Aid to Russia*, 20, 93, 112-117; Sherwood, *Roosevelt and Hopkins*, 791-793, 796, 802.

[96] *Cong. Rec. – House of Representatives*, 77th Cong., 1st Sess. (1941) pt. 7; Folsom, Jr., and Folsom, *FDR Goes to War*, 230-235, 340-342n40-44; Herring, Jr., *Aid to Russia*, 20, 93, 112-117, 120-122, 124-128; Sherwood, *Roosevelt and Hopkins*, 791-793, 796, 802.

[97] *Cong. Rec. – House of Representatives*, 77th Cong., 1st Sess. (1941) pt. 7; Dawson, *The Decision to Aid Russia*, 273, 274-278, 279-281; Herring, Jr., *Aid to Russia*, 20, 93, 112-117, 120-122, 124-128.

[98] *Cong. Rec. – House of Representatives*, 77th Cong., 1st Sess. (1941) pt. 7; Dawson, *The Decision to Aid Russia*, 273, 274-278, 279-281; Folsom, Jr., and Folsom, *FDR Goes to War*, 230-235, 340-342n40-44; Herring, Jr., *Aid to Russia*, 20, 93, 112-117, 120-122, 124-128; McMeekin, *Stalin's War*, 349-350, 722n4.

[99] *Cong. Rec. – House of Representatives*, 77th Cong., 1st Sess. (1941) pt. 7; Dawson, *The Decision to Aid Russia*, 279-281; McMeekin, *Stalin's War*, 349-350, 722n4.

[100] *Cong. Rec. – House of Representatives*, 77th Cong., 1st Sess. (1941) pt. 7; Herring, Jr., *Aid to Russia*, 20, 93, 112-117.

[101] *Cong. Rec. – House of Representatives*, 77th Cong., 1st Sess. (1941) pt. 7; Dawson, *The Decision to Aid Russia*, 279-281.

[102] *Cong. Rec. – House of Representatives*, 77th Cong., 1st Sess. (1941) pt. 7; Dawson, *The Decision to Aid Russia*, 279-281.

[103] *Congressional Record – United States Senate*, 77th Congress, 1st Session (1941), pt. 8, Government Publishing Office, https://www.govinfo.gov/content/pkg/GPO-CRECB-1941-pt8/pdf/GPO-CRECB-1941-pt8-4.pdf.

[104] Dawson, *The Decision to Aid Russia*, 276.

[105] *Cong. Rec. – United States Senate*, 77th Cong. 1st Sess. (1941) pt.8.

[106] Ibid.

[107] U.S. President, "Franklin Roosevelt Administration: Stalin Replies to Roosevelt Letter of 30 October 1941 (November 4, 1941)," *The White House*, Washington, D.C., 4 November 1941, https://www.jewishvirtuallibrary.org/stalin-replies-to-roosevelt-letter-of-october-30-1941-november-1941.

[108] Deane, *The Strange Alliance*, 89; McMeekin, *Stalin's War*, 380-381, 382-384, 389-392; U.S. Department of State, *Soviet Supply Protocols*, 1-3, 9-12; U.S. President, "Franklin Roosevelt Administration."

[109] Jones, *The Roads to Russia*, 94-95; U.S. President, "Box 8 Roosevelt to Stalin May – December 1942."

[110] Sherwood, *Roosevelt and Hopkins*, 254; Stettinius, Jr., *Lend-Lease*, 237.

[111] U.S. Department of State, *Soviet Supply Protocols*, 1-3, 9-12.

[112] Alexander Werth, *Russia at War, 1941-1945: A History* (New York: Carroll & Graf Publishers, 1992), xiii-xv, 148-149.

[113] The Daily Iowan (Unattributed Report), "Soviets Have Suffered Heavy Defeat But Are Not Finished: Foreign Observers Declare Reds Need Planes 'Desperately'," *The Daily Iowan*, 30 October 1941, http://dailyiowan.lib.uiowa.edu/DI/1941/di1941-10-30.pdf.

[114] Kelly, *Saving Stalin*, 26-29; Sherwood, *Roosevelt and Hopkins*, 395-396; The Daily Iowan, "Soviets Have Suffered."

[115] The New York Times (Unattributed Report), "MISS BOURKE-WHITE PRAISES STALIN; Back After Photographing Him in Moscow, She Says He Has Extraordinary Personality,"

The New York Times, 3 November 1941, https://www.nytimes.com/1941/11/03/archives/miss-bourkewhite-praises-stalin-back-after-photographing-him-in.html.

[116] The New York Times, "MISS BOURKE-WHITE PRAISES STALIN."

[117] Hill, *The Great Patriotic War of the Soviet Union*, 180.

[118] Alexander Hill, "British Lend-Lease Aid and the Soviet War Effort, June 1941-June 1942," *The Journal of Military History*, Vol. 71, No. 3 (July 2007), 773-808, https://www.jstor.org/stable/30052890; Ministry of Foreign Affairs of the U.S.S.R., *Stalin's Correspondence*, "No. 1: Personal Message from Mr. Churchill to Monsieur Stalin," 8 July 1941, 11; Reynolds and Pechatnov, *The Kremlin Letters*, 23.

[119] Ministry of Foreign Affairs of the U.S.S.R., *Stalin's Correspondence*, "No. 10: Personal Message from Premier Stalin to the Prime Minister, Mr. Churchill," 3 September 1941, 20-22; Reynolds and Pechatnov, *The Kremlin Letters*, 40-41.

[120] Churchill, *Memoirs*, 481-482; Ministry of Foreign Affairs of the U.S.S.R., *Stalin's Correspondence*, "No. 10," 3 September 1941, 20-22, italics and parentheses in the original; Reynolds and Pechatnov, *The Kremlin Letters*, 40-41.

[121] McMeekin, *Stalin's War*, 330-334; Ministry of Foreign Affairs of the U.S.S.R., *Stalin's Correspondence*, "No. 10," 3 September 1941, 20-22; Reynolds and Pechatnov, *The Kremlin Letters*, 40-41; Sokolov, *The Role of the Soviet Union in the Second World War*, 53-55.

[122] McMeekin, *Stalin's War*, 330-334; Ministry of Foreign Affairs of the U.S.S.R., *Stalin's Correspondence*, "No. 10," 3 September 1941, 20-22; Reynolds and Pechatnov, *The Kremlin Letters*, 40-41; Sokolov, *The Role of the Soviet Union in the Second World War*, 53-55.

[123] Harrison, *Soviet Planning in Peace and War*, 115-119; Hill, "British Lend-Lease Aid and the Soviet War Effort," 775-779; Ministry of Foreign Affairs of the U.S.S.R., *Stalin's Correspondence*, "No. 10," 3 September 1941, 20-22; Reynolds and Pechatnov, *The Kremlin Letters*, 40-41; U.S. Department of State, *Soviet Supply Protocols*, 9-12, 13-15.

[124] Harrison, *Soviet Planning in Peace and War*, 119-121; Hill, "British Lend-Lease Aid and the Soviet War Effort," 781-783, 785-787.

[125] Churchill, *Memoirs*, 476-479; Ministry of Foreign Affairs of the U.S.S.R., *Stalin's Correspondence*, "No. 10," 3 September 1941, 20-22; Reynolds and Pechatnov, *The Kremlin Letters*, 40-41.

[126] Ministry of Foreign Affairs of the U.S.S.R., *Stalin's Correspondence*, "No. 10," 3 September 1941, 20-22; Pownall, *Chief of Staff*, 39-40, 41-42; Reynolds and Pechatnov, *The Kremlin Letters*, 40-41.

[127] Hill, "British Lend-Lease Aid and the Soviet War Effort," 781-783, 785-787.

[128] Ministry of Foreign Affairs of the U.S.S.R., *Stalin's Correspondence*, "No. 11: Prime Minister Churchill to Monsieur Stalin," 4 September 1941, 22-23.

[129] Ministry of Foreign Affairs of the U.S.S.R., *Stalin's Correspondence*, "No. 11: Prime Minister Churchill to Monsieur Stalin," 4 September 1941, 22-23.

[130] Pownall, *Chief of Staff*, 39-40, 41-42.

[131] Ibid.

[132] Alanbrooke, *War Diaries*, 416-417; Hill, "British Lend-Lease Aid and the Soviet War Effort," 785-787, 788-792, 793-794; U.S. Department of State, *Soviet Supply Protocols*, 13-15, 16-17.

[133] Carl-Frederik Geust, "Aircraft Deliveries to the Soviet Union," *Lend-Lease History and People*, 6 July 2019, https://lend-lease.net/articles-en/aircraft-deliveries-to-the-soviet-union/; Hill, *The Great Patriotic War of the Soviet Union*, 181.

[134] Herring, *Aid to Russia*, 229-231, 236-237, 340-342; Hill, *The Great Patriotic War of the Soviet Union*, 187; U.S. Department of State, *Soviet Supply Protocols*, 9-12, 13-15.

[135] Dawson, *The Decision to Aid Russia*, 294.

[136] Koster, *Operation Snow*, 15-17, 204-205, 215; Steil, *The Battle of Bretton Woods*, 55-57.

[137] Dawson, *The Decision to Aid Russia*, 296-298; Herring, Jr., *Aid to Russia*, 317-319, 322-324; Sherwood, *Roosevelt and Hopkins*, 278-280, 328, 644, 657-658, 746-747, 752, 755-757.

[138] Jones, *The Roads to Russia*, 103-105, 107; McMeekin, *Stalin's War*, 364-367, 403-405; Van Tuyll, *Feeding the Bear*, 26-27; Weeks, *Russia's Life-Saver*, 45, 131-133.

[139] Steil, *The Battle of Bretton Woods*, 53-55.

[140] Fitzgibbon, "The Hiss-Chambers Case,"; VENONA Decrypts, "13. Hoover to Matthew Connelly, 12 September 1945," *Internet Archive Wayback Machine*, https://web.archive.or g/web/20071114214743/https://www.cia.gov/library/center-for-the-study-of-intelligen ce/csi-publications/books-and-monographs/venona-soviet-espionage-and-the-americ an-response-1939-1957/13.gif.

[141] Koster, *Operation Snow*, 1-4, 5-8, 19-22, 37-41; McMeekin, *Stalin's War*, 261-264; Steil, *The Battle of Bretton Woods*, 53-55; VENONA Decrypts, "13. Hoover to Matthew Connelly."

[142] Koster, *Operation Snow*, 1-4, 5-8, 19-22, 37-41; McMeekin, *Stalin's War*, 261-264; Steil, *The Battle of Bretton Woods*, 53-55.

[143] Koster, *Operation Snow*, 132-135, 137, 215; McMeekin, *Stalin's War*, 261-264, 379; Steil, *The Battle of Bretton Woods*, 53-55; VENONA Decrypts, "13. Hoover to Matthew Connelly."

[144] Koster, *Operation Snow*, 160-165; McMeekin, *Stalin's War*, 379, 396, 399; VENONA Decrypts, "13. Hoover to Matthew Connelly."

[145] U.S. Department of the Treasury, "Diaries of Henry Morgenthau, Jr., April 27, 1933-July 27, 1945," Series 1: Morgenthau Diaries, "Memo for Secretary: 471 – 6/6/41 HDW," 6 June 1941.

[146] Ibid., "Diaries of Henry Morgenthau, Jr.," Series 2, "Russian Clearance Problems."

[147] Koster, *Operation Snow*, 137, 165; McMeekin, *Stalin's War*, 43-44, 261-164; U.S. Department of the Treasury, "Diaries of Henry Morgenthau, Jr.," Series 1, "Memo for Secretary."

[148] Koster, *Operation Snow*, 132-135, 137, 203-204, 215; U.S. Department of the Treasury, "Diaries of Henry Morgenthau, Jr.," Series 1, "Memo for Secretary."

[149] McMeekin, *Stalin's War*, 261-164, 379; Steil, *The Battle of Bretton Woods*, 129, 137-140; U.S. Department of the Treasury, "Diaries of Henry Morgenthau, Jr.," Series 1, "Memo for Secretary."

[150] U.S. Department of the Treasury, "Diaries of Henry Morgenthau, Jr.," Series 1, "Memo for Secretary."

[151] Kaiser, *No End Save Victory*, 234, 250; Koster, *Operation Snow*, 111-112, 117, 123; Steil, *The Battle of Bretton Woods*, 55-57; VENONA Decrypts, "13. Hoover to Matthew Connelly."

[152] U.S. Department of the Treasury, "Diaries of Henry Morgenthau, Jr.," Series 2, "Russian Clearance Problems."

[153] Koster, *Operation Snow*, 132-135, 137, 215; McMeekin, *Stalin's War*, 261-264, 379; U.S. Department of the Treasury, "Diaries of Henry Morgenthau, Jr.," Series 1, "Memo for Secretary,"; VENONA Decrypts, "13. Hoover to Matthew Connelly."

[154] Koster, *Operation Snow*, 132-136, 137; U.S. Department of the Treasury, "Diaries of Henry Morgenthau, Jr."

[155] Steil, *The Battle of Bretton Woods*, 53-55; U.S. Department of the Treasury, "Diaries of Henry Morgenthau, Jr.," Series 1, "Memo for Secretary."

[156] Hull, *The Memoirs of Cordell Hull*, 1062-1067, 1074-1076; Steil, *The Battle of Bretton Woods*, 53-55.

[157] U.S. Department of the Treasury, "Diaries of Henry Morgenthau, Jr.," Series 1, "Memo for Secretary."

[158] Hull, *The Memoirs of Cordell Hull*, 1062-1067, 1074-1076; Kaiser, *No End Save Victory*, 259, 335; Koster, *Operation Snow*, 132-135, 137, 203-204, 215; Steil, *The Battle of Bretton Woods*, 53-55.

[159] Kaiser, *No End Save Victory*, 234, 250; Koster, *Operation Snow*, 125-127, 130; U.S. Department of the Treasury, "Diaries of Henry Morgenthau, Jr.,"

[160] Koster, *Operation Snow*, 132-135, 137.

[161] Francis Pike, *Hirohito's War: The Pacific War, 1941-1945* (New York: Bloomsbury Academic, 2016), xxvi, 108, 111, 115, 133, 137, 141, 147, 156-157, 160, 163-164, 170-173.

[162] Koster, *Operation Snow*, 132-135, 137; Kurt Schuler and Andrew Rosenberg, *The Bretton Woods Transcripts* (New York: Center for Financial Stability, 2013), 41; U.S. Department of the Treasury, "Diaries of Henry Morgenthau, Jr.," Series 1, "Suggested Approach for Elimination of United States-Japanese Tension," 17 November 1941.

[163] Hull, *The Memoirs of Cordell Hull*, 1062-1067, 1074-1076; Koster, *Operation Snow*, 132-135, 137; U.S. Department of the Treasury, "Diaries of Henry Morgenthau, Jr.," Series 1, "Suggested Approach."

[164] U.S. Department of the Treasury, "Diaries of Henry Morgenthau, Jr.," Series 1, "Suggested Approach."

[165] Steil, *The Battle of Bretton Woods*, 53-55; U.S. Department of the Treasury, "Diaries of Henry Morgenthau, Jr.," Series 1, "Suggested Approach."

[166] Koster, *Operation Snow*, 132-135, 136-138; McMeekin, *Stalin's War*, 379n; Steil, *The Battle of Bretton Woods*, 53-55; U.S. Department of the Treasury, "Diaries of Henry Morgenthau, Jr.," Series 1, "Suggested Approach."

[167] Kaiser, *No End Save Victory*, 234, 250; Steil, *The Battle of Bretton Woods*, 53-55; U.S. Department of the Treasury, "Diaries of Henry Morgenthau, Jr.," Series 1, "Suggested Approach."

[168] Carter, "Russian War Relief," 67; Steil, *The Battle of Bretton Woods*, 53-55.

[169] Kaiser, *No End Save Victory*, 17, 50, 259, 335; Koster, *Operation Snow*, 139-140; Liddell Hart, *History of the Second World War*, 269, 272-276, 276-278; Pike, *Hirohito's War*, xxvi, 108, 111, 115, 133, 137, 141, 147, 156-157, 160, 163-164, 170-173.

[170] McMeekin, *Stalin's War*, 376-377.

[171] Carell, *Hitler Moves East*, 136-142, 144-146, 148, 155-157; Clark, *Barbarossa*, 184-185, 190-193, 202; McMeekin, *Stalin's War*, 376-377; Sokolov, *Marshal K. K. Rokossovsky*, 137-140, 140-143, 147-149, 150-153; Zhukov, *Marshal of Victory Vol. 1*, 281-282, 285, 287-289.

[172] Folsom, Jr., and Folsom, *FDR Goes to War*, 228; Koster, *Operation Snow*, 160-165.

[173] U.S. President, "Executive Order 9066, February 19, 1942,"; Emily Yellin, *Our Mothers' War: American Women at Home and at the Front During World War II* (New York: Simon & Schuster, 2004), 40-41.

[174] Koster, *Operation Snow*, 10-11, 19-22, 37-41; Kenneth D. Rose, *Myth and the Greatest Generation: A Social History of Americans in World War II* (New York: Routledge, 2007), 5, 31, 82-83; Steil, *The Battle of Bretton Woods*, 57-58; VENONA Decrypts, "13. Hoover to Matthew Connelly,"; Weeks, *Russia's Life-Saver*, 23, 45.

[175] Jordan, *Major Jordan's Diaries*, 41-43.

[176] Chambers, *Witness*, 415-417, 421-424; *Cong. Rec. – House of Representatives*, 80th Cong., 2nd Sess. (1948); Fitzgibbon, "The Hiss-Chambers Case,"; Sudoplatov and Sudoplatov,

Special Tasks, 222, 226-227, 227-229, 230; VENONA Decrypts, "Silvermaster Folder NY 65-14603 'Alger Hiss."

[177] Chairman of the Board, Tennessee Valley Authority, "Lend-Lease Program With Russia," 23 and 26 September 1942, *National Archives at Atlanta*, https://www.archives.gov/atlanta/exhibits/item81_full.html; Eisenhower, *Crusade in Europe*, 69-70, 489-490; Feis, *Churchill, Roosevelt, Stalin*, 9-12; Folsom, Jr., and Folsom, *FDR Goes to War*, 228, 246-249, 251.

CHAPTER 3

[1] The New York Times (Unattributed Report), "HARMONY IN DRIVES FOR RELIEF SOUGHT; Meeting of Organizations for Aid Abroad to Be Held Soon, E. C. Carter Reports," *The New York Times*, 3 January 1942, https://www.nytimes.com/1942/01/03/archives/harmony-in-drives-for-relief-sought-meeting-of-organizations-for.html.

[2] Deane, *The Strange Alliance*, 88-89, 103, 202; Feis, *Churchill, Roosevelt, Stalin*, 9-12; Hull, *The Memoirs of Cordell Hull*, 967, 973-974, 979-981; McMeekin, *Stalin's War*, 517-518, 536-537; Sherwood, *Roosevelt and Hopkins*, 791-793, 796, 802; Standley and Ageton, *Admiral Ambassador to Russia*, 355-359; Stettinius, Jr., *Lend-Lease*, 248-249, 250, 252, 253-254, 257.

[3] Alanbrooke, *War Diaries*, 416-417; Hill, "British Lend-Lease Aid and the Soviet War Effort," 785-787, 788-792, 793-794; McMeekin, *Stalin's War*, 516, 517-518, 534-536; The New York Times, "HARMONY IN DRIVES FOR RELIEF SOUGHT; U.S. Department of State, *Soviet Supply Protocols*, 13-15, 16-17.

[4] Arnold, *Global Mission*, 211-212, 385-387; Alexander B. Dolitsky, Victor D. Glazkov, and Henry Varnum Poor, *Pipeline to Russia: The Alaska-Siberia Air Route in World War II*, trans. James F. Gebhardt (Anchorage: Alaska Affiliated Areas Program National Park Service, 2016), 79-80, 84-85; Van Tuyll, *Feeding the Bear*, 22-23; Weeks, *Russia's Life-Saver*, 3-4, 7-8.

[5] Walling, *Forgotten Sacrifice*, 9-10; David Wragg, *Sacrifice for Stalin: The Cost and Value of the Arctic Convoys Re-Assessed* (Barnsley, South Yorkshire: Pen & Sword Maritime, 2005), xii-xv, 72-73.

[6] Ministry of Foreign Affairs of the U.S.S.R., *Stalin's Correspondence*, "No. 58: Prime Minister to Premier Stalin," 31 July 1942, 57; Reynolds and Pechatnov, *The Kremlin Letters*, 133-134; U.S. President, "Map Room Papers Box 8 Stalin to Roosevelt July – December 1942."

[7] Alanbrooke, *War Diaries*, 416-417; Hill, "British Lend-Lease Aid and the Soviet War Effort," 775-779, 781-783, 785-787, 788-792, 793-794; U.S. Department of State, *Soviet Supply Protocols*, 13-15, 16-17.

[8] Whitehall History Publishing – Ministry of Defence, *The Royal Navy and the Arctic Convoys*, 5-7; Wragg, *Sacrifice for Stalin*, 57-58.

[9] Sir Ian Campbell and Donald MacIntyre, *The Kola Run: A Record of Arctic Convoys 1941-1945* (London: Frederick Muller Limited, 1959), 19-21; Michael Wadsworth, *Arctic Convoy PQ8: The Story of Capt Robert Brundle and the SS Harmatris* (Barnsley, South Yorkshire: Pen & Sword Maritime, 2009), 4-5, 71-72.

[10] Campbell and MacIntyre, *The Kola Run*, 13-15; Hill, "British Lend-Lease Aid and the Soviet War Effort," 781-783, 785-787; Wadsworth, *Arctic Convoy PQ8*, 2-3; Whitehall History Publishing – Ministry of Defence, *The Royal Navy and the Arctic Convoys*, 5-7.

[11] Sherwood, *Roosevelt and Hopkins*, 544-546; Stettinius, Jr., *Lend-Lease*, 230-232.

[12] McMeekin, *Stalin's War*, 425-427.

[13] Chairman of the Board, Tennessee Valley Authority, "Lend-Lease Program With Russia,"; Sherwood, *Roosevelt and Hopkins*, 544-546; Stettinius, Jr., *Lend-Lease*, 230-232.

[14] McMeekin, *Stalin's War*, 534-536; Vail Motter, *The Persian Corridor*, 3-5.

[15] Evgenii Altunin, "On the History of the Alaska-Siberia Ferrying Route," *The Journal of Slavic Military Studies*, Vol. 10, Issue 2 (June 1997), 85-96, https://www.tandfonline.com/doi/abs/10.1080/13518049708430292?journalCode=fslv20; Geust, "Aircraft Deliveries to the Soviet Union,"; McMeekin, *Stalin's War*, 534-536; Vail Motter, *The Persian Corridor*, 124-127; Weeks, *Russia's Life-Saver*, 131-133.

[16] Otis Hays, Jr., *The Alaska-Siberia Connection: The World War II Air Route* (College Station: Texas A&M University Press, 1996), xi-xii, 22-25, 38-39; Stettinius, Jr., *Lend-Lease*, 237-238, 240-242, 244; Vail Motter, *The Persian Corridor*, 124-127.

[17] McMeekin, *Stalin's War*, 534-536; The New York Times (Unattributed Report), "JAPAN LETS RUSSIA GET OUR SUPPLIES; Map in Lend-Lease Report to Congress Reveals Shipments Made by Route to Siberia THESE ARE UNMOLESTED Cargoes Moving in Russian Vessels Are Mostly of Food So Far, Capital Hears," *The New York Times*, 13 March 1943, https://www.nytimes.com/1943/03/13/archives/japan-lets-russia-get-our-supplies-map-in-lendlease-report-to.html.

[18] Altunin, "On the History of the Alaska-Siberia Ferrying Route," 85-87; Arnold, *Global Mission*, 211-212, 385-387; Dolitsky, Glazkov, and Poor, *Pipeline to Russia*, 69-70; Geust, "Aircraft Deliveries to the Soviet Union,"; Hays, Jr., *The Alaska-Siberia Connection*, 38-39, 51-52; McMeekin, *Stalin's War*, 420, 422, 438-439, 518-519; Weeks, *Russia's Life-Saver*, 114-115.

[19] Hill, *The Great Patriotic War of the Soviet Union*, 185; Vail Motter, *The Persian Corridor*, 136-138; Weeks, *Russia's Life-Saver*, 25-27.

[20] Walter S. Dunn, *The Soviet Economy and the Red Army, 1930-1945* (Westport, CT: Praeger, 1995), 80-81; Whitehall History Publishing – Ministry of Defence, *The Royal Navy and the Arctic Convoys*, 129-130.

[21] Ministry of Foreign Affairs of the U.S.S.R., *Stalin's Correspondence*, "No. 138: Personal and Secret Message from Premier J. V. Stalin to the Prime Minister, Mr. W. Churchill," 2 April 1943, "No. 145: Personal and Secret Message from Premier J. V. Stalin to the Prime Minister, Mr. W. Churchill," 12 April 1943, 117-118; Reynolds and Pechatnov, *The Kremlin Letters*, 227, 232; U.S. President, "Map Room Papers Box 8 Roosevelt to Stalin January – June 1943."

[22] Geust, "Aircraft Deliveries to the Soviet Union,"; Hill, *The Great Patriotic War of the Soviet Union*, 185; McMeekin, *Stalin's War*, 420, 422, 518-519; Van Tuyll, *Feeding the Bear*, 26-28; Weeks, *Russia's Life-Saver*, 25-27.

[23] Ulysses S. Grant, *The Complete Personal Memoirs of Ulysses S. Grant* (Lexington, KY: Seven Treasures Publications, 2009), 131-132; Weigley, *The American Way of War*, 128-129, 150-152, 162-163, 357-359.

[24] Dunn, *The Soviet Economy and the Red Army*, 80-81; Hill, *The Great Patriotic War of the Soviet Union*, 185; Whitehall History Publishing – Ministry of Defence, *The Royal Navy and the Arctic Convoys*, 129-130; Weeks, *Russia's Life-Saver*, 25-27; Whitehall History Publishing – Ministry of Defence, *The Royal Navy and the Arctic Convoys*, x-xii.

[25] Whitehall History Publishing – Ministry of Defence, *The Royal Navy and the Arctic Convoys*, 5-7; Wragg, *Sacrifice for Stalin*, 65-66.

[26] Hill, *The Great Patriotic War of the Soviet Union*, 172-173, 174-176; George Mellinger, *Soviet Lend-Lease Fighter Aces of World War II* (Oxford, Osprey Publishing, 2006), 25, 26-27; Zaloga, *Soviet Lend-Lease Tanks*, 6-8.

[27] Alexander Hill, "British 'Lend-Lease' Tanks and the Battle for Moscow, November-December 1941 – A Research Note," *The Journal of Slavic Military Studies*, Vol. 19, Issue 2 (September 2006), 289-294, https://www.tandfonline.com/doi/abs/10.1080/1351804060 0697811; Loza, *Commanding the Red Army's Sherman Tanks*, xvii-xviii, 41-43; McMeekin, *Stalin's War*, 381-383; Zaloga, *Soviet Lend-Lease Tanks*, 6-8, 18-20, 22-24.

[28] Ibid.; Ministry of Foreign Affairs of the U.S.S.R., *Stalin's Correspondence*, "No. 10," 3 September 1941, 20-22, "No. 20: "Personal Message from Premier Stalin to Prime Minister Churchill," 8 November 1941, 33-34, "No. 22: Message from Premier Stalin to Prime Minister Churchill," 23 November 1941, 35-36, "No. 4: J. V. Stalin to F. Roosevelt," 3 October 1941, and "No. 6: J. V. Stalin to F. Roosevelt," 4 November 1941; Reynolds and Pechatnov, *The Kremlin Letters*, 40-41, 67-68, 72-73, Sherwood, *Roosevelt and Hopkins*, 327-330, 337-341, 387-388; 396-398.

[29] Hill, *The Great Patriotic War of the Soviet Union*, 174-176; McMeekin, *Stalin's War*, 381-383; Zaloga, *Soviet Lend-Lease Tanks*, 6-8.

[30] Robert M. Citino, *Death of the Wehrmacht: The German Campaigns of 1942* (Lawrence: University Press of Kansas, 2007), 152-153, 180-182.

[31] Deane, *The Strange Alliance*, 89; McMeekin, *Stalin's War*, 403-405, 407-409; Stettinius, Jr., *Lend-Lease*, 229; U.S. Department of State, *Soviet Supply Protocols*, 13-15, 16-17.

[32] Office, Chief of Finance War Department, "Lend-Lease Shipments World War II,"; Sherwood, *Roosevelt and Hopkins*, 544-546; Stettinius, *Lend-Lease*, 230-232.

[33] Ministry of Foreign Affairs of the U.S.S.R., *Stalin's Correspondence*, "No. 16: His Excellency Joseph Stalin, President of the Soviet People's Commissars of the U.S.S.R.," 16 March 1942, 22.

[34] Ministry of Foreign Affairs of the U.S.S.R., *Stalin's Correspondence*, "No. 17: Personal Message from the President to Mr. Stalin," 12 April 1942, 22-23; Reynolds and Pechatnov, *The Kremlin Letters*, 96-97.

[35] Ministry of Foreign Affairs of the U.S.S.R., *Stalin's Correspondence*, "No. 18: J. V. Stalin F. Roosevelt," 20 April 1942, 23-24; Reynolds and Pechatnov, *The Kremlin Letters*, 98.

[36] Campbell and MacIntyre, *The Kola Run*, 19-21; Wragg, *Sacrifice for Stalin*, 67-68.

[37] Ministry of Foreign Affairs of the U.S.S.R., "No 19: For Mr. Stalin," 4 May 1942, 24; U.S. President, "Map Room Papers Box 8 Roosevelt to Stalin May – December 1942,"; Molotov and Chuev, *Molotov Remembers*, 1-3, 41-43, 52-53.

[38] Ministry of Foreign Affairs of the U.S.S.R., *Stalin's Correspondence*, "No. 20: J. V. Stalin to F. Roosevelt," 15 May 1942, 24-25; Reynolds and Pechatnov, *The Kremlin Letters*, 110; Sherwood, *Roosevelt and Hopkins*, 544-546.

[39] Franklin Delano Roosevelt and Winston Churchill, "Texts of Roosevelt-Churchill Messages," *The New York Times*, 12 June 1972, https://www.nytimes.com/1972/06/12/ar chives/texts-of-rooseveltchurchill-messages.html#:~:text=Letter%20by%20Roosevelt%2 0to%20Churchill%2C%20March%2018%2C%201942%3A,either%20your%20Foreign%20 Office%20or%20my%20State%20Department; Standley and Ageton, *Admiral Ambassador to Russia*, 154, 248; Walling, *Forgotten Sacrifice*, 121-122.

[40] Campbell and MacIntyre, *The Kola Run*, 19-21, 22, 24-26; Brian B. Schofield, *The Russian Convoys* (London: B. T. Batsford, 1964), 43-45, 47-48; Whitehall History Publishing – Ministry of Defence, *The Royal Navy and the Arctic Convoys*, 3, 5-7, 17-19, 21-22.

[41] Whitehall History Publishing – Ministry of Defence, *The Royal Navy and the Arctic Convoys*, 13-15.

[42] Schofield, *The Russian Convoys*, 43-45, 47-48; Whitehall History Publishing – Ministry of Defence, *The Royal Navy and the Arctic Convoys*, 13-15; Walling, *Forgotten Sacrifice*, 52-53, 55.

[43] Leonard Mosley, *The Reich Marshal: A Biography of Hermann Goering* (New York: Dell Publishing Company, 1975), 350-353, 355-359; Schofield, *The Russian Convoys*, 37-38, 39-41, 43-44, 51-53; Whitehall History Publishing – Ministry of Defence, *The Royal Navy and the Arctic Convoys*, 21-22.

[44] Georges Blond, *Ordeal Below Zero: The Heroic Story of the Arctic Convoys in World War II* (London: Souvenir Press, 1959), 24-26; Walling, *Forgotten Sacrifice*, 44, 56-57; Whitehall History Publishing – Ministry of Defence, *The Royal Navy and the Arctic Convoys*, 72-73.

[45] Whitehall History Publishing – Ministry of Defence, *The Royal Navy and the Arctic Convoys*, 72-73.

[46] The German Naval Staff, "War Diary: German Naval Staff Operations Division September 1942," *Internet Archive*, https://archive.org/stream/wardiarygermann371942 germ/wardiarygermann371942germ_djvu.txt; Whitehall History Publishing – Ministry of Defence, *The Royal Navy and the Arctic Convoys*, 72-73.

[47] Campbell and MacIntyre, *The Kola Run*, 36-37, 41-42; Mason, *Arctic Warriors*, 103; Schofield, *The Russian Convoys*, 64-66; Walling, *Forgotten Sacrifice*, 128-129.

[48] Blond, *Ordeal Below Zero*, 66-67, 69-71; Schofield, *The Russian Convoys*, 69-71, 72-74; Walling, *Forgotten Sacrifice*, 149-150.

[49] British Admiralty, "Supplement to The London Gazette of Friday, 13th October, 1950: Convoys to North Russia, 1942," *The London Gazette*, 17 October 1950, https://www.ibibl io.org/hyperwar/UN/UK/LondonGazette/39041.pdf; Broome, *Convoy is to Scatter*, 190-191, 206-207; Mark Lardas, *Arctic Convoys 1942: The Luftwaffe Cuts Russia's Lifeline* (London: Bloomsbury Publishing Plc, 2022), 4-7, 60-61; The New York Times (Unattributed Report), "U.S. Freighters in Convoy," *The New York Times*, 9 July 1942, https://www.nytimes.com/1942/07/09/archives/us-freighters-in-convoy.html; Walling, *Forgotten Sacrifice*, 166-167, 169-171; Richard Woodman, *Arctic Convoys 1941-1945* (London: John Murray Ltd., 1994), 258.

[50] Broome, *Convoy is to Scatter*, 190-191, 206-207; Campbell and MacIntyre, *The Kola Run*, 87-89; Charlie Erswell and John R. McKay, *Surviving the Arctic Convoys: The Wartime Memoir of Leading Seaman Charlie Erswell* (Barnsley, South Yorkshire: Pen & Sword Maritime, 2021), 33-34; Lardas, *Arctic Convoys 1942*, 64-66, 72-73; The New York Times, "U.S. Freighters in Convoy,"; Walling, *Forgotten Sacrifice*, 169-171; Woodman, *Arctic Convoys 1941-1945*, 259-262.

[51] British Admiralty, "Supplement to The London Gazette,"; Broome, *Convoy is to Scatter*, 190-191, 206-207; Erswell and McKay, *Surviving the Arctic Convoys*, 33-34; Schofield, *The Russian Convoys*, 79-80, 83-84, 85, 87-88, 91-92; Walling, *Forgotten Sacrifice*, 172-173.

[52] Broome, *Convoy is to Scatter*, 190-191, 206-207, 209-210; Erswell and McKay, *Surviving the Arctic Convoys*, 34-35; Lardas, *Arctic Convoys 1942*, 64-66, 72-73; The New York Times, "U.S. Freighters in Convoy."

[53] Arseni G. Golovko, *With the Red Fleet: The War Memoirs of the Late Arseni G. Golovko*, ed. Sir Aubrey Mansergh, trans. Peter Broomfield (London: Putnam, 1965), 96-97, 98-100.

[54] Golovko, *With the Red Fleet*, 102-103; Lardas, *Arctic Convoys 1942*, 64-66, 72-73.

[55] Golovko, *With the Red Fleet*, 103-105, 107-109; The New York Times, "U.S. Freighters in Convoy."

[56] UK Prime Minister, "Former Naval Person to President: Personal and Secret," 14 July 1942, *Churchill Archive for Schools*, https://www.churchillarchiveforschools.com/theme

s/the-themes/key-events-and-developments-in-world-history/was-churchill-really-wo
rried-about-the-battle-of-the-atlantic-and-if-so-why/the-sources/source-8.

[57] Alanbrooke, *War Diaries*, 254; Deane, *The Strange Alliance*, 109; Golovko, *With the Red Fleet*, 107-109; Ministry of Foreign Affairs of the U.S.S.R., *Stalin's Correspondence*, "No. 56: W. Churchill to J. V. Stalin," 18 July 1942, 52-55 and "No. 57: Message from Premier Stalin to Prime Minister Churchill," 23 July 1942; Reynolds and Pechatnov, *The Kremlin Letters*, 124-127, 129; Standley and Ageton, *Admiral Ambassador to Russia*, 157.

[58] Alanbrooke, *War Diaries*, 285-286; Chuikov, *The Battle for Stalingrad*, 116-120, 194; Churchill, *Memoirs*, 478-479; Glantz and House, *When Titans Clashed*, 143-147, 171-172, 176-177, 186-187, 190; Hellbeck, *Stalingrad*, 87-88, 138-139; Ministry of Foreign Affairs of the U.S.S.R., *Stalin's Correspondence*, "No. 58: Prime Minister to Premier Stalin," 31 July 1942, 57; Reynolds and Pechatnov, *The Kremlin Letters*, 132-133; Roosevelt and Churchill, "Texts of Roosevelt-Churchill Messages,"; Sherwood, *Roosevelt and Hopkins*, 545; Standley and Ageton, *Admiral Ambassador to Russia*, 307; U.S. President, "Map Room Papers Box 8 Stalin to Roosevelt July – December 1942,"; Werth, *Russia at War*, 148-149, 152-153, 171, 243, 249-252. In these communications with Roosevelt, Stalin repeatedly called attention to the Red Army Air Forces' preference for the U.S. P-39, rating the "Aircobra [sic]" favorably in comparison to other attack aircraft.

[59] Mason, *Arctic Warriors*, 155; The New York Times (Unattributed Report), "SOVIET HAILS VICTORY OF MURMANSK CONVOY; Russians Guard Allied Vessels in Air and Sea Fight," *The New York Times*, 20 July 1942, https://www.nytimes.com/1942/07/20/archive s/soviet-hails-victory-of-murmansk-convoy-russians-guard-allied.html; Walling, *Forgotten Sacrifice*, 270-271.

[60] Stettinius, Jr., *Lend-Lease*, 230-232; U.S. Department of State, *Soviet Supply Protocols*, 9-12, 13-15, 16-17. As further clarified by Roosevelt's former speechwriter Robert Sherwood, a close friend of Hopkins, 84 Liberty ships reportedly left U.S. ports for North Russia between April and June 1942 after the president's urgent directive in March, carrying 522,000 tons of supplies on board. Inclement weather is said to have forced some of the ships to either return or to temporarily dock in British ports, while vicious enemy attacks also inflicted losses. Yet 44 Liberty ships successfully sailed with the spring convoys and delivered much of the material, safely bringing 300,000 tons of Lend-Lease cargo from the United States to the North Russian ports by the end of the First Protocol period on 30 June 1942, while the men of the very large Convoy PQ-18 and its successors in the JW series of Arctic convoys subsequently delivered more material between late 1942 and early 1943, much of which arrived safely, fueling the Red Army's ongoing fight. See McMeekin, *Stalin's War*, 403-405, 407-409; and Sherwood, *Roosevelt and Hopkins*, 544-546.

[61] Sokolov, *The Role of the Soviet Union in the Second World War*, 53-55; Stettinius, Jr., *Lend-Lease*, 249, 252; Van Tuyll, *Feeding the Bear*, 83.

[62] Chuikov, *The Battle for Stalingrad*, 116-120, 194; Craig, *Enemy at the Gates*, 102-103, 106-107, 140-143; Hellbeck, *Stalingrad*, 98-102, 117-125; Werth, *Russia at War*, 152-153, 157, 162-164.

[63] Reynolds and Pechatnov, *The Kremlin Letters*, 94, 96; Roosevelt and Churchill, "Texts of Roosevelt-Churchill Messages,"; Sherwood, *Roosevelt and Hopkins*, 545; U.S. President, "Map Room Papers Box 8 Stalin to Roosevelt July – December 1942."

[64] Glantz and House, *When Titans Clashed*, 143-147, 171-172, 176-177, 186-187, 190.

[65] Erswell and McKay, *Surviving the Arctic Convoys*, 34-35; Roosevelt and Churchill, "Texts of Roosevelt-Churchill Messages,"; U.S. President, U.S. President, "Map Room Papers Box

8 Stalin to Roosevelt July – December 1942,"; Dwight Jon Zimmerman, "Lend-Lease to Russia: The Persian Corridor," *DefenseMediaNetwork*, 8 November 2012, https://www.de fensemedianetwork.com/stories/lend-lease-to-russia-the-persian-corridor/.

[66] Chuikov, *The Battle for Stalingrad*, 125-126, 157-162, 175; Glantz and House, *When Titans Clashed*, 143-147, 171-172, 176-177, 186-187, 190; Hellbeck, *Stalingrad*, 173, 181.

[67] David Carlton, *Churchill and the Soviet Union* (Manchester: Manchester University Press, 2000), 101-102.

[68] McMeekin, *Stalin's War*, 407-408; Weeks, *Russia's Life-Saver*, 112-113.

[69] Carlton, *Churchill and the Soviet Union*, 101-102.

[70] Mason, *Arctic Warriors*, 11-12, 13-15; Peter C. Smith, *Arctic Victory: The Story of Convoy PQ 18* (London: William Kimber & Co. Limited, 1975), 31; Walling, *Forgotten Sacrifice*, 213-215; Woodman, *Arctic Convoys 1941-1945*, 262-264.

[71] Erswell and McKay, *Surviving the Arctic Convoys*, 38-39; Mason, *Arctic Warriors*, 54-55; Walling, *Forgotten Sacrifice*, 213-215.

[72] Erswell and McKay, *Surviving the Arctic Convoys*, 43-44; Smith, *Arctic Victory*, 11-12; The German Naval Staff, "War Diary,"; Walling, *Forgotten Sacrifice*, 213-215; Woodman, *Arctic Convoys 1941-1945*, 262-264.

[73] Walling, *Forgotten Sacrifice*, 213-215.

[74] Eswell and McKay, *Surviving the Arctic Convoys*, 44-45; Lardas, *Arctic Convoys 1942*, 74-75; Smith, *Arctic Victory*, 192-193; Woodman, *Arctic Convoys 1941-1945*, 264-265, 266; Whitehall History Publishing – Ministry of Defence, *The Royal Navy and the Arctic Convoys*, 78-79.

[75] Landas, *Arctic Convoys 1942*, 74-75; Mason, *Arctic Warriors*, 71-73; Whitehall History Publishing – Ministry of Defence, *The Royal Navy and the Arctic Convoys*, 80-81.

[76] Erswell and McKay, *Surviving the Arctic Convoys*, 52-53; Smith, *Arctic Victory*, 192-193; Woodman, *Arctic Convoys 1941-1945*, 267-270; Whitehall History Publishing – Ministry of Defence, *The Royal Navy and the Arctic Convoys*, 80-81.

[77] Schofield, *The Russian Convoys*, 116-117; The German General Staff, "War Diary,"; Whitehall History Publishing – Ministry of Defence, *The Royal Navy and the Arctic Convoys*, 80-81, 82-83; Woodman, *Arctic Convoys 1941-1945*, 267-270.

[78] Mason, *Arctic Warriors*, 87-89, 90; Smith, *Arctic Victory*, 194-196; Woodman, *Arctic Convoys 1941-1945*, 271-272, 273-275.

[79] Blond, *Ordeal Below Zero*, 149-150; Landas, *Arctic Convoys 1942*, 82-83; McMeekin, *Stalin's War*, 419-420, 422; Smith, *Arctic Victory*, 197-199, 201-202; The German Naval Staff, "War Diary,"; Whitehall History Publishing – Ministry of Defence, *The Royal Navy and the Arctic Convoys*, 80-81; Woodman, *Arctic Convoys 1941-1945*, 276-280, 282-283.

[80] McMeekin, *Stalin's War*, 419-420, 422; Smith, *Arctic Victory*, 203-205; Sokolov, *The Role of the Soviet Union in the Second World War*, 53-55, 57-59; Woodman, *Arctic Convoys 1941-1945*, 276-280, 282-283.

[81] Thomas, Leona J. *Through Ice and Fire: A Russian Arctic Convoy Diary, 1942*, (Stroud, Gloucestershire: Fonthill Media Limited, 2015), 147-148.

[82] Mason, *Arctic Warriors*, 155-156.

[83] Hellbeck, *Stalingrad*, 173, 181; Stephen J. Thorne, "Hitler, Raeder, and the demise of the *Kriegsmarine*," *Legion: Canada's Military History Magazine*, 2 October 2019, https://legio nmagazine.com/en/hitler-raeder-and-the-demise-of-the-kriegsmarine/.

[84] K. C. Fraser, "73 North: The Battle of the Barents' Sea 1942," *Reference Reviews*, Vol. 14, No. 6 (1 June 2000), 14, https://www.emerald.com/insight/content/doi/10.1108/rr.2000

.14.6.14.281/full/html; Landas, *Arctic Convoys 1942*, 4-7, 82-83, 84; Mosley, *The Reich Marshal*, 350-353, 353-355, 355-359; Whitehall History Publishing – Ministry of Defence, *The Royal Navy and the Arctic Convoys*, 89-90; George Walker, "Fiasco in the Barents' Sea," *Naval History Magazine*, Vol. 32, No. 2 (April 2018), 14-17, https://www.usni.org/magaz ines/naval-history-magazine/2018/april/contact.

[85] Schofield, *The Russian Convoys*, 132-135; Walling, *Forgotten Sacrifice*, 246-248.

[86] Blond, *Ordeal Below Zero*, 152-153; Campbell and MacIntyre, *The Kola Run*, 159-162; Fraser, "73 North," 14; Whitehall History Publishing – Ministry of Defence, *The Royal Navy and the Arctic Convoys*, 92-94; Walker, "Fiasco in the Barents' Sea," 15-16."

[87] Whitehall History Publishing – Ministry of Defence, *The Royal Navy and the Arctic Convoys*, 97-98.

[88] Campbell and MacIntyre, *The Kola Run*, 159-162; Fraser, "73 North,"; Schofield, *The Russian Convoys*, 132-135; Thorne, "Hitler, Raeder, and the demise of the *Kriegsmarine*,"; Walker, "Fiasco in the Barents' Sea," 15-16,"; Walling, *Forgotten Sacrifice*, 246-248.

[89] Erswell and McKay, *Surviving the Arctic Convoys*, 93-95; Whitehall History Publishing – Ministry of Defence, *The Royal Navy and the Arctic Convoys*, 101-102.

[90] Blond, *Ordeal Below Zero*, 158-160; Campbell and MacIntyre, *The Kola Run*, 164-165; Fraser, "73 North,"; Whitehall History Publishing – Ministry of Defence, *The Royal Navy and the Arctic Convoys*, 101-102; Walker, "Fiasco in the Barents' Sea," 15-16."

[91] Blond, *Ordeal Below Zero*, 152-153, 161-163; Fraser, "73 North," 14; Pastorfield-Li, "An excerpt from an interview with a Soviet soldier,"; Stephen J. Thorne, "Raeder's defence: German admiral fights for his doomed fleet," *Legion: Canada's Military History Magazine*, 30 October 2019, https://legionmagazine.com/en/raeders-defence-german-admiral-fig hts-for-his-doomed-fleet/; Walker, "Fiasco in the Barents' Sea," 17; Whitehall History Publishing – Ministry of Defence, *The Royal Navy and the Arctic Convoys*, 101-102.

[92] Chuikov, *The Battle for Stalingrad*, 215-217, 227-229; Pastorfield-Li, "An excerpt from an interview with a Soviet soldier."

[93] Herman Melton, *Liberty's War: An Engineer's Memoir of the Merchant Marine, 1942-45*, ed. Will Melton (Annapolis, MD: Naval Institute Press, 2017), 31, 33.

[94] Campbell and MacIntyre, *The Kola Run*, 164-165; Fraser, "73 North," 14; Melton, *Liberty's War*, 34-35, 37, 72-73; Walker, "Fiasco in the Barents' Sea," 17.

[95] Campbell and MacIntyre, *The Kola Run*, 164-165; Erswell and McKay, *Surviving the Arctic Convoys*, 96-98; Melton, *Liberty's War*, 74-76.

[96] Fraser, "73 North," 14; *The National Archives of the UK*, "PREMIER 3 393/8," "First Sea Lord," 14 December 1942; Walker, "Fiasco in the Barents' Sea," 17.

[97] Hellbeck, *Stalingrad*, 173, 181; *The National Archives of the UK*, "PREMIER 3 393/8," "Prime Minister to Premier Stalin," 29 December 1942.

[98] *The National Archives of the UK*, "PREMIER 3 393/8" "Prime Minister," n. d.

[99] Ibid., "Foreign Secretary. First Lord. First Sea Lord," 9 January 1943.

[100] Ibid.

[101] Alanbrooke, *War Diaries*, 319-320, 327-328, 387; Arnold, *Global Mission*, 259; Churchill, *Memoirs*, 742-744, 745-747; Eisenhower, *Crusade in Europe*, 69-70; Sherwood, *Roosevelt and Hopkins*, 713-714; Standley and Ageton, *Admiral Ambassador to Russia*, 331-333; U.S. President, "Map Room Papers Box 8 Stalin to Roosevelt July – December 1942,"; U.S. President, "Map Room Papers Box 8 Roosevelt to Stalin January – June 1943."

[102] *The National Archives of the UK*, "PREMIER 3 393/8," "Copy. Secret." 2 January 1943; U.S. Department of State, *Soviet Supply Protocols*, 32-34, 35-36, 46-47.

[103] Office, Chief of Finance War Department, "Lend-Lease Shipments World War II,"; *The National Archives of the UK*, "PREMIER 3 393/8," "Prime Minister to Premier Stalin," 10 January 1943, and "Premier Stalin to Premier Churchill," 15 January 1943.

[104] The National Archives of the UK, "PREMIER 3 393/8," "Prime Minister," 18 January 1943, and "Most Secret. Mr. Keenlyside," 19 January 1943.

[105] Ibid., "Stratagem No. 100. Prime Minister to Foreign Secretary," 19 January 1943.

[106] Ministry of Foreign Affairs of the U.S.S.R., *Stalin's Correspondence*, "No. 103: For Marshal Stalin from President Roosevelt and Prime Minister Churchill," 19 August 1943, 83; Reynolds and Pechatnov, *The Kremlin Letters*, 287-288; *The National Archives of the UK*, "PREMIER 3 393/8," "Stratagem No. 100. Prime Minister to Foreign Secretary," 19 January 1943; U.S. President, "Map Room Papers Box 8 Stalin to Roosevelt July – December 1942,"; U.S. President, "Map Room Papers Box 8 Roosevelt to Stalin January – June 1943."

[107] *The National Archives of the UK*, "PREMIER 3 393/8,", "Telescope No. 152. Following for Keenlyside for Ministry of War Transport," 20 January 1943.

[108] Erswell and McKay, *Surviving the Arctic Convoys*, 93-95; *The National Archives of the UK*, "PREMIER 3 393/8," "Telescope No. 152. Following for Keenlyside for Ministry of War Transport," 20 January 1943.

[109] Kotelnikov, *Lend-Lease and Soviet Aviation*, 173-175, 191-192, 193-195; Loza, *Attack of the Airacobras*, 30-31, 47-49, 52-53, 57-62; Melton, *Liberty's War*, 48-49.

[110] Melton, *Liberty's War*, 48-49.

[111] Kotelnikov, *Lend-Lease and Soviet Aviation*, 173-175, 191-192, 193-195; Loza, *Attack of the Airacobras*, 30-31, 47-49, 52-53, 57-62; Melton, *Liberty's War*, 50, 74-76; Senior British Naval Officer, North Russia, "Report of SBNO (extracts) – December 1942."

[112] Erswell and McKay, *Surviving the Arctic Convoys*, 96-98; Senior British Naval Officer, North Russia, "Report of SBNO (extracts) – Feb-Apr 1943."

[113] Loza, *Attack of the* Airacobras, 39-42; Mellinger, *Soviet Lend-Lease Fighter Aces*, 45-47, 48, 59-61; Melton, *Liberty's War*, 74-76; Rickenbacker, *Rickenbacker*, 407-408, 409.

[114] U.S. President, "Map Room Papers Box 8 Stalin to Roosevelt July – December 1942,"; U.S. President, "Map Room Papers Box 8 Roosevelt to Stalin January – June 1943."

[115] Melton, *Liberty's War*, 74-76.

[116] Erswell and McKay, *Surviving the Arctic Convoys*, 96-98, 107-109, 109-111; *The National Archives of the UK*, "PREMIER 3 393/8," "Prime Minister," 18 January 1943, and "Most Secret. Mr. Keenlyside," 19 January 1943; Sherwood, *Roosevelt and Hopkins*, 791-793, 796; U.S. President, "Map Room Papers Box 8 Roosevelt to Stalin January – June 1943."

[117] Ministry of Foreign Affairs of the U.S.S.R., *Stalin's Correspondence*, "No. 103: For Marshal Stalin from President Roosevelt and Prime Minister Churchill," 19 August 1943, 83; Reynolds and Pechatnov, *The Kremlin Letters*, 287-288; U.S. President, "Map Room Papers Box 8 Roosevelt to Stalin January – June 1943."

[118] Arnold, *Global Mission*, 211-212, 385-387; Van Tuyll, *Feeding the Bear*, 117-119; Weeks, *Russia's Life-Saver*, 115-117, 120-121.

[119] Associated Press, "Rickenbacker and Two of Stimson's Aides In Moscow on a Mission for War Secretary," *The New York Times*, 24 June 1943, https://www.nytimes.com/1943/0 6/24/archives/rickenbacker-and-two-of-stimsons-aides-in-moscow-on-a-mission-for. html; Rickenbacker, *Rickenbacker*, 389.

[120] Jones, *The Roads to Russia*, 139-140.

[121] Ibid., 61-62; McMeekin, *Stalin's War*, 403-404.

[122] Standley and Ageton, *Admiral Ambassador*, 153.

[123] Ibid., 160.

[124] Associated Press, "Rickenbacker and Two of Stimson's Aides in Moscow,"; Rickenbacker, *Rickenbacker*, 399-400.

[125] Denny, "SOVIET FLIERS LAND PLANE AT NORTH POLE,"; Rickenbacker, *Rickenbacker*, 399-400, 407-408.

[126] Rickenbacker, *Rickenbacker*, 409.

[127] Arnold, *Global Mission*, 259; Associated Press, "RICKENBACKER HOME FROM MOSCOW TRIP; He Reports to Stimson on the Results of Tour Abroad," *The New York Times*, 12 August 1943, https://www.nytimes.com/1943/08/12/archives/rickenback er-home-from-moscow-trip-he-reports-to-stimson-on-the.html; Rickenbacker, *Rickenbacker*, 400-401.

[128] Rickenbacker, *Rickenbacker*, 402-403.

[129] McMeekin, *Stalin's War*, 534-536; The New York Times, "JAPAN LETS RUSSIA GET OUR SUPPLIES."

[130] Associated Press, "RICKENBACKER HOME FROM MOSCOW TRIP,"; Rickenbacker, *Rickenbacker*, 402-403.

[131] Rickenbacker, *Rickenbacker*, 402-403.

[132] McMeekin, *Stalin's War*, 534-536; Office, Chief of Finance War Department, "Lend-Lease Shipments World War II,"; The New York Times, "JAPAN LETS RUSSIA GET OUR SUPPLIES,"; U.S. Department of State, *Soviet Supply Protocols*, 55, 57-61, 66-71, 76, 79-83.

[133] Ministry of Foreign Affairs of the U.S.S.R., *Stalin's Correspondence*, "No. 138: Personal and Secret Message from Premier J. V. Stalin to the Prime Minister, Mr. W. Churchill," 2 April 1943, 112; Reynolds and Pechatnov, *The Kremlin Letters*, 227.

[134] Ministry of Foreign Affairs of the U.S.S.R., *Stalin's Correspondence*, "No. 138: Personal and Secret Message from Premier J. V. Stalin to the Prime Minister, Mr. W. Churchill," 2 April 1943, 112; Reynolds and Pechatnov, *The Kremlin Letters*, 227.

[135] Dunn, *The Red Army and the Soviet Economy*, 80-81; Hill, *The Great Patriotic War of the Soviet Union*, 185; Vail Motter, *The Persian Corridor*, 136-138; Weeks, *Russia's Life-Saver*, 25-27; Whitehall History Publishing – Ministry of Defence, *The Royal Navy and the Arctic Convoys*, x-xii, 129-130.

[136] Churchill, *Memoirs*, 742-744, 745-747; Ministry of Foreign Affairs of the U.S.S.R., *Stalin's Correspondence*, "No. 199: Personal and Most Secret Message from the Prime Minister, Mr. Winston Churchill, to Marshal Stalin," 1 October 1943, 166-169; Reynolds and Pechatnov, *The Kremlin Letters*, 316-318.

[137] Arnold, *Global Mission*, 211-212, 385-387; Dolitsky, Glazkov, and Poor, Pipeline to Russia, 64-66, 79-80, 84-85.

[138] McMeekin, *Stalin's War*, 518-519; U.S. Department of State, *Soviet Supply Protocols*, 55, 57-61, 66-71, 76, 79-83.

[139] Ministry of Foreign Affairs of the U.S.S.R., *Stalin's Correspondence*, "No. 165: Personal and Secret Message from Premier J. V. Stalin to the Prime Minister, Mr. W. Churchill," 24 June 1943, 136-138; Reynolds and Pechatnov, *The Kremlin Letters*, 267-270.

[140] Carlton, *Churchill and the Soviet Union*, 101-102; McMeekin, *Stalin's War*, 406-408.

[141] Ministry of Foreign Affairs of the U.S.S.R., *Stalin's Correspondence*, "No. 165," 136-138; Reynolds and Pechatnov, *The Kremlin Letters*, 267-270.

[142] Mason, *Arctic Warriors*, 155-156; Melton, *Liberty's War*, 74-76; Ministry of Foreign Affairs of the U.S.S.R., *Stalin's Correspondence*, "No. 103: For Marshal Stalin from

President Roosevelt and Prime Minister Churchill," 19 August 1943, 83; Reynolds and Pechatnov, *The Kremlin Letters*, 287-288; U.S. Department of State, *Soviet Supply Protocols*, 55, 57-61, 66-71, 76, 79-83; U.S. President, "Map Room Papers Box 8 Roosevelt to Stalin January – June 1943,"; *The National Archives of the UK*, "PREMIER 3 393/8," "Stratagem No. 100. Prime Minister to Foreign Secretary," 19 January 1943; Thomas, *Through Ice and Fire*, 147-148.

[143] Eisenhower, *Crusade in Europe*, 29; Jones, *The Roads to Russia*, 65, 110-111; Frank N. Schubert, "The Persian Gulf Command: Lifeline to the Soviet Union," *Pars Times – Greater Iran & Beyond* (March 2005), 305-315; Van Tuyll, *Feeding the Bear*, 5, 49.

[144] Vail Motter, *The Persian Corridor*, 141-143, 259-262, 319-320, 341-344; Van Tuyll, *Feeding the Bear*, 26-27, 51, 73.

[145] Jones, *The Roads to Russia*, 49, 65, 110-111; Schubert, "The Persian Gulf Command," 308-309; Van Tuyll, *Feeding the Bear*, 26-27, 51, 73; U.S. President, "Map Room Papers Box 8 Roosevelt to Stalin January – June 1943."

[146] William H. Lawrence, "LEND-LEASE HELP TO RUSSIA TO RISE; Proposals for New Protocol, to Go Into Effect June 30, Delivered to Moscow GAIN FROM SHORTER ROUTE Opening of Mediterranean to speed Supply – Stettinius Gives Figures to April 30," *The New York Times*, 15 June 1943, https://www.nytimes.com/1943/06/15/archives/lendleas e-help-to-russia-to-rise-proposals-for-new-protocol-to-go.html; Stettinius, Jr., *Lend-Lease*, 240-242, 244-246, 248; Weeks, *Russia's Life-Saver*, 111-112; Zimmerman, "Lend-Lease to Russia."

[147] Jones, *The Roads to Russia*, 139-140, 143, 208-209; Ministry of Foreign Affairs of the U.S.S.R., *Stalin's Correspondence*, "No. 199: Personal and Most Secret Message from the Prime Minister, Mr. Winston Churchill, to Marshal Stalin," 1 October 1943, 166-169; Office, Chief of Finance War Department, "Lend-Lease Shipments World War II,"; Reynolds and Pechatnov, *The Kremlin Letters*, 316-318; U.S. President, "Map Room Papers Box 8 Roosevelt to Stalin,"; Vail Motter, *The Persian Corridor and Aid to Russia*, 215-217.

[148] Vail Motter, *The Persian Corridor*, 19-20, 21-23, 26-27, 93-96, 143-147, 149, 152-155; Zimmerman, "Lend-Lease to Russia."

[149] Office, Chief of Finance War Department, "Lend-Lease Shipments World War II,"; Stettinius, Jr., *Lend-Lease*, 240-242, 244-246, 248; Vail Motter, *The Persian Corridor and Aid to Russia*, 139, 240-241; Van Tuyll, *Feeding the Bear*, 54.

[150] Dunn, *The Red Army and the Soviet Economy*, 74; Office, Chief of Finance War Department, "Lend-Lease Shipments World War II,"; U.S. Department of State, *Soviet Supply Protocols*, 55, 57-61, 66-71, 76, 79-83; Vail Motter, *The Persian Corridor and Aid to Russia*, 312-313; Zimmerman, "Lend-Lease to Russia."

[151] Schubert, "The Persian Gulf Command," 310-312; Sherwood, *Roosevelt and Hopkins*, 545, 799; Stettinius, Jr., *Lend-Lease*, 241; Zimmerman, "Lend-Lease to Russia."

[152] Dawson, *The Decision to Aid Russia*, 198; Schubert, "The Persian Gulf Command," 305-307; Weeks, *Russia's Life-Saver*, 116; Zimmerman, "Lend-Lease to Russia."

[153] Stettinius, Jr., *Lend-Lease*, 240-242, 244-246, 248; U.S. Department of State, *Soviet Supply Protocols*, 55, 57-61, 66-71, 76, 79-83; Zimmerman, "Lend-Lease to Russia."

[154] Hellbeck, *Stalingrad*, 173, 181; McMeekin, *Stalin's War*, 409-410, 412-414, 416-417, 423-424, 425-427; Sokolov, *Marshal K. K. Rokossovsky*, 173-175, 177, 179-181, 215; Zhukov, *Marshal of Victory Vol. 2*, 79-80, 287-289, 411.

[155] Jones, *The Roads to Russia*, 110-111, 112-113, 139-140, 143; Vail Motter, *The Persian Corridor*, 312-313, 316-319; Van Tuyll, *Feeding the Bear*, 5, 26-27, 49; Weeks, *Russia's Life-Saver*, 111-112.

[156] "The New York Times (Unattributed Report), "HULL PRAISES RED ARMY; Says Stalingrad Marks Troops as Equal of Any in War," *The New York Times*, 4 February 1943, https://www.nytimes.com/1943/02/04/archives/hull-praises-red-army-says-stalingrad -marks-troops-as-equal-of-any.html; TIME (Unattributed Report), "World Battlefronts: THE BATTLE OF RUSSIA: The Beginning of Disaster?" TIME, Vol. XLI, No. 4 (25 January 1943), 1-2, https://content.time.com/time/subscriber/article/0,33009,850230,00.html.

[157] Dunn, *The Soviet Economy and the Red Army*, 80-81; Hill, *The Great Patriotic War of the Soviet Union*, 185; Schubert, "The Persian Gulf Command," 313-315; Weeks, *Russia's Life-Saver*, 25-27; Zimmerman, "Lend-Lease to Russia."

[158] See, for example, Eisenhower, *Crusade in Europe*, 25, 69-70; Glantz, *Colossus Reborn*, 22, 27, 40-41, 43, 58, 88-89; Hill, *The Great Patriotic War of the Soviet Union*, 185; Zimmerman, "Lend-Lease to Russia."

[159] Hill, *The Great Patriotic War of the Soviet Union*, 187-188, 190; Sokolov, *The Role of the Soviet Union in the Second World War*, 53-55.

[160] McMeekin, *Stalin's War*, 419-420, 422; U.S. Department of State, *Soviet Supply Protocols*, 55, 57-61, 66-71, 76, 79-83; Van Tuyll, *Feeding the Bear*, 5, 26-27, 49; Zimmerman, "Lend-Lease to Russia."

[161] Arnold, *Global Mission*, 248-249; Baer, *One Hundred Years of Sea Power*, 165; Blake W. Smith, *Warplanes to Alaska* (Blaine, WA: Hancock House Publishers, 1998), 14, 17, 45-47; Stettinius, Jr., *Lend-Lease*, 257.

[162] Arnold, *Global Mission*, 254; U.S. Department of State, *Soviet Supply Protocols*, 55, 57-61, 66-71, 76, 79-83.

[163] Arnold, *Global Mission*, 211-212, 385-387; Dolitsky, Glazkov, and Poor, *Pipeline to Russia*, 10, 52-53, 55-57; Smith, *Warplanes to Alaska*, 23-27, 29-31; Weeks, *Russia's Life-Saver*, 122.

[164] Hays, Jr., *The Alaska-Siberia Connection*, 37-38, 41, 43-45, 49; Smith, *Warplanes to Alaska*, 45-47, 54-56.

[165] Dolitsky, Glazkov, and Poor, *Pipeline to Russia*, 36-37, 40-41, 47-49; Hays, Jr., *The Alaska-Siberia Connection*, 45, 47.

[166] Hays, Jr., *The Alaska-Siberia Connection*, 49; Smith, *Warplanes to Alaska*, 55-56; Weeks, *Russia's Life-Saver*, 1-4, 4-7, 114-115.

[167] Arnold, *Global Mission*, 211-212, 385-387; Hays, Jr., *The Alaska-Siberia Connection*, 57-58; Office, Chief of Finance War Department, "Lend-Lease Shipments World War II,"; U.S. Department of State, *Soviet Supply Protocols*, 32-34, 35-36, 46-47.

[168] Jordan, *Major Jordan's Diaries*, 19; Smith, *Warplanes to Alaska*, 94-95, 98-99.

[169] Van Tuyll, *Feeding the Bear*, 116-117; Weeks, *Russia's Life-Saver*, 120.

[170] Sokolov, *The Role of the Soviet Union in the Second World War*, 53-55, 57-59.

[171] Dunn, *The Soviet Economy and the Red Army*, 80-81; Hill, *The Great Patriotic War of the Soviet Union*, 185; McMeekin, *Stalin's War*, 534-536; The New York Times, "JAPAN LETS RUSSIA GET OUR SUPPLIES."

[172] Dolitsky, Glazkov, and Poor, *Pipeline to Russia*, 52-53, 55-57; McMeekin, *Stalin's War*, 534-536; Smith, *Warplanes to Alaska*, 113-115, 122; The New York Times, "JAPAN LETS RUSSIA GET OUR SUPPLIES."

[173] Erswell and McKay, *Surviving the Arctic Convoys*, 107-109, 109-111, 131-135, 135-137, 142-144, 148-149.

[174] Whitehall History Publishing – Ministry of Defence, *The Royal Navy and the Arctic Convoys* x-xii.

[175] Schofield, *The Russian Convoys*, 206.

[176] Whitehall History Publishing – Ministry of Defence, *The Royal Navy and the Arctic Convoys*, x-xii. Jones provides the exact figures for the equipment transported by PQ-18 as totaling, "4,000 Vehicles, 800 Tanks, 550 Aircraft, 11,000 Tons of TNT, 157,500 Tons of miscellaneous and very valuable cargo."

[177] Chuikov, *The Battle for Stalingrad*, 236-239, 322-324; Whitehall History Publishing – Ministry of Defence, *The Royal Navy and the Arctic Convoys*, x-xii.

CHAPTER 4

[1] Carlton, *Churchill and the Soviet Union*, 101-102; Standley and Ageton, *Admiral Ambassador*, 153, 160; *The National Archives of the UK*, "PREMIER 3 393/8," "Prime Minister to Premier Stalin," 10 January 1943, and "Premier Stalin to Premier Churchill," 15 January 1943.

[2] Churchill, *Memoirs*, 742-744, 745-747; Ministry of Foreign Affairs of the U.S.S.R., *Stalin's Correspondence*, "No. 199: Personal and Most Secret Message from the Prime Minister, Mr. Winston Churchill, to Marshal Stalin," 1 October 1943, 166-169; Molotov and Chuev, *Molotov Remembers*, 1-3, 37-39, 41-43, 52-53; Reynolds and Pechatnov, *The Kremlin Letters*, 316-318; U.S. President, "Map Room Papers Box 8 Roosevelt to Stalin May – December 1942."

[3] Walling, *Forgotten Sacrifice*, 261-262.

[4] Ibid.; Whitehall History Publishing – Ministry of Defence, *The Royal Navy and the Arctic Convoys*, 108-109.

[5] Walling, *Forgotten Sacrifice*, 261-262.

[6] *The National Archives of the UK*, "ADM 199/77: North Russia convoys JW and RA reports: JW 54 A, JW 54 B, JW 55 A, JW 55 B, JW 56 A, JW 56 B, RA 5'4 A, RA 54 B, RA 55 A, RA 55 B, RA 56," 1943-1944, 52-53.

[7] *The National Archives of the UK*, "ADM 199/77," 56-57.

[8] Whitehall History Publishing – Ministry of Defence, *The Royal Navy and the Arctic Convoys*, 109-110.

[9] Walling, *Forgotten Sacrifice*, 252-255.

[10] *The National Archives of the UK*, "ADM 199/77," 61-62.

[11] Ibid.; Walling, *Forgotten Sacrifice*, 261-262; Whitehall History Publishing – Ministry of Defence, *The Royal Navy and the Arctic Convoys*, 111-115.

[12] *The National Archives of the UK*, "ADM 199/77," 336-337, 340-341.

[13] Whitehall History Publishing – Ministry of Defence, *The Royal Navy and the Arctic Convoys*, 111-115.

[14] *The National Archives of the UK*, "ADM 199/77," 341-343; Whitehall History Publishing – Ministry of Defence, *The Royal Navy and the Arctic Convoys*, 111-115.

[15] *The National Archives of the UK*, "ADM 199/77," 341-343; Whitehall History Publishing – Ministry of Defence, *The Royal Navy and the Arctic Convoys*, 111-115.

[16] *The National Archives of the UK*, "ADM 199/77," 343-344; Walling, *Forgotten Sacrifice*, 252-255.

[17] Walling, *Forgotten Sacrifice*, 252-255.

[18] Whitehall History Publishing – Ministry of Defence, *The Royal Navy and the Arctic Convoys*, 111-115.

[19] Walling, *Forgotten Sacrifice*, 252-255; Whitehall History Publishing – Ministry of Defence, *The Royal Navy and the Arctic Convoys*, 111-115.

[20] *The National Archives of the UK*, "ADM 199/77," 343-344.

[21] Ibid.

[22] Whitehall History Publishing – Ministry of Defence, *The Royal Navy and the Arctic Convoys*, 115-117.

[23] William Smith, *Churchill's Arctic Convoys: Strength Triumphs Over Adversity* (Barnsley, South Yorkshire: Pen & Sword Maritime, 2022), 116, 157-158.

[24] Smith, *Churchill's Arctic Convoys*, 157-158.

[25] Ibid., 158-159; Walling, *Forgotten Sacrifice*, 261-262.

[26] Smith, *Churchill's Arctic Convoys*, 159-160.

[27] Admiralty Naval Staff, *Battle Summary No. 27: Attack on the "Tirpitz" (Operation "Tungsten") 3rd April, 1944*, (London: Tactical, Torpedo and Staff Duties Division – Historical Section, 1944), 1-3, 5-7, https://www.navy.gov.au/sites/default/files/documents/Battle_Summary_27.pdf; *The National Archives of the UK*, "ADM 199/77," 347-349, 352-353; Whitehall History Publishing – Ministry of Defence, *The Royal Navy and the Arctic Convoys*, 115-117.

[28] Smith, *Churchill's Arctic Convoys*, 160-162; Walling, *Forgotten Sacrifice*, 261-262.

[29] *Imperial War Museum*, "Documents.2114: Private Papers of Lieutenant P S Cockrell RNVR," Box No: 92/45/1.

[30] *Imperial War Museum*, "Documents.2114,"; Whitehall History Publishing – Ministry of Defence, *The Royal Navy and the Arctic Convoys*, 120-122.

[31] *Imperial War Museum*, "Documents.2114,"; Smith, *Churchill's Arctic Convoys*, 170.

[32] Smith, *Churchill's Arctic Convoys*, 170.

[33] *Imperial War Museum*, "Documents.2114." Parentheses in the original, bracket quotes mine.

[34] Ibid.; Smith, *Churchill's Arctic Convoys*, 173-175; Whitehall History Publishing – Ministry of Defence, *The Royal Navy and the Arctic Convoys*, 120-122.

[35] *Imperial War Museum*, "Documents.2114,"; Smith, *Churchill's Arctic Convoys*, 173-175; Whitehall History Publishing – Ministry of Defence, *The Royal Navy and the Arctic Convoys*, 120-122.

[36] Smith, *Churchill's Arctic Convoys*, 173-175; Whitehall History Publishing – Ministry of Defence, *The Royal Navy and the Arctic Convoys*, 120-122.

[37] *Imperial War Museum*, "Documents.2114,"; Smith, *Churchill's Arctic Convoys*, 173-175.

[38] *Imperial War Museum*, "Documents.2114; Whitehall History Publishing – Ministry of Defence, *The Royal Navy and the Arctic Convoys*, 120-122.

[39] *Imperial War Museum*, "Documents.2114,"; Smith, *Churchill's Arctic Convoys*, 173-175; Whitehall History Publishing – Ministry of Defence, *The Royal Navy and the Arctic Convoys*, 120-122.

[40] Whitehall History Publishing – Ministry of Defence, *The Royal Navy and the Arctic Convoys*, 120-122.

[41] *Imperial War Museum*, "Documents.2114."; Smith, *Churchill's Arctic Convoys*, 173-175; Whitehall History Publishing – Ministry of Defence, *The Royal Navy and the Arctic Convoys*, 120-122.

[42] *Imperial War Museum,* "Documents.2114."

[43] Ibid.

[44] Ibid.; Smith, *Churchill's Arctic Convoys,* 173-175; Whitehall History Publishing – Ministry of Defence, *The Royal Navy and the Arctic Convoys,* 120-122.

[45] *Imperial War Museum,* "Documents.2114."

[46] Ibid.; Smith, *Churchill's Arctic Convoys,* 173-175; Whitehall History Publishing – Ministry of Defence, *The Royal Navy and the Arctic Convoys,* 120-122.

[47] Erswell and McKay, *Surviving the Arctic Convoys,* 33-34, 96-98, 107-109, 109-111, 131-135, 135-137, 142-144, 148-149; *Imperial War Museum,* "Documents.2114,"; Mason, *Arctic Warriors,* 155-156; Melton, *Liberty's War,* 74-76; Smith, *Churchill's Arctic Convoys,* 173-175; Thomas, *Through Ice and Fire,* 147-148; Whitehall History Publishing – Ministry of Defence, *The Royal Navy and the Arctic Convoys,* 120-122.

[48] Smith, *Churchill's Arctic Convoys,* 173-175; Walling, *Forgotten Sacrifice,* 270-271; Whitehall History Publishing – Ministry of Defence, *The Royal Navy and the Arctic Convoys,* 120-122.

[49] Jones, *The Roads to Russia,* 49, 65, 110-111; McMeekin, *Stalin's War,* 534-536; Schubert, "The Persian Gulf Command," 308-309; Van Tuyll, *Feeding the Bear,* 26-27, 51, 73; U.S. President, "Map Room Papers Box 8 Roosevelt to Stalin January – June 1943,"; Vail Motter, *The Persian Corridor,* 124-127.

CHAPTER 5

[1] Harrison, *Accounting For War,* 149-152, 152-154.

[2] Folsom, Jr., and Folsom, *FDR Goes to War,* 246-249, 251; McMeekin, *Stalin's War,* 347-350, 352-357, 370-371.

[3] Chairman of the Board, Tennessee Valley Authority, "Lend-Lease Program With Russia,"; U.S. President, "Statement on Raw Materials, Munition Assignments, and Shipping Adjustment Boards."

[4] Hill, *The Great Patriotic War of the Soviet Union,* 183, 187.

[5] Ibid., 183, 187; Weeks, *Russia's Life-Saver,* 115-117.

[6] Dunn, *The Red Army and the Soviet Economy,* 74; Jones, *The Roads to Russia,* 139, 152; McMeekin, *Stalin's War,* 409-410, 412-414, 416-417, 423-424, 425-427.

[7] Weeks, *Russia's Life-Saver,* 126-127.

[8] Glantz, *Colossus Reborn,* 22, 27, 40-41, 43, 58.

[9] Ibid., 62-63, 69, 71-72. 76-77, 80, 83, 87, 98-101, 140, 190, 244-245, 390, 393, 407, 494-495, 510, 525-527, 541, 610-613, 642n47, 645n66, 658n54; McMeekin, *Stalin's War,* 457-462, 465-473.

[10] Glantz, *Colossus Reborn,* 62-63, 69, 71-72. 76-77, 80, 83, 87, 98-101, 140, 190, 244-245, 390, 393, 407, 494-495, 510, 525-527, 541, 610-613, 642n47, 645n66, 658n54; McMeekin, *Stalin's War,* 457-462, 465-473.

[11] Hill, *The Great Patriotic War of the Soviet Union,* 239; Weeks, *Russia's Life-Saver,* 124-126.

[12] Ibid., 143; Weeks, *Russia's Life-Saver,* 122.

[13] Rickenbacker, *Rickenbacker,* 403.

[14] Hill, *The Great Patriotic War of the Soviet Union,* 184, 186-187; Loza, *Commanding the Red Army's Sherman Tanks,* 57; McMeekin, *Stalin's War,* 417, 430, 460-461, 542, 642.

[15] Glantz, *Colossus Reborn,* 172-173.

[16] Stettinius, Jr., *Lend-Lease,* 234-235.

[17] Werth, *Russia at War,* 171, 243, 249-252.

[18] Zaloga, *Soviet Lend-Lease Tanks,* 34-35.

[19] Forczyk, Robert A. *Tank Warfare on the Eastern Front 1943-1945: Red Steamroller* (Barnsley, South Yorkshire: Pen & Sword, 2017), 231, 245; Hill, *The Great Patriotic War,* 185-186.

[20] Stettinius, Jr., *Lend-Lease,* 254.

[21] Kotelnikov, *Lend-Lease and Soviet Aviation,* 144-145.

[22] Curtis, "Lend-Lease."

[23] Hill, *The Great Patriotic War of the Soviet Union,* 187.

[24] Ibid., 215; Khrushchev, *Khrushchev Remembers,* 238-239.

[25] Weeks, *Russia's Life-Saver,* 133.

[26] Nikolai Litvin, *800 Days on the Eastern* Front, 9, 50; Khrushchev, *Khrushchev Remembers,* 238-239.

[27] Sokolov, *The Role of the Soviet Union in the Second World War,* 57-59; U.S. Department of the Treasury, "Diaries of Henry Morgenthau, Jr.," Series 2, "Russian Clearance Problems."

[28] Harrison, *Accounting For War,* 149-152, 152-154.

[29] McMeekin, *Stalin's War,* 605-608; U.S. Department of State, *Soviet Supply Protocols,* 147-149, 155-156.

[30] The New York Times, "HULL PRAISES RED ARMY."

[31] Bourke-White, *Portrait of Myself,* 183-184,187-188.

[32] Detroit Evening Times, "Drive on Caucasus Oil Smashed,"; Smelser and Davies II, *The Myth of the Eastern Front,* 35-38.

[33] Detroit Evening Times, "Drive on Caucasus Oil Smashed,"; Smelser and Davis II, *The Myth of the Eastern Front,* 35-38.

[34] Smelser and Davis II, *The Myth of the Eastern Front,* 7-8, 9-11.

[35] Melvin Small, "How We Learned to Love the Russians: American Media and the Soviet Union During World War II," *The Historian,* Vol. 36, No. 3 (May 1974), 455-478, https://www.jstor.org/stable/24443747.

[36] Wendell Willkie, "STALIN: 'GLAD TO SEE YOU, MR. WILLKIE' Through LIFE Roosevelt's personal representative reports on his interview on war in the Kremlin," *LIFE,* 5 October 1942, 35-38.

[37] Willkie, "STALIN: 'GLAD TO SEE YOU, MR. WILLKIE,'" 35.

[38] Leland Stowe, "Stowe, in Visit to Rzhev Sector Which Is Ideal for Mechanized Warfare, Marvels at Success of Russian Defenders," *Indianapolis Times,* 5 September 1942, https://newspapers.library.in.gov/?a=d&d=IPT19420905.1.5&e=-------en-20--1--txt-txIN-------. For one such example of Stowe's quoting of a young Red Army major parroting Stalin's line on Lend-Lease tanks and expressing a desire to receive more, "Airacobras or other first-class American .... warplanes," see Leland Stowe, "Russian Question: When Will U.S. Help?" *Indianapolis Times,* 3 November 1942, https://newspapers.library.in.gov/?a=d&d=IPT19421103.1.20&e=-------en-20--1--txt-txIN-------.

[39] Stowe, "Stowe, in Visit to Rzhev Sector."

[40] Leland Stowe, "The Evolution of the Red Army," *Foreign Affairs,* October 1943, https://www.foreignaffairs.com/articles/russian-federation/1943-10-01/evolution-red-army.

[41] Detroit Evening Times (Unattributed Report), "Drive on Caucasus Oil Smashed, Reds Claim Nazis Lose 95,000 at Kharkov, Huge Battle Reported Near End, *Detroit Evening Times,* 31 May 1942, https://chroniclingamerica.loc.gov/lccn/sn88063294/1942-05-31/ed-1/seq-1/ocr/; Madera Tribune (Unattributed Report), "Reds Approaching Kiev; RUSS

ARMIES CUT GERMAN DEFENSE ARC; Berlin Command Has Ordered Evacuation Of Key City Started," *Madera Tribune,* 11 October 1943, https://cdnc.ucr.edu/cgi-bin/cdnc?a=d &d=MT19431011.2.14&e=-------en--20--1--txt-txIN--------1.

[42] Leland Stowe, "Miracles of Red Army Credited In Large Part to Its Women: Thousands Serve as Guards, Gunners, Telegraphers, Storekeepers and Nurses," *Evening Star,* 31 October 1942, https://www.newzpaperarchive.com/gazete/evening_star/1942-10-31/7; The Brainerd Daily Dispatch, "BATTLE ON DON RIVER BANK; Report Big Air-Sea Battle Fought," *The Brainerd Daily Dispatch* (Unattributed Report), 10 July 1942, https://newsp aperarchive.com/brainerd-daily-dispatch-jul-10-1942-p-1/.

[43] Conrad H. Lanza, "Russo-German War Part II: Second Phase of the War – Smolensk and Uman," *The Field Artillery Journal* (July 1942), 512-522, https://tradocfcoeccafcoepfwpro d.blob.core.usgovcloudapi.net/fires-bulletin-archive/1942/JUL_1942/JUL_1942_FULL_ EDITION.pdf; Small, "How We Learned to Love the Russians," 457-462; Leland Stowe, "Nazi Army Fears Second Winter Of War in Russia, Reds Claim; Captured Germans Say Morale of Hitler's Forces Is Low as Bitter Cold Sets In," *Evening Star,* 2 November 1942, https://www.newzpaperarchive.com/gazete/evening_star/1942-11-02/26.

[44] Carter, "Russian War Relief," 67; Jordan, *Major Jordan's Diaries,* 9; The New York Times, "Addresses of Litvinoff, Hopkins and Green,"; The New York Times (Unattributed Report), "MILLION A MONTH AID IS SHIPPED TO SOVIET; Russian War Relief Hopes to Continue Rate Through 1943," *The New York Times,* 27 April 1943, https://www.nytimes.com/1943 /04/27/archives/million-a-month-aid-is-shipped-to-soviet-russian-war-relief-hopes.html.

[45] Carter, "Russian War Relief," 67; Jordan, *Major Jordan's Diaries,* 9; The New York Times, "Addresses of Litvinoff, Hopkins and Green,"; McMeekin, *Stalin's War,* 487-488.

[46] *Cong. Rec. – House of Representatives,* 81st Cong. 1st and 2nd Sess. (1949-1950); Jordan, *Major Jordan's Diaries,* 36-38, 40-41, 42-44; McMeekin, *Stalin's War,* 531-534.

[47] Associated Press, "U.S., Britain To Ask Russian Clarification," *The Tampa Tribune,* 6 October 1942, https://www.newspapers.com/newspage/327196525/.

[48] Associated Press, "U.S., Britain to Ask."

[49] Clark Lee, "Threat of Allies-Stalin Crisis Averted, A. P. War Writer Says; Cassidy, Back From Moscow, Sees Russia Satisfied on Second Front Issue," *Evening Star,* 28 February 1943, https://chroniclingamerica.loc.gov/lccn/sn83045462/1943-02-28/ed-1/seq-18/.

[50] Lee, "Threat of Allies-Stalin Crisis Averted."

[51] TIME (Unattributed Report), "INTERNATIONAL: Die, But Do Not Retreat," *TIME,* Vol. XLI, No. 1 (4 January 1943), 1-6, https://content.time.com/time/subscriber/article/0,33 009,790648,00.html.

[52] William H. Lawrence, "STALIN LAUDS U.S. FOR AID TO SOVIET; Cites 'Remarkable' Production Job in Long Interview With Johnston and Harriman," *The New York Times,* 28 June 1944, https://www.nytimes.com/1944/06/28/archives/stalin-lauds-us-for-aid-to-soviet-cites-remarkable-production-job.html; Small, "How We Learned to Love the Russians," 457-462.

[53] Eric Johnston, "My Talk with Joseph Stalin," *Reader's Digest,* (October 1944), 1-10; U.S. Department of State, "Foreign Relations of the United States: Diplomatic Papers, 1944, Europe, Volume IV – The Ambassador in the Soviet Union (Harriman) to the Secretary of State," 11 July 1944, https://history.state.gov/historicaldocuments/frus1944v04/d884.

[54] Small, "How We Learned to Love the Russians," 457-462; The New York Times (Unattributed Report), "FORD TIRE FACTORY WILL GO TO RUSSIA: It Is Being Bought by Our Government for Shipment Under Lend-Lease Plan," *The New York Times,* 31 October

1942, https://www.nytimes.com/1942/10/31/archives/ford-tire-factory-will-go-to-russi a-it-is-being-bought-by-our.html.

[55] Bullitt, *For the President*, 576-580, 587; Henry Raymont, "Bullitt Letter to Roosevelt in 1943 Urged Invasion of Balkans to Deter Soviet Advance," *The New York Times*, 26 April 1970, https://www.nytimes.com/1970/04/26/archives/bullitt-letter-to-roosevelt-in-194 3-urged-invasion-of-balkans-to.html; Small, "How We Learned to Love the Russians," 457-462; Smelser and Davies II, *The Myth of the Eastern Front*, 31-34.

[56] William L. White, *Report on the Russians* (New York: Harcourt, Brace and Company, 1945), 43-44.

[57] White, *Report on the Russians*, 122-123.

[58] *Congressional Record – United States Senate*, 78th Congress, 1st Session (1943), pt. 3, Government Publishing Office, https://babel.hathitrust.org/cgi/pt?id=umn.31951d0209 4619s&view=1up&seq=1.

[59] *Cong. Rec. – United States Senate*, 78th Cong., 1st Sess. (1943) pt. 3.

[60] Ibid.

[61] Ibid.

[62] Ibid.

[63] Ibid.

[64] *Cong. Rec. – United States Senate*, 78th Cong., 1st Sess. (1943) pt. 3; Ministry of Foreign Affairs of the U.S.S.R., *Stalin's Correspondence*, "No. 58: Prime Minister to Premier Stalin," 31 July 1942, 57; Reynolds and Pechatnov, *The Kremlin Letters*, 132-133; Sherwood, *Roosevelt and Hopkins*, 545; U.S. President, "Map Room Papers Box 8 Stalin to Roosevelt July – December 1942."

[65] *Cong. Rec. – United States Senate*, 78th Cong., 1st Sess. (1943) pt. 3.

[66] McMeekin, *Stalin's War*, 464-465, 517-518, 538; Sherwood, *Roosevelt and Hopkins*, 705; Standley and Ageton, *Admiral Ambassador to Russia*, 331-333, 335-338. 339-343, 346-349.

[67] McMeekin, *Stalin's War*, 464-465, 517-518, 538; Sherwood, *Roosevelt and Hopkins*, 705; Standley and Ageton, *Admiral Ambassador to Russia*, 331-333, 335-338. 339-343, 346-349.

[68] *Congressional Record – United States Senate and House of Representatives*, 78th Cong., 1st Sess. (1943) pt? https://www.govinfo.gov/content/pkg/GPO-CRECB-1943-pt2/pdf /GPO-CRECB-1943-pt2-6.pdf; McMeekin, *Stalin's War*, 464-465, 517-518, 538.

[69] *Cong. Rec. – United States Senate and House of Representatives*, 78th Cong., 1st Sess. (1943); Standley and Ageton, *Admiral Ambassador to Russia*, 331-333, 335-338. 339-343, 346-349.

[70] *Cong. Rec. – United States Senate and House of Representatives*, 78th Cong., 1st Sess. (1943); Standley and Ageton, *Admiral Ambassador to Russia*, 331-333, 335-338. 339-343, 346-349.

[71] *Cong. Rec. – United States Senate and House of Representatives*, 78th Cong., 1st Sess. (1943).

[72] Ibid.; Sherwood, *Roosevelt and Hopkins*, 705.

[73] *Cong. Rec. – United States Senate and House of Representatives*, 78th Cong., 1st Sess. (1943); McMeekin, *Stalin's War*, 464-465, 517-518, 538.

[74] McMeekin, *Stalin's War*, 517-518, 534-536.

[75] *Cong. Rec. – United States Senate and House of Representatives*, 78th Cong., 1st Sess. (1943); McMeekin, *Stalin's War*, 464-465, 517-518, 538; Standley and Ageton, *Admiral Ambassador to Russia*, 331-333, 335-338, 339-343, 346-349; The New York Times (Unattributed Report), "STANDLEY'S TALK STIRS WASHINGTON; Observers Wonder Whether the Ambassador Spoke for Himself or Government EFFECT ON BILL POSSIBLE

Restrictive Amendments Might Be Attached to Lend-Lease Act, It Is Declared," *The New York Times*, 9 March 1943, https://www.nytimes.com/1943/03/09/archives/standleys-talk-stirs-washington-observers-wonder-whether-the.html.

[76] The New York Times, "STANDLEY'S TALK STIRS WASHINGTON,"; U.S. Department of State, "'Lend-Lease Act,' March 11, 1941," *Peace and War – United States Foreign Policy 1931-1941*, https://www.ibiblio.org/hyperwar/Dip/PaW/200.html.

[77] *Cong. Rec. – House of Representatives*, 77th Cong., 1st Sess. (1941) pt. 7; Folsom, Jr., and Folsom, *FDR Goes to War*, 230-235, 340-342n40-44; Herring, Jr., *Aid to Russia*, 20, 93, 112-117, 120-122, 124-128; Sherwood, *Roosevelt and Hopkins*, 791-793, 796, 802; Standley and Ageton, *Admiral Ambassador to Russia*, 331-333, 335-338, 339-343, 346-349; The New York Times, "STANDLEY'S TALK STIRS WASHINGTON."

[78] *Cong. Rec. – United States Senate and House of Representatives*, 78th Cong., 1st Sess. (1943); McMeekin, *Stalin's War*, 464-465, 517-518, 538; Standley and Ageton, *Admiral Ambassador to Russia*, 331-333, 335-338, 339-343, 346-349.

[79] Standley and Ageton, *Admiral Ambassador to Russia*, 331-333, 335-338. 339-343, 346-349; The New York Times, "STANDLEY'S TALK STIRS WASHINGTON."

[80] *Cong. Rec. – United States Senate and House of Representatives*, 78th Cong., 1st Sess. (1943); McMeekin, *Stalin's War*, 464-465, 517-518, 538; Standley and Ageton, *Admiral Ambassador to Russia*, 331-333, 335-338, 339-343, 346-349; The New York Times, "STANDLEY'S TALK STIRS WASHINGTON."

[81] *Congressional Record – United States Senate*, 78th Congress, 1st Session (1943), pt? Government Publishing Office, https://www.senate.gov/about/resources/pdf/russell-cr-1943.pdf.

[82] *Cong. Rec. -United States Senate*, 78th Cong., 1st Sess. (1943).

[83] *Cong. Rec. – United States Senate and House of Representatives*, 78th Cong., 1st Sess. (1943); McMeekin, *Stalin's War*, 464-465, 517-518, 538; Standley and Ageton, *Admiral Ambassador to Russia*, 331-333, 335-338, 339-343, 346-349; The New York Times, "STANDLEY'S TALK STIRS WASHINGTON."

[84] *Cong. Rec. – United States Senate*, 78th Cong., 1st Sess. (1943) pt. 3; William H. Lawrence, "SENATE VOTES 82-0; President Signs Bill – Says Axis Weakens as Our Aid Grows TOTAL NOW $9,632,000,000 Litvinoff Hails Help to Red Army and Says Soviet People Deeply Appreciate It A LEND-LEASE TOAST WITH LEND-LEASE MILK LEND-LEASE VOTED, PRESIDENT SIGNS," *The New York Times*, 12 March 1943, https://www.nytimes.com/1943/03/12/archives/senate-votes-820-president-signs-bill-says-axis-weakens-as-our-aid.html.

[85] The New York Times (Unattributed Report), LITVINOFF'S THANKS PUBLISHED IN RUSSIA; Excerpts From Speech by Roosevelt Printed," *The New York Times*, 14 March 1943, https://www.nytimes.com/1943/03/14/archives/litvinoffs-thanks-published-in-russia-excerpts-from-speech-by.html.

[86] Lawrence, "SENATE VOTES 82-0,"; The New York Times, "LITVINOFF'S THANKS PUBLISHED IN RUSSIA."

[87] Sherwood, *Roosevelt and Hopkins*, 733; Standley and Ageton, *Admiral Ambassador to Russia*, 355-359.

[88] Carlton, *Churchill and the Soviet Union*, 101-102; Sherwood, *Roosevelt and Hopkins*, 733; Standley and Ageton, *Admiral Ambassador to Russia*, 355-359.

[89] *National Archives and Records Administration*, "Letter from Joseph E. Davies,"; Sherwood, *Roosevelt and Hopkins*, 306-308, 733; Standley and Ageton, *Admiral Ambassador to Russia*, 355-359.

[90] McMeekin, Stalin's War, 452-453, 454-455, 737n35; Martin Weil, *A Pretty Good Club: The Founding Fathers of the U.S. Foreign Service* (New York: W. W. Norton & Company, 1978), 136-137.

[91] Sherwood, *Roosevelt and Hopkins*, 733; Standley and Ageton, *Admiral Ambassador to Russia*, 355-359.

[92] Office, Chief of Finance War Department, "Lend-Lease Shipments World War II,"; U.S. Department of State, *Soviet Supply Protocols*, 9-12, 13-15, 49, 51-53.

[93] *Congressional Record – United States Senate*, 78th Congress, 2nd Session (1943) pt. 7, Government Publishing Office, https://www.govinfo.gov/content/pkg/GPO-CRECB-1943-pt7/pdf/GPO-CRECB-1943-pt7-7-1.pdf.

[94] McMeekin, *Stalin's War*, 536-537; Sherwood, *Roosevelt and Hopkins*, 432-433, 565-566, 567-568.

[95] *Congressional Record – United States Senate*, 78th Congress, 2nd Session (1944) pt.? Government Publishing Office, https://babel.hathitrust.org/cgi/pt?id=umn.319510d02094618u&view=1up&seq=1.

[96] *Cong. Rec. – United States Senate*, 78th Cong., 2nd Sess. (1944).

[97] Ibid.

[98] *Cong. Rec. – United States Senate*, 78th Cong., 2nd Sess. (1944).

[99] Arnold, *Global Mission*, 211-212, 385-387.

[100] Bohlen, *Witness to History*, 149-150; Carlton, *Churchill and the Soviet Union*, 106-107.

[101] Arnold, *Global Mission*, 466-470; Bohlen, *Witness to History*, 149-150; U.S. Department of State, "Foreign Relations of the United States: Diplomatic Papers, The Conferences at Cairo and Tehran, 1943," White House Files – Log of the Trip, 27 November-2 December 1943, https://history.state.gov/historicaldocuments/frus1943CairoTehran/d353.

[102] Arnold, *Global Mission*, 466-470; Bohlen, *Witness to History*, 149-150; U.S. Department of State, "Foreign Relations: The Conferences at Cairo and Tehran."

[103] Alanbrooke, *War Diaries*, 254; Arnold, *Global Mission*, 466-470; Bohlen, *Witness to History*, 149-150; Carlton, *Churchill and the Soviet Union*, 106-107; Pownall, *Chief of Staff*, 29; U.S. Department of State, "Foreign Relations: The Conferences at Cairo and Tehran,"; Zaloga, *Soviet Lend-Lease Tanks*, 4.

[104] Alanbrooke, *War Diaries*, 486-487; Carlton, *Churchill and the Soviet Union*, 106-107.

[105] Alanbrooke, *War Diaries*, 486-487; Bohlen, *Witness to History*, 149-150; Carlton, *Churchill and the Soviet Union*, 106-107; U.S. Department of State, "Foreign Relations: The Conferences at Cairo and Tehran."

[106] The New York Times (Unattributed Report), "GENERAL IS REDUCED AFTER DUTY IN SOVIET; Faymonville Now a Colonel – Michela Also to Lose Rank," *The New York Times*, 18 November 1943, https://www.nytimes.com/1943/11/18/archives/general-is-reduced-after-duty-in-soviet-faymonville-now-a-colonel.html.

[107] Deane, *The Strange Alliance*, 88-89, 103.

[108] Ibid., 88-89.

[109] Ibid.; Rickenbacker, *Rickenbacker*, 403-404, 418-419; U.S. Department of State, "Foreign Relations: The Conferences at Cairo and Tehran."

[110] Bullitt, *For the President*, 576-580; Raymont, "Bullitt Letter to Roosevelt."

[111] Bullitt, *For the President*, 576-580; Jones, *The Roads to Russia*, 39; Sherwood, *Roosevelt and Hopkins*, 306-308.

[112] Bullitt, *For the President*, 587-588, 602-604; Raymont, "Bullitt Letter to Roosevelt."

[113] Thomas Fleming, *The New Dealers' War: Franklin D. Roosevelt and the War Within World War II* (New York: Basic Books, 2001), 204-205, 464-465; McMeekin, *Stalin's War*, 450-452, 731n31-33; Weigley, *The American Way of War*, 128-129, 150-152, 162-163, 357-359.

[114] George H. Earle, "F.D.R.'s Tragic Mistake!" *Confidential*, 14 (August 1958), http://www.oldmagazinearticles.com/1943-german-peace-feelers_pdf; Heinrich Hohne, *Canaris: Hitler's Master Spy*, trans. J. Maxwell Brownjohn (New York: Cooper Square Press, 1999), 483-484; McMeekin, *Stalin's War*, 450-452, 737n31-33; Michael Mueller, *Canaris: The Life and Death of Hitler's Spymaster*, trans. Geoffrey Brooks (Annapolis, MD: Naval Institute Press, 2007), 220-221; Sherwood, *Roosevelt and Hopkins*, 791; John Waller, *The Unseen War in Europe: Espionage and Conspiracy in the Second World War* (New York: Random House, 1996), 280-285; Weil, *A Pretty Good* Club, 136-137.

[115] Earle, "F.D.R.'s Tragic Mistake!" 14; Folsom, Jr., and Folsom, *FDR Goes to War*, 246-249; Hohne, *Canaris*, 483-484; McMeekin, *Stalin's War*, 450-452, 731n31-33; Waller, *The Unseen War in Europe*, 280-285.

[116] Earle, "F.D.R.'s Tragic Mistake!" 14.

[117] Ibid.; Fleming, *The New Dealers' War*, 204-205, 464-465; McMeekin, *Stalin's War*, 450-452, 731n31-33; Mueller, *Canaris*, 220-221.

[118] Earle, "F.D.R.'s Tragic Mistake!" 14; Fleming, *The New Dealers' War*, 204-205, 464-465; Folsom, Jr., and Folsom, *FDR Goes to War*, 246-249; McMeekin, *Stalin's War*, 450-452, 731n31-33; Weil, *A Pretty Good Club*, 136-137.

[119] Bullitt, *For the President*, 587-588; Folsom, Jr., and Folsom, *FDR Goes to War*, 251; Raymont, "Bullitt Letter to Roosevelt."

[120] Bullitt, *For the President*, 593-599; Deane, *The Strange Alliance*, 88-89, 103; Kaiser, *No End Save Victory*, 337, 392; Sherwood, *Roosevelt and Hopkins*, 376-377; Standley and Ageton, *Admiral Ambassador to Russia*, 308-309.

[121] Bullitt, *For the President*, 593-599; Folsom, Jr., and Folsom, *FDR Goes to War*, 246-249, 251; Kaiser, *No End Save Victory*, 337, 341, 392-394; Raymont, "Bullitt Letter to Roosevelt."

[122] *Cong. Rec. – House of Representatives*, 81st Cong. 1st and 2nd Sess. (1949-1950); Jordan, *Major Jordan's Diaries*, 36-38, 40-41, 42-44; McMeekin, *Stalin's War*, 531-534; The New York Times (Unattributed Report), "RUSSIA AND THE BOMB," *The New York Times*, 24 September 1949, https://www.nytimes.com/1949/09/24/archives/russia-and-the-bomb.html; U.S. Air Force, *Project Rand*, 1-7, 43-54.

[123] Bullitt, *For the President*, 593-599; Folsom, Jr., and Folsom, *FDR Goes to War*, 246-249, 251.

[124] *Cong. Rec. – House of Representatives*, 81st Cong. 1st and 2nd Sess. (1949-1950); Daily News (Unattributed Report), "Uranium Missing but Most Recovered," *Daily News*, 19 May 1949; https://trove.nla.gov.au/newspaper/article/2804617?downloadScope=page; Jordan, *Major Jordan's Diaries*, 48-49; The New York Times (Unattributed Report), "THAT LOST URANIUM," *The New York Times*, 20 May 1949, https://www.nytimes.com/1949/05/20/archives/that-lost-uranium.html.

[125] *Cong. Rec. – House of Representatives*, 81st Cong. 1st and 2nd Sess. (1949-1950); Jordan, *Major Jordan's Diaries*, 48-49.

[126] Associated Press, "RICKENBACKER HOME FROM MOSCOW TRIP,"; Rickenbacker, *Rickenbacker*, 418-419.

[127] *Wilson Center Digital Archive, Collection 27*, "Cold War Origins."

[128] Jordan, *Major Jordan's Diaries*, 38-39.

[129] McMeekin, *Stalin's War*, 397-398, 487-489; U.S. Air Force, *Project Rand*, 27-34; Weeks, *Russia's Life-Saver*, 22-24, 47-49.

[130] Pastorfield-Li, "An excerpt from an interview with a Soviet soldier,"; Weeks, *Russia's Life-Saver*, 129-131.

[131] John Beasant, *Stalin's Silver: The Sinking of the USS John Barry* (New York: St. Martin's Press, 1999), 4-6, 8-9, 10-13; Weeks, *Russia's Life-Saver*, 129-131, 131-133.

[132] Associated Press, "US Warship Sunk in 1944 Yields Treasure," *The Christian Science Monitor*, 10 November 1995, https://www.csmonitor.com/layout/set/amphtml/1995/1110/10144.html.

[133] Beasant, *Stalin's Silver*, 116-117, 118-120, 121-123; Arthur Clark, "The Silver Ship," *Saudi Aramco World*, Vol. 48, No. 2 (March/April 1997), https://archive.aramcoworld.com/issue/199702/the.silver.ship.html; Associated Press, "US Warship Sunk in 1944,"; Michael Huggins, "Saudi treasure fails to find buyer," *UPI*, 16 November 1995, https://www.upi.com/amp/Archives/1995/11/16/Saudi-treasure-fails-to-find-buyer/4576816498000/; Weeks, *Russia's Life-Saver*, 129-131, 131-133.

[134] Beasant, *Stalin's Silver*, 143-145, 161-163; Clark, "The Silver Ship,"; Tara Patel, "Giant pliers pluck treasure from the deep," *New Scientist*, Issue 1956 (17 December 1994), https://www.newscientist.com/article/mg14419561-300-giant-pliers-pluck-treasure-from-the-deep/; Reuters, "Liberty Ship, Sunk off Oman, Begins Yielding Treasure Trove: Eighteen tons of silver coins minted for Saudi Arabia and worth some $70 million have been recovered," *The Journal of Commerce online*, 14 November 1994, https://www.joc.com/maritime-news/liberty-ship-sunk-oman-begins-yielding-treasure-trove_19941114.html; Weeks, *Russia's Life-Saver*, 129-131, 131-133.

[135] Beasant, *Stalin's Silver*, 143-145, 153-157; Clark, "The Silver Ship,"; Orlando Sentinel (Unattributed Report), "Silver Salvaged from Ship Sunk in WWII Displayed," *Orlando Sentinel*, 27 November 1994, https://www.orlandosentinel.com/news/os-xpm-1994-11-28-9411270345-story.html; Reuters, "Liberty Ship, Sunk off Oman."

[136] Beasant, *Stalin's Silver*, 41-42, 43-45, 147-149; Reagan Fancher, *The Holy Warrior: Osama Bin Laden and His Jihadi Journey in the Soviet-Afghan War* (Wilmington, DE: Vernon Press, 2023), xvii, 41, 51, 73-74, 75-79, 81-83, 85, 89, 99-100, 110-115, 118-119; Weeks, *Russia's Life-Saver*, 129-131.

[137] Associated Press, "US Warship Sunk in 1944,"; Clark, "The Silver Ship,"; Huggins, "Saudi treasure fails to find buyer,"; Orlando Sentinel, "Silver Salvaged from Ship,"; Patel, "Giant pliers pluck treasure,"; Weeks, *Russia's Life-Saver*, 129-131.

[138] Associated Press, "US Warship Sunk in 1944,"; Beasant, *Stalin's Silver*, 143-145, 153-157; Clark, "The Silver Ship,"; Huggins, "Saudi treasure fails to find buyer,"; Orlando Sentinel, "Silver Salvaged from Ship,"; Patel, "Giant pliers pluck treasure,"; Reuters, "Liberty Ship, Sunk off Oman,"; Weeks, *Russia's Life-Saver*, 131-133.

[139] White, *Report on the Russians*, 102.

[140] Ibid.

[141] Jordan, *Major Jordan's Diaries*, 49-50; White, *Report on the Russians*, 102.

[142] Roosevelt, *Great Speeches*, 126-128.

[143] Franklin D. Roosevelt, "Lend-Lease," *The New York Times*, 27 August 1943, 16, https://www.nytimes.com/1943/08/27/archives/lendlease.html.

[144] Beasant, *Stalin's Silver*, 64-67; Harriman and Abel, *Special Envoy*, 316; Roosevelt, "Lend-Lease,"; U.S. President, "Lend-Lease Policy Toward the Soviet Union."

[145] Beasant, *Stalin's Silver*, 55-57, 64-67; *Cong. Rec. – United States Senate and House of Representatives*, 78th Cong. 2nd Sess. (1944) pt.6; McMeekin, *Stalin's War*, 364-366, 658-659; U.S. President, "Report to Congress on Reverse Lend-Lease."

[146] Harriman and Abel, *Special Envoy*, 319.

[147] Arnold, *Global Mission*, 587; Van Tuyll, *Feeding the Bear*, 71-73.

[148] Arnold, *Global Mission*, 587; Van Tuyll, *Feeding the Bear*, 71-73, 79-80, 81.

[149] Beasant, *Stalin's Silver*, 55-58, 64-67; *Cong. Rec. – United States Senate and House of Representatives*, 78th Cong, 2nd Sess. (1944) pt. 6; U.S. President, "Report to Congress on Reverse Lend-Lease."

[150] Beasant, *Stalin's Silver*, 64-67; *Cong. Rec. – United States Senate and House of Representatives*, 78th Cong, 2nd Sess. (1944) pt.6; U.S. President, "Report to Congress on Reverse Lend-Lease."

[151] *Cong. Rec. – House of Representatives*, 80th Cong., 2nd Sess. (1948); Fitzgibbon, "The Hiss-Chambers Case,"; Koster, *Operation Snow*, 152-157, 160-165; McMeekin, *Stalin's War*, 570, 571, 573, 575, 580, 657; Sudoplatov and Sudoplatov, *Special Tasks*, 222, 226-227, 227-229, 230; VENONA Decrypts, "Silvermaster Folder NY 65-14603 'Alger Hiss."

[152] Koster, *Operation Snow*, 15-17, 171-172, 179-181; McMeekin, *Stalin's War*, 396; VENONA Decrypts, "13. Hoover to Matthew Connelly."

[153] George Racey Jordan, *Gold Swindle: The Story of Our Dwindling Gold* (New York: The Bookmailer, Inc., 1959), 8-10; U.S. Department of the Treasury, "Part 3093 – Gold Mining (Limitation Order L-208)," *Federal Register*, 9 October 1942, https://www.govinfo.gov/content/pkg/FR-1942-10-09/pdf/FR-1942-10-09.pdf.

[154] Jordan, *Gold Swindle*, 8-10; U.S. Department of the Treasury, "Part 3093 – Gold Mining."

[155] Jordan, *Gold Swindle*, 12-14, 42-43, 44-46.

[156] Ibid., 12-14, 95-96; Koster, *Operation Snow*, 166, 167-168; Schuler and Rosenberg, *The Bretton Woods Transcripts*, 41; Steil, *The Battle of Bretton Woods*, 268-270, 273-274.

[157] Joint Chiefs of Staff, "Directive to the Commander in Chief of the U.S. Occupation Forces (JCS 1067) (April 1945)," German History in Documents and Images, https://ghdi.ghi-dc.org/sub_document.cfm?document_id=2297.

[158] Joint Chiefs of Staff, "Directive to the Commander in Chief."

[159] McMeekin, *Stalin's War*, 581; Schuler and Rosenberg, *The Bretton Woods Transcripts*, 41; VENONA Decrypts, "13. Hoover to Matthew Connelly."

[160] National Security Agency, "Koltsov's Account of a Conversation with 'Jurist,'" 4 August 1944, https://www.nsa.gov/portals/75/documents/news-features/declassified-documents/venona/dated/1944/4aug_conversaion_harry_dexter_white.pdf.

[161] Koster, *Operation Snow*, 165.

[162] *Cong. Rec. – House of Representatives*, 80th Cong., 2nd Sess. (1948); Fitzgibbon, "The Hiss-Chambers Case,"; Schuler and Rosenberg, *The Bretton Woods Transcripts*, 41; Sudoplatov and Sudoplatov, *Special Tasks*, 222, 226-227, 227-229, 230; VENONA Decrypts, "13. Hoover to Matthew Connelly."

[163] *Cong. Rec. – House of Representatives*, 80th Cong., 2nd Sess. (1948); Fitzgibbon, "The Hiss-Chambers Case,"; McMeekin, *Stalin's War*, 606; Sudoplatov and Sudoplatov, *Special Tasks*, 222, 226-227, 227-229, 230.

[164] *Cong. Rec. – House of Representatives*, 80th Cong., 2nd Sess. (1948); Chambers, *Witness*, 415-417, 421-424, 425-427, 441-443; Fitzgibbon, "The Hiss-Chambers Case,"; Koster, *Operation Snow*, 15, 132-135; Sudoplatov and Sudoplatov, *Special Tasks*, 222, 226-227, 227-229, 230; VENONA Decrypts, "13. Hoover to Matthew Connelly."

[165] Elinor Lipper, *Eleven Years in Soviet Prison Camps* (London: The World Affairs Book Club, 1950), 111-114; Henry A. Wallace, *Soviet Asia Mission* (New York: Reynal and Hitchcock Publishers, 1946), 34-37, 38-41.

[166] Lipper, *Eleven Years in Soviet Prison Camps*, 111-114; Wallace, *Soviet Asia Mission*, 34-37, 38-41.

[167] Vadim J. Birstein, "Three Days in 'Auschwitz without Gas Chambers': Henry A. Wallace's Visit to Magadan in 1944," *Wilson Center: Cold War International History Project*, https://www.wilsoncenter.org/publication/three-days-auschwitz-without-gas-chambers-henry-wallaces-visit-to-magadan-1944.

[168] Birstein, "Three Days in 'Auschwitz without Gas Chambers,'"; Wallace, *Soviet Asia Mission*, 41-44, 47-49, 58, 62-65, 99-100.

[169] Jordan, *Gold Swindle*, 8-10, 12-14, 42-43, 44-46; Lipper, *Eleven Years in Soviet Prison Camps* 111-114, 117-119; U.S. Department of the Treasury, "Part 3093 – Gold Mining."

[170] Birstein, "Three Days in 'Auschwitz without Gas Chambers,'"; Lipper, *Eleven Years in Soviet Prison Camps*, 127-129, 134-135; Wallace, *Soviet Asia Mission*, 41-44, 70-73.

[171] Evans and Romerstein, *Stalin's Secret Agents*, 117-120, 126-128, 147-149; Folsom, Jr., and Folsom, *FDR Goes to War*, 240, 241-245, 246-249; *The National Archives of the UK*, "PREMIER 3 393/8" "Prime Minister," n. d.

[172] McMeekin, *Stalin's War*, 441-443, 445-447, 450; Ministry of Foreign Affairs of the U.S.S.R., *Stalin's Correspondence*, "No. 103: For Marshal Stalin from President Roosevelt and Prime Minister Churchill," 19 August 1943, 83; Reynolds and Pechatnov, *The Kremlin Letters*, 287-288; U.S. President, "Map Room Papers Box 8 Roosevelt to Stalin January – June 1943."

[173] Folsom, Jr., and Folsom, *FDR Goes to War*, 240, 241-245, 246-249.

[174] Earle, "F.D.R.'s Tragic Mistake!" 14; Folsom, Jr., and Folsom, *FDR Goes to War*, 246-249; Ministry of Foreign Affairs of the U.S.S.R., *Stalin's Correspondence*, "No. 103: For Marshal Stalin from President Roosevelt and Prime Minister Churchill," 19 August 1943, 83; Reynolds and Pechatnov, *The Kremlin Letters*, 287-288; U.S. President, "Map Room Papers Box 8 Roosevelt to Stalin January – June 1943."

[175] McMeekin, *Stalin's War*, 441-443, 445-447, 450.

[176] Ion Mihai Pacepa and Ronald J. Rychlak, *Disinformation: Former Spy Chief Reveals Secret Strategies for Undermining Freedom, Attacking Religion, and Promoting Terrorism* (New York: Midpoint Trade Books, 2013), v, 5, 8-9, 49-51.

[177] Stephane Courtois, Mark Kramer, Nicolas Werth, and Jean-Louis Panne, *The Black Book of Communism: Crimes, Terror, Repression* (Cambridge, MA: Harvard University Press, 1999), trans. Jonathan Murphy, 26; Michael Fumento, "A Church Arson Epidemic? It's Smoke and Mirrors," *The Wall Street Journal*, 8 July 1996, https://www.wsj.com/articl es/SB836760439744561500; Ronald J. Rychlak, "Cardinal Stepinac, Pope Pius XII, and the Roman Catholic Church during the Second World War," *Catholic Social Science Review*, Vol. 14 (2009), 367-383, https://www.pdcnet.org/cssr/content/cssr_2009_0014_0367_0383.

[178] Christopher Andrew and Oleg Gordievsky, *KGB: The Inside Story of its Foreign Operations from Lenin to Gorbachev* (New York: HarperCollins, 1990), 343.

[179] Evans and Romerstein, *Stalin's Secret Agents*, 195-198, 207, 228; Folsom, Jr., and Folsom, *FDR Goes to War*, 240, 241-245, 246-249; Robert K. Wilcox, T*arget: Patton: The Plot to Assassinate General George S. Patton* (Washington, D.C.: Regnery, 2010), 215-217, 227-230.

[180] John Loftus, *The Belarus Secret* (New York: Alfred A. Knopf, 1982), 48; Charles Lutton, "Stalin's War: Victims and Accomplices," *Journal of Historical Review*, Vol. 20 (2001), 4, http://vho.org/GB/Journals/JHR/1/4/Lutton371.html.

[181] Andrew and Gordievsky, *KGB*, 343; Loftus, *The Belarus Secret*, 48; Lutton, "Stalin's War," 4; Wilcox, *Target: Patton*, 337-338, 446n10-11.

182 Andrew and Gordievsky, *KGB*, 343; Loftus, *The Belarus Secret*, 48; Lutton, "Stalin's War," 4; Wilcox, *Target: Patton*, 337-338, 446n10-11.

183 Chambers, *Witness*, 415-417, 421-424, 425-427, 441-443; *Cong. Rec. – House of Representatives*, 80th Cong., 2nd Sess. (1948); Fitzgibbon, "The Hiss-Chambers Case,"; Koster, *Operation Snow*, 15, 132-135; McMeekin, *Stalin's War*, 606; Sudoplatov and Sudoplatov, *Special Tasks*, 222, 226-227, 227-229, 230; VENONA Decrypts, "13. Hoover to Matthew Connelly."

184 McMeekin, *Stalin's War*, 474-478, 478-481, 482-485, 492-494, 496-498, 511-515.

185 Evans and Romerstein, *Stalin's Secret Agents*, 147-149; McMeekin, *Stalin's War*, 492-494, 496-497, 511-515, 743n17; Laurence E. Salisbury. "Report on China," *Far Eastern Survey*, Vol. 13, No. 23 (15 November 1944), 211-213, https://www.jstor.org/stable/3022138.

186 Evans and Romerstein, *Stalin's Secret Agents*, 147-149; McMeekin, *Stalin's War*, 492-494, 496-497, 511-515, 743n17.

187 Folsom, Jr., and Folsom, *FDR Goes to War*, 240, 241-245, 246-249; McMeekin, *Stalin's War*, 492-494, 496-497, 511-515; Salisbury, "Report on China," 211-213.

188 Frank Dorn, *Walkout: With Stilwell in Burma* (New York: Thomas Y. Crowell Co., 1971), 75-76; McMeekin, *Stalin's War*, 746n54; Anthony Kubek, *How the Far East Was Lost: American Foreign Policy and the Creation of Communist China*, 1941-1949 (New York: Twin Circle Publishing Company, 1972), 205-206, 209; Salisbury, "Report on China," 211-213.

189 Dorn, *Walkout*, 75-76; Kubek, *How the Far East Was Lost*, 205-206, 209; McMeekin, *Stalin's War*, 511-515, 746n53.

190 Evans and Romerstein, *Stalin's Secret Agents*, 149, 152; McMeekin, *Stalin's War*, 511-515, 746n53; Rayfield, *Stalin and His Hangmen*, 201, 313; Salisbury, "Report on China," 211-213; Wilcox, *Target: Patton*, 357, 447n7-8.

191 McMeekin, *Stalin's War*, 474-478, 478-481, 482-485; TIME (Unattributed Report), "THE BALKANS: Area of Decision," *TIME*, 9 October 1944, 1-5, https://content.time.com/time/subscriber/article/0,33009,803304-1,00.html.

192 Evans and Romerstein, *Stalin's Secret Agents*, 149, 152; McMeekin, *Stalin's War*, 474-478, 478-481, 482-485; Rayfield, *Stalin and His Hangmen*, 201, 313; TIME, "THE BALKANS," 1-5; Wilcox, *Target: Patton*, 357, 447n7-8.

193 Evans and Romerstein, *Stalin's Secret Agents*, 149, 152; Rayfield, *Stalin and His Hangmen*, 201, 313; TIME, "THE BALKANS," 1-5; Wilcox, *Target: Patton*, 357, 447n7-8.

194 Folsom, Jr., and Folsom, *FDR Goes to War*, 240, 241-245, 246-249; McMeekin, *Stalin's War*, 474-478, 478-481, 482-485; Rayfield, *Stalin and His Hangmen*, 201, 313; Wilcox, *Target: Patton*, 357, 447n7-8.

195 TIME, "THE BALKANS," 1-5.

196 Evans and Romerstein, *Stalin's Secret Agents*, 149, 152; Folsom, Jr., and Folsom, *FDR Goes to War*, 240, 241-245, 246-249; McMeekin, *Stalin's War*, 474-478, 478-481, 482-485; TIME, "THE BALKANS," 1-5.

197 Folsom, Jr., and Folsom, *FDR Goes to War*, 240, 241-245, 246-249; McMeekin, *Stalin's War*, 474-478, 478-481, 482-485; Rayfield, *Stalin and His Hangmen*, 201, 313; TIME, "THE BALKANS," 1-5; Wilcox, *Target: Patton*, 357, 447n7-8.

198 Evans and Romerstein, *Stalin's Secret Agents*, 86, 113, 132, 151, 227; Folsom, Jr., and Folsom, *FDR Goes to War*, 240, 241-245, 246-249; Wilcox, *Target: Patton*, 241, 252-253.

199 David McCullough, *Truman* (New York: Touchstone, 1992), 254, 257, 345-348; Wilcox, *Target: Patton*, 241, 252-253.

[200] McMeekin, *Stalin's War*, 605-608; Office, Chief of Finance War Department, "Lend-Lease Shipments World War II."

[201] McMeekin, *Stalin's War*, 605-608; Office, Chief of Finance War Department, "Lend-Lease Shipments World War II,"; U.S. Department of State, *Soviet Supply Protocols*, 95-97, 104-107, 141-145.

[202] McMeekin, *Stalin's War*, 605-608; Suvorov, *The Chief Culprit*, 266-267, 268-274, 274-277; U.S. Department of State, *Soviet Supply Protocols*, 147-149, 155-156.

[203] Fest, *Hitler*, 747-750.

[204] James F. Byrnes, *Speaking Frankly* (New York: Harper & Brothers, 1947), 263.

[205] Suvorov, *The Chief Culprit*, 270-275, 275-277; Weeks, *Stalin's Other War*, 175-180.

[206] Evans and Romerstein, *Stalin's Secret Agents*, 205-206; Samuel Lyman Atwood Marshall, *Pork Chop Hill: The American Fighting Man in Action Korea, Spring, 1953* (New York: Berkley Books, 2000); 4-5, 7-12; Kim Il Sung, *The Selected Works of Kim Il Sung* (New York: Prism Key Press, 2011), 7-8, 8-10; Radzinsky, *Stalin*, 517-519; Suvorov, *The Chief Culprit*, 266-267, 268-274, 274-277; Weeks, *Stalin's Other War*, 180-181.

[207] U.S. Air Force, *Project Rand*, 27-34, 43-54.

[208] Koster, *Operation Snow*, 171-172.

[209] Ibid.

[210] Ibid.

[211] Ibid.; Alexei Markov, "Stalin's secret war plans," *Saturday Evening Post*, 20 September 1952, https://vividmaps.com/stalins-secret-war-plans/amp/; Marshall, *Pork Chop Hill*, 4-5, 7-12; James S. Olson and Randy Roberts, *Where the Domino Fell: America and Vietnam, 1945-2010* (Hoboken, NJ: 2014), vii-viii, 62-65; U.S. Air Force, *Project Rand*, 27-34, 43-54.

[212] *Congressional Record – United States Senate*, 79th Congress, 1st Session (1946), pt. 2, Government Publishing Office, https://www.govinfo.gov/content/pkg/GPO-CRECB-1946-pt2/pdf/GPO-CRECB-1946-pt2-3.pdf.

[213] *Cong. Rec. – United States Senate*, 79th Cong., 1st Sess. (1946) pt. 2.

[214] Ibid.

[215] Ibid.

[216] Ibid.

[217] *Parliamentary Record – House of Commons*, 1st Session (1946), http://hansard.millbanksystems.com/commons/1946/apr/16/russia-british-empire-war-assistance.

[218] British Admiralty, "Supplement to The London Gazette"; *Parl. Rec. – House of Commons*, 1st Sess. (1946).

[219] *Parl. Rec. – House of Commons*, 1st Sess. (1946); Whitehall History Publishing – Ministry of Defence, *The Royal Navy and the Arctic Convoys*, x-xi, 129-130.

[220] Harrison, *Accounting For War*, 152-154; Weeks, *Russia's Life-Saver*, 131-133.

[221] U.S. Department of State, *Soviet Supply Protocols*, 95-97, 104-107, 141-145; U.S. President, "Map Room Papers Box 8 Stalin to Roosevelt July – December 1942," *The White House*, Washington, D.C., 1942, *National Archives and Records Service Franklin D. Roosevelt Library*, http://www.fdrlibrary.marist.edu/_resources/images/mr/mr0051a.pdf.

CONCLUSION

[1] Folsom, Jr., and Folsom, *FDR Goes to War*, 251.

[2] Harrison, *Accounting For War*, 131-132, 133, 134-136, 139-146, 146-149; Jones, *The Roads to Russia*, 37, 39, 120-122; Weeks, *Russia's Life-Saver*, 82-83, 110-111, 111-112.

[3] Deane, *The Strange Alliance*, 88-89, 103; Rickenbacker, *Rickenbacker*, 402-403; Sherwood, *Roosevelt and Hopkins*, 791-793, 796, 802, 812-814; Standley and Ageton, *Admiral Ambassador to Russia*, 308-309, 312-313; Stettinius, Jr., *Lend-Lease*, 254-255, 257; The New York Times, "HULL PRAISES RED ARMY."

[4] Earle, "F.D.R.'s Tragic Mistake!" 14; Folsom, Jr., and Folsom, *FDR Goes to War*, 246-249; Hohne, *Canaris*, 483-484; McMeekin, *Stalin's War*, 450-452, 731n31-33; Ministry of Foreign Affairs of the U.S.S.R., *Stalin's Correspondence*, "No. 165: Personal and Secret Message from Premier J. V. Stalin to the Prime Minister, Mr. W. Churchill," 24 June 1943, 136-138; Reynolds and Pechatnov, *The Kremlin Letters*, 267-270; Roosevelt and Churchill, "Texts of Roosevelt-Churchill Messages,"; Sherwood, *Roosevelt and Hopkins*, 545; Standley and Ageton, *Admiral Ambassador to Russia*, 307, 328; *The National Archives of the UK*, "PREMIER 3 393/8," "Foreign Secretary. First Lord. First Sea Lord," 9 January 1943,"; Waller, *The Unseen War in Europe*, 280-285.

[5] McMeekin, *Stalin's War*, 516, 517-518; Reynolds and Pechatnov, *The Kremlin Letters*, 133-134; U.S. President, "Map Room Papers Box 8 Stalin to Roosevelt July – December 1942," *The White House*, Washington, D.C., 1942, *National Archives and Records Service Franklin D. Roosevelt Library*, http://www.fdrlibrary.marist.edu/_resources/images/mr/mr0051a.pdfMcMeekin, *Stalin's War*, 331-332, 347-349, 424-427.

[6] Harrison, *Accounting For War*, 149-152, 152-154; Weeks, *Stalin's Other War*, 175-180.

[7] Ronald Reagan, *An American Life* (New York: Threshold Editions, 2011), 12-15, 619-623, 651-655.

[8] Edward Girardet, *Killing the Cranes: A Reporter's Journey Through Three Decades of War in Afghanistan* (White River Junction, VT: Chelsea Green Publishing, 2011), 111, 174, 285; Ronald Reagan, *The Reagan Diaries*, ed. Douglas Brinkley (New York: Harper Perennial, 2009), 102-103, 117-118, 128-129.

[9] McCullough, *Truman*, 382, 398; Weeks, *Russia's Life-Saver*, 131-133.

[10] Khrushchev, *Khrushchev Remembers*, 436.

[11] Ibid.

[12] Edmund Conway, "Reborn Russia clears Soviet debt," *The Telegraph*, 22 August 2006, https://www.telegraph.co.uk/finance/2945924/Reborn-Russia-clears-Soviet-debt.html; Weeks, *Russia's Life-Saver*, 134.

[13] William Inboden, *The Peacemaker: Ronald Reagan, the Cold War, and the World on the Brink* (New York: Dutton, 2022), 3-5, 7-8; Paul Kengor, The Crusader: Ronald Reagan and the Fall of Communism (New York: Harper Perennial, 2007), 66-69; Peter Schweitzer, *Reagan's War: The Epic Story of His Forty-Year Struggle and Final Triumph Over Communism* (New York: Anchor Books, 2003), 125-127.

[14] Leonid I. Brezhnev, *Leonid I. Brezhnev: Pages From His Life*, trans. The Academy of Sciences of the U.S.S.R. (New York: Simon & Schuster, 1978), 243, 246-249, 309-312, 313-317, 318-320; Khrushchev, *Khrushchev Remembers*, 457-459, 498-499.

[15] Kim Il Sung, *The Selected Works of Kim Il-Sung* (New York: Prism Key Press, 2011), 51-53; Brian Latell, *Castro's Secrets: Cuban Intelligence, The CIA, and the Assassination of John F. Kennedy* (New York: Palgrave MacMillan, 2013), 7, 51, 67-68; Marshall, *Pork Chop* Hill, 4-5, 7-12; Olson and Roberts, *Where the Domino Fell*, vii-viii, 62-65; Juan Reinaldo Sanchez and Axel Gylden, *The Double Life of Fidel Castro: My 17 Years as Personal Bodyguard to El Lider Maximo*, trans. Catherine Spencer (New York: St. Martin's Griffin, 2016), 129-130. As recalled here by his former bodyguard, Juan Reinaldo Sanchez, Castro appears to have been particularly brutal in his language, often ranting and raving against

U.S. presidents as, "*hijos de perra* (sons of bitches) or *hijos de puta* (essentially the same, of the non-canine variety)," before elaborating further on the Cuban dictator's more graphic expletives and explaining that, "Ronald Reagan and his successor George H. W. Bush were without doubt the American presidents he most maligned." Parentheses in the original.

[16] Reagan, *The Reagan Diaries*, 73, 77-79, 85-87, 94-98, 117.

[17] Leonid I. Brezhnev, *Trilogy: Little Land, Rebirth, The Virgin Lands* (New York: International Publishers, 1980), 10-11; Inboden, *The Peacemaker*, 3-11, 87-89, 208-210; Kengor, *The Crusader*, 66-69, 78, 81-83; Schweitzer, *Reagan's War*, 178-179, 183-186.

[18] Steve Coll, *Ghost Wars: The Secret History of the CIA, Afghanistan, and bin Laden, from the Soviet Invasion to September 10, 2001* (New York: Penguin Books, 2005), 42-46; Geoffrey Wawro, *Quicksand: America's Pursuit of Power in the Middle East* (New York: The Penguin Press, 2010), 378. Crucially, however, as Steve Coll explains here, the original amount of funds that the Carter administration half-heartedly allocated to the CIA's covert action aid program in support of the Afghan resistance fighters totaled only U.S. $500,000, hardly enough to effectively aid the guerrillas let alone boost their fortunes in overthrowing the regime, as emphasized at the time by Pakistani President Muhammad Zia ul-Haq, and a sum that paled in comparison to the aid later provided by the Congress during Ronald Reagan's presidency. Moreover, it is important to note here that while Reagan's efforts to arm the Afghan rebels gained momentum only in 1983, the insurgents had already been persevering in the field for nearly four years by that point against the Soviet 40th Army and Air Force, with all of its superior conventional armored forces and air supremacy, with almost negligible aid from the West whereas the Red Army of 1941, while vastly unprepared for the Nazi surprise attack, remained fully capable of resisting its German opponent even with combat aircraft despite losing many fighters to Berlin's initial aerial bombings and began receiving immediate and enormous shipments of material from the Anglo-American Allies by the end of that year, thanks to fairly weak and limited congressional opposition to Roosevelt and Hopkins's efforts to include Stalin's fighting forces in Lend-Lease.

[19] The Russian General Staff, *The Soviet-Afghan War: How a Superpower Fought and Lost*, ed. Lester W. Grau, trans. Michael A. Gress (Lawrence: University Press of Kansas, 2002), 8-10, 10-11.

[20] Gregory Feifer, *The Great Gamble: The Soviet War in Afghanistan* (New York: Harper Perennial, 2010), 1-4, 14-18, 21-22, 25-29; Hussein Haqqani, *Pakistan: Between Mosque and Military* (Washington, D.C.: Carnegie Endowment for International Peace, 117, 122, 152-153, 162-165; Fancher, *The Holy Warrior*, vii, xi-xii, 17-18; Elisabeth Leake, *Afghan Crucible: The Soviet Invasion and the Making of Modern Afghanistan* (New York: Oxford University Press, 2022), 23-26, 79-82.

[21] Ali Ahmad Jalali, *A Miliary History of Afghanistan: From the Great Game to the Global War on Terror* (Lawrence: University Press of Kansas, 2017), 341-344, 366-368, 369, 372-374, 379, 380; Coll, *Ghost Wars*, 60-63; Mohammad Yousaf and Mark Adkin, *Afghanistan – The Bear Trap: The Defeat of a Superpower* (Barnsley, South Yorkshire: Pen & Sword, 2001), 1-3, 8-10, 18-19.

[22] Coll, *Ghost Wars*, 42-46; Inboden, *The Peacemaker*, 208-210; Kengor, *The Crusader*, 228-229, 230-232; Schweitzer, *Reagan's War*, 118, 202-204, 234-235, 255; U.S. Department of the Treasury, "Diaries of Henry Morgenthau, Jr.," Series 2, "Russian Clearance Problems."

23 Fancher, *The Holy Warrior*, 18-19, 20-21, 30-31, 32, 45, 176n183, 183n75-76; Robert M. Gates, *From the Shadows: The Ultimate Insider's Story of Five Presidents and How They Won the Cold War* (New York: Simon and Schuster, 1996), 431; Yousaf and Adkin, 13-15, *Afghanistan*, 18-19.

24 Fancher, *The Holy Warrior*, 18-19, 20-21, 30-31; Kaplan, *Soldiers of God*, 14-15, 168-170, 171-172.

25 Corey Robin, "Radical writer Alexander Cockburn dead at 71," *Al-Jazeera*, 23 July 2012, https://www.aljazeera.com/amp/opinions/2012/7/23/radical-writer-alexander-cockbu rn-dead-at-71.

26 Kaplan, *Soldiers of God*, 15; Robin, "Radical writer Alexander Cockburn."

27 Kaplan, *Soldiers of God*, 15; Robin, "Radical writer Alexander Cockburn,"; Barnett R. Rubin, "The 'Overlooked' War in Afghanistan," *The New York Times*, 17 October 1986, http s://www.nytimes.com/1986/10/17/opinion/the-overlooked-war-in-afghanistan.html.

28 William J. Casey, *Scouting the Future: The Public Speeches of William J. Casey*, ed. and comp. Herbert E. Meyer (Washington, D.C.: Regnery, 1989), 119-120, 123, 125, 135, 143, 161-163, 170-171, 183-186; Cassidy, "Soviet Offensive Is Speeded By American War Supplies,"; Davies, *Mission to Moscow*, 275-277, 278-280; Debra Denker, "Along Afghanistan's War-Torn Frontier," *National Geographic*, Vol. 167, No. 6 (June 1985), 772-797; Edward Girardet, "Afghanistan: Soviet 'migratory genocide' and failed UN talks," *The Christian Science Monitor, 6 December 1983*, https://www.csmonitor.com/1983/1206/12 0648.html' Robert D. Kaplan, *Soldiers of God: With Islamic Warriors in Afghanistan and Pakistan* (New York: Vintage, 2001), 176-178; National Archives and Record Administration, "Letter from Joseph E. Davies,"; Howell Raines, "REAGAN HINTING AT ARMS FOR AFGHAN REBELS," *The New York Times*, 10 March 1981, https://www.nytimes.com/1981 /03/10/world/reagan-hinting-at-arms-for-afghan-rebels.html; Reagan, *The Reagan Diaries*, 128, 411; Radek Sikorski, *Dust of the Saints: A Journey Through War-Torn Afghanistan* (New York: Paragon House, 1990), 173-175, 215. 268; Small, "How We Learned to Love the Russians," 465-469, 473-475; Stowe, "Sows, in Visit to Rzhev Sector,"; The New York Times, "MISS BOURKE-WHITE PRAISES STALIN."

29 Girardet, *Killing the Cranes*, 279; Kaplan, *Soldiers of God*, 135, 143, 187-188, 189.

30 Denker, "Along Afghanistan's War-Torn Frontier," 773-774, 783-785, 787-788; Edward Girardet, "Soviets step up war against reporters in Afghanistan," *The Christian Science Monitor*, 23 October 1984, https://www.csmonitor.com/1984/1023/102339.html.

31 Girardet, "Afghanistan."

32 Fancher, *The Holy Warrior*, 33-36, 178n219, 183-184n86-89; Kaplan, *Soldiers of God*, 36-38, 40-41, 172-173, 187, 189.

33 Bourke-White, *Portrait of Myself*, 183-184,187-188; Denker, "Along Afghanistan's War-Torn Frontier," 773-774, 783-785, 787-788; Feifer, *The Great Gamble*, 117-118, 208-212; Girardet, "Afghanistan,"; W. Eric Gustafson and William L. Richter, "Pakistan in 1980: Weathering the Storm," *Asian Survey*, Vol. 21, No. 2 (February 1981), 162-171, https://www.jstor.org/stable/2643761; Kaplan, *Soldiers of God*, 128, 187, 189; Sikorski, *Dust of the Saints*, 41, 53, 143, 152, 207-209; The Russian General Staff, *The Soviet-Afghan War*, 131-133, 170, 223-227; Mughees Uddin, "Image of Pakistan in the *New York Times* (1980-1990)," *Journal of Pakistan Vision*, Vol. 11, No. 1 (2010), 12-43, http://pu.edu.pk/images/j ournal/studies/PDF-FILES/Artical%20No-2.pdf; UPI Archives, "Afghan aircraft on operations against anti-communist guerrillas violated Pakistani," *UPI*, 1 November 1983,

https://www.upi.com/Archives/1983/11/01/Afghan-aircraft-on-operations-against-ant
i-communist-guerrillas-violated-Pakistani/7902436510800/.

34 DNA Web Team "Did Hollywood film Rambo 3 predict the Taliban takeover of
Afghanistan? Know the truth," *DNA*, 23 August 2021, https://www.dnaindia.com/world/
report-did-hollywood-film-rambo-3-predict-the-taliban-takeover-of-afghanistan-know-the-
truth-sylvester-stallone-hollywood-cia-mujahideen-soviet-invasion-2907298; James
Pittaway, "The Afghan War Isn't Over Until the Afghans Say So," *The Washington Post*, 29
December 1985, https://www.washingtonpost.com/archive/opinions/1985/12/29/the-
afghan-war-isnt-over-until-the-afghans-say-so/b18a7068-8918-4122-983c-6411a365d3
d0/; Girardet, *Killing the Cranes*, 6, 56, 100-101, 104, 276; Richard Weintraub, "AFGHAN
REBELS BUTTRESS SIEGE." *The Washington Post*, 30 December 1987, https://www.wash
ingtonpost.com/archive/politics/1987/12/30/afghan-rebels-buttress-siege/76f3b734-6
61e-40e6-b4c0-e0a0523aedee/.

35 Inboden, *The Peacemaker*, 208-210, 320-321; *Congressional Record – United States
Senate*, 98th Congress, 1st Session, pt. 21(1983), https://www.govinfo.gov/content/pk
g/GPO-CRECB-1983-pt21/pdf/GPO-CRECB-1983-pt21-2-1.pdf;   U.S.   President,
"Proclamation 5033 – Afghanistan Day, 1983," *The White House*, Washington, D.C., 21
March 1983, *The American Presidency Project*, https://www.presidency.ucsb.edu/docum
ents/proclamation-5033-afghanistan-day-1983.

36 *Congressional Record – United States Senate and House of Representatives*, 100th
Congress, 1st Session, pt. 3 (1987), https://www.congress.gov/100/crecb/1987/02/23/GP
O-CRECB-1987-pt3-9.pdf; George Crile, *Charlie Wilson's War: The Extraordinary Story of
How the Wildest Man in Congress and a Rogue CIA Agent Changed the History of Our Times*
(New York: Grove Press, 2003), 4-7, 107-109. 110-113; Lynn Winthrop, "11/11/03 FILE
STORY: During book signing, Wilson recalls efforts to arm Afghans," *The Lufkin Daily
News*, 11 November 2003, https://web.archive.org/web/20071120055652/http://lufkind
ailynews.com/hp/content/region/ettoday/cww/stories/book_signing.html.

37 *Cong. Rec. – United States Senate*, 98th Cong., 1st Sess. (1983); *Cong. Rec. – United States
Senate and House of Representatives*, 100th Cong., 1st Sess. (1987); Crile, *Charlie Wilson's
War*, 324-328, 330, 334, 338; Fancher, *The Holy Warrior*, 30, 32-33, 45-56, 53, 176-177n192;
Haqqani, *Pakistan*, 162-165; Tom Kenworthy, "Congressman Charlie Wilson, Not Holding
his Fire," The Washington Post, 20 August 1990, *https://www.washingtonpost.com/archive
/lifestyle/1990/08/20/congressman-charlie-wilson-not-holding-his-fire/4597c5fa-1e05-416
2-9e4a-e4aefc697f9d/*; Reagan, *The Reagan Diaries*, 128-129; Peter Roff, "Capital Q&A:
Sen. Gordon Humphrey," *UPI*, 10 October 2001, https://www.upi.com/amp/Archives/2
001/10/10/Capital-QA-Sen-Gordon-Humphrey/5671002686400/.

38 Casey, *Scouting the* Future, 119-120, 123, 125, 135, 143, 161-163, 170-171, 183-186; Crile,
Charlie Wilson's War, 76-79, 243; Sherwood, *Roosevelt and Hopkins*, 791-793, 796, 812;
Yousaf and Adkin, Afghanistan, 62-63, 81, 120; Winthrop, "11/11/03 FILE STORY."

39 William Borders, " Pakistan's Plight: At Odds With U.S. and Fearful of Soviet; News
Analysis American Embassy Is in Ruins Aid Halted Under U.S. Legislation," *The New York
Times*, 2 January 1980, https://www.nytimes.com/1980/01/02/archives/pakistans-plight
-at-odds-with-us-and-fearful-of-soviet-news.html; Casey, *Scouting the* Future, 119-120,
123, 125, 135, 143, 161-163, 170-171, 183-186; Chairman of the Board, Tennessee Valley
Authority, "Lend-Lease Program With Russia,"; Gustafson and Richter, "Pakistan in 1980,"
162-165; Reagan, *The Reagan Diaries*, 128, 411; Nathaniel Sheppard, Jr., "Senator Says
U.S. Ready to Support Rebel Capital," *Chicago Tribune*, 15 May 1988, https://www.chicag

otribune.com/news/ct-xpm-1988-05-15-8803170824-story.html; *The National Security Archive*, "Ambassador Dean Cable, 'Subject: Afghanistan,'" 10 December 1986, https://nsa rchive.gwu.edu/document/18133-document-11-ambassador-dean-cable-subject; Uddin, "Image of Pakistan," 15-17, 22-23; Lally Weymouth, "Moscow's 'Invisible War' of Terror Inside Pakistan," *The Washington Post*, 13 March 1988, https://www.washingtonpost.co m/archive/opinions/1988/03/13/moscows-invisible-war-of-terror-inside-pakistan/6e9 6dd11-56a5-4d1e-bc64-c333f41af17e/.

[40] *Cong. Rec. – United States Senate*, 98th Cong., 1st Sess. (1983); Fancher, *The Holy Warrior*, 29; Kengor, *The Crusader*, 165-167, 168-169, 170-173; Leake, *Afghan Crucible*, 79-82, 129; Joseph E. Persico, *Casey: The Lives and Secrets of William J. Casey: From the OSS to the CIA* (New York: Penguin Books, 1991), 225-226, 230-231, 281, 309-313; U.S. President, "National Security Decision Directive Number 75: U.S. Relations with the USSR," The White House, Washington, D.C., 17 January 1983, *Ronald Reagan Presidential Library & Museum*, https://www.reaganlibrary.gov/public/archives/reference/scanned-nsdds/ns dd75.pdf.

[41] *Cong. Rec. – United States Senate*, 98th Cong., 1st Sess. (1983); *Cong. Rec. – United States Senate and House of Representatives*, 100th Cong., 1st Sess. (1987); Persico, *Casey*, 225-226, 230-231, 281, 309-313; Wawro, *Quicksand*, 380-382, 385-386, 390-394.

[42] Leake, *Afghan Crucible*, 134-135; Pittaway, "The Afghan War Isn't Over Until the Afghans Say So,"; U.S. President, "Remarks Following a Meeting With Afghan Resistance Leaders and Members of Congress," *The White House*, Washington, D.C., 12 November 1987, *Ronald Reagan Presidential Library & Museum*, https://www.reaganlibrary.gov/archives/speech /remarks-following-meeting-afghan-resistance-leaders-and-members-congress.

[43] *Congressional Record – United States Senate*, 100th Congress, 1st Session, pt. 17 (1987), https://www.govinfo.gov/content/pkg/GPO-CRECB-1987-pt17/pdf/GPO-CRECB-1987-pt17-7-2.pdf; Crile, *Charlie Wilson's War*, 356; Fancher, *The Holy Warrior*, 54, 188n147-149; Kaplan, *Soldiers of God*, 187-188; Kengor, *The Crusader*, 232-233; Barnett, R. Rubin, *Afghanistan: What Everyone Needs to Know* (New York: Oxford University Press, 2020), 72-73; Sikorski, *Dust of the Saints*, 268; U.S. President, "National Security Decision Directive Number 166: U.S. Policy, Programs and Strategy in Afghanistan," *The White House*, Washington, D.C., 27 March 1985, https://www.reaganlibrary.gov/public/archives/refer ence/scanned-nsdds/nsdd166.pdf.

[44] Rodric Braithwaite, *Afgantsy: The Russians in Afghanistan 1979-89* (New York: Oxford University Press, 2013), 203-205; Fancher, *The Holy Warrior*, 44, 182n60; Mark Galeotti, *Afghanistan: The Soviet Union's Last War* (London: Frank Cass & Co. Ltd, 1995), 18, 195-196; Artemy M. Kalinovsky, *A Long Goodbye: The Soviet Withdrawal from Afghanistan* (Cambridge, MA: Harvard University Press, 2011), 23-24.

[45] *Cong. Rec. – United States Senate*, 100th Cong., 1st Sess. (1987); Kotelnikov, *Lend-Lease and Soviet Aviation*, 173-175, 191-192, 193-195; Loza, *Attack of the Airacobras*, 1-3, 4-8, 12-16, 316-319, 320-323; Office, Chief of Finance War Department, "Lend-Lease Shipments World War II,"; Rubin, *Afghanistan*, 52-54, 57-59, 72-73; U.S. Department of State, *Soviet Supply Protocols*, 55, 57-61, 66-71, 76, 79-83; U.S. President, "Remarks Following a Meeting With Afghan Resistance Leaders and Members of Congress."

[46] Casey, *Scouting the Future*, 119-120, 123, 125, 135, 143, 161-163, 170-171, 183-186; *Cong. Rec. – United States Senate and House of Representatives*, 100th Cong., 1st Sess. (1987); Crile, *Charlie Wilson's War*, 276-279, 285-287, 294-296; Reagan, *The Reagan*

Diaries, 128, 411; U.S. President, "Remarks Following a Meeting With Afghan Resistance Leaders and Members of Congress,"; Winthrop, "11/11/03 FILE STORY."

[47] Wawro, *Quicksand*, 385-386, 394-397. It is important to briefly note here that *Quicksand*, despite being written by a brilliant, astute, and rightly renowned scholar and military historian, contains many glaring and significant factual errors regarding al-Qaeda leader Osama bin Laden's religious and philosophical beliefs, motivations, character traits, and even his physical health and stamina. Wawro, notwithstanding his accurate assessment of Islamabad's traditional views of Afghanistan's strategic importance to Pakistani national security, errs on these same pages in his depiction of bin Laden as a recipient of CIA aid, a freelance warmonger always bent on killing Westerners and Arab tyrants for no reason other than allegedly being one of the Islamist "bigots" supposedly running amok, an insulin-dependent diabetic, and a radical takfiri fanatic rather than the independent actor, ruthless but pragmatic operator, physically healthy and active man, and traditional but militant Salafist that the al-Qaeda leader consistently proved himself to be, both during and after the Soviet-Afghan War. These popular but inaccurate assertions, which are unfortunately believed and parroted by far too many people, are by no means minor, nitpicky "gotcha" issues, but are quite serious, misinformative myths that have been thoroughly, convincingly, and repeatedly debunked by many dedicated scholars and biographers of bin Laden, including, first and foremost, top biographers such as Peter Bergen and Michael Scheuer. To be sure, and in all fairness to an otherwise top-notch and rightly respected academic, bin Laden's life and actions are neither Wawro's forte nor his major focus in *Quicksand*, and the work, like his many others, remains more than worth exploring and is highly recommended to readers. For several rigorously researched and more historically accurate accounts of bin Laden's true and well-documented motivations, actions, overall solid physical health, and militant but genuine religious convictions, both during his formative guerrilla years in the Soviet-Afghan War and throughout his life, see Peter Bergen, *The Rise and Fall of Osama bin Laden* (New York: Simon & Schuster, 2022), 42-43; Fancher, *The Holy Warrior*, 40-45, 48-52, 181-183n27-75, 184-187n93-128; and Michael Scheuer, *Osama bin Laden* (New York: Oxford University Press, 2012), 48-49, 50-52, 52-54, 54-59, 59-71, 71-75, 75-78.

[48] Haqqani, *Pakistan*, 162-165; Persico, *Casey*, 225-226, 230-231, 281, 309-313; Serge Schmemann, "AFGHAN WAR, AFTER 6 YEARS, BECOMES A SOVIET FACT OF LIFE," *The New York Times*, 18 February 1986, https://www.nytimes.com/1986/02/18/world/afghan -war-after-6-years-becomes-a-soviet-fact-of-life.html; Yousaf and Adkin, *Afghanistan*, 23-25, 27-29, 113-115, 120-122, 140, 143.

[49] Haqqani, *Pakistan*, 162-165; Kaplan, *Soldiers of God*, 40-41; Jalali, *A Military History of Afghanistan*, 414-418, 418-424; Leake, *Afghan Crucible*, 24-25, 28-29, 112-115, 201; Yousaf and Adkin, *Afghanistan*, 83-84, 107-108.

[50] Abid Hussein, "What is behind a resurgence of violent attacks in Pakistan?" *Al-Jazeera*, 26 December 2022, https://www.aljazeera.com/news/2022/12/26/what-is-behind-a-resurgence-of-violent-attacks-in-pakistan; Salman Masood, "Pakistan Raids a Prison After Militants Seize a Hostage," *The New York Times*, 20 December 2022, https://www.ny times.com/2022/12/20/world/asia/pakistan-taliban-prison-raid-hostages.html; Nic Robertson, "Pakistan's Taliban problem is America's too," *CNN*, 15 December 2022, https://www.msn.com/en-us/news/world/pakistan-s-taliban-problem-is-america-s-to o/ar-AA15llfd?ocid=entnewsntp&cvid=32d31213599f4d698ade9430bcb0d3f3; The Hindu (Unattributed Report), "Pakistan Taliban kill 6 security personnel in multiple

attacks in Baluchistan," *The Hindu*, 25 December 2022, https://www.thehindu.com/new s/international/pakistan-taliban-kill-security-personnel-in-multiple-attacks-in-balochi stan/article66305106.ece; Abdul Salam Zaeef, *My Life with the Taliban*, ed. Alex van Linschoten, trans. Felix Kuehn (London: Hurst & Company, 2010), 31, 35-37, 38.

[51] Haqqani, *Pakistan*, 162-165, 173-175, 179-183; *The National Security Archive*, "Cable from Ambassador Dean to Secretary of State: "Subject: Discussion with Rajiv Gandhi on Afghanistan," 11 July 1987, https://nsarchive.gwu.edu/document/18136-document-14-cable-ambassador-dean; Yousaf and Adkin, *Afghanistan*, 62, 69, 81, 88, 116, 136, 158, 165211-212, 231, 234.

[52] Coll, *Ghost Wars*, 42-46; Riaz Haq, "Pakistani Air Force: The Only Air Force That Shot Down Multiple Russian fighter Pilots in Combat Since WWII," *Haq's Musings*, 16 March 2022, http://www.riazhaq.com/2022/03/pakistan-air-force-only-air-force-that.html?m= 1; News Desk, ""Did Pakistan's F-16 shoot down Russian vice president's fighter jet?" *Global Village Space*, 14 May 2020, https://www.globalvillagespace.com/did-pakistans-f-16-shoot-down-russian-vice-presidents-fighter-jet/; Yousaf and Adkin, *Afghanistan*, 33, 94-98, 122-124, 126-128.

[53] William Branigin, "Guerrillas Use Cease-Fire To Rearm," *The Washington Post*, 18 October 1983, https://www.washingtonpost.com/archive/politics/1983/10/18/guerrilla s-use-cease-fire-to-rearm/5c2bced3-1da9-49bb-bc17-b623367406d2/; Fancher, *The Holy Warrior*, 33; Mark Galeotti, *The Panjshir Valley 1980-86: The Lion Tames the Bear in Afghanistan* (Oxford, UK: Osprey Publishing, 2021), 63-66; Edward Girardet, "Soviet truce with Afghan rebels fades," *The Christian Science Monitor*, 18 August 1983, https://www.csmonitor.com/1983/0818/081856.html; Jalali, *A Military History of Afghanistan*, 404-405; Kaplan, *Soldiers of God*, 38-41; Yousaf and Adkin, *Afghanistan*, 71; The New York Times (Unattributed Report), "An AFGHAN REBEL AND SOVIET REPORTEDLY AGREE TO A TRUCE," *The New York Times*, 25 May 1983, https://www.nyt imes.com/1983/05/25/world/an-afghan-rebel-and-soviet-reportedly-agree-to-a-truce. html.

[54] Branigin, "Guerrillas Use Cease-Fire To Rearm,"; Fancher, *The Holy Warrior*, 33; Galeotti, *The Panjshir Valley 1980*-86, 63-66; Girardet, "Soviet truce with Afghan rebels fades,"; Kaplan, *Soldiers of God*, 38-41; The New York Times, "AN AFGHAN REBEL AND SOVIET,"; Yousaf and Adkin, *Afghanistan*, 129-130, 141, 231.

[55] Casey, *Scouting the* Future, 119-120, 123, 125, 135, 143, 161-163, 170-171, 183-186; Haqqani, *Pakistan*, 162-165; Persico, *Casey*, 368; Reagan, *The Reagan Diaries*, 128, 411; *The National Security Archive*, "Cable from Secretary of State to Amembassy New Delhi: 'Subject: Armacost Pre-summit Discussions with Vorontsov on Afghanistan," 20 November 1987, https: //nsarchive.gwu.edu/document/18138-document-16-cable-secretary-state; U.S. President, "Remarks Following a Meeting With Afghan Resistance Leaders and Members of Congress,"; Yousaf and Adkin, *Afghanistan*, 23-25, 27-29, 113-115.

[56] Bill Keller, "A BIG AFGHAN TOWN IS SEIZED BY REBELS," *The New York Times*, 15 August 1988, https://www.nytimes.com/1988/08/15/world/a-big-afghan-town-is-seized-by-rebels.html; Persico, *Casey*, 225-226, 230-231, 281, 309-313; U.S. President, "Remarks Following a Meeting With Afghan Resistance Leaders and Members of Congress,"

[57] Davies, *Mission to Moscow*, 275-277; Jones, *The Roads to Russia*, 39; *National Archives and Record Administration*, "Letter from Joseph E. Davies,"; Sherwood, *Roosevelt and Hopkins*, 306-308.

[58] Persico, *Casey*, 225-226, 230-231, 281, 309-313; Yousaf and Adkin, *Afghanistan*, 105-106, 117.

[59] *Cong. Rec. – United States Senate*, 98th Cong., 1st Sess. (1983).

[60] *Cong. Rec. – United States Senate and House of Representatives*, 100th Cong., 1st Sess. (1987); Kenworthy, "Congressman Charlie Wilson, Not Holding his Fire,"; Rubin, *Afghanistan*, 72-73; Roff, "Capital Q&A,"; Yousaf and Adkin, *Afghanistan*, 105-106, 117-119, 140, 143, 152-153; Winthrop, "11/11/03 FILE STORY."

[61] Persico, *Casey*, 368; Yousaf and Adkin, *Afghanistan*, 23-26, 26-30.

[62] Arthur Bonner, "AN ODYSSEY WITH AFGHAN REBELS: TRANSPORTING VITAL ARMS SUPPLY," *The New York Times*, 31 October 1985, https://www.nytimes.com/1985/10/31/world/an-odyssey-with-afghan-rebels-transporting-vital-arms-supply.html; *Cong. Rec. – United States Senate and House of Representatives*, 100th Cong., 1st Sess. (1987); Denker, "Along Afghanistan's War-Torn Frontier," 783-785, 787-788; Fancher, *The Holy Warrior*, 31, 46; Girardet, "Afghanistan,"; Feifer, *The Great Gamble*, 117-118, 208-212; Kaplan, *Soldiers of God*, 174, 178-179, 187-188, 189; The Russian General Staff, *The Soviet-Afghan War*, 131-133, 170, 223-227; Zaeef, *My Life with the Taliban*, 21-23, 27-29.

[63] *Cong. Rec. – United States Senate and House of Representatives*, 100th Cong., 1st Sess. (1987); Persico, *Casey*, 368; *The National Security Archive*, "Memorandum of Conversation: Special Working Group on Afghanistan, March 22, 1988," 22 March 1988, http://nsarchive.gwu.edu/document/18260-national-security-archive-doc-08-memorandum; *The National Security Archive*, "Ambassador Dean's Cable. Subject: Gandhi/Ryzhkov Meeting: Discussion of Afghanistan," 27 November 1987, https://nsarchive.gwu.edu/document/18139-document-17-ambassador-dean-s-cable-subject; U.S. Department of State, "U.S.-Soviet Relations: Testing Gorbachev's 'New Thinking.' Current Policy No. 985.," Washington, D.C., Bureau of Public Affairs, 1 July 1987, https://files.eric.ed.gov/fulltext/ED286807.pdf.

[64] Bonner, "AN ODYSSEY WITH AFGHAN REBELS,"; Jack Anderson and Dale van Atta, "Afghan Rebel Aid Enriches Generals," *The Washington Post*, 8 May 1987, https://www.washingtonpost.com/archive/local/1987/05/08/afghan-rebel-aid-enriches-generals/40243b90-55d4-421b-80b7-929c3e4b1075/; Fancher, *The Holy Warrior*, 30, 175n170-171; Persico, *Casey*, 368; Yousaf and Adkin, *Afghanistan*, 81-83; Roff, "Capital Q&A."

[65] Coll, *Ghost Wars*, 93-98, 101-102, 103-106; Persico, *Casey*, 368; *The National Security Archive*, "Cable from Ambassador Raphel, Islamabad, to Secretary of State, Washington: Subject: USCINCCENT Visit to Pakistan: The Pak Military on Afghanistan," 5 June 1988, https://nsarchive.gwu.edu/document/18152-document-26-cable-ambassador-raphel; Yousaf and Adkin, *Afghanistan*, 78-80, 81-83, 87-89, 90-91, 92; U.S. President, "Remarks Following a Meeting With Afghan Resistance Leaders and Members of Congress."

[66] Inboden, *The Peacemaker*, 1-4, 10-13, 22, 25, 28; Roff, "Capital Q&A,"; *The National Security Archive*, "Cable from Secretary of State to U.S. Embassy Islamabad. Subject: Marker Call on Armacost, December 9," 10 December 1988, https://nsarchive.gwu.edu/document/17565-document-x7-cable-secretary-state-u-s.

[67] *The National Security Archive*, "Cable from Secretary of State to U.S. Embassy Islamabad,"; U.S. President, "Proclamation 5033."

[68] U.S. President, "Letter to the Presidium of the Supreme Soviet of the U.S.S.R. on the 50th Anniversary of Diplomatic Relations Between the United States and the Soviet Union," *The White House*, Washington, D.C., 16 November 1983, *The American Presidency Project*, https://www.presidency.ucsb.edu/documents/letter-the-presidium-the-supreme-soviet-the-ussr-the-50th-anniversary-diplomatic-relations.

[69] Braithwaite, *Afgantsy*, 203-205; Coll, *Ghost Wars*, 65-66, 67, 72; Fancher, *The Holy Warrior*, 43-44, 182n57-60; Galeotti. *Afghanistan*, 18, 195-196; Kalinovsky, *A Long Goodbye*, 43; Kaplan, *Soldiers of God*, 176-177; Robert Pear, "Arming Afghan Guerrillas: A Huge Effort Led by U.S.," *The New York Times*, 18 April 1988, https://www.nytimes.com/1988/04/18/world/arming-afghan-guerrillas-a-huge-effort-led-by-us.html#:~:text=Wit h%20help%20from%20China%20and%20many%20Moslem%20nations%2C,to%20driv e%20the%20Soviet%20Army%20from%20their%20country.; Wawro, *Quicksand*, 381-382, 385-386, 390-394; Yousaf and Adkin, *Afghanistan*, 81-83, 105-106.

[70] Neamatollah Nojumi, *The Rise of the Taliban in Afghanistan: Mass Mobilization, Civil War, and the Future of the Region* (London: Palgrave MacMillan, 2002), 51-52, 119, 122, 127, 135, 144, 149, 153, 189; Ahmed Rashid, *Jihad: The Rise of Militant Islam in Central Asia* (New York: Penguin Books, 2002), 5-7, 36-40, 42-46; Zaeef, *My Life with the Taliban*, 47-49, 62-65.

[71] Bonner, "AN ODYSSEY WITH AFGHAN REBELS,"; Feifer, *The Great Gamble*, 318-220, 238-241; Jalali, *A Military History of Afghanistan*, 424-426; Kalinovsky, *A Long Goodbye*, 43; Kaplan, *Soldiers of God*, 176-177; Leake, *Afghan Crucible*, 245-246, 254-255; McMeekin, *Stalin's War*, 651-653, 657, 664-665; Ahmed Rashid, *Taliban: The Power of Militant Islam in Afghanistan and Beyond* (London: I. B. Tauris, 2010), 17-20, 21, 31-35; Weeks, *Russia's Life-Saver*, 129-131, 131-133; U.S. Department o f State, "Regional Issues and U.S.-Soviet Relations: Current Policy No. 1089," Washington, D.C., Bureau of Public Affairs, 25 August 1988, https://babel.hathitrust.org/cgi/pt?id=umn.31951002961446p&view=1up&seq=3&skin=2021&q1=afghanistan.

[72] *Cong. Rec. – United States Senate and House of Representatives*, 100th Cong., 1st Sess. (1987); Inboden, *The Peacemaker*, 9, 42-44; Kengor, *The Crusader*, 251-255; Schweitzer, *Reagan's War*, 52-54, 57-59, 61-62, 73, 85-87, 117.

[73] McMeekin, *Stalin's War*, 517-518, 536-537.

[74] *Cong. Rec. – United States Senate*, 78th Cong., 2nd Sess. (1944); Deane, *The Strange Alliance*, 87-89, 168-169, 202; Eisenhower, *Crusade in Europe*, 489-490; Feis, *Churchill, Roosevelt, Stalin*, 9-12; Harriman and Abel, *Special Envoy*, 190, 192; Rickenbacker, *Rickenbacker*, 403-404, 418-419; Roosevelt and Churchill, "Texts of Roosevelt-Churchill Messages,"; Sherwood, *Roosevelt and Hopkins*, 545; U.S. Department of State, "Foreign Relations: The Conferences at Cairo and Tehran,"; Weigley, *The American Way of War*, 128-129, 150-152, 162-163, 357-359.

[75] *The National Security Archive*, "Cable from Secretary of State to U.S. Embassy Islamabad,"; U.S. Department of State, "Regional Issues and U.S.-Soviet Relations,"; U.S. President, "Proclamation 5033."

[76] Bonner, "AN ODYSSEY WITH AFGHAN REBELS,"; Nojumi, *The Rise of the Taliban in Afghanistan*, 51-52, 119, 122, 127, 135, 144, 149, 153, 189; Rashid, *Taliban*, 17-20, 21, 31-35; U.S. Department of State, "Regional Issues and U.S.-Soviet Relations,"; Zaeef, *My Life with the Taliban*, 93-95, 115-118, 146-147.

[77] *Cong. Rec. – United States Senate*, 78th Cong., 2nd Sess. (1944); Deane, *The Strange Alliance*, 87-89, 168-169, 202; McMeekin, *Stalin's War*, 650-652, 653-657; Weeks, *Stalin's Other War*, 175-180; Zaeef, *My Life with the Taliban*, 93-95, 115-118, 146-147.

[78] Nojumi, *The Rise of the Taliban in Afghanistan*, 51-52, 119, 122, 127, 135, 144, 149, 153, 189; Rashid, *Taliban*, 17-20, 21, 31-35; Zaeef, *My Life with the Taliban*, 93-95, 115-118, 146-147.

[79] Hull, *The Memoirs of Cordell Hull*, 967, 973-974; The New York Times, "MISS BOURKE-WHITE PRAISES STALIN."

[80] Haqqani, *Pakistan*, 62-65; 87-89, 90-94, 103-104; Kaplan, *Soldiers of God*, 135, 143, 187-188, 189; Kenworthy, "Congressman Charlie Wilson, Not Holding his Fire,"; Rashid, *Jihad*, 5-7, 36-40, 42-46; Rubin, *Afghanistan*, 72-73; Zaeef, *My Life with the Taliban*, 62-64, 65.

[81] Pear, "Arming Afghan Guerrillas,"; Persico, *Casey*, 368; *The National Security Archive*, "Cable from Secretary of State to U.S. Embassy Islamabad,"; U.S. President, "Remarks Following a Meeting With Afghan Resistance Leaders and Members of Congress."

[82] David Binder, "Soviet Brigade: How the U.S. Traced It," *The New York Times*, 13 September 1979, https://www.nytimes.com/1979/09/13/archives/soviet-brigade-how-the-us-traced-it-how-dispute-developed.html.

[83] Inboden, *The Peacemaker*, 9, 42-44; Kengor, *The Crusader*, 251-255; Reagan, *An American Life*, 619-623, 651-655; Schweitzer, *Reagan's War*, 52-54, 57-59, 61-62, 73, 85-87, 117.

[84] *The National Security Archive, Vol. II*, "The Costs of Soviet Involvement in Afghanistan: An Intelligence Assessment," https://nsarchive2.gwu.edu/NSAEBB/NSAEBB57/us8.pdf.

[85] Pear, "Arming Afghan Guerrillas,"; Persico, *Casey*, 368; Reagan, *An American Life*, 619-623, 651-655; *The National Security Archive*, "Cable from Secretary of State to U.S. Embassy Islamabad,"; U.S. President, "Remarks Following a Meeting With Afghan Resistance Leaders and Members of Congress."

[86] *The National Security Archive*, "Cable from Ambassador Raphel, Islamabad, to Secretary of State, Washington," 5 June 1988.

[87] Braithwaite, *Afgantsy*, 203-205; Galeotti, *Afghanistan*, 18, 195-196; Haqqani, *Pakistan*, 62-65; 87-89, 90-94, 103-104; Kalinovsky, *A Long Goodbye*, 23-24; Kengor, *The Crusader*, 257-260, 274-275; Kenworthy, "Congressman Charlie Wilson, Not Holding his Fire,"; Rubin, *Afghanistan*, 72-73; *The National Security Archive*, "Cable from Ambassador Raphel, Islamabad, to Secretary of State, Washington," 5 June 1988; Yousaf and Adkin, *Afghanistan*, 105-106, 117-119, 140, 143, 152-153; Winthrop, "11/11/03 FILE STORY."

[88] *The National Security Archive, Vol. II*, "The Costs of Soviet Involvement in Afghanistan."

[89] *The National Security Archive*, "Cable from Secretary of State to U.S. Embassy Islamabad,"; U.S. Department of State, "Regional Issues and U.S.-Soviet Relations,"; U.S. President, "Proclamation 5033."

[90] Feifer, *The Great Gamble*, 251-253, 254; Galeotti, *The Panjshir Valley*, 1980-86, 86-88, 88-89; Jalali, *A Military History of Afghanistan*, 424-426; Kalinovsky, *A Long Goodbye*, 43; Rashid, *Taliban*, 17-20, 21. 31-35; Rubin, *Afghanistan*, 72-73; *The National Security Archive*, "Cable from Secretary of State to U.S. Embassy Islamabad,"; The Soviet General Staff, *The Soviet-Afghan War*, xxii-xxv, 13-14; U.S. President, "Remarks Following a Meeting With Afghan Resistance Leaders and Members of Congress,"; Zaeef, *My Life with the Taliban*, 47-49.

[91] Loza, *Attack of the* Airacobras, 39-42; Mellinger, *Soviet Lend-Lease Fighter Aces*, 45-47, 48, 59-61; Melton, *Liberty's War*, 74-76; Office, Chief of Finance War Department, "Lend-Lease Shipments World War II,"; Rickenbacker, *Rickenbacker*, 407-408, 409; U.S. Department of State, *Soviet Supply Protocols*, 55, 57-61, 66-71, 76, 79-83.

[92] Rashid, *Jihad*, 5-7, 36-40, 42-46; Zaeef, *My Life with the Taliban*, 62-64, 65.

[93] Hull, *The Memoirs of Cordell Hull*, 967.

[94] McMeekin, *Stalin's War*, 622-627; Weeks, *Russia's Life-Saver*, 131-133; Ministry of Foreign Affairs of the U.S.S.R., *Stalin's Correspondence*, "No. 103: For Marshal Stalin from President Roosevelt and Prime Minister Churchill," 19 August 1943, 83; Reynolds and

Pechatnov, *The Kremlin Letters*, 287-288; U.S. Department of State, *Soviet Supply Protocols*, 95-97, 147-149; U.S. Department of State, "The Yalta Conference,".; U.S. President, "Map Room Papers Box 8 Roosevelt to Stalin January – June 1943."

95 Natalie Musumeci, "Ukraine revealed secret battle plans left behind by Russian troops and claimed they showed Russia planned a 15-day war," *Yahoo News*, 2 March 2022, https://news.yahoo.com/ukraine-revealed-secret-battle-plans-211801990.html?guccounter=1.

96 John Nagl, "Why the Russian doomsday scenario hasn't happened – yet," *NBC*, 28 December 2022, https://www.nbcnews.com/think/opinion/russia-ukraine-war-shocked-putin-military-vets-rcna63365; The New York Times (Unattributed Report, "Ukraine Battles for Control of Key Black Sea Peninsula," *The New York Times*, 22 November 2022, https://www.nytimes.com/live/2022/11/22/world/russia-ukraine-war-news.

97 Paul McLeary, Erin Banco, and Lara Seligman, "First Javelins. Then HIMARS. Now Patriot. What's Next?" *Politico*, 29 December 2022, https://www.politico.com/news/2022/12/29/himars-patriot-russia-ukraine-biden-00075708; Nagl, "Why the Russian doomsday scenario hasn't happened."

98 Craig Hooper, "Ukraine Converts $21.9 Billion In U.S. Military Surplus Into Fearsome Force," *Forbes*, 26 December 2022, https://www.forbes.com/sites/craighooper/2022/12/26/ukraine-converts-219-billion-in-us-military-surplus-into-fearsome-force/?sh=407dff56370a.

99 Inboden, *The Peacemaker*, 1-4, 10-13, 22, 25, 28; Reagan, *An American Life*, 619-623, 651-655; *The National Security Archive*, "Cable from Secretary of State to U.S. Embassy Islamabad,"; U.S. Department of State, "Regional Issues and U.S.-Soviet Relations,"; U.S. President, "Proclamation 5033."

100 Euronews (Unattributed Report), "US slams 'loose talk' on nuclear weapons after Putin comments," *Euronews*, 8 December 2022, https://www.euronews.com/2022/12/08/us-slams-loose-talk-on-nuclear-weapons-after-putin-comments; John Haltiwanger and Charles R. Davis, "Putin's nuclear threats are stirring fears of a nightmare scenario. Here's what's in his arsenal and what could happen if he orders the unthinkable," *Business Insider*, 24 December 2022, https://www.businessinsider.com/ukraine-war-putin-russia-nuclear-weapons-threats-what-could-happen-2022-10; Tim Lister, "Putin floats possibility that Russia may abandon 'no first use' nuclear doctrine," *CNN*, 9 December 2022, https://www.cnn.com/2022/12/09/europe/russia-putin-nuclear-weapons-intl/index.html.

101 Phelan Chatterjee, "Ukraine War: Zelensky's visit shows neither Ukraine nor US want peace, Russia says," *BBC*, 22 December 2022, https://www.bbc.com/news/world-us-canada-64066584; Inboden, *The Peacemaker*, 1-4, 10-13, 22, 25, 28; Al-Jazeera (Unattributed Report), "Russia accuses US of fighting proxy war in Ukraine," *Al-Jazeera*, 22 December 2022, https://www.aljazeera.com/news/2022/12/22/russia-accuses-us-of-fighting-proxy-war-in-ukraine.

102 Casey, *Scouting the Future*, 119-120, 123, 125, 135, 143, 161-163, 170-171, 183-186; Crile, *Charlie Wilson's War*, 76-79, 243; Sherwood, *Roosevelt and Hopkins*, 791-793, 796, 812; Yousaf and Adkin, Afghanistan, 62-63, 81, 120; Winthrop, "11/11/03 FILE STORY."

103 Chris Alexander, "Lend-Lease for Ukraine: US revives WWII anti-Hitler policy to defeat Putin," *Atlantic Council*, 9 April 2022, https://www.atlanticcouncil.org/blogs/ukrainealert/lend-lease-for-ukraine-us-revives-wwii-anti-hitler-policy-to-defeat-putin/; Catie Edmondson, "Congress Clears Bill to Allow Lending Arms to Ukraine: House passage of the measure, which invoked the World War II-era Lend-Lease Act, sent it to President Biden for his

signature," *The New York Times*, 28 April 2022, https://www.nytimes.com/2022/04/28/us /politics/ukraine-lend-lease-arms.html; Amy B. Wang, "Biden signs Ukraine lend-lease act into law, expediting military aid," *The Washington Post*, 9 May 2022, https://www.wa shingtonpost.com/politics/2022/05/09/president-biden-ukraine-lend-lease-signing/; *Congressional Record – United States Senate*, "S. 3522, Ukraine Democracy Defense Lend-Lease Act of 2022," Congressional Budget Office, 6 April 2022, https://www.cbo.gov/syst em/files/2022-04/s3522.pdf.

104 *The National Security Archive*, "Cable from Secretary of State to Amembassy New Delhi," 20 November 1987; *The National Security Archive*, "Cable from Ambassador Raphel, Islamabad, to Secretary of State, Washington," 5 June 1988.

105 Matt Berg and Lara Seligman, "Zelenskyy makes his case in D.C. for more U.S. support for Ukraine: In his first foreign trip since Russia invaded, the Ukrainian leader urges Biden, and the U.S. Congress, for more money and weapons," *Politico*, 21 December 2022, https://www.politico.com/news/2022/12/21/zelenskyy-washington-ukraine-whit e-house-00074954; Michael Crowley, "Congress Proposes More Than $44 Billion for Ukraine: The spending bill unveiled Tuessday includes billions more for the country than President Biden had requested," *The New York Times*, 20 December 2022, https://www.ny times.com/2022/12/20/us/politics/congress-aid-ukraine.html; Holly Ellyatt, Christina Wilkie, and Chelsey Cox, "Against all odds, 'Ukraine didn't fall,' Zelenskyy says in historic address to U.S. Congress," *CNBC*, 23 December 2022, https://www.cnbc.com/2022/12/2 1/ukraine-war-live-updates-latest-news-on-russia-and-the-war-in-ukraine.html.

106 Natasha Bertrand, Kylie Atwood, Kevin Liptak, and Alex Marquardt, "Austin's assertion that US wants to 'weaken' Russia underlines Biden strategy shift," *CNN*, 26 April 2022, https://www.cnn.com/2022/04/25/politics/biden-administration-russia-strategy/inde x.html; Giulia Carbonaro, "U.S. Wants Russia 'Weakened' So It Can Never Invade Again," *Newsweek*, 25 April 2022, https://www.newsweek.com/us-wants-russia-weakened-so-that-it-can-never-invade-again-1700570; Missy Ryan and Annabelle Timsit, "U.S. wants Russian military 'weakened' from Ukraine invasion, Austin says," *The Washington Post*, 25 April 2022, https://www.washingtonpost.com/world/2022/04/25/russia-weakened-lloyd-austin-ukraine-visit/.

107 Alexander, "Lend-Lease for Ukraine,"; *Congressional Record – United States Senate*, "S. 3522,"; Edmondson, "Congress Clears Bill,"; Wang, "Biden signs Ukraine lend-lease act into law."

108 Melkulangara K. Bhadrakumar, "West lost the plot in Ukraine: the strategy of forcing Russia to its knees is not going to work," *The Tribune*, 15 January 2023, https://www.trib uneindia.com/news/comment/west-lost-the-plot-in-ukraine-464493; Samantha Schmidt, Isabelle Khurshudyan, Serhii Korolchuk, "Captured Russian tanks and equipment are coveted trophies – and a headache: Ukrainian forces have seized hundreds of tanks and other military vehicles, but many are languishing as they wait for repairs and spare parts," *The Washington Post*, 27 December 2022, https://www.washingtonpost.com/world/2022 /12/27/ukraine-russia-tanks-military-vehicles/; President Volodymir Zelensky, "Full Transcript of Zelensky's Speech Before Congress" The Ukrainian president delivered an emotional appeal for further American support, vowing that his country would prevail in its war with Russia" *The New York Times*, 21 December 2022, https://www.nytimes.com/ 2022/12/21/us/politics/zelensky-speech-transcript.html.

109 Jerusalem Post Staff, "US may not maintain military support for Ukraine, Navy secretary says: However, several key US security officials have expressed concern over

continued and potential escalations in the Ukraine-Russia conflict," *The Jerusalem Post,* 12 January 2023, https://www.jpost.com/international/article-728360; Tatiana Vorozhko, "Former US Secretary of State Details Her Support for Arming Ukraine," *VOA,* 13 January 2023, https://www.voanews.com/a/former-us-secretary-of-state-details-her-support-for-arming-ukraine-/6917776.html.

[110] Alyssa Lukpat and Emily Cochrane, "Rand Paul holds up $40 billion in aid for Ukraine: Mr. Paul had sought to alter the bill to include requiring that an inspector general monitor the spending," *The New York Times,* 12 May 2022, https://www.nytimes.com/2022/05/12/world/europe/rand-paul-ukraine-aid.html.

[111] Lukpat and Cochrane, "Rand Paul holds up $40 billion in aid for Ukraine."

[112] Paul Adams and Alexandra Fouche, "Russia fires new waves of missiles at Ukraine and hits energy infrastructure," *BBC,* 14 January 2023, https://www.bbc.com/news/world-europe-64278733; Amnesty International (Unattributed Report), "Ukraine: Devastating power cuts undermining civilian life as Christmas approaches," *Amnesty International,* 21 December 2022, https://www.amnesty.org/en/latest/news/2022/12/ukraine-devastatin g-power-cuts-undermining-civilian-life-as-christmas-approaches/; Business Standard (Unattributed Report), "Russian strikes will cause emergency power cuts across country: Ukraine," *Business Standard,* 15 January 2023, https://www.business-standard.com/arti cle/international/russian-strikes-will-cause-emergency-power-cuts-across-country-uk raine-123011500046_1.html; Lars Paulsson, "How Europe Is Muddling Through Putin's Energy War," *The Washington Post,* 15 January 2023, https://www.washingtonpost.com/business/energy/how-europe-is-muddling-through-putins-energy-war/2023/01/14/22 2c46ee-93e0-11ed-90f8-53661ac5d9b9_story.html; Karina Zaiets and Stephen J. Beard, "Russian missile attacks on Ukraine power grids cut electricity, heat and water to millions," *USA Today,* 24 December 2022, https://www.usatoday.com/in-depth/graphics /2022/12/24/russian-missile-attacks-ukraine-electricity-heat-water/10901300002/.

[113] *The National Security Archive,* "Cable from Ambassador Raphel, Islamabad, to Secretary of State, Washington," 5 June 1988.

[114] Ministry of Foreign Affairs of the U.S.S.R., *Stalin's Correspondence,* "No. 103: For Marshal Stalin from President Roosevelt and Prime Minister Churchill," 19 August 1943, 83; Reynolds and Pechatnov, *The Kremlin Letters,* 287-288; U.S. President, "Map Room Papers Box 8 Roosevelt to Stalin January – June 1943."

[115] Lolita C. Baldor, "Expanded US training for Ukraine forces begins in Germany," *AP News,* 16 January 2023, https://apnews.com/article/russia-ukraine-politics-germany-7ae8c22dfd9379e77f172bd2b3ab5fb7; Dan Lamothe, "U.S. begins expanded training of Ukrainian forces for large-scale combat," *The Washington Post,* 15 January 2023, https://www.washingtonpost.com/national-security/2023/01/15/us-military-ukraine-t raining-germany-grafenwoehr/.

[116] Alexander, "Lend-Lease for Ukraine,"; *Congressional Record – United States Senate,* "S. 3522,"; Edmondson, "Congress Clears Bill,"; Wang, "Biden signs Ukraine lend-lease act into law."

[117] Baldor, "Expanded US training for Ukraine forces begins in Germany,"; Lamothe, "U.S. begins expanded training of Ukrainian forces."

[118] Alexander, "Lend-Lease for Ukraine,"; *Congressional Record – United States Senate,* "S. 3522,"; Edmondson, "Congress Clears Bill,"; Wang, "Biden signs Ukraine lend-lease act into law."

[119] Guy Faulconbridge and Tom Balmforth, "Russia takes Avdiivka from Ukraine, biggest gain in nine months," *Reuters*, 18 February 2024, https://www.reuters.com/world/europ e/ukrainian-troops-withdraw-avdiivka-ammunition-shortage-bites-2024-02-17/; Tim Lister and Maria Kostenko, "Russia raises its flag in Avdiivka, then presses the advantage on a vulnerable Ukraine," *CNN*, 18 February 2024, https://amp.cnn.com/cnn/2024/02/18/eu rope/russia-flag-avdiivka-pressures-ukraine-intl/index.html; Maria Kostenko and Manveena Suri, "Zelensky pleads for help to plug 'artificial' weapons deficit amid signs of Russia seizing advantage," *CNN*, 17 February 2024, https://amp.cnn.com/cnn/2024/02/ 17/europe/zelensky-pleads-plug-artificial-weapons-deficit-intl/index.html; Aliaksandr Kudrytski, "Ukraine Enters Third Year of War as Stalled Aid Dims Outlook," *Bloomberg*, 24 February 2024, https://www.bloomberg.com/news/articles/2024-02-24/ukraine-enters-third-year-of-war-as-stalled-us-aid-dimsoutlook?utm_campaign=pol&utm_medium= bd&utm_source=applenews; Anatol Lieven, "Ukraine Can't Win the War," *TIME*, 24 February 2024, https://time.com/6695261/ukraine-forever-war-danger/.

[120] Faulconbridge and Balmforth, "Russia takes Avdiivka from Ukraine,"; Lister and Kostenko, "Russia raises its flag in Avdiivka,"; Kostenko and Suri, "Zelensky pleade for help,"; Kudrytski, "Ukraine Enters Third Year of War,"; Lieven, "Ukraine Can't Win the War."

[121] Ministry of Foreign Affairs of the U.S.S.R., *Stalin's Correspondence*, "No. 103: For Marshal Stalin from President Roosevelt and Prime Minister Churchill," 19 August 1943, 83; Reynolds and Pechatnov, *The Kremlin Letters*, 287-288; U.S. President, "Map Room Papers Box 8 Roosevelt to Stalin January – June 1943."

[122] U.S. Department of State, *Soviet Supply Protocols*, 55, 57-61, 66-71, 76, 79-83.

[123] McMeekin, *Stalin's War*, 534-536; Whitehall History Publishing – Ministry of Defence, *The Royal Navy and the Arctic Convoys*, 3, 5-7, 17-19, 21-22; *The National Security Archive*, *Vol. II*, "The Costs of Soviet Involvement in Afghanistan,"; Vail Motter, *The Persian Corridor*, 124-127.

[124] Pear, "Arming Afghan Guerrillas,"; Persico, *Casey*, 368; Reagan, *An American Life*, 619-623, 651-655; *The National Archives of the UK*, "PREMIER 3 393/8," "Telescope No. 152. Following for Keenlyside for Ministry of War Transport," 20 January 1943; *The National Security Archive*, "Cable from Secretary of State to U.S. Embassy Islamabad,"; *The National Security Archive, Vol. II*, "The Costs of Soviet Involvement in Afghanistan,"; U.S. President, "Remarks Following a Meeting With Afghan Resistance Leaders and Members of Congress."

[125] Jones, *The Roads to Russia*, 103-105, 107; Mason, *Arctic Warriors*, 209-210; McMeekin, *Stalin's War*, 364-367, 403-405; Melton, *Liberty's War*, 67-68; Thomas, *Through Ice and Fire*, 147-148; Vail Motter, *The Persian Corridor*, 124-127; Van Tuyll, *Feeding the Bear*, 26-27; Walling, *Forgotten Sacrifice*, 9-10, 270-271; Woodman, *Arctic Convoys 1941-1945*, 308-309; Weeks, *Russia's Life-Saver*, 45, 131-133.

[126] Arnold, *Global Mission*, 259; Eisenhower, *Crusade in Europe*, 69-70, 489-490; Harriman and Abel, *Special Envoy*, 190, 192; Hull, *The Memoirs of Cordell Hull*, 1167-1168, 1171-1173; Rickenbacker, *Rickenbacker*, 400-401, 402-403; Standley and Ageton, *Admiral Ambassador to Russia*, 308-309, 312-313.

[127] Ministry of Foreign Affairs of the U.S.S.R., *Stalin's Correspondence*, "No. 138: Personal and Secret Message from Premier J. V. Stalin to the Prime Minister, Mr. W. Churchill," 2 April 1943, "No. 145: Personal and Secret Message from Premier J. V. Stalin to the Prime Minister, Mr. W. Churchill," 12 April 1943, 117-118; Pear, "Arming Afghan Guerrillas,"; Persico, *Casey*, 368; Reagan, *An American Life*, 619-623, 651-655; *The National Archives of*

the UK, "PREMIER 3 393/8," "Foreign Secretary. First Lord. First Sea Lord," 9 January 1943; *The National Security Archive*, "Cable from Secretary of State to U.S. Embassy Islamabad,"; *The National Security Archive, Vol. II*, "The Costs of Soviet Involvement in Afghanistan,"; Reynolds and Pechatnov, *The Kremlin Letters*, 227, 232; U.S. President, "Map Room Papers Box 8 Roosevelt to Stalin January – June 1943,"; U.S. President, "Remarks Following a Meeting With Afghan Resistance Leaders and Members of Congress."

EPILOGUE

[1] U.S. Department of State, "Foreign Relations: The Conferences at Cairo and Tehran."

[2] Liddell Hart, *History of the Second World War*, 908-910.

[3] Arnold, *Global Mission*, 211-212, 385-387; U.S. Department of State, "The Yalta Conference,"; Dolitsky, Glazkov, and Poor, *Pipeline to Russia*, 64-66, 79-80, 84-85; ; Hays, Jr., *The Alaska-Siberia Connection*, 37-38, 41, 43-45, 49; Jones, *The Roads to Russia*, 266-269; Mason, *Arctic Warriors*, 209-210; McMeekin, *Stalin's War*, 650-652, 653-657; Melton, *Liberty's War*, 67-68; Smith, *Warplanes to Alaska*, 45-47, 54-56; Sokolov, *The Role of the Soviet Union in the Second World War*, 53-55; Stettinius, Jr., *Lend-Lease*, 249, 252; Thomas, *Through Ice and Fire*, 147-148; Vail Motter, *The Persian Corridor*, 141-143, 259-262, 319-320, 341-344; Van Tuyll, *Feeding the Bear*, 137-140, 141-143; Weeks, *Russia's Life-Saver*, 135-136; Whitehall History Publishing – Ministry of Defence, *The Royal Navy and the Arctic Convoys*, 78-79; Woodman, *Arctic Convoys 1941-1945*, 264-265, 266, 308-309.

[4] Sokolov, *The Role of the Soviet Union in the Second World War*, 53-55, 57-59.

[5] Harrison, *Accounting For War*, 149-152, 152-154; Jones, *The Roads to Russia*, 37, 39, 120-122; Weeks, *Russia's Life-Saver*, 82-83, 110-111, 111-112.

[6] *Cong. Rec. – House of Representatives*, 81st Cong. 1st and 2nd Sess. (1949-1950); Jordan, *Major Jordan's Diaries*, 36-38, 40-41, 42-44; Kotkin, *Stalin*, 103; McMeekin, *Stalin's War*, 531-534; Radzinsky, *Stalin*, 47-49, 59-64; Rayfield, *Stalin and His Hangmen*, 25-32, 32-34; Suvorov, *The Chief Culprit*, 1-2, 58-59.

[7] Harrison, *Accounting For War*, 128-131, 146-149, 149-152, 152-154; Van Tuyll, *Feeding the Bear*, xii, 3-4, 27, 71, 83-84, 122-124.

[8] U.S. Department of State, "The Yalta Conference."

[9] Carter, "Russian War Relief," 67; Jordan, *Major Jordan's Diaries*, 9; The New York Times, "Addresses of Litvinoff, Hopkins and Green,"; McMeekin, *Stalin's War*, 487-488.

[10] Coll, *Ghost Wars*, 42-46; Haq, "Pakistani Air Force,"; Inboden, *The Peacemaker*, 208-210; Kengor, *The Crusader*, 228-229, 230-232; Schweitzer, *Reagan's War*, 118, 202-204, 234-235, 255; Gates, *From the Shadows*, 431.

[11] Chambers, *Witness*, 425-427, 441-443; *Cong. Rec. – House of Representatives*, 80th Cong., 2nd Sess. (1948); U.S. Department of State, "The Yalta Conference,"; Fitzgibbon, "The Hiss-Chambers Case,"; Koster, *Operation Snow*, 140-143, 152-157; McMeekin, *Stalin's War*, 606; Sudoplatov and Sudoplatov, *Special Tasks*, 222, 226-227, 227-229, 230; VENONA Decrypts, "Silvermaster Folder NY 65-14603 'Alger Hiss."

[12] McMeekin, *Stalin's War*, 347-350, 352-357, 370-371.

[13] Folsom, Jr., and Folsom, *FDR Goes to War*, 228, 251.

[14] Bullitt, *For the President*, 576-580, 587-588, 593-599; Earle, "F.D.R.'s Tragic Mistake!" 14; Folsom, Jr., and Folsom, *FDR Goes to War*, 246-249; Raymont, "Bullitt Letter to Roosevelt,"; Sherwood, *Roosevelt and Hopkins*, 544-545, 791-793, 796, 802; Standley and Ageton,

Admiral Ambassador to Russia, 355-359; U.S. President, "Map Room Papers Box 8 Roosevelt to Stalin January – June 1943."

[15] Eisenhower, *Crusade in Europe*, 25, 489-490; Ministry of Foreign Affairs of the U.S.S.R., *Stalin's Correspondence*, "No. 20: J. V. Stalin to F. Roosevelt," 15 May 1942, 24-25; Reynolds and Pechatnov, *The Kremlin Letters*, 110; Rickenbacker, *Rickenbacker*, 400-401, 402-403; Sherwood, *Roosevelt and Hopkins*, 544-546; Standley and Ageton, *Admiral Ambassador to Russia*, 308-309, 312-313.

[16] Rickenbacker, *Rickenbacker*, 400-401, 402-403; Sherwood, *Roosevelt and Hopkins*, 306-308; Standley and Ageton, *Admiral Ambassador to Russia*, 308-309, 312-313.

[17] Merridale, *Ivan's War*, 124, 394-395; Werth, *Russia at War*, 148-149, 152-153, 171, 243, 249-252.

[18] Earle, "F.D.R.'s Tragic Mistake!" 14; Fleming, *The New Dealers' War*, 204-205, 464-465; Folsom, Jr., and Folsom, *FDR Goes to War*, 246-249; McMeekin, *Stalin's War*, 450-452, 731n31-33; Weil, *A Pretty Good Club*, 136-137.

[19] Dolitsky, Glazkov, and Poor, *Pipeline to Russia*, 64-66, 79-80, 84-85; Eisenhower, *Crusade in Europe*, 25, 489-490; Hays, Jr., *The Alaska-Siberia Connection*, 37-38, 41, 43-45; Jones, *The Roads to Russia*, 266-269; McMeekin, *Stalin's War*, 419-420, 422, 650-652, 635-657; U.S. Department of State, "Foreign Relations: The Conferences at Cairo and Tehran,"; Van Tuyll, *Feeding the Bear*, 5, 26-27, 49; Zimmerman, "Lend-Lease to Russia."

[20] Weigley, *The American Way of War*, 316-317, 357-359.

[21] Eisenhower, *Crusade in Europe*, 69; Weigley, *The American Way of War*, 318-319, 330-332, 352-354.

[22] *Cong. Rec. – House of Representatives*, 81st Cong. 1st and 2nd Sess. (1949-1950).

[23] Jordan, *Major Jordan's Diaries*, 45-47; National Security Agency, "Koltsov's Account of a Conversation with 'Jurist,'"; Romerstein and Breindel, *The Venona Secrets*, 484-490.

[24] *Cong. Rec. – House of Representatives*, 81st Cong. 1st and 2nd Sess. (1949-1950); Fitzgibbon, "The Hiss-Chambers Case,"; Jordan, *Major Jordan's Diaries*, 36-38, 40-41, 42-44; McMeekin, *Stalin's War*, 531-534.

[25] Deane, *The Strange Alliance*, 89; McMeekin, *Stalin's War*, 403-405, 407-409; Stettinius, Jr., *Lend-Lease*, 229; U.S. Department of State, *Soviet Supply Protocols*, 13-15, 16-17.

[26] Glantz, *Colossus Reborn*, 142-143, 244; Jordan, *Major Jordan's Diaries*, 10-13.

[27] *Cong. Rec. – House of Representatives*, 81st Cong. 1st and 2nd Sess. (1949-1950); Jordan, *Major Jordan's Diaries*, 10-13.

[28] *Cong. Rec. – House of Representatives*, 81st Cong. 1st and 2nd Sess. (1949-1950); Fitzgibbon, "The Hiss-Chambers Case,"; Jordan, *Major Jordan's Diaries*, 10-13.

[29] Jordan, *Major Jordan's Diaries*, 5-7, 8-9, 10-13, 15-16; Sherwood, *Roosevelt and Hopkins*, 588.

[30] *Cong. Rec. – House of Representatives*, 81st Cong. 1st and 2nd Sess. (1949-1950); Jordan, *Major Jordan's Diaries*, 10-13.

[31] Bourke-White, *Portrait of Myself*, 186, 191; Carter, "Russian War Relief," 67; Kelly, *Saving Stalin*, 26-29; Small, "How We Learned to Love the Russians," 457-462; Smelser and Davies II, *The Myth of the Eastern Front*, 18-20, 27, 31-34, 35-36; Stowe, "Stowe, in Visit to Rzhev Sector,"; The New York Times, "Addresses of Litvinoff, Hopkins and Green,"; The New York Times, "MILLION A MONTH AID IS SHIPPED TO SOVIET,"; Willkie, "STALIN: 'GLAD TO SEE YOU, MR. WILLKIE," 35.

[32] Bullitt, *For the President*, 576-580, 587-588, 593-599; Deane, *The Strange Alliance*, 88-89, 103; Earle, "F.D.R.'s Tragic Mistake!" 14; Folsom, Jr., and Folsom, *FDR Goes to War*, 246-249; Raymont, "Bullitt Letter to Roosevelt."

[33] Alanbrooke, *War Diaries*, 486-487; Bohlen, *Witness to History*, 149-150; Carlton, *Churchill and the Soviet Union*, 106-107; Churchill, *Memoirs*, 476-479; Pownall, *Chief of Staff*, 29; *The National Archives of the UK*, "Foreign Secretary. First Lord. First Sea Lord," 9 January 1943; U.S. Department of State, "Foreign Relations: The Conferences at Cairo and Tehran,"; Zaloga, *Soviet Lend-Lease Tanks*, 4.

[34] Grant, *The Complete Personal Memoirs*, 131-132. Italics mine.

[35] Eisenhower, *The Papers of Dwight David Eisenhower*, 66; Weigley, *The American Way of War*, 316-317, 357-359.

[36] Glantz and House, *When Titans Clashed*, 52-53, 58, 71-73, 103, 105, 142-143, 175-176; Harrison, *Accounting For War*, 128-131, 146-149, 149-152, 152-154; Hill, *The Great Patriotic War of the Soviet Union*, 185, 187-188; Merridale, *Ivan's War*, 124, 128, 262, 264-265, 394-395; Van Tuyll, *Feeding the Bear*, xii, 3-4, 27, 71, 83-84, 122-124; Weeks, *Russia's Life-Saver*, 82-83, 110-111, 111-112.

[37] Erswell and McKay, *Surviving the Arctic Convoys*, 43-44; Smith, *Arctic Victory*, 11-12; The German Naval Staff, "War Diary,"; Walling, *Forgotten Sacrifice*, 213-215; Woodman, *Arctic Convoys 1941-1945*, 262-264.

[38] Ibid., 419-420, 422; UK Prime Minister, "Former Naval Person to the President," 14 July 1942; U.S. Department of State, *Soviet Supply Protocols*, 55, 57-61, 66-71, 76, 79-83.

[39] Mosley, *The Reich Marshal*, 350-353, 353-355, 355-359.

[40] Erswell and McKay, *Surviving the Arctic Convoys*, 107-109, 109-111, 131-135, 135-137, 142-144, 148-149; Jones, *The Roads to Russia*, 139-140; Vail Motter, *The Persian Corridor*, 141-143, 259-262, 319-320, 341-344; Van Tuyll, *Feeding the Bear*, 26-27, 51, 73.

[41] Churchill, *Memoirs*, 742-744, 745-747; Ministry of Foreign Affairs of the U.S.S.R., *Stalin's Correspondence*, "No. 199: Personal and Most Secret Message from the Prime Minister, Mr. Winston Churchill, to Marshal Stalin," 1 October 1943, 166-169; Reynolds and Pechatnov, *The Kremlin Letters*, 316-318. It is interesting to note that in these late 1943 telegram exchanges with Churchill, after Molotov, "insisted" on the resumption of the Arctic convoys, Stalin again emphasized the North Russian route's importance and ridiculed the Iranian one, stating, "As experience has shown, delivery of armaments and military supplies to the U.S.S.R. through Persian ports cannot compensate in any way for those supplies which were not delivered by the northern route." While agreeing to send a series of four convoys each consisting of thirty-five U.S. and British ships between November 1943 and February 1944, Churchill subsequently informed Roosevelt that he had, "received a telegram from U.J. ['Uncle Joe,' Stalin's pseudonym] .... The Soviet machine is quite convinced that it can get everything by bullying, and I am sure it is a matter of some importance to show that this is not necessarily always true," to no avail as the president still refused to attach conditions to Soviet Lend-Lease.

[42] Dunn, *The Soviet Economy and the Red Army*, 74, 75; Sokolov, *The Role of the Soviet Union in the Second World War*, 53-55, 57-59.

[43] Dunn, *The Soviet Economy and the Red Army*, 74, 75, 80-81; Harrison, *Accounting For War*, 128-131, 146-149, 149-152; Hill, *The Great Patriotic War of the Soviet Union*, 185, 187-188; McMeekin, *Stalin's War*, 516, 517-518, 534-536; Weeks, *Russia's Life-Saver*, 45-46, 131-133.

[44] McMeekin, *Stalin's War*, 5-6; Walling, *Forgotten Sacrifice*, 276; Weeks, *Russia's Life-Saver*, ix-x.

[45] Hohne, *Canaris*, 479-480; McMeekin, *Stalin's War*, 452-453, 454-455, 737n34.

[46] Hohne, *Canaris*, 479-480, 483-484; McMeekin, *Stalin's War*, 452-453, 454-455, 737n34.

[47] Hohne, *Canaris*, 479-480; McMeekin, *Stalin's War*, 452-453, 454-455, 737n34.

[48] McMeekin, *Stalin's War*, 5-6; Walling, *Forgotten Sacrifice*, 276; Weeks, *Russia's Life-Saver*, ix-x.

49 Eisenhower, *Crusade in Europe*, 25, 69-70, 489-490; Rickenbacker, *Rickenbacker*, 402-403.

50 Blond, *Ordeal Below Zero*, 152-153, 157-162; Erswell and McKay, *Surviving the Arctic Convoys*, 107-109, 109-111, 131-135, 135-137, 142-144, 148-149; Landas, *Arctic Convoys 1942*, 82-83; Mason, *Arctic Warriors*, 155-156; McMeekin, *Stalin's War*, 419-420, 422; Melton, *Liberty's War*, 74-76; Smith, *Arctic Victory*, 197-199, 201-202; The German Naval Staff, "War Diary,"; *The National Archives of the UK*, "PREMIER 3 393/8," "Prime Minister," 18 January 1943, and "Most Secret. Mr. Keenlyside," 19 January 1943; Thomas, *Through Ice and Fire*, 147-148; Woodman, *Arctic Convoys 1941-1945*, 276-280, 282-283.

51 Dolitsky, Glazkov, and Poor, *Pipeline to Russia*, 60-63, 72-75, 79-80, 84-85; Hays, Jr., *The Alaska-Siberia Connection*, 38-39, 51-52, 57-58; Ministry of Foreign Affairs of the U.S.S.R., *Stalin's Correspondence*, "No. 20: J. V. Stalin to F. Roosevelt," 15 May 1942, 24-25; Office, Chief of Finance War Department, "Lend-Lease Shipments World War II,"; Reynolds and Pechatnov, *The Kremlin Letters*, 110; Sherwood, *Roosevelt and Hopkins*, 544-546; Smith, *Warplanes to Alaska*, 161-165, 173-176; U.S. Department of State, *Soviet Supply Protocols*, 55, 57-61, 66-71, 76, 79-83; Vail Motter, *The Persian Corridor and Aid to Russia*, 312-313; Zimmerman, "Lend-Lease to Russia."

BIBLIOGRAPHY

Published Primary Sources

Adero, Malaika. *Up South: Stories, Studies, and Letters of This Century's Black Migrations*. New York: New Press, 1993.

Alanbrooke, Field-Marshal Lord. *War Diaries 1939-1945*. London: Phoenix Press, 2001.

Arnold, Henry H. *Global Mission*. New York: Harper & Brothers, 1949.

Bohlen, Charles E. *Witness to History, 1929-1969*. Edited by Robert H. Phelps. New York: Norton, 1973.

Bourke-White, Margaret. *Eyes on Russia*. New York: Simon and Schuster, 1931.

———. *Portrait of Myself*. New York: Simon and Schuster, 1963.

Brezhnev, Leonid I. *Leonid I. Brezhnev: Pages From His Life*. New York: Simon & Schuster, 1978. Translated by The Academy of Sciences of the U.S.S.R.

———. *Trilogy: Little Land, Rebirth, The Virgin Lands*. New York: International Publishers, 1980.

Broome, Jack. *Convoy is to Scatter*. London: William Kimber and Co. Limited, 1972.

Bullitt, Orville H. *For the President – Personal and Secret: Correspondence Between Franklin D. Roosevelt and William C. Bullitt*. Boston: Houghton Mifflin, 1972.

Byrnes, James F. *Speaking Frankly*. New York: Harper & Brothers, 1947.

Campbell, Sir Ian, and Donald MacIntyre. *The Kola Run: A Record of Arctic Convoys, 1941-1945*. London: Frederick Muller Limited, 1959.

Carell, Paul. *Hitler Moves East 1941-1943*. Edited and translated by Ewald Osers. New York: Bantam Books, 1966.

Casey, William J. *Scouting the Future: The Public Speeches of William J. Casey*. Edited and compiled by Herbert E. Meyer. Washington, D.C.: Regnery, 1989.

Chambers, Whittaker. *Witness*. Southbend, IN: Regnery, 1952.

Chuikov, Vasili. *The Battle for Stalingrad*. New York: Ballantine Books, 1968. Edited and translated by Harold Silver.

Churchill, Winston S. *Memoirs of the Second World War*. Boston: Houghton Mifflin Company, 1987.

Cudahy, John. *Archangel: The American War with Russia*. Chicago: A.C. McClurg, 1924.

Davies, Joseph E. *Mission to Moscow*. New York: Simon and Schuster, 1941.

Deane, John R. *The Strange Alliance: The Story of Our Efforts at Wartime Cooperation with Russia*. New York: The Viking Press, 1947.

Dorn, Frank. *Walkout: With Stilwell in Burma*. New York: Thomas Y. Crowell Co., 1971.

Eisenhower, Dwight D. *Crusade in Europe*. New York: Avon Books, 1968.

———. *The Papers of Dwight David Eisenhower: The War Years*, Vol. 1. Edited by Alfred D. Chandler, Jr. Baltimore: Johns Hopkins Press, 1970.

Erswell, Charlie, and John R. McKay. *Surviving the Arctic Convoys: The Wartime Memoir of Leading Seaman Charlie Erswell.* Barnsley, South Yorkshire: Pen & Sword Maritime, 2021.

Feis, Herbert. *Churchill, Roosevelt, Stalin: The War They Waged and the Peace They Sought.* Princeton: Princeton University Press, 1967.

Francis, David R. *Russia From the American Embassy: April, 1916-November, 1918.* New York: Charles Scribner's Sons, 1921.

Gates, Robert M. *From the Shadows: The Ultimate Insider's Story of Five Presidents and How They Won the Cold War.* New York: Simon and Schuster, 1996.

Girardet, Edward. *Killing the Cranes: A Reporter's Journey Through Three Decades of War in Afghanistan.* White River Junction, VT: Chelsea Green Publishing, 2011.

Golovko, Arseni G. *With the Red Fleet: The War Memoirs of the Late Admiral Arseni G. Golovko.* Edited by Sir Aubrey Mansergh. Translated by Peter Broomfield. London: Putnam, 1965.

Grant, Ulysses S. *The Complete Personal Memoirs of Ulysses S. Grant.* Lexington, KY: Seven Treasures Publications, 2009.

Graves, William S. *America's Siberian Adventure 1918-1920.* New York: Peter Smith Publishing, Inc., 1941.

Guderian, Heinz. *Panzer Leader.* Edited and translated by Constantine Fitzgibbon. New York: Da Capo Press, 1996.

Harriman, William Averell, and Elie Abel. *Special Envoy to Churchill and Stalin 1941-1946.* New York: Random House, 1975.

Hill, Alexander. *The Great Patriotic War of the Soviet Union: A Documentary Reader.* New York: Routledge, 2010.

Hitler, Adolf. *Mein Kampf.* Translated by Ralph Manheim. New York: Mariner Books, 1999.

Hull, Cordell. *The Memoirs of Cordell Hull,* Vol II. New York: The MacMillan Company, 1948.

Il Sung, Kim. *The Selected Works of Kim Il Sung.* New York: Prism Key Press, 2011.

Ironside, Field-Marshal Lord. *Archangel: 1918-1919.* Uckfield, East Sussex, UK: Naval & Military Press, 2007.

Jordan, George Racey. *Major Jordan's Diaries.* New York: Harcourt, Brace, and Company, 1952.

———. *Gold Swindle: The Story of Our Dwindling Gold.* New York: The Bookmailer, Inc., 1959.

Kaplan, Robert D. *Soldiers of God: With Islamic Warriors in Afghanistan and Pakistan.* New York: Vintage, 2001.

Khrushchev, Nikita S. *Khrushchev Remembers.* Edited and translated by Strobe Talbott. New York: Bantam Books, 1971.

Lenin, Vladmir I. *Lenin Collected Works,* Vol. 41. Translated by Yuri Sdobnikov. Moscow: Progress Publishers, 1977.

Lipper, Elinor. *Eleven Years in Soviet Prison Camps.* London: The World Affairs Book Club, 1950.

Litvin, Nikolai. *800 Days on the Eastern Front: A Russian Soldier Remembers World War II*. Edited and translated by Stuart Britton. Lawrence: University Press of Kansas, 2007.

Loza, Dmitriy. *Commanding the Red Army's Sherman Tanks: The World War II Memoirs of Hero of the Soviet Union Dmitriy Loza*. Edited and translated by James F. Gebhardt. Lincoln: University of Nebraska Press, 1996.

Marshall, Samuel Lyman Atwood. *Pork Chop Hill: The American Fighting Man in Action Korea, Spring, 1953*. New York: Berkley Books, 2000.

Mason, Alfred Grossmith. *Arctic Warriors: A Personal Account of Convoy PQ18*. Edited by Julie Grossmith Deltrice. Barnsley, South Yorkshire: Pen & Sword Maritime, 2013.

Melton, Herman E. *Liberty's War: An Engineer's Memoir of the Merchant Marine, 1942-45*. Edited by Will Melton. Annapolis, MD: Naval Institute Press, 2017.

Molotov, Vyacheslav and Felix Chuev. *Molotov Remembers: Inside Kremlin Politics*. Edited and translated by Ivan R. Dee. Lanham, MD: Rowman & Littlefield, 1993.

Moore, Joel R., Harry H. Meade, and Lewis E. Jahns. *History of the American Expedition Fighting the Bolsheviks: U.S. Military Intervention in Soviet Russia, 1918-1919*. Detroit: Polar Bear Publishing, 1920.

Pacepa, Ion Mihai, and Ronald J. Rychlak. *Disinformation: Former Spy Chief Unveils Secret Strategies for Undermining Freedom, Attacking Religion, and Promoting Terrorism*. New York: Midpoint Trade Books, 2013.

Poole, DeWitt Clinton. *An American Diplomat in Bolshevik Russia*. Edited by Lorraine M. Lees and William S. Rodner. Madison: The University of Wisconsin Press, 2014.

Pownall, Sir Henry. *Chief of Staff: The Diaries of Lieutenant-General Sir Henry Pownall*, Vol. 2. Edited by Brian Bond. Hamden, CT: Archon Books, 1974.

Reagan, Ronald. *The Reagan Diaries*. Edited by Douglas Brinkley. New York: Harper Perennial, 2009.

———. *An American Life*. New York: Threshold Editions, 2011.

Reynolds, David, and Vladimir Pechatnov. *The Kremlin Letters: Stalin's Wartime Correspondence with Churchill and Roosevelt*. New Haven: Yale University Press, 2018.

Rickenbacker, Edward V. *Rickenbacker*. New York: Fawcett Crest, 1969.

Roosevelt, Franklin Delano. *Great Speeches*. Edited by John Grafton. Mineola, NY: Dover Publications, 1999.

Sanchez, Juan Reinaldo, and Axel Gylden. *The Double Life of Fidel Castro: My 17 Years as Personal Bodyguard to El Lider Maximo*. Translated by Catherine Spencer. New York: St. Martin's Griffin, 2016.

Schofield, Brian B. *The Russian Convoys*. London: B. T. Batsford, 1964.

Schuler, Kurt, and Andrew Rosenberg. *The Bretton Woods Transcripts*. New York: Center for Financial Stability, 2013.

Scott, John. *Behind the Urals: An American Worker in Russia's City of Steel*. Bloomington: Indiana University Press, 1973.

Sherwood, Robert E. *Roosevelt and Hopkins: An Intimate History*. New York: Ishi Press, 2020.

Sikorski, Radek. *Dust of the Saints: A Journey Through War-Torn Afghanistan.* New York: Paragon House, 1990.

Stalin, Joseph V. *Selected Works.* Honolulu, HI: University Press of the Pacific, 2002.

———. *The Great Patriotic War of the Soviet Union.* Edited and translated by Harry F. Ward. New York: International Publishers, 1945.

Standley, William Harrison, and Arthur Ainsley Ageton. *Admiral Ambassador to Russia.* Chicago: Henry Regnery Company, 1955.

Stettinius, Jr., Edward R. *Lend-Lease: Weapon for Victory.* New York: Pocket Books, 1944.

Sudoplatov, Pavel, and Anatoli Sudoplatov. *Special Tasks: The Memoirs of an Unwanted Witness – A Soviet Spymaster.* New York: Little, Brown, and Company, 1995.

The Russian General Staff. *The Soviet-Afghan War: How a Superpower Fought and Lost.* Edited by Lester W. Grau. Translated by Michael A. Gress. Lawrence: The University Press of Kansas, 2002.

Thomas, Leona J. *Through Ice and Fire: A Russian Arctic Convoy Diary, 1942.* Stroud, Gloucestershire: Fonthill Media Limited, 2015.

U.S. Air Force. *Project Rand Research Memorandum: The Soviet Union and the Atom: The 'Secret Phase.'* Santa Monica, CA: The Rand Corporation, 1957.

White, William L. *Report on the Russians.* New York: Harcourt, Brace and Company, 1945.

Yousaf, Mohammad, and Mark Adkin. *Afghanistan – The Bear Trap: The Defeat of a Superpower.* Barnsley, South Yorkshire: Pen & Sword, 2001.

Zaeef, Abdul Salam. *My Life with the Taliban.* Edited by Alex van Linschoten. Translated by Felix Kuehn. London: Hurst & Company, 2010.

Zhukov, Georgy. *Marshal of Victory Vol. 1: The WWII Memoirs of General Georgy Zhukov through 1941.* Edited and translated by Geoffrey Roberts. Mechanicsburg, PA: Stackpole Books, 2015.

———. *Marshal of Victory Vol. 2: The WWII Memoirs of General Georgy Zhukov, 1941-1945,* Edited and translated by Geoffrey Roberts. Mechanicsburg, PA: Stackpole Books, 2015.

Digital Primary Sources/Archival Material

Adams, Paul, and Alexandra Fouche. "Russia fires new waves of missiles at Ukraine and hits energy infrastructure." *BBC,* 14 January 2023. Accessed 15 January 2023. https://www.bbc.com/news/world-europe-64278733.

Admiralty Naval Staff. *Battle Summary No. 27: Attack on the "Tirpitz" (Operation "Tungsten") 3rd April, 1944.* London: Tactical, Torpedo and Staff Duties Division – Historical Section, 1944. Accessed 25 February 2024. https://www. navy.gov.au/sites/default/files/documents/Battle_Summary_27.pdf.

Alexander, Chris. "Lend-Lease for Ukraine: US revives WWII anti-Hitler policy to defeat Putin." *Atlantic Council,* 9 April 2022. Accessed 28 April 2022. *Alpha History Authors.* "Russian Revolution Documents." Accessed 21 March 2022. https://alphahistory.com/russianrevolution/russian-revolution-documents/.

Altunin, Evgenii. "On the History of the Alaska-Siberia Ferrying Route." *The Journal of Slavic Military Studies*, Vol. 10, Issue 2, June 1997, 85-96. Accessed 27 March 2022. https://www.tandfonline.com/doi/abs/10.1080/1351804970 8430292?journalCode=fslv20.

Amnesty International (Unattributed Report). "Ukraine: Devastating power cuts undermining civilian life as Christmas approaches." *Amnesty International*, 21 December 2022. Accessed 7 January 2023. https://www.amnesty.org/en/late st/news/2022/12/ukraine-devastating-power-cuts-undermining-civilian-lif e-as-christmas-approaches/.

Anderson, Jack, and Dale van Atta. "Afghan Rebel Aid Enriches Generals." *The Washington Post*, 8 May 1987. Accessed 22 February 2022. https://www.washi ngtonpost.com/archive/local/1987/05/08/afghan-rebel-aid-enriches-gener als/40243b90-55d4-421b-80b7-929c3e4b1075/.

Architect Staff. "The USA, the USSR, and Architecture: An exhibition at the Canadian Centre for Architecture explores American influences on Soviet culture." *Architect*, 15 November 2019. Accessed 15 July 2022. https://www.ar chitectmagazine.com/design/exhibits-books-etc/the-usa-the-ussr-and-arc hitecture_o.

Associated Press. "ALLIES PAY TRIBUTE TO YANKS OVERSEAS: Troop in Russia Feast on Delicious Wild Turkey." *The Morning Oregonian*, 29 November 1918. Accessed 24 January 2022. https://oregonnews.uoregon.edu/lccn/sn830251 38/1918-11-29/ed-1/seq-18/.

———. "U.S., Britain To Ask Russian Clarification." *The Tampa Tribune*, 6 October 1942. Accessed 17 September 2022. https://www.newspapers.com/newspag e/327196525/.

———. "Rickenbacker and Two of Stimson's Aides In Moscow on a Mission for War Secretary." *The New York Times*, 24 June 1943. Accessed 17 April 2022. https://www.nytimes.com/1943/06/24/archives/rickenbacker-and-two-of-stimsons-aides-in-moscow-on-a-mission-for.html.

———. "RICKENBACKER HOME FROM MOSCOW TRIP; He Reports to Stimson on the Results of Tour Abroad." *The New York Times*, 12 August 1943. Accessed 17 April 2022. https://www.nytimes.com/1943/08/12/archives/ric kenbacker-home-from-moscow-trip-he-reports-to-stimson-on-the.html.

———. "US Warship Sunk in 1944 Yields Treasure." *The Christian Science Monitor*, 10 November 1995. Accessed 21 November 2022. https://www.csmonitor.co m/layout/set/amphtml/1995/1110/10144.html.

Baldor, Lolita. "Expanded US training for Ukraine forces begins in Germany." *AP News*, 16 January 2023. Accessed 16 January 2023. https://apnews.com/ article/russia-ukraine-politics-germany-7ae8c22dfd9379e77f172bd2b3ab5fb7.

Beers, Henry P. "U.S. Naval Forces in Northern Russia (Archangel and Murmansk) 1918-1919." *Office of Records Administration, Records Officer, Navy Department*, 1943. Accessed 6 March 2021, https://babel.hathitrust.org/cgi/pt?id=mdp.39 015011359273&view=1up&seq=1.

Berg, Matt, and Lara Seligman. "Zelenskyy makes his case in D.C. for more U.S. support for Ukraine: In his first foreign trip since Russia invaded, the Ukrainian leader urges Biden, and the U.S. Congress, for more money and weapons." *Politico*, 21 December 2022. Accessed 23 December 2022. https://

www.politico.com/news/2022/12/21/zelenskyy-washington-ukraine-white-house-00074954.

Bertrand, Natasha, Kylie Atwood, Kevin Liptak, and Alex Marquardt. "Austin's assertion that US wants to 'weaken' Russia underlines Biden strategy shift." *CNN*, 26 April 2022. https://www.cnn.com/2022/04/25/politics/biden-admi nistration-russia-strategy/index.html.

Bhadrakumar, Melkulangara K. "West lost the plot in Ukraine: The strategy of forcing Russia to its knees is not going to work." *The Tribune*, 15 January 2023. Accessed 15 January 2023. https://www.tribuneindia.com/news/comment/west-lost-the-plot-in-ukraine-464493.

Binder, David. "Soviet Brigade: How the U.S. Traced It." *The New York Times*, 13 September 1979. Accessed 25 February 2024. https://www.nytimes.com/1979/09/13/archives/soviet-brigade-how-the-us-traced-it-how-dispute-developed .html.

Birstein, Vadim J. "Three Days in 'Auschwitz without Gas Chambers': Henry A. Wallace's Visit to Magadan in 1944." *Wilson Center: Cold War International History Project.* Accessed 17 March 2022. https://www.wilsoncenter.org/pub lication/three-days-auschwitz-without-gas-chambers-henry-wallaces-visit-to-magadan-1944.

Bonner, Arthur. "AN ODYSSEY WITH AFGHAN REBELS: TRANSPORTING VITAL ARMS SUPPLY." *The New York Times*, 31 October 1985. Accessed 4 June 2022. https://www.nytimes.com/1985/10/31/world/an-odyssey-with-afgha n-rebels-transporting-vital-arms-supply.html.

Borders, William. "Pakistan's Plight: At odds With U.S. and Fearful of Soviet; News Analysis American Embassy Is in Ruins Aid Halted Under U.S. Legislation." *The New York Times*, 2 January 1980. Accessed 17 April 2022. https://www.nytimes .com/1980/01/02/archives/pakistans-plight-at-odds-with-us-and-fearful-of -soviet-news.html.

Bourke-White, Margaret. "SILK STOCKINGS IN THE FIRST FIVE-YEAR PLAN; Despite the Soviet Drive and the New Order of Things, Russia's Women Are Still Feminine." *The New York Times*, 14 February 1932. Accessed 7 October 2022. https://www.nytimes.com/1932/02/14/archives/silk-stockings-in-the -fiveyear-plan-despite-the-soviet-drive-and.html.

Brainerd Daily Dispatch (Unattributed Report). "BATTLE ON DON RIVER BANK; Report Big Air-Sea Battle Fought." *Brainerd Daily Dispatch*, 10 July 1942. Accessed 27 June 2022. https://newspaperarchive.com/brainerd-daily-dispatch-jul-10-1942-p-1/.

Branigin, William. "Guerrillas Use Cease-Fire To Rearm." *The Washington Post*, 18 October 1983. Accessed 31 October 2022. https://www.washingtonpost.c om/archive/politics/1983/10/18/guerrillas-use-cease-fire-to-rearm/5c2bce d3-1da9-49bb-bc17-b623367406d2/.

British Admiralty. "Supplement to The London Gazette of Friday, 13th October, 1950: Convoys to North Russia, 1942." *The London Gazette*, 17 October 1942. Accessed 4 June 2022. https://www.ibiblio.org/hyperwar/UN/UK/LondonG azette/39041.pdf.

Brisson, Irene. "How Albert Kahn helped the Soviet Union industrialize." *Detroit Curbed.* 13 December 2019. Accessed 15 July 2022. https://detroit.cu rbed.com/2019/12/13/21012559/albert-kahn-russia-ussr-detroit-world-war-ii.

Business Standard (Unattributed Report). "Russian strikes will cause emergency power cuts across country: Ukraine." *Business Standard,* 15 January 2023. Accessed 15 January 2023. https://www.business-standard.com/article/inte rnational/russian-strikes-will-cause-emergency-power-cuts-across-country -ukraine-123011500046_1.html.

Carbonaro, Giulia. "U.S. Wants Russia 'Weakened' So It Can Never Invade Again." *Newsweek,* 25 April 2022. Accessed 3 January 2023. https://www.news week.com/us-wants-russia-weakened-so-that-it-can-never-invade-again-1 700570.

Carter, Edward C. "Russian War Relief." *The Slavonic and East European Review: America Series,* Vol. 3, No. 2 (Aug. 1944), 61-74. Accessed 13 June 2022. https://www-jstor-org.libproxy.library.unt.edu/stable/3020236?seq=1#meta data_info_tab_contents.

Cassidy, Henry C. "Soviet Offensive Is Speeded by American War Supplies; U.S. HELP SPEEDS SOVIET OFFENSIVE." *The New York Times,* 6 March 1943. Accessed 7 April 2022. https://www.nytimes.com/1943/03/06/archives/sovi et-offensive-is-speeded-by-american-war-supplies-us-help-speeds.html.

Chairman of the Board, Tennessee Valley Authority. "Lend-Lease Program With Russia." *National Archives at Atlanta,* 23 and 26 September 1942. Accessed 17 June 2022. https://www.archives.gov/atlanta/exhibits/item81-tag.html.

Chatterjee, Phelan. "Ukraine war: Zelensky's visit shows neither Ukraine nor US want peace, Russia says." *BBC,* 22 December 2022. Accessed 3 January 2023. https://www.bbc.com/news/world-us-canada-64066584.

Chief of the Imperial General Staff. "Revolutionary Russia – A British View: Poole, F C," 1-37. 12 January 1919. "King's Collections: The Serving Soldier." King's College London. Accessed 4 January 2022. https://kingscollections.or g/servingsoldier/collection/revolutionary-russia-a-british-view/.

Clark, Arthur. "The Silver Ship." *Saudi Aramco World,* Vol. 48, No. 2 (March/April 1997). Accessed 21 November 2022. https://archive.aramcoworld.com/issue /199702/the.silver.ship.htm.

Columbia University Library Digital Collections. "Allen Wardwell, RWR Chairman, to Herbert H. Lehman." Russian War Relief, Inc., 14 October 1942. Accessed 13 June 2022. http://www.columbia.edu/cu/lweb/digital/collectio ns/rbml/lehman/pdfs/0941/ldpd_leh_0941_0014.pdf.

Conway, Edmund. "Reborn Russia clears Soviet debt," *The Telegraph,* 22 August 2006. Accessed 9 December 2022. https://www.telegraph.co.uk/finance/294 5924/Reborn-Russia-clears-Soviet-debt.html.

Cornell University Library. *Proceedings of the Brest-Litovsk Peace Conference: The Peace Negotiations Between Russia and the Central Powers – 21 November, 1917-3 March, 1918.* Washington, D.C.: Government Publishing Office, 1918.

Cornell University Library Digital Collections. "What Russia Means to Us: A Speech by Albert Einstein. English Version." Jewish Council for Russian War Relief, 25 October 1942. Accessed 13 June 2022. https://digital.library.cornel l.edu/catalog/ss:21072652.

Crawford, Christina E. "Soviet Planning Praxis: From Tractors to Territory." *Centerpiece,* Vol. 29, No. 2 (Spring 2015). Weatherford Center for International Affairs, Harvard University. Accessed 15 July 2022. https://wcfia.harvard.edu /publications/centerpiece/spring2015/feature-crawford.

Crowley, Michael. "Congress Proposes More Than $44 Billion for Ukraine: The spending bill unveiled Tuesday includes billions more for the country than President Biden had requested." *The New York Times*, 20 December 2022. Accessed 23 December 2022. https://www.nytimes.com/2022/12/20/us/politics/congress-aid-ukraine.html.

Curtis, Michael. "Lend-Lease: How U.S. Kept the Soviets Afloat in World War II." *American Thinker*. 13 June 2020. Accessed 20 September 2020. https://www.americanthinker.com/articles/2020/06/lendlease_how_the_us_kept_the_soviets_afloat_in_world_war_ii.html. Fordham University Sourcebook. "World War II in Europe." https://sourcebooks.fordham.edu/mod/modsbook45.asp#War%20In%20Europe.

Daily News (Unattributed Report). "Uranium Missing but Most Recovered." *Daily News*, 19 May 1949. Accessed 23 March 2022. https://trove.nla.gov.au/newspaper/article/2804617?downloadScope=page.

Dawsey, Jason. "Trotsky's Struggle Against Stalin: Joseph Stalin was a hangman whose noose could reach across oceans." The National World War II Museum – New Orleans, 12 September 2018. Accessed 6 January 2022. https://www.nationalww2museum.org/war/articles/trotskys-struggle-against-stalin.

Deml, John. "'Get the Rope!': Anti-German Violence in World War I-era Wisconsin." *Atlantic Monthly*, Vol. 11, No. 1 (January 1919), 101-102. Accessed 7 January 2022. http://historymatters.gmu.edu/d/1/.

Denker, Debra. "Along Afghanistan's War-Torn Frontier. *National Geographic*, Vol. 167, No. 6, June 1985, 772-797.

Denny, Harold. "SOVIET FLIERS LAND PLANE AT NORTH POLE FOR A BASE FOR FLIGHTS TO AMERICA; CAMP MADE ON ICE Party Begins Clearing of Field for Permanent Scientific Station THREE PLANES TO FOLLOW Buildings Will Be Erected for Four Men Who Will Remain a Year Near Pole RADIO REPORTS TO STALIN Expedition Sends Regrets for Fear Caused by Failure of Wireless Before Landing Field Base at Pole Planned SOVIET FLIERS LAND NEAR NORTH POLE Dog Will Warn of Bears Climax to Years of Effort SOVIET FLIERS WHO LANDED NEAR NORTH POLE," *The New York Times*, 22 May 1937. Accessed 13 November 2022. https://www.nytimes.com/1937/05/22/archives/soviet-fliers-land-plane-at-north-pole-for-a-base-for-flights-to.html.

Detroit Evening Times (Unattributed Report). "Drive on Caucasus Oil Smashed, Reds Claim Nazis Lose 95,000 at Kharkov, Huge Battle Reported Near End." *Detroit Evening Times*, 31 May 1942. Accessed 27 June 1942. https://chroniclingamerica.loc.gov/lccn/sn88063294/1942-05-31/ed-1/seq-1/ocr/.

Deutscher Reichsanzeiger (Unattributed Report). "Treaty of peace between Finland and Germany. Signed at Berlin, 7 March, 1918." *Deutscher Reichsanzeiger*, 8 March 1918. Accessed 10 April 2022. https://documentsdedroitinternational.fr/ressources/TdP/1918-03-07-TraitedeBerlin(Finlande)(enanglais).pdf.

DNA Web Team. "Did Hollywood film Rambo 3 predict the Taliban takeover of Afghanistan? Know the truth." *DNA*, 23 August 2021. Accessed 29 December 2022. https://www.dnaindia.com/world/report-did-hollywood-film-rambo-3-predict-the-taliban-takeover-of-afghanistan-know-the-truth-sylvester-stallone-hollywood-cia-mujahideen-soviet-invasion-2907298.

Dreilinger, Danielle. "Built in the U.S.S.R. (by Detroit)." *LSA Magazine* (Fall 2019). University of Michigan. Accessed 15 July 2022. https://lsa.umich.edu/lsa/new s-events/all-news/search-news/built-in-the-u-s-s-r---by-detroit-.html.

Duranty, Walter. "RUSSIANS HUNGRY, BUT NOT STARVING; Deaths From Diseases Due to Malnutrition High, Yet the Soviet Is Entrenched. LARGER CITIES HAVE FOOD Ukraine, North Caucasus and Lower Volga Regions Suffer From Shortages. KREMLIN'S 'DOOM' DENIED Russians and Foreign Observers In Country See No Ground for Predictions of Disaster." *The New York Times*, 31 March 1933. Accessed 19 July 2022. https://www.nytimes.com/1933/03/3 1/archives/russians-hungry-but-not-starving-deaths-from-diseases-due-to. html.

———. "RUSSIAN REDS SEE MECHANIZED ARMY; 2,000 Delegates to Congress Review Great Parade in Moscow's Red Square. BIG NEW TANKS DISPLAYED Voroshiloff Says Bolsheviki Are Ready 'to Hold Every Inch of the Fatherland.'" *The New York Times*, 10 February 1934. Accessed 19 July 2022. https://www.nytimes.com/1934/02/10/archives/russian-reds-see-mechani zed-army-2000-delegates-to-congress-review.html.

———. "SOVIET WAR GAMES OPEN ON BIG SCALE; Manoeuvres in Kiev Region Said to Be the Largest Ever Held by Red Army." *The New York Times*, 15 September 1935. Accessed 19 July 2022. https://www.nytimes.com/1935/09/ 15/archives/soviet-war-games-open-on-big-scale-manoeuvres-in-kiev-regi on-said.html.

Earle, George H. "F.D.R.'s Tragic Mistake!" *Confidential*, 14 (August 1958). Accessed 15 October 2022. http://www.oldmagazinearticles.com/1943-german-peace-feelers_pdf.

Edmondson, Catie. "Congress Clears Bill to Allow Lending Arms to Ukraine: House passage of the measure, which invoked the World War II-era Lend-Lease Act, sent it to President Biden for his signature." *The New York Times*, 28 April 2022. Accessed 7 May 2022. https://www.nytimes.com/2022/04/28 /us/politics/ukraine-lend-lease-arms.html.

Egorov, Boris. "How the newborn Soviet state took capitalist help hushed it up." *Russia Beyond.* 25 July 2018. Accessed 15 July 2022. https://www.rbth.com/h istory/328834-soviet-state-took-capitalist-help/amp.

Ellyatt, Holly, Christina Wilkie, and Chelsey Cox. "Against all odds, 'Ukraine didn't fall,' Zelenskyy says in historic address to U.S. Congress." *CNBC*, 23 December 2022. Accessed 26 December 2022. https://www.cnbc.com/2022 /12/21/ukraine-war-live-updates-latest-news-on-russia-and-the-war-in-uk raine.html.

Euronews (Unattributed Report). "US slams 'loose talk' on nuclear weapons after Putin comments." *Euronews*, 8 December 2022. Accessed 2 January 2023. Http s://www.euronews.com/2022/12/08/us-slams-loose-talk-on-nuclear-weap ons-after-putin-comments.

Faulconbridge, Guy, and Tom Balmforth. "Russia takes Avdiivka from Ukraine, biggest gain in nine months." *Reuters*, 18 February 2024. Accessed 21 February 2024. https://www.reuters.com/world/europe/ukrainian-troops-withdraw-avdiivka-ammunition-shortage-bites-2024-02-17/.

Fish, Hamilton. "Article 6." *The New York Times*, 6 October 1941. Accessed 8 September 2020. https://www.nytimes.com/1941/10/06/archives/article-6-no-title.html.

Fitzgibbon, William. "The Hiss-Chambers Case: A Chronology Since 1934." *The New York Times*, 12 June 1949.

Fraser, K. C. "73 North: The Battle of the Barents' Sea 1942." *Reference Reviews*, Vol. 14, No. 6 (1 June 2000), 14. Accessed 19 July 2022. https://www.emerald.com/insight/content/doi/10.1108/rr.2000.14.6.14.281/full/html.

Fumento, Michael. "A Church Arson Epidemic? It's Smoke and Mirrors." *The Wall Street Journal*, 8 July 1996. Accessed 4 February 2023. https://www.wsj.com/articles/SB836760439744561500.

Geust, Carl-Frederik. "Aircraft Deliveries to the Soviet Union." *Lend-Lease History and People.* 6 July 2019. Accessed 7 October 2020. https://lend-lease.net/articles-en/aircraft-deliveries-to-the-soviet-union/.

Girardet, Edward. "Soviet truce with Afghan rebels fades." *The Christian Science Monitor*, 18 August 1983. Accessed 3 October 2022. https://www.csmonitor.com/1983/0818/081856.html.

———. "Afghanistan: Soviet 'migratory genocide' and failed UN talks." *The Christian Science Monitor*, 6 December 1983. Accessed 27 December 2022. https://www.csmonitor.com/1983/1206/120648.html.

———. "Soviets step up war against reporters in Afghanistan." *The Christian Science Monitor*, 23 October 1984. Accessed 24 September 2022. https://www.csmonitor.com/1984/1023/102339.html.

Gustafson, W. Eric, and William L. Richter. "Pakistan in 1980: Weathering the Storm." *Asian Survey*, Vol. 21, No. 2, February 1981, 162-171. Accessed 23 July 2022. https://www.jstor.org/stable/2643761.

Haltiwanger, John, and Charles R. Davis. "Putin's nuclear threats are stirring fears of a nightmare scenario. Here's what's in his arsenal and what could happen if he orders the unthinkable." *Business Insider*, 24 December 2022. Accessed 5 January 2023. https://www.businessinsider.com/ukraine-war-putin-russia-nuclear-weapons-threats-what-could-happen-2022-10.

Haq, Riaz. "Pakistani Air Force: The Only Air Force That Shot Down Multiple Russian Fighter Pilots in Combat Since WWII." *Haq's Musings*, 16 March 1988. Accessed 14 October 2022. http://www.riazhaq.com/2022/03/pakistan-air-force-only-air-force-that.html?m=1.

Herndon, James S., and Joseph O. Baylen. "Col. Philip R. Faymonville and the Red Army, 1934-43." *Slavic Review: Interdisciplinary Quarterly of Russian, Eurasian, and East European Studies*, Vol. 34, Issue 3 (September 1975). Accessed 19 July 2022. https://www.cambridge.org/core/services/aop-cambridge-core/content/view/2473C57D215570C91E8F1F5B225876DD/S0037677900071722a.pdf/col_philip_r_faymonville_and_the_red_army_193443.pdf.

Hill, Alexander. "British 'Lend-Lease' Tanks and the Battle for Moscow, November-December 1941 – A Research Note." *The Journal of Slavic Military Studies*, Vol. 19, Issue 2, September 2006, 289-294. Accessed 21 April 2022. https://www.tandfonline.com/doi/full/10.1080/13518040600697811?needAccess=true.

———. "British Lend-Lease Aid and the Soviet War Effort, June 1941-June 1942." *The Journal of Military History*, Vol. 71, No. 3, July 2007, 773-808. Accessed 24 April 2022. https://www.jstor.org/stable/30052890.

Historic Detroit (Unattributed Report). "Albert Kahn (March 21, 1869-Dec. 8, 1942)." *HistoricDetroit.org.* Accessed 15 July 2022. https://historicdetroit.org/architects/albert-kahn.

Hooper, Craig. "Ukraine Converts $21.9 Billion In U.S. Military Surplus Into Fearsome Force." *Forbes,* 26 December 2022. Accessed 15 January 2023. Https://www.forbes.com/sites/craighooper/2022/12/26/ukraine-converts-219-billion-in-us-military-surplus-into-fearsome-force/?sh=407dff56370a.

Huggins, Michael. "Saudi treasure fails to find buyer." *UPI,* 16 November 1995. Accessed 21 November 2022. https://www.upi.com/amp/Archives/1995/11/16/Saudi-treasure-fails-to-find-buyer/4576816498000/.

Hussein, Abid. "What is behind a resurgence of violent attacks in Pakistan?" *Al-Jazeera,* 26 December 2022. Accessed 28 December 2022. https://www.aljazeera.com/news/2022/12/26/what-is-behind-a-resurgence-of-violent-attacks-in-pakistan.

Imperial War Museum. "Documents.2114: Private Papers of Lieutenant P S Cockrell RNVR." Box No: 92/45/1.

Al-Jazeera (Unattributed Report). "Russia accuses US of fighting proxy war in Ukraine." *Al-Jazeera,* 22 December 2022. Accessed 3 January 2023. https://www.aljazeera.com/news/2022/12/22/russia-accuses-us-of-fighting-proxy-war-in-ukraine.

Jerusalem Post Staff. "US may not maintain military support for Ukraine, Navy secretary says: However, several key US security officials have expressed concern over continued and potential escalations in the Ukraine-Russia conflict." *The Jerusalem Post,* 12 January 2023. Accessed 15 January 2023. https://www.jpost.com/international/article-728360.

Johnston, Eric. "My Talk with Joseph Stalin." *Reader's Digest* (October 1944), 1-10.

Joint Chiefs of Staff. "Directive to the Commander in Chief of the U.S. Occupation Forces (JCS 1067) (April 1945)." German History in Documents and Images (GHDI). Accessed 29 November 2022. https://ghdi.ghi-dc.org/sub_document.cfm?document_id=2297.

Keller, Bill. "A BIG AFGHAN TOWN IS SEIZED BY REBELS." *The New York Times,* 15 August 1988. Accessed 23 June 2022. https://www.nytimes.com/1988/08/15/world/a-big-afghan-town-is-seized-by-rebels.html.

Kenworthy, Tom. "Congressman Charlie Wilson, Not Holding his Fire." *The Washington Post,* 20 August 1990. Accessed 10 April 2022. https://www.washingtonpost.com/archive/lifestyle/1990/08/20/congressman-charlie-wilson-not-holding-his-fire/4597c5fa-1e05-4162-9e4a-e4aefc697f9d/.

Kostenko, Maria, and Manveena Suri. "Zelensky pleads for help to plug 'artificial' weapons deficit amid signs of Russia seizing advantage." *CNN,* 17 February 2024. Accessed 22 February 2024. https://amp.cnn.com/cnn/2024/02/17/europe/zelensky-pleads-plug-artificial-weapons-deficit-intl/index.html.

Kudrytski, Aliaksandr. "Ukraine Enters Third Year of War as Stalled Aid Dims Outlook." *Bloomberg,* 24 February 2024. Accessed 25 February 2024. https://www.bloomberg.com/news/articles/2024-02-24/ukraine-enters-third-year-of-war-as-stalled-us-aid-dims-outlook?utm_campaign=pol&utm_medium=bd&utm_source=applenews.

Lamothe, Dan. "U.S. begins expanded training of Ukrainian forces for large-scale combat." *The Washington Post*, 15 January 2023. Accessed 16 January 2023. https://www.washingtonpost.com/national-security/2023/01/15/us-military-ukraine-training-germany-grafenwoehr/.

Lanza, Conrad H. "Russo-German War Part II: Second Phase of the War – Smolensk and Uman," *The Field Artillery Journal*, July 1942. Accessed 19 July 2022. https://tradocfcoeccafcoepfwprod.blob.core.usgovcloudapi.net/fires-bulletin-archive/1942/JUL_1942/JUL_1942_FULL_EDITION.pdf.

Lawrence, William H. "SENATE VOTES 82-0; President Signs Bill – Says Axis Weakens as Our Aid Grows TOTAL NOW $9,632,000,000 Litvinoff Hails Help to Red Army and Says Soviet People Deeply Appreciate It A LEND-LEASE TOAST WITH LEND-LEASE MILK LEND-LEASE VOTED, PRESIDENT SIGNS," *The New York Times*, 12 March 1943. Accessed 25 November 2022. https://www.nytimes.com/1943/03/12/archives/senate-votes-820-president-signs-bill-says-axis-weakens-as-our-aid.html.

———. "LEND-LEASE HELP TO RUSSIA TO RISE; Proposals for New Protocol, to Go Into Effect June 30, Delivered to Moscow GAIN FROM SHORTER ROUTE Opening of Mediterranean to Speed Supply – Stettinius Gives Figures to April 30." *The New York Times*, 15 June 1943. https://www.nytimes.com/1943/06/15/archives/lendlease-help-to-russia-to-rise-proposals-for-new-protocol-to-go.html.

———. "STALIN LAUDS U.S. FOR AID TO SOVIET; Cites 'Remarkable' Production Job in Long Interview With Johnston and Harriman," *The New York Times*, 28 June 1944. Accessed 2 August 2022. https://www.nytimes.com/1944/06/28/archives/stalin-lauds-us-for-aid-to-soviet-cites-remarkable-production-job.html.

Lee, Clark. "Threat of Allies-Stalin Crisis Averted, A. P. War Writer Says; Cassidy, Back From Moscow, Sees Russia Satisfied on Second Front Issue," *Evening Star*, 28 February 1943. Accessed 14 September 2022. https://chroniclingamerica.loc.gov/lccn/sn83045462/1943-02-28/ed-1/seq-18/.

Lieven, Anatol. "Ukraine Can't Win the War." *TIME*, 24 February 2024. Accessed 25 February 2024. https://time.com/6695261/ukraine-forever-war-danger/.

Lister, Tim. "Putin floats possibility that Russia may abandon 'no first use' nuclear doctrine." *CNN*, 9 December 2022. Accessed 7 January 2023. https://www.cnn.com/2022/12/09/europe/russia-putin-nuclear-weapons-intl/index.html.

Lister, Tim, and Maria Kostenko. "Russia raises its flag in Avdiivka, then presses the advantage on a vulnerable Ukraine." *CNN*, 18 February 2024. Accessed 22 February 2024. https://amp.cnn.com/cnn/2024/02/18/europe/russia-flag-avdiivka-pressures-ukraine-intl/index.html.

Lukacs, John. "America and Russia, Americans and Russians." *American Heritage*, Vol. 43, No. 1 (February-March 1992). Accessed 2 March 2021, https://www.americanheritage.com/america-and-russia-americans-and-russians.

Lukpat, Alyssa, and Emily Cochrane. "Rand Paul holds up $40 billion in aid for Ukraine: Mr. Paul had sought to alter the bill to include requiring than an inspector general monitor the spending," *The New York Times*, 12 May 2022. Accessed 6 December 2022. https://www.nytimes.com/2022/05/12/world/europe/rand-paul-ukraine-aid.html.

Lutton, Charles. "Stalin's War: Victims and Accomplices." *Journal for Historical Review*, Vol. 20 (2001), 4. Accessed 30 January 2023. http://vho.org/GB/Journ als/JHR/1/4/Lutton371.html.

Madera Tribune (Unattributed Report). "RUSSIANS REACH SAN JACINTO LACK OF GAS CAUSES HALT LONG FLIGHT Pole Vaulting Plane Made Forced Landing in Cow Pasture Near Town VILLAGE IN TURMOIL Flyers Were Unaware That March Field Is But 20 Miles Away," *The Madera Tribune*, 14 July 1937. Accessed 13 November 2022. https://cdnc.ucr.edu/?a=d&d=MT193707 14.2.18&e=-------en--20--1--txt-txIN--------.

———. "Reds Approaching Kiev; RUSS ARMIES CUT GERMAN DEFENSE ARC; Berlin Command Has Ordered Evacuation Of Key City Started." *Madera Tribune*, 11 October 1943. Accessed 26 June 2022. https://cdnc.ucr.edu/cgi-bin/cdnc?a=d&d=MT19431011.2.14&e=-------en--20--1--txt-txIN--------1.

Majstorovic, Vojin. "H-Diplo Roundtable XXIV-5 on McMeekin, *Stalin's War*," review of *Stalin's War* by Sean McMeekin, *H-War, H-Net Reviews*, 26 September 2022. Accessed 15 October 2022. https://networks.h-net.org/node/28443/di scussions/10685214/h-diplo-roundtable-xxiv-5-stalin%E2%80%99s-war#_T oc111672159.

Manning, Mary J. "Being German, Being American: In World War I, They Faced Suspicion, Discrimination Here at Home." *Prologue* (Summer 2014), 14-22. *National Archives and Records Administration*. Accessed 7 January 2022. https://www.archives.gov/files/publications/prologue/2014/summer/germ ans.pdf.

Markov, Alexei. "Stalin's secret war plans." *Saturday Evening Post*, 20 September 1952. Accessed 22 November 2022. https://vividmaps.com/stalins-secret-war-plans/amp/.

Masood, Salman. "Pakistan Raids a Prison After Militants Seize a Hostage." *The New York Times*, 20 December 2022. Accessed 28 December 2022. https://ww w.nytimes.com/2022/12/20/world/asia/pakistan-taliban-prison-raid-hosta ges.html.

McCormick, Anne O'Hare. "When Henry Ford Was the Hero of the Soviet Union." *The New York Times*. 9 April 1947. Accessed 15 July 2022. https://www.nytimes.com/1947/04/09/archives/when-henry-ford-was-the-hero-of-the-soviet-union.html.

McLeary, Paul, Erin Banco, and Lara Seligman. "First Javelins. Then HIMARS. Now Patriot. What's Next?" *Politico*, 29 December 2022. Accessed 29 December 2022. https://www.politico.com/news/2022/12/29/himars-patriot-russia-uk raine-biden-00075708.

Musumeci, Natalie. "Ukraine revealed secret battle plans left behind by Russian troops and claimed they showed Russia planned a 15-day war." *Yahoo News*, 2 March 2022. Accessed 15 December 2022. https://news.yahoo.com/ukraine -revealed-secret-battle-plans-211801990.html?guccounter=1.

National Archives and Records Administration. "Letter from Joseph E. Davies to Samuel Rosenman, January 22, 1945." *Harry S. Truman Presidential Library & Museum*. Accessed 14 September 2022. https://www.trumanlibrary.gov/lib rary/research-files/letter-joseph-e-davies-samuel-rosenman.

News Desk. "Did Pakistan's F-16 shoot down Russian vice president's fighter jet?" *Global Village Space*, 14 May 2020. Accessed 16 December 2022. https://

www.globalvillagespace.com/did-pakistans-f-16-shoot-down-russian-vice-presidents-fighter-jet/.

Pastorfield-Li, Justin. "An Excerpt from an Interview with a Soviet soldier who survived the Battle of Stalingrad." *Digital Public Library of America*, "World War II's Eastern Front: Operation Barbarossa." 19 January 2008. Accessed 5 September 2020. https://dp.la/primary-source-sets/world-war-ii-s-eastern-front-operation-barbarossa/sources/1696.

Melnikova-Raich, Sonia. "The Soviet Problem with Two 'Unknowns': How an American Architect and a Soviet Negotiator Jump-Started the Industrialization of Russia, Part I: Albert Kahn." *The Journal of the Society for Industrial Archaeology*, Vol. 36, No. 2 (January 2010), 57-80. Accessed 15 July 2022. https://www.researchgate.net/publication/262098142_The_Soviet_Problem_with_Two_Unknowns_How_an_American_Architect_and_a_Soviet_Negotiator_Jump-Started_the_Industrialization_of_Russia_Part_I_Albert_Kahn.

Ministry of Foreign Affairs of the U.S.S.R. *Stalin's Correspondence with Churchill, Attlee, Roosevelt and Truman 1941-45*. New York: E. P. Dutton & Co., Inc., 1958.

Nagl, John. "Why the Russian doomsday scenario hasn't happened – yet." *NBC*, 28 December 2022. Accessed 29 December 2022. https://www.nbcnews.com/think/opinion/russia-ukraine-war-shocked-putin-military-vets-rcna63365.

National Security Agency. "Koltsov's Account of a Conversation with 'Jurist,'" 4 August 1944. Accessed 10 March 2022. https://www.nsa.gov/portals/75/documents/news-features/declassified-documents/venona/dated/1944/4aug_conversaion_harry_dexter_white.pdf.

Office, Chief of Finance War Department. "Lend-Lease Shipments World War II." 31 December 1946. Accessed 2 September 2020. http://ibiblio.org/hyperwar/USA/ref/LL-Ship/index.html.

Orlando Sentinel (Unattributed Report). "Silver Salvaged from Ship Sunk in WWII Displayed." *Orlando Sentinel*, 27 November 1994. Accessed 21 November 2022. https://www.orlandosentinel.com/news/os-xpm-1994-11-28-9411270345-story.html.

Patel, Tara. "Giant pliers pluck treasure from the deep." *New Scientist*, Issue 1956 (27 December 1994). Accessed 21 November 2022. https://www.newscientist.com/article/mg14419561-300-giant-pliers-pluck-treasure-from-the-deep/.

Paulsson, Lars. "How Europe is Muddling Through Putin's Energy War." *The Washington Post*, 15 January 2023. Accessed 15 January 2023. https://www.washingtonpost.com/business/energy/how-europe-is-muddling-through-putins-energy-war/2023/01/14/222c46ee-93e0-11ed-90f853661ac5d9b9_story.html.

Pear, Robert. "Arming Afghan Guerrillas: A Huge Effort Led by U.S." *The New York Times*, 18 April 1988. Accessed 28 May 2022. https://www.nytimes.com/1988/04/18/world/arming-afghan-guerrillas-a-huge-effort-led-by-us.html#:~:text=With%20help%20from%20China%20and%20many%20Moslem%20nations%2C,to%20drive%20the%20Soviet%20Army%20from%20their%20country.

Pershing, General John J. "MY EXPERIENCES IN THE WORLD WAR; Enemy Growing Exhausted. New Offensives Planned. Wearing Down the Germans. Artillery and Tanks Needed. Our Plans Badly Disrupted. 1,200,000 Yankee Soldiers in France. A Regiment Sent to Russia. Against Dissipating a Great Effort Force to Russia to Guard Stores. First American Army Ordered. Harbord Named to Head S.O.S." *The New York Times*, 7 March 1931. Accessed 19 July 2022. https:

//www.nytimes.com/1931/03/07/archives/my-experiences-in-the-world-war-enemy-growing-exhausted-new.html.

Pittaway, James. "The Afghan War Isn't Over Until the Afghans Say So." *The Washington Post*, 29 December 1985. Accessed 1 December 2022. https://www.washingtonpost.com/archive/opinions/1985/12/29/the-afghan-war-isnt-over-until-the-afghans-say-so/b18a7068-8918-4122-983c-6411a365d3d0/.

Primary Sources: The 1920s. "Red Scare." Accessed 15 July 2022. https://cnu.libguides.com/1920s/redscare.

Raines, Howell. "REAGAN HINTNG AT ARMS FOR AFGHAN REBELS." *The New York Times*, 10 March 1981. Accessed 17 June 2022. https://www.nytimes.com/1981/03/10/world/reagan-hinting-at-arms-for-afghan-rebels.html.

Raymont, Henry. "Bullitt Letter to Roosevelt in 1943 Urged Invasion of Balkans to Deter Soviet Advance." *The New York Times*, 26 April 1970. https://www.nytimes.com/1970/04/26/archives/bullitt-letter-to-roosevelt-in-1943-urged-invasion-of-balkans-to.html.

Reuters. "Liberty Ship, Sunk off Oman, Begins Yielding Treasure Trove: Eighteen tons of silver coins minted for Saudi Arabia and worth some $70 million have been recovered." *The Journal of Commerce online*, 14 November 1994. Accessed 21 November 2022. https://www.joc.com/maritime-news/liberty-ship-sunk-oman-begins-yielding-treasure-trove_19941114.html.

Rhodes, Benjamin D. "The Anglo-American Intervention at Archangel, 1918-1919: The Role of the 339th Infantry." *The International History Review*, Vol. 8, No. 3 (August 1986), 367-388. Accessed 21 February 2021. https://www.jstor.org/stable/40105628?seq=1.

Roberts, Geoffrey. "Stalin's War: Distorted history of a complex second World War." *The Irish Times*, 8 May 2021. Accessed 16 February 2024. https://www.irishtimes.com/culture/books/stalin-s-war-disorted-history-of-a-complex-second-world-war-1.4551057.

Robertson, Nic. "Pakistan's Taliban problem is America's too." *CNN*, 15 December 2022. Accessed 16 December 2022. https://www.msn.com/en-us/news/world/pakistan-s-taliban-problem-is-america-s-too/ar-AA15llfd?ocid=entnewsntp&cvid=32d31213599f4d698ade9430bcb0d3f3.

Robin, Corey. "Radical writer Alexander Cockburn dead at 71." *Al-Jazeera*, 23 July 2012. Accessed 26 November 2022. https://www.aljazeera.com/amp/opinions/2012/7/23/radical-writer-alexander-cockburn-dead-at-71.

Roff, Peter. "Capital Q&A: Sen. Gordon Humphrey." *UPI*, 10 October 2001. Accessed 24 August 2022. https://www.upi.com/amp/Archives/2001/10/10/Capital-QA-Sen-Gordon-Humphrey/5671002686400/.

Roosevelt, Franklin Delano. "Lend-Lease." *The New York Times*, 27 August 1943. Accessed 19 September 2020. https://www.nytimes.com/1943/08/27/archives/lendlease.html.

Roosevelt, Franklin Delano, and Winston Churchill. "Texts of Roosevelt-Churchill Messages." *The New York Times*, 12 June 1972. Accessed 17 April 2022. https://www.nytimes.com/1972/06/12/archives/texts-of-rooseveltchurchill-messages.html#:~:text=Letter%20by%20Roosevelt%20to%20Churchill%2C%20March%2018%2C%201942%3A,either%20your%20Foreign%20Office%20or%20my%20State%20Department.

Roosevelt, Theodore. "Theodore Roosevelt on the Sinking of the Lusitania, 1915." *The Gilder Lehman Institute of American History.* 23 June 1915. Accessed 7 January 2022. https://www.gilderlehrman.org/sites/default/files/inline-pdfs /t-08003.pdf.

Rubin, Barnett R. "The 'Overlooked' War in Afghanistan." *The New York Times,* 17 October 1986. Accessed 26 November 2022. https://www.nytimes.com/19 86/10/17/opinion/the-overlooked-war-in-afghanistan.html.

Ryan, Missy, and Annabelle Timsit. "US wants Russian military 'weakened' from Ukraine invasion, Austin says." *The Washington Post,* 25 April 2022. Accessed 4 June 2022. https://www.washingtonpost.com/world/2022/04/25 /russia-weakened-lloyd-austin-ukraine-visit/.

Rychlak, Ronald J. "Cardinal Stepinac, Pope Pius XII, and the Roman Catholic Church During the Second World War." *Catholic Social Science Review,* Vol. 14 (2009), 367-383. Accessed 3 February 2023. https://www.pdcnet.org/cssr/con tent/cssr_2009_0014_0367_0383.

Salisbury, Laurence E. "Report on China." *Far Eastern Survey,* Vol. 13, No. 23 (15 November 1944), 211-213. Accessed 4 February 2023. https://www.jstor.org/ stable/3022138.

Schmemann, Serge. "AFGHAN WAR, AFTER 6 YEARS, BECOMES SOVIET FACT OF LIFE." *The New York Times,* 18 February 1986. Accessed 14 April 2022. https://www.nytimes.com/1986/02/18/world/afghan-war-after-6-years-bec omes-a-soviet-fact-of-life.html.

Schmidt, Samantha, Isabelle Khurshudyan, and Serhii Korolchuk. "Captured Russian tanks and equipment are coveted trophies – and a headache: Ukrainian forces have seized hundreds of tanks and other military vehicles, but many are languishing as they wait for repairs and spare parts." *The Washington Post,* 27 December 2022. Accessed 5 January 2023. https://www.Washingtonpost.com/w orld/2022/12/27/ukraine-russia-tanks-military-vehicles/.

Schubert, Frank N. "The Persian Gulf Command: Lifeline to the Soviet Union." *Pars Times – Greater Iran & Beyond* (March 2005), 305-315. Accessed 28 June 2022. https://www.parstimes.com/history/persian_gulf_command.pdf.

Senior British Naval Officer, North Russia. "Halcyon Class Ships: SBNO Reports." 1941-1944. *Halcyon Class and Survey Ships of World War Two.* Accessed 23 October 2022. http://www.halcyon-class.co.uk/SBNOreports/sb no_reports.htm.

Seventeen Moments in Soviet History: An on-line archive of primary sources. Michigan State University. Accessed 15 June 2022. https://soviethistory.msu. edu/home.

Sheppard, Jr., Nathaniel. "Senator Says U.S. Ready to Support Rebel Capital." *Chicago Tribune,* 15 May 1988. Accessed 17 February 2022. https://www.chic agotribune.com/news/ct-xpm-1988-05-15-8803170824-story.html.

Shpotov, Boris M. "The Ford Motor Company in the Soviet Union in the 1920s-1930s: Strategy, identify, performance, reception, adaptability." Institute of World History, Russian Academy of Sciences (n. d.), 1-7. Accessed 15 July 2022. https://studylib.net/doc/8309060/the-ford-motor-company-in-the-soviet-u nion-in-the-1920s.

———. "Business without Entrepreneurship: the Ford Motor Company and the Soviet Industrialization, 1920s-1930s." Institute of World History, Russian

Academy of Sciences (n. d.), 1-13. Accessed 15 July 2022. https://ebha.org/eb ha2007/pdf/Shpotov.pdf.

Small, Melvin. "How We Learned to Love the Russians: American Media and the Soviet Union During World War II." *The Historian*, Vol. 36, No. 3 (May 1974), 455-478. Accessed 17 June 2022. https://www.jstor.org/stable/24443747.

Smith, Gibson Bell. "Guarding the Railroad, Taming the Cossacks: The U.S. Army in Russia, 1918-1920." *Prologue*, Vol. 34, No. 4 (Winter 2002). National Archives and Records Administration. Accessed 24 December 2021. https://www.archiv es.gov/publications/prologue/2002/winter/us-army-in-russia-1.html.

Sokolov, Boris V. "The Role of Lend-Lease in Soviet Military Efforts, 1941-1945." *The Journal of Slavic Military Studies*, Vol. 7, Issue 3, September 1994. Accessed 24 April 2022. https://www.tandfonline.com/doi/abs/10.1080/135180494084 30160.

Stateside Staff. "Detroit architect Albert Kahn helped pave the way for Soviet victory in WWII." *Michigan Radio*. 10 August 2018. Accessed 15 July 2022. https://www.michiganradio.org/arts-culture/2018-08-10/detroit-architect-a lbert-kahn-helped-pave-the-way-for-soviet-victory-in-wwii?_amp=true.

Stowe, Leland. "Stowe, In Visit to Rzhev Sector, Which Is Ideal for Mechanized Warfare, Marvels art Success of Russian Defenders." *Indianapolis Times*, 5 September 1942. Accessed 15 June 2022. https://newspapers.library.in.gov/?a =d&d=IPT19420905.1.5&e=-------en-20--1--txt-txIN-------.

———. "Miracles of Red Army Credited In Large Part to Its Women; Thousands Serves as Guards, Gunners, Telegraphers, Storekeepers and Nurses." *Evening Star*, 31 October 1942. Accessed 24 July 2022. https://www.newzpaperarchive .com/gazete/evening_star/1942-10-31/7.

———. "Nazi Army Fears Second Winter Of War in Russia, Reds Claim; Captured Germans Say Morale of Hitler's Forces Is Low as Bitter Cold Sets In." *Evening Star*, 2 November 1942. Accessed 23 July 2022. https://www.newzpa perarchive.com/gazete/evening_star/1942-11-02/26.

———. "Russian Question: When Will U.S. Help?" *Indianapolis Times*, 3 November 1942. Accessed 23 July 2022. https://newspapers.library.in.gov/?a =d&d=IPT19421103.1.20&e=-------en-20--1--txt-txIN-------.

———. "The Evolution of the Red Army." *Foreign Affairs*, October 1943. Accessed 24 June 2022. https://www.foreignaffairs.com/articles/russian-fed eration/1943-10-01/evolution-red-army.

Temple, Herbert. "LUSITANIA TORPEDOED: Sinking of Great Liner May Involve United States – Fate of Passengers and Crew Uncertain – Victim of Submarine Sinks off Irish Coast in Thirty Minutes." *The San Diego Union-Tribune*, 7 May 1915. Accessed 7 January 2022. https://www.sandiegouniontr ibune.com/news/150-years/sd-me-150-years-may-7-20180425htmlstory.html.

The Alaska Daily Empire (Unattributed Report). "Yankees Back From Russia Deny Mutiny." *The Alaska Daily Empire*, 15 July 1919. Accessed 23 January 2022. https://chroniclingamerica.loc.gov/lccn/sn84020657/1919-07-15/ed-1/seq1/.

The American Sentinel (Unattributed Report). "Still, One Never Knows his Allies up Here." *The American Sentinel*, No. 8, 1 February 1919. Accessed 4 January 2022. https://quod.lib.umich.edu/p/polar/3241550.0001.008/3?pag e=root;size=100;view=text.

———. "Yanks Took Part in Big Fighting Here: Historians Will Find Americans Played Important Role in Campaign in North Russia." *The American Sentinel,* No. 25, 31 May 1919. Accessed 4 January 2022. https://quod.lib.umich.edu/p/polar/3241550.0001.025/1?view=image&size=150.

The Daily Iowan (Unattributed Report). "Soviets Have Suffered Heavy Defeat But Are Not Finished: Foreign Observers Declare Reds Need Planes 'Desperately.'" *The Daily Iowan,* 30 October 1941. Accessed 30 June 2022. http://dailyiowan.lib.uiowa.edu/DI/1941/di1941-10-30.pdf.

The German General Staff. "Erich Ludendorff on the Opening of the 1918 Spring Offensive, 21 March 1918." *Source Records of the Great War,* Vol. VI. Edited by Charles F. Horne. New York: National Alumni, 1923. Accessed 8 April 2022. https://www.firstworldwar.com/source/kaiserbattle_ludendorff.htm.

The German Naval Staff. "War Diary: German Naval Staff Operations Division September 1942." *Internet Archive.* Accessed 1 May 2022. https://archive.org/stream/wardiarygermann371942germ/wardiarygermann371942germ_djvu.txt.

The Harvard Crimson (Unattributed Report). "BENEFIT TUESDAY NIGHT FOR RUSSIAN WAR RELIEF." *The Harvard Crimson,* 18 February 1944. Accessed 13 June 2022. https://www.thecrimson.com/article/1944/2/18/benefit-tuesday-night-for-russian-war/.

The Hindu (Unattributed Report). "Pakistan Taliban kill 6 security personnel in multiple attacks in Balochistan." *The Hindu,* 25 December 2022. Accessed 28 December 2022. https://www.thehindu.com/news/international/pakistan-taliban-kill-security-personnel-in-multiple-attacks-in-balochistan/article66305106.ece.

The National Security Archive. "Ambassador Dean Cable, 'Subject" Afghanistan." 10 December 1986. Accessed 17 April 2022. https://nsarchive.gwu.edu/document/18133-document-11-ambassador-dean-cable-subject.

———. "Cable from Ambassador Dean to Secretary of State: 'Subject: Discussion with Rajiv Gandhi on Afghanistan," 11 July 1987. Accessed 14 April 2022. https://nsarchive.gwu.edu/document/18136-document-14-cable-ambassador-dean.

———. "Cable from Secretary of State to Amembassy New Delhi: 'Subject: Armacost Pre-summit Discussions with Vorontsov on Afghanistan," 20 November 1987. Accessed 4 June 2022. https://nsarchive.gwu.edu/document/18138-document-16-cable-secretary-state.

———. "Ambassador Dean's Cable. Subject: Gandhi/Ryzhkov Meeting: Discussion of Afghanistan," 27 November 1987. Accessed 12 June 2022. https://nsarchive.gwu.edu/document/18139-document-17-ambassador-dean-s-cable-subject.

———. "Memorandum of Conversation: Special Working Group on Afghanistan, March 22, 1988," 22 March 1988. Accessed 24 June 2022. https://nsarchive.gwu.edu/document/18260-national-security-archive-doc-08-memorandum.

———. "Cable from Ambassador Raphel, Islamabad, to Secretary of State, Washington: 'Subject: USCINCCENT Visit to Pakistan: The Pak Military on Afghanistan," 5 June 1988. Accessed 17 June 2022. https://nsarchive.gwu.edu/document/18152-document-26-cable-ambassador-raphel.

———. "Cable from Secretary of State to U.S. Embassy Islamabad. Subject: Marker Call on Armacost, December 9," 10 December 1988. Accessed 23 June 2022. https://nsarchive.gwu.edu/document/17565-document-x7-cable-secretary-state-u-s.

The National Security Archive, Volume II. "Episode 1 Cold War Documents: Roosevelt-Litvinov – The White House, November 16, 1933." Accessed 7 January 2022. https://nsarchive2.gwu.edu/coldwar/documents/episode-1/fdr-ml.htm.

———. "The Costs of Soviet Involvement in Afghanistan: An Intelligence Assessment." Accessed 27 July 2022. https://nsarchive2.gwu.edu/NSAEBB/NSAEBB57/us8.pdf.

The National Archives of the UK. "The Cabinet Papers: The Western Front." British War Cabinet. "Cabinet Conclusion 1. The Western Front. 27 May 1918." Accessed 8 April 2022. http://filestore.nationalarchives.gov.uk/pdfs/small/cab-23-6-wc-419-41.pdf.

———. "Spotlights on history: Allied intervention in Russia, 1918-19." Accessed 24 December 2021. https://www.nationalarchives.gov.uk/pathways/firstworldwar/spotlights/allies.htm.

———. "PREMIER 3 393/8: Convoy JW 52." December 1942-February 1943.

———. "ADM 199/77: North Russia convoys JW and RA reports: JW 54 A, JW 54 B, JW 55 A, JW 55 B, JW 56 A, JW 56 B, RA 54 A, RA 54 B, RA 55 A, RA 55 B, RA 56." 1943-1944.

The Navy Department Library. "Lend-Lease Act, 11 March 1941." Naval History and Heritage Command. Accessed 28 September 2020. https://www.history.navy.mil/research/library/online-reading-room/title-list-alphabetically/l/lend-lease-act-11-march-1941.html.

The New York Times (Unattributed Report). "GRAVES TO LEAD OUR SIBERIAN ARMY." *The New York Times,* 8 August 1918. Accessed 4 March 2021. https://www.nytimes.com/1918/08/08/archives/graves-to-lead-our-siberian-army-former-assistant-chief-of-general.html.luk

———. "ALLIES TO QUIT ARCHANGEL IN EARLY SPRING; Baker Announces That All Our Forces in North Russia Will Be Withdrawn. ORDERED BY PRESIDENT Secretary Baker Instructed to Give Reasons to Military Committees of Congress. WARNING OF MASSACRE R.E. Simmons Tells Senate Committee Slaughter Would Follow Withdrawal of Allies in North. ALLIES TO QUIT ARCHANGEL SOON RED PROPAGANDISTS BUSY IN ARCHANGEL American Soldiers Get Leaflets Urging Them to Demand That They Be Sent Home." *The New York Times,* 18 February 1919. Accessed 19 July 2022. https://www.nytimes.com/1919/02/18/archives/allies-to-quit-archangel-in-early-spring-baker-announces-that-all.html.

———. "THIRD TALK HELD BY STALIN ON AID; Harriman and Beaverbrook See Premier Again After a Long Parley Together PRIORITIES ARE DISCUSSED Biggest Task Is to Find Ships to Carry Arms and Supplies Diverted From Britain." *The New York Times,* 1 October 1941. Accessed 15 November 2022. https://www.nytimes.com/1941/10/01/archives/third-talk-held-by-stalin-on-aid-harriman-and-beaverbrook-see.html.

———. "MISS BOURKE-WHITE PRAISES STALIN; Back After Photographing Him in Moscow, She Says He Has Extraordinary Personality." *The New York*

Times, 3 November 1941. Accessed 3 September 2022. https://www.nytimes.c om/1941/11/03/archives/miss-bourkewhite-praises-stalin-back-after-phot ographing-him-in.html.

———. "HARMONY IN DRIVES FOR RELIEF SOUGHT; Meeting of Organizations for Aid Abroad to Be Held Soon, E. C. Carter Reports." *The New York Times*, 3 January 1942. Accessed 17 June 2022. https://www.nytimes.com/1942/01/03/arc hives/harmony-in-drives-for-relief-sought-meeting-of-organizations-for.html.

———. "Addresses of Litvinoff, Hopkins and Green at Russian War Relief Rally in Madison Sq. Garden." *The New York Times*, 23 June 1942. Accessed 13 June 2022. https://www.nytimes.com/1942/06/23/archives/addresses-of-litvinoff -hopkins-and-green-at-russian-war-relief.html.

———. "U.S. Freighters in Convoy." *The New York Times*, 9 July 1942. Accessed 12 May 2022. https://www.nytimes.com/1942/07/09/archives/us-freighters- in-convoy.html.

———. "SOVIET HAILS VICTORY OF MURMANSK CONVOY; Russians Guard Allied Vessels in Air and Sea Fight." *The New York Times*, 20 July 1942. Accessed 12 May 2022. https://www.nytimes.com/1942/07/20/archives/sovi et-hails-victory-of-murmansk-convoy-russians-guard-allied.html.

———. "FORD TIRE FACTORY WILL GO TO RUSSIA; It Is Being Bought by Our Government for Shipment Under Lend-Lease Plan." *The New York Times*, 31 October 1942. Accessed 4 June 2022. https://www.nytimes.com/1942/10/31/ archives/ford-tire-factory-will-go-to-russia-it-is-being-bought-by-our.html.

———. "HULL PRAISES RED ARMY; Says Stalingrad Marks Troops as Equal of Any in War." *The New York Times*, 4 February 1943. Accessed 27 October 2021. https://www.nytimes.com/1943/02/04/archives/hull-praises-red-army-says -stalingrad-marks-troops-as-equal-of-any.html.

———. "STANDLEY'S TALK STIRS WASHINGTON; Observers Wonder Whether the Ambassador Spoke for Himself or Government EFFECT ON BILL POSSIBLE Restrictive Amendments Might Be Attached to Lend-Lease, It Is Declared." *The New York Times*, 9 March 1943. Accessed 2 February 2023. Https://www. nytimes.com/1943/03/09/archives/standleys-talk-stirs-washington-observ ers-wonder-whether-the.html.

———. "JAPAN LETS RUSSIA GET OUR SUPPLIES; Map in Lend-Lease Report to Congress Reveals Shipments Made by Route to Siberia THESE ARE UNMOLESTED Cargoes Moving in Russian Vessels Are Mostly of Food So Far, Capital Hears." *The New York Times*, 13 March 1943. Accessed 21 February 2022. https://www.nytimes.com/1943/03/13/archives/japan-lets-russia-get -our-supplies-map-in-lendlease-report-to.html.

———. "LITVINOFF'S THANKS PUBLISHED IN RUSSIA; Excerpts From Speech by Roosevelt Printed." *The New York Times*, 14 March 1943. Accessed 2 February 2023. https://www.nytimes.com/1943/03/14/archives/litvinoffs-th anks-published-in-russia-excerpts-from-speech-by.html.

———. "MILLION A MONTH AID IS SHIPPED TO SOVIET; Russian War Relief Hopes to Continue Rate Through 1943." *The New York Times*, 27 April 1943. Accessed 4 June 2022. https://www.nytimes.com/1943/04/27/archives/milli on-a-month-aid-is-shipped-to-soviet-russian-war-relief-hopes.html.

———. "GENERAL IS REDUCED AFTER DUTY IN SOVIET; Faymonville Now a Colonel – Michela Also to Lose Rank." *The New York Times*, 18 November

1943. Accessed 9 December 2022. https://www.nytimes.com/1943/11/18/arc hives/general-is-reduced-after-duty-in-soviet-faymonville-now-a-colonel.html.

———. "THAT LOST URANIUM." *The New York Times*, 20 May 1949. Accessed 14 March 2022. https://www.nytimes.com/1949/05/20/archives/that-lost-uranium.html.

———. "RUSSIA AND THE BOMB." *The New York Times*, 24 September 1949. Accessed 27 March 2022. https://www.nytimes.com/1949/09/24/archives/r ussia-and-the-bomb.html.

———. "AN AFGHAN REBEL AND SOVIET REPORTEDLY AGREE TO A TRUCE." *The New York Times*, 25 May 1983. Accessed 7 September 2022. Https://www. nytimes.com/1983/05/25/world/an-afghan-rebel-and-soviet-reportedly-agr ee-to-a-truce.html.

———. "Ukraine Battles for Control of Key Black Sea Peninsula." *The New York Times*, 22 November 2022. Accessed 12 December 2022. https://www.nytime s.com/live/2022/11/22/world/russia-ukraine-war-news.

Thorne, Stephen J. "Hitler, Raeder, and the demise of the *Kriegsmarine.*" *Legion: Canada's Military History Magazine*, 2 October 2019. Accessed 2 June 2022. https://legionmagazine.com/en/hitler-raeder-and-the-demise-of-the-krieg smarine/.

———. "Raeder's defence: German admiral fights for his doomed fleet." *Legion: Canada's Military History Magazine*, 30 October 2019. Accessed 2 June 2022. https://legionmagazine.com/en/raeders-defence-german-admiral-fights-fo r-his-doomed-fleet/.

TIME (Unattributed Report). "Die, But Do Not Retreat." *TIME*, Vol. XLI, No. 1, 4 January 1943, 1-6. Accessed 24 September 2022. https://content.time.com/ti me/subscriber/article/0,33009,790648,00.html.

———. "World Battlefronts: THE BATTLE OF RUSSIA: The Beginning of Disaster?" *TIME*, Vol. XLI, No. 4, 25 January 1943, 1-2. Accessed 9 September 2022. https:// content.time.com/time/subscriber/article/0,33009,850230,00.html.

———. "THE BALKANS: Area of Decision." *TIME*, 9 October 1944, 1-5. Accessed 2 February 2023. https://content.time.com/time/subscriber/article/0,33009 ,803304-1,00.html.

Uddin, Mughees. "Image of Pakistan in the *New York Times* (1980-1990)." *Journal of Pakistan Vision*, Vol. 11, No. 1, 2010, 12-43. Accessed 5 September 2022. http://pu.edu.pk/images/journal/studies/PDF-FILES/Artical%20No-2.pdf.

UK Parliament. *Parliamentary Record – House of Commons. House of Commons Debates*, 17 October 1918. Accessed 23 March 2022. https://hansard.parliam ent.uk/Commons/1918-10-17/debates/8bea1019-0383-4875-9914-7bf2dbd e4f29/ArchangelGovernment.

———. *Parliamentary Record – House of Commons. House of Commons Debates*, 16 April 1946. Accessed 12 July 2022. http://hansard.millbanksystems.com/co mmons/1946/apr/16/russia-british-empire-war-assistance.

UK Prime Minister. "Papers of David Lloyd George, 1st Earl Lloyd-George of Dwyfor (as filmed by the AJPC) [microfilm]: [M1124-1125], 1903-1944." Series F/File 2/01/1932. "L. S. Amery to Lloyd George," 24 December 1918.

———. "Former Naval Person to the President." *No. 10 Downing Street*, 14 July 1942. Accessed 23 April 2022. *Churchill Archive for Schools*. https://www.chu rchillarchiveforschools.com/themes/the-themes/key-events-and-developm

ents-in-world-history/was-churchill-really-worried-about-the-battle-of-the
-atlantic-and-if-so-why/the-sources/source-8.

UPI Archives. "Afghan aircraft on operations against anti-communist guerrillas
violated Pakistani." *UPI*, 1 November 1983. Accessed 2 December 2022. https:
//www.upi.com/Archives/1983/11/01/Afghan-aircraft-on-operations-again
st-anti-communist-guerrillas-violated-Pakistani/7902436510800/.

U.S. Congress. *Congressional Record – Senate.* 65th Congress, 3rd Session, pt. 1,
2 December 1918-4 January 1919. Government Publishing Office. Accessed 28
February 2021. https://babel.hathitrust.org/cgi/pt?id=uc1.31210026472934
&view=1up&seq=3.

———. *Congressional Record – Senate.* 65th Congress, 3rd Session, pt. 4, 12-24
February 1919. Government Publishing Office. Accessed 28 February 2021. Https
://babel.hathitrust.org/cgi/pt?id=uc1.31210023079575&view=1up&seq=5.

———. *Congressional Record – House of Representatives.* 66th Congress, 2nd
Session, pt.1, 1 June 1920. Government Publishing Office. Accessed 15 July
2022. https://babel.hathitrust.org/cgi/pt?id=hvd.32044019271584&view=1
up&seq=7&skin=2021.

———. *Congressional Record – House of Representatives.* 77th Congress, 1st
Session, pt. 7, 12 August 1941-20 October 1941. Government Publishing
Office. Accessed 2 February 2023. https://babel.hathitrust.org/cgi/pt?id=uc1
.31210018789337&view=1up&seq=1&q1=rich%20amendment.

———. *Congressional Record – Senate.* 77th Congress, 1st Session, pt. 8, 28
October 1941. Government Publishing Office. Accessed 9 October 2020.
https://www.govinfo.gov/content/pkg/GPO-CRECB-1941-pt8/pdf/GPO-CR
ECB-1941-pt8-4.pdf.

———. *Congressional Record – Senate.* 78th Congress, 1st Session, pt. 3, 1 and 2
March 1943. Government Publishing Office. Accessed 12 November 2020.
https://babel.hathitrust.org/cgi/pt?id=umn.31951d02094619s&view=1up&s
eq=1.

———. *Congressional Record – Senate and House of Representatives.* 78th
Congress, 1st Session, pt.? 9 March 1943. Government Publishing Office.
Accessed 23 November 2022. https://www.govinfo.gov/content/pkg/GPO-C
RECB-1943-pt2/pdf/GPO-CRECB-1943-pt2-6.pdf.

———. *Congressional Record – Senate and House of Representatives.* 78th
Congress, 2nd Session, pt. 7, 1 November 1943. Governing Publishing Office.
Accessed 11 October 2022. https://www.govinfo.gov/content/pkg/GPO-CRE
CB-1943-pt7/pdf/GPO-CRECB-1943-pt7-7-1.pdf.

———. *Congressional Record – Senate.* 78th Congress, 2nd Session, pt.? 26 April
1944. Government Publishing Office. Accessed 27 October 2022. https://babe
l.hathitrust.org/cgi/pt?id=umn.31951d02094618u&view=1up&seq=2.

———. *Congressional Record – Senate and House of Representatives.* 78th
Congress, 2nd Session, pt. 6, 5 September 1944. Government Publishing Office.
Accessed 27 August 2022. https://www.govinfo.gov/content/pkg/GPO-CREC
B-1944-pt6/pdf/GPO-CRECB-1944-pt6-7.pdf.

———. *Congressional Record – Senate.* 79th Congress, 1st Session, pt. 2, 21
February 1946. Government Publishing Office. Accessed 30 June 2022. https:
//www.govinfo.gov/content/pkg/GPO-CRECB-1946-pt2/pdf/GPO-CRECB-1
946-pt2-3.pdf.

———. *Congressional Record – House of Representatives.* 80th Congress, 2nd Session, pt.? 17 August 1948. Government Publishing Office. Accessed 21 September 2022. https://web.archive.org/web/20100721003156/http://www.law.umkc.edu/faculty/projects/ftrials/hiss/8-17testimony.html.

———. *Congressional Record – House of Representatives.* 81st Congress, 1st and 2nd Sessions, 1949-1950, pts.? 5 and 7 December 1949, 23, 24, 25, and 26 January 1950, and 2, 3, and 7 March 1950. Government Publishing Office. Accessed 5 August 2022. https://www.ibiblio.org/hyperwar/NHC/NewPDFs/USAAF/United%20States%20Strategic%20Bombing%20Survey/USSBS%20Shipment%20of%20Atomic%20Material%20to%20the%20Soviet%20Union%20during%20WWII.pdf.

———. *Congressional Record – Senate.* 98th Congress, 1st Session, pt. 21, 24 October 1983. Accessed 28 May 2022. https://www.govinfo.gov/content/pkg/GPO-CRECB-1983-pt21/pdf/GPO-CRECB-1983-pt21-2-1.pdf.

———. *Congressional Record – Senate and House of Representatives.* 100th Congress, 1st Session, pt2 17, 23 February 1987. Accessed 23 March 2022. https://www.congress.gov/100/crecb/1987/02/23/GPO-CRECB-1987-pt3-9.pdf.

———. *Congressional Record – Senate.* 100th Congress, 1st Session, pt. 17, 15 September 1987. Accessed 18 March 2022. https://www.govinfo.gov/content/pkg/GPO-CRECB-1987-pt17/pdf/GPO-CRECB-1987-pt17-7-2.pdf.

———. *Congressional Record – Senate.* "S. 3522, Ukraine Democracy Defense Lend-Lease Act of 2022." Congressional Budget Office, 26 April 2022. Accessed 5 June 2022. https://www.cbo.gov/system/files/2022-04/s3522.pdf.

U.S. Department of Justice. "Red Radicalism as Described by its own Leaders." 1920. Government Publishing Office. Accessed 15 July 2022. https://babel.hathitrust.org/cgi/pt?id=umn.31951001556727y&view=1up&seq=1&skin=2021.

U.S. Department of State. "Telegram with a Translation of the Zimmermann Telegram." 24 February 1917. *National Archives and Records Administration.* Accessed 14 June 2022. https://www.archives.gov/education/lessons/zimmermann.

———. "Papers Relating to the Foreign Relations of the United States, Russia, 1918, Volume I: The Acting Secretary of State to Consul General at Moscow, March 11, 1918." 11 March 1918. Accessed 4 January 2022. https://history.state.gov/historicaldocuments/frus1918Russiav01/d398.

———. "The Secretary of State to the Allied Ambassadors." 17 July 1918. Accessed 4 January 2022. http://pbma.grobbel.org/aide_memoire.htm.

———. "Papers Relating to the Foreign Relations of the United States, Russia, 1919: The Acting Secretary of State to the **Chargé** in Russia (Poole)." 29 March 1919. Accessed 20 March 2022. https://history.state.gov/historicaldocuments/frus1919Russia/d685.

———. "'Lend-Lease Act,' March 11, 1941." *Peace and War – United States Foreign Policy 1931-1941.* Accessed 3 February 2023. https://www.ibiblio.org/hyperwar/Dip/PaW/200.html.

———. "Foreign Relations of the United States Diplomatic Papers, 1941, General, The Soviet Union, Volume I: The Ambassador in the Soviet Union (Steinhardt) to the Secretary of State." 26 June 1941. Accessed 30 June 2022. https://history.state.gov/historicaldocuments/frus1941v01/d839.

————. "Foreign Relations of the United States: Diplomatic Papers, The Conferences at Cairo and Tehran, 1943." White House Files – Log of the Trip. 27 November-2 December 1943. Accessed 20 September 2022. https://history .state.gov/historicaldocuments/frus1943CairoTehran/d353.

————. "Foreign Relations of the United States: Diplomatic Papers, 1944, Europe, Volume IV – The Ambassador in the Soviet Union (Harriman) to the Secretary of State." 11 July 1944. Accessed 27 August 2022. https://history.stat e.gov/historicaldocuments/frus1944v04/d884.

————. "The Yalta Conference, 1945." Accessed 17 February 2024. https://histo ry.state.gov/milestones/1937-1945/yalta-conf#:~:text=The%20Americans%2 0and%20the%20British,territories%20liberated%20from%20Nazi%20Germany.

————. *Soviet Supply Protocols*. Washington, D.C.: Government Publishing Office, 1948. Accessed 21 September 2022. https://lend-lease.net/files/Sovie t_Supply_Protocols.pdf.

————. "U.S.-Soviet Relations: Testing Gorbachev's 'New Thinking.' Current Policy No. 985." Washington, D.C., Bureau of Public Affairs, 1 July 1987. Accessed 7 August 2022. Https://files.eric.ed.gov/fulltext/ED286807.pdf.

————. "Regional Issues and U.S.-Soviet Relations: Current Policy No. 1089." Washington, D.C., Bureau of Public Affairs, 25 August 1988. Accessed 7 May 2022. https://babel.hathitrust.org/cgi/pt?id=umn.31951002961446p&view=1up&s eq=1&skin=2021&q1=afghanistan.

U.S. Department of the Treasury. "Diaries of Henry Morgenthau, Jr., April 27, 1933-July 27, 1945." *Franklin D. Roosevelt Presidential Library & Museum*. Accessed 10 March 2022. http://www.fdrlibrary.marist.edu/archives/collecti ons/franklin/index.php?p=collections/findingaid&id=535&q=&rootcontenti d=189777.

————. "Part 3093 – Gold Mining (Limitation Order L-208)." *Federal Register*, 9 October 1942. Accessed 17 June 2022. https://www.govinfo.gov/content/pkg /FR-1942-10-09/pdf/FR-1942-10-09.pdf.

U.S. President. "President Woodrow Wilson's Proclamation of Neutrality." 4 August 1914. *Naval History and Heritage Command. The White House*, Washington, D.C. Accessed 14 June 2022. https://www.history.navy.mil/resea rch/publications/documentary-histories/wwi/1914/ttl-president-woodro.html.

————. "April 19, 1916: Message Regarding German Actions." *The White House*, Washington, D.C. 2 April 1918. University of Virginia – Miller Center: "Presidential Speeches – Woodrow Wilson Presidency." Accessed 14 June 2022. https://millercenter.org/the-presidency/presidential-speeches/april-1 9-1916-message-regarding-german-actions.

————. "April 2, 1917: Address to Congress Requesting a Declaration of War Against Germany." *The White House*, Washington, D.C. 2 April 1918. University of Virginia – Miller Center: "Presidential Speeches – Woodrow Wilson Presidency." Accessed 14 June 2022. https://millercenter.org/the-presidency/presidential-speeches/april-2-1917-address-congress-requestin g-declaration-war.

————. "April 6, 1917: Proclamation 1364." *The White House*, Washington, D.C. 6 April 1917. University of Virginia – Miller Center: "Presidential Speeches – Woodrow Wilson Presidency." Accessed 14 June 2022. https://millercenter.or g/the-presidency/presidential-speeches/april-6-1917-proclamation-1364.

———. "Proclamation 1496 – Thanksgiving Day, 1918." *The American Presidency Project*, 16 November 1918. Accessed 3 January 2022. https://www.presidency.ucsb.edu/documents/proclamation-1496-thanksgiving-day-1918.

———. "American Troops in Siberia: Message from the President of the United States." *The White House*, Washington, D.C. 22 July 1919. Accessed 19 February 2021, https://babel.hathitrust.org/cgi/pt?id=loc.ark:/13960/t01z4q15t&view=1up&seq=2.

———. "Franklin Roosevelt Administration: Stalin Replies to Roosevelt's Letter of October 30, 1941 (November 4, 1941)." *The White House*, Washington, D.C., 4 November 1941. Accessed 17 March 2022. https://www.jewishvirtuallibrary.org/stalin-replies-to-roosevelt-letter-of-october-30-1941-november-1941.

———. "Statement on Raw Materials, Munition Assignments, Shipping Adjustment Boards." *The White House*, Washington, D.C. 26 January 1942. Accessed 7 January 2022. https://www.presidency.ucsb.edu/documents/statement-raw-materials-munition-assignments-and-shipping-adjustment-boards.

———. "Executive Order 9066, February 19, 1942." *The White House*, Washington, D.C. 19 February 1942. *National Archives and Records Administration*. Accessed 17 January 2022. https://www.archives.gov/historical-docs/todays-doc/?dod-date=219.

———. "Map Room Papers Box 8 Roosevelt to Stalin May – December 1942." *The White House*, Washington, D.C.: 1942. *National Archives and Records Service Franklin D. Roosevelt Library*. Accessed 20 October 2022. http://www.fdrlibrary.marist.edu/_resources/images/mr/mr0051.pdf.

———. "Map Room Papers Box 8 Stalin to Roosevelt July – December 1942." *The White House*, Washington, D.C.: 1942. *National Archives and Records Service Franklin D. Roosevelt Library*. Accessed 20 October 2022. http://www.fdrlibrary.marist.edu/_resources/images/mr/mr0051a.pdf.

———. "Map Room Papers Box 8 Roosevelt to Stalin January – June 1943." *The White House*, Washington, D.C.: 1943. *National Archives and Records Service Franklin D. Roosevelt Library*. Accessed 27 October 2022. http://www.fdrlibrary.marist.edu/_resources/images/mr/mr0052.pdf.

———. "Report to Congress on Reverse Lend-Lease." *The White House*, Washington, D.C. 11 November 1943. *The American Presidency Project*. Accessed 30 October 2020. https://www.presidency.ucsb.edu/documents/report-congress-reverse-lend-lease.

———. "Lend-Lease Policy toward the Soviet Union." *The White House*, Washington, D.C. 3 July 1945. National Archives and Records Administration. Accessed 17 January 2022. https://www.trumanlibrary.gov/node/401220.

———. "NSDD 75: U.S. Relations with the USSR." *The White House*, Washington, D.C., 17 January 1983. *Ronald Reagan Presidential Library & Museum*. Accessed 27 February 2022.

———. "Proclamation 5033 – Afghanistan Day." *The White House*, Washington, D.C., 21 March 1983. *The American Presidency Project*. Accessed 22 May 2022. https://www.presidency.ucsb.edu/documents/proclamation-5033-afghanistan-day-1983.

———. "Letter to the Presidium of the Supreme Soviet of the U.S.S.R. on the 50th Anniversary of Diplomatic Relations Between the United States and the Soviet Union." *The White House*, Washington, D.C., 16 November 1983. *The*

American Presidency Project. Accessed 7 January 2022. https://www.presiden
cy.ucsb.edu/documents/letter-the-presidium-the-supreme-soviet-the-ussr-
the-50th-anniversary-diplomatic-relations.

———. "NSDD 166: U.S. Policy, Programs and Strategy in Afghanistan." *The
White House*, Washington, D.C., 27 March 1985. *Ronald Reagan Presidential
Library & Museum*. Accessed 17 August 2022. https://www.reaganlibrary.gov/
public/archives/reference/scanned-nsdds/nsdd166.pdf.

———. "Remarks Following a Meeting With Afghan Resistance Leaders and
Members of Congress." *The White House*, Washington, D.C., 12 November
1987. *Ronald Reagan Presidential Library & Museum*. Accessed 27 February
2022. https://www.reaganlibrary.gov/archives/speech/remarks-following-m
eeting-afghan-resistance-leaders-and-members-congress.

VENONA Decrypts. "13. Hoover to Matthew Connelly, 12 September 1945."
Internet Archive Wayback Machine, 12 September 1945. Accessed 29 June
2022. https://web.archive.org/web/20071114214743/https://www.cia.gov/li
brary/center-for-the-study-of-intelligence/csi-publications/books-and-mo
nographs/venona-soviet-espionage-and-the-american-response-1939-1957
/13.gif.

———. "Silvermaster Folder NY 65-14603 'Alger Hiss.'" *Internet Archive
Wayback Machine*, n. d. Accessed 12 June 2022. https://web.archive.org/web/
20120310003840/http://www.education-research.org/PDFs/splitfiles/splitp
rocessed/Silvermaster006_Folder/Silvermaster006_page106.pdf.

Vershinin, Alexander. "Christie's chassis: An American tank for the Soviets."
Russia Beyond. 18 May 2015. Accessed 15 July 2022. https://www.rbth.com/d
efence/2015/05/18/christies_chassis_an_american_tank_for_the_soviets_4
6135.html.

Vorozhko, Tatiana. "Former US Secretary of State Details Her Support for
Arming Ukraine." *VOA*, 13 January 2023. Accessed 15 January 2023. https://w
ww.voanews.com/a/former-us-secretary-of-state-details-her-support-for-ar
ming-ukraine-/6917776.html.

Walker, George. "Fiasco in the Barents' Sea." *Naval History Magazine*, Vol. 32,
No. 2 (April 2018), 14-17. Accessed 29 June 2022. https://www.usni.org/maga
zines/naval-history-magazine/2018/april/contact.

Wang, Amy B. "Biden signs Ukraine lend-lease act into law, expediting military
aid." *The Washington Post*, 9 May 2022. Accessed 15 May 2022. https://www
.washingtonpost.com/politics/2022/05/09/president-biden-ukraine-lend-
lease-signing/.

Weintraub, Richard M. "AFGHAN REBELS BUTTRESS SIEGE." *The Washington
Post*, 30 December 1987. Accessed 1 December 2022. https://www.washingto
npost.com/archive/politics/1987/12/30/afghan-rebels-buttress-siege/76f3b
734-661e-40e6-b4c0-e0a0523aedee/.

Weymouth, Lally. "Moscow's 'Invisible War' of Terror Inside Pakistan." *The
Washington Post*, 13 March 1988. Accessed 24 April 2022. https://www.washi
ngtonpost.com/archive/opinions/1988/03/13/moscows-invisible-war-of-te
rror-inside-pakistan/6e96dd11-56a5-4d1e-bc64-c333f41af17e/.

Whitehall History Publishing – Ministry of Defence. *The Royal Navy and the
Arctic Convoys: A Naval Staff History*. Edited by Malcolm Llewelyn-Jones.
London: Routledge, 2007.

Willkie, Wendell. "STALIN: GLAD TO SEE YOU, MR. WILLKIE' Through LIFE Roosevelt's personal representative reports on his interview on war in the Kremlin." *LIFE*, 5 October 1942, 35-38.

Wilson Center Digital Archive, Collection 27. "Cold War Origins." Accessed 17 September 2020. https://digitalarchive.wilsoncenter.org/collection/27/cold-war-origins/3.

Winthrop, Lynn. "11/11/03 FILE STORY: During book signing, Wilson recalls efforts to arm Afghans." *The Lufkin Daily News*, 11 November 2003. Accessed 17 April 2022. https://web.archive.org/web/20071120055652/http://lufkinda ilynews.com/hp/content/region/ettoday/cww/stories/book_signing.html.

Zaiets, Karina, and Stephen J. Beard. "Russian missile attacks on Ukraine power grids cut electricity, heat and water to millions: Ukrainians are living with less electricity since Russia began unleashing missiles to attack power across the country, causing blackouts." *USA Today*, 24 December 2022. Accessed 5 January 2023. https://www.usatoday.com/in-depth/graphics/2022/12/24/ru ssian-missile-attacks-ukraine-electricity-heat-water/10901300002/.

Zelensky, President Volodymyr. "Full Transcript of Zelensky's Speech Before Congress: The Ukrainian president delivered an emotional appeal for further American support, vowing that his country would prevail in its war with Russia." *The New York Times*, 21 December 2022. Accessed 23 December 2022. https://www.nytimes.com/2022/12/21/us/politics/zelensky-speech-tr anscript.html.

Zimmerman, Dwight Jon. "Lend-Lease to Russia: The Persian Corridor." *DefenseMediaNetwork*, 8 November 2012. Accessed 28 June 2022. https://w ww.defensemedianetwork.com/stories/lend-lease-to-russia-the-persian-corridor/.

Secondary Sources

Andrew, Christopher, and Oleg Gordievsky. *KGB: The Inside Story of its Foreign Operations from Lenin to Gorbachev*. New York: HarperCollins, 1990.

Baer, George W. *One Hundred Years of Sea Power: The U.S. Navy, 1890-1990*. Stanford, CA: Stanford University Press.

Beasant, John. *Stalin's Silver: The Sinking of the USS John Barry*. New York: St. Martin's Press, 1999.

Bergen, Peter. *The Rise and Fall of Osama bin Laden*. New York: Simon & Schuster, 2022.

Blond, Georges. *Ordeal Below Zero: The Heroic Story of the Arctic Convoys in World War II*. London: Souvenir Press, 1956.

Bradley, John. *Allied Intervention in Russia*. New York: Basic Books, 1968.

Braithwaite, Rodric. *Afgantsy: The Russians in Afghanistan 1979-89*. New York: Oxford University Press, 2013.

Carlton, David. *Churchill and the Soviet Union*. Manchester: Manchester University Press, 2000.

Carrell, Paul. *Hitler Moves East 1941-1943*. Translated by Ewald Osers. New York: Bantam Books, 1966.

Citino, Robert M. *Death of the Wehrmacht: The German Campaigns of 1942*. Lawrence: University Press of Kansas, 2007.

Clark, Alan. *Barbarossa: The Russian-German Conflict 1941-45*. New York: Signet Books, 1966.

Coll, Steve. *Ghost Wars: The Secret History of the CIA, Afghanistan, and bin Laden, from the Soviet Invasion to September 10, 2001*. New York: Penguin Books, 2005.

Courtois, Stephane, Mark Kramer, Nicolas Werth, and Jean-Louis Panne. *The Black Book of Communism: Crimes, Terror, Repression*. Translated by Jonathan Murphy. Cambridge, MA: Harvard University Press, 1999.

Craig, William. *Enemy at the Gates: The Battle for Stalingrad*. Old Saybrook, CT: Konecky & Konecky, 1973.

Crile, George. *Charlie Wilson's War: The Story of How the Wildest Man in Congress and a Rogue CIA Agent Changed the History of Our Times*. New York: Grove Press, 2003.

Daniels, Robert Vincent. *The Stalin Revolution: The Foundations of the Totalitarian Era*. New York: Houghton Mifflin, 1965.

Dawson, Raymond H. *The Decision to Aid Russia, 1941: Foreign Policy and Domestic Politics*. Chapel Hill: The University of North Carolina Press, 1959.

Dobson, Christopher, and John Miller. *The Day They Almost Bombed Moscow: The Allied War in Russia 1918-1920*. New York: Simon & Schuster, 1986.

Dunn, Walter S. *The Soviet Economy and the Red Army, 1930-1945*. Westport, CT: Praeger, 1995.

Dolitsky, Alexander B., Victor D. Glazkov, and Henry Varnum Poor. *Pipeline to Russia: The Alaska-Siberia Air Route in World War II*. Translated by James F. Gebhardt. Anchorage: Alaska Affiliated Areas Program National Park Service, 2016.

Ellis, Frank. *Barbarossa 1941: Reframing Hitler's Invasion of Stalin's Soviet Empire*. Lawrence: University Press of Kansas, 2015.

Evans, M. Stanton, and Herbert Romerstein. *Stalin's Secret Agents: The Subversion of Roosevelt's Government*. New York: Threshold Editions, 2013.

Fancher, Reagan. *The Holy Warrior: Osama Bin Laden and His Jihadi Journey in the Soviet-Afghan War*. Wilmington, DE: Vernon Press, 2023.

Feifer, Gregory. *The Great Gamble: The Soviet War in Afghanistan*. New York: Harper Perennial, 2010.

Fest, Joachim C. *Hitler*. Translated by Richard and Clara Winston. New York: Harcourt, 1974.

Fleming, Thomas. *The New Dealers' War: Franklin D. Roosevelt and The War Within World War II*. New York: Basic Books, 2001.

Folsom, Jr., Burton, and Anita Folsom. *FDR Goes to War: How Expanded Executive Power, Spiraling National Debt, and Restricted Civil Liberties Shaped Wartime America*. New York: Threshold Editions, 2013.

Forczyk, Robert A. *Tank Warfare on the Eastern Front 1943-1945: Red Steamroller*. Barnsley, South Yorkshire: Pen & Sword, 2017.

Galeotti, Mark. *Afghanistan: The Soviet Union's Last War*. London: Frank Cass & Co. Ltd., 1995.

———. *The Panjshir Valley 1980-86: The Lion Tames the Bear in Afghanistan*. Oxford, UK: Osprey Publishing, 2021.

Gilbert, Martin. *The First World War: A Complete History*. New York: Owl Books, 1996.

Glantz, David M. *Stumbling Colossus: The Red Army on the Eve of World War*. Lawrence: University Press of Kansas, 1998.

———. *Colossus Reborn: The Red Army at War, 1941-1943*. Lawrence: University Press of Kansas, 2005.

Glantz, David M. and Jonathan M. House. *When Titans Clashed: How the Red Army Stopped Hitler*. Lawrence: University Press of Kansas, 2015.

Halliday, E. M. *When Hell Froze Over: The Secret War Between the U.S. and Russia at the Top of the World*. New York: Simon & Schuster, 2000.

Haqqani, Hussein. *Pakistan: Between Mosque and Military*. Washington, D.C.: Carnegie Endowment for International Peace, 2005.

Harrison, Mark. *Soviet Planning in Peace and War 1938-1945*. Cambridge, UK: Cambridge University Press, 1985.

———. *Accounting For War: Soviet Production, Employment, and the Defence Burden, 1940-1945*. Cambridge, UK: Cambridge University Press, 1996.

Hays, Jr., Otis. *The Alaska-Siberia Connection: The World War II Air Route*. College Station: Texas A&M Press, 1996.

Hellbeck, Jochen. *Stalingrad: The City That Defeated the Third Reich*. New York: PublicAffairs, 2015.

Herring Jr., George C. *Aid to Russia 1941-1946: Strategy, Diplomacy, The Origins of the Cold War*. New York: Columbia University Press, 1973.

Hohne, Heinz. *Canaris: Hitler's Master Spy*. Translated by J. Maxwell Brownjohn. New York: Cooper Square Press, 1999.

House, John M. *Wolfhounds and Polar Bears: The American Expeditionary Force in Siberia, 1918-1920*. Tuscaloosa: University of Alabama Press, 2016.

Inboden, William. *The Peacemaker: Ronald Reagan, the Cold War, and the World on the Brink*. New York: Dutton, 2022.

Jalali, Ali Ahmad. *A Military History of Afghanistan: From the Great Game to the Global War on Terror*. Lawrence: University Press of Kansas, 2017.

Jones, Robert Huhn. *The Roads to Russia: United States Lend-Lease to the Soviet Union*. Norman: University of Oklahoma Press, 1969.

Kaiser, David. *No End Save Victory: How FDR Led the Nation into War*. New York: Basic Books, 2015.

Kalinovsky, Artemy M. *A Long Goodbye: The Soviet Withdrawal from Afghanistan*. Cambridge, MA: Harvard University Press, 2011.

Kelly, John. *Saving Stalin: Roosevelt, Churchill, and the Cost of Allied Victory in Europe*. New York: Hatchette Books, 2020.

Kenez, Peter. *The Birth of the Propaganda State*. New York: University of Cambridge Press, 1985.

Kengor, Paul. *The Crusader: Ronald Reagan and the Fall of Communism*. New York: Harper Perennial, 2007.

Kennan, George F. *Soviet-American Relations, 1917-1920, Vol. II: The Decision to Intervene*. Princeton: Princeton University Press, 1958.

Khlevniuk, Oleg V. *Stalin: New Biography of a Dictator*. Edited and translated by Nora Seligman Favorov. New Haven, CT: Yale University Press, 2015.

Kinvig, Clifford. *Churchill's Crusade: The British Invasion of Russia 1918-1920*. London: Hambledon Continuum, 2007.

Koster, John. *Operation Snow: How a Soviet Mole in FDR's White House Triggered Pearl Harbor*. Washington, D.C.: Regnery History, 2015.

Kotelnikov, Vladimir. *Lend-Lease and Soviet Aviation in the Second World War*. West Midlands, UK: Helion & Company, 2017.

Kotkin, Stephen. *Stalin: Paradoxes of Power, 1878-1928*. New York: Penguin Press, 2014.

———. *Stalin: Waiting for Hitler, 1929-1941*. New York: Penguin Press, 2017.

Kubek, Anthony. *How the Far East Was Lost: American Foreign Policy and the Creation of Communist China, 1941-1949*. New York: Twin Circle Publishing Company, 1972.

Lardas, Mark. *Arctic Convoys 1942: The Luftwaffe Cuts Russia's Lifeline*. London: Bloomsbury Publishing Plc, 2022.

Latell, Brian. *Castro's Secrets: Cuban Intelligence, the CIA, and the Assassination of John F. Kennedy*. New York: Palgrave MacMillan, 2013.

Leake, Elisabeth. *Afghan Crucible: The Soviet Invasion and the Making of Modern Afghanistan*. New York: Oxford University Press, 2022.

Liddell Hart, B. H. *The Real War 1914-1918*. New York: Little, Brown and Company, 1963

———. *History of the Second World War*. London: Pan Books, 2011.

Lincoln, William Bruce. *Red Victory: A History of the Russian Civil War 1918-1921*. Boston: Da Capo Press, 1999.

Liulevicius, Vejas Gabriel. *War Land on the Eastern Front: Culture, National Identity and German Occupation in World War I*. Cambridge, UK: Cambridge University Press, 2005.

Loftus, John. *The Belarus Secret*. New York: Alfred A. Knopf, 1982.

Loza, Dmitriy. *Attack of the Airacobras: Soviet Aces, American P-39s, and the Air War Against Germany*. Edited and translated by James F. Gebhardt. Lawrence: University Press of Kansas, 2002.

Marshall, Samuel Lyman Atwood. *World War I*. New York: Mariner Books, 2001.

Mawdsley, Evan. *The Russian Civil War*. London: Pegasus Books, 2009.

McCullough, David. *Truman*. New York: Touchstone, 1992.

McMeekin, Sean. *The Russian Revolution: A New History*. New York: Basic Books, 2017.

———. *Stalin's War: A New History of World War II*. New York: Basic Books, 2021.

Mellinger, George. *Soviet Lend-Lease Fighter Aces of World War II*. Oxford: Osprey Publishing, 2006.

Merridale, Catherine. *Ivan's War: Life and Death in the Red Army, 1939-1945*. New York: Metropolitan, 2007.

Moorehead, Alan. *The Russian Revolution*. New York: Harper & Brothers, 1958.

Mosley, Leonard. *The Reich Marshal: A Biography of Hermann Goering*. New York: Dell Publishing Company, 1975.

Motter, Thomas H. Vail. *The Persian Corridor: United States Army in World War II – The Middle East Theater*. Washington, D.C.: Office of the Chief of Military History, Department of the Army, 1952.

Mueller, Michael. *Canaris: The Life and Death of Hitler's Spymaster.* Annapolis, MD: Naval Institute Press, 2007. Translated by Geoffrey Brooks.

Nojumi, Neamatollah. *The Rise of the Taliban in Afghanistan: Mass Mobilization, Civil War, and the Future of the Region.* London: Palgrave MacMillan, 2002.

Nelson, James Carl. *The Polar Bear Expedition: The Heroes of America's Forgotten Invasion of Russia 1918-1919.* New York: William Morrow, 2020.

Olson, James S., and Randy Roberts. *Where the Domino Fell: America and Vietnam, 1945-2010.* Hoboken, NJ: Wiley-Blackwell, 2014.

Persico, Joseph E. *Casey: The Lives and Secrets of William J. Casey: From the OSS to the CIA.* New York: Penguin Books, 1991.

Pike, Francis. *Hirohito's War: The Pacific War, 1941-1945.* New York: Bloomsbury Academic, 2016.

Radzinsky, Edvard. *The Last Tsar: The Life and Death of Nicholas II.* Translated by Marian Schwartz. New York: Anchor Books, 1993.

———. *Stalin: The Girst In-Depth Biography Based on Explosive New Documents from Russia's Secret Archives.* Translated by Harry T. Willets. New York: Anchor Books, 1997.

———. *Alexander II: The Last Great Tsar.* Translated by Antonina W. Bouis. New York: Free Press, 2006.

Rashid, Ahmed. *Jihad: The Rise of Militant Islam in Central Asia.* New York: Penguin Books, 2002.

———. *Taliban: The Power of Militant Islam in Afghanistan and Beyond.* London: I. B. Tauris, 2010.

Rayfield, Donald. *Stalin and His Hangmen: The Tyrant and Those Who Killed for Him.* New York: Random House, 2005.

Richard, Carl J. *When the United States Invaded Russia: Woodrow Wilson's Siberian Disaster.* Lanham, MD: Rowman & Littlefield, 2013.

Romerstein, Herbert, and Eric Breindel. *The Venona Secrets: The Definitive Exposé of Soviet Espionage in America.* Washington, D.C.: Regnery History, 2000.

Rose, Kenneth D. *Myth and the Greatest Generation: A Social History of Americans in World War II.* New York: Routledge, 2007.

Rubin, Barnett R. *Afghanistan: What Everyone Needs to Know.* New York: Oxford University Press, 2020.

Ruddy, Daniel. *Theodore the Great: Conservative Crusader.* Washington, D.C.: Regnery History, 2016.

Scheuer, Michael. *Osama bin Laden.* New York: Oxford University Press, 2012.

Smelser, Ronald, and Edward J. Davies II. *The Myth of the Eastern Front: The Nazi-Soviet War in American Popular Culture.* Cambridge, UK: Cambridge University Press, 2008.

Smith, Blake W. *Warplanes to Alaska.* Blaine, Washington: Hancock House Publishers, 1998.

Smith, Peter C. *Arctic Victory: The Story of Convoy PQ 18.* London: William Kimber & Co. Limited, 1975.

Smith, William. *Churchill's Arctic Convoys: Strength Triumphs Over Adversity.* Barnsley, South Yorkshire: Pen & Sword Maritime, 2022.

Sokolov, Boris V. *The Role of the Soviet Union in the Second World War: A Re-Examination.* West Midlands, UK: Helion & Company, 2013.

———. *Marshal K. K. Rokossovsky: The Red Army's Gentleman Commander.* Edited and translated by Stuart Britton. Warwick, UK: Helion & Company, 2015.

Steil, Benn. *The Battle of Bretton Woods: John Maynard Keynes, Harry Dexter White, and the Making of a New World Order.* Princeton, NJ: Princeton University Press.

Sutton, Antony C. *National Suicide: Military Aid to the Soviet Union.* Las Vegas, NV: Dauphin Publications, Inc., 1973.

Suvorov, Viktor. *The Chief Culprit: Stalin's Grand Design to Start World War II.* Annapolis, MD: Naval Institute Press, 2013.

Swettenham, John. *Allied Intervention in Russia 1918-1919.* Oxfordshire: Routledge, 2019.

Tsouras, Peter G. *Civil War Quotations: In the Words of the Commanders.* New York: Sterling Publishing Co., Inc., 1998.

Van Tuyll, Hubert P. *Roads to Russia: American Aid to the Soviet Union, 1941-1945.* Westport, CT: Greenwood Press, 1989.

Wadsworth, Michael. *Arctic Convoy PQ8: The Story of Capt Robert Brundle and the SS Harmatris.* Barnsley, South Yorkshire: Pen & Sword Maritime, 2009.

Waller, John H. *The Unseen War in Europe: Espionage and Conspiracy in the Second World War.* New York: Random House, 1996.

Walling, Michael G. *Forgotten Sacrifice: The Arctic Convoys of World War II.* Oxford: Osprey Publishing, 2016.

Wawro, Geoffrey. *A Mad Catastrophe: The Outbreak of World War I and the Collapse of the Habsburg Empire.* New York: Basic Books, 2015.

———. *Sons of Freedom: The Forgotten American Soldiers Who Defeated Germany in World War I.* New York: Basic Books, 2018.

———. *Quicksand: America's Pursuit of Power in the Middle East.* New York: The Penguin Press, 2010.

Weeks, Albert L. *Stalin's Other War: Soviet Grand Strategy, 1939-1941.* Lanham, MD: Rowman & Littlefield Publishers, Inc., 2003.

———. *Russia's Life-Saver: Lend-Lease Aid to the U.S.S.R. in World War II.* Lanham, MD: Rowman & Littlefield Publishers, Inc., 2010.

Weil, Martin. *A Pretty Good Club: The Founding Fathers of the U.S. Foreign Service.* New York: W. W. Norton & Company, 1978.

Werth, Alexander. *Russia at War, 1941-1945: A History.* New York: Carroll & Graf, 1992.

Wilcox, Robert K. *Target Patton: The Plot to Assassinate General George S. Patton.* Washington, D.C.: Regnery, 2010.

Willett, Robert. *Russian Sideshow: America's Undeclared War 1918-1920.* McLean, VA: Potomac Books, 2006.

Woodman, Richard. *Arctic Convoys 1941-1945.* London: John Murray Ltd, 1994.

Wragg, David. *Sacrifice for Stalin: The Cost and Value of the Arctic Convoys Re-Assessed.* Barnsley, South Yorkshire: Pen & Sword Maritime, 2005.

Yellin, Emily. *Our Mothers' War: American Women at Home and at the Front During World War II.* New York: Simon & Schuster, 2004.

Zaloga, Steven J., and James Grandsen. *Soviet Tanks and Combat Vehicles of World War Two.* London: Arms and Armour Press, 1984.

Zaloga, Steven J. *Soviet Lend-Lease Tanks of World War II.* Oxford: Osprey Publishing, 2017.

INDEX